Unmasking Biblical Faiths

Who am I?
I am told I am many things;
some may well be true.
I am Homo sapiens,
cousin to the chimpanzee,
a warm-blooded mammal
spawned in some protozoan sea;
Adam's child of dust from the stars,
shaped with spit and spittle
by the finger of God;
raised like cotton in the hot Delta bottom
land of the muddy Mississippi;
Baptist of the postwar South by tradition,
critic of convention by training,
skeptic by confession,
humanist by disposition;
reason's servant by profession,
raising horizons,
altering perceptions.
Epitaphs are for others to write, he thought.
Yet in water he did write
prematurely
by flesh, blood, and bone
a conflicted legacy;
his wry curiosity
scribbling
bold forgettable marginalia
on conventional views
of reality. (6-26-13)

Unmasking Biblical Faiths

*The Marginal Relevance of the Bible
for Contemporary Religious Faith*

CHARLES W. HEDRICK

▲ CASCADE *Books* • Eugene, Oregon

UNMASKING BIBLICAL FAITHS
The Marginal Relevance of the Bible for Contemporary Religious Faith

Copyright © 2019 Charles W. Hedrick. All rights reserved. Except for brief quotations in critical publications or reviews, no part of this book may be reproduced in any manner without prior written permission from the publisher. Write: Permissions, Wipf and Stock Publishers, 199 W. 8th Ave., Suite 3, Eugene, OR 97401.

Cascade Books
An Imprint of Wipf and Stock Publishers
199 W. 8th Ave., Suite 3
Eugene, OR 97401

www.wipfandstock.com

PAPERBACK ISBN: 978-1-5326-1302-9
HARDCOVER ISBN: 978-1-5326-1304-3
EBOOK ISBN: 978-1-5326-1303-6

Cataloguing-in-Publication data:

Names: Hedrick, Charles W., author.

Title: Unmasking biblical faiths : the marginal relevance of the Bible for contemporary religious faith / Charles W. Hedrick.

Description: Eugene, OR: Cascade Books, 2019. | Includes bibliographical references and index.

Identifiers: ISBN: 978-1-5326-1302-9 (paperback). | ISBN: 978-1-5326-1304-3 (hardcover). | ISBN: 978-1-5326-1303-6 (ebook).

Subjects: LCSH: Faith and reason. | Religion and culture—United States. | Bible—Influence. | Popular culture—United States.

Classification: BS538.7 H433 2019 (print). | BS540 (epub).

Manufactured in the U.S.A.   JANUARY 9, 2019

Biblical quotations marked (RSV) are taken from the Revised Standard Version of the Bible copyright © 1946, 1952, and 1971 National Council of the Churches of Christ in the United States of America. Used by permission. All rights reserved worldwide.

Other biblical quotations, unless otherwise noted, are the author's own translations.

For my students at Missouri State University 1980–2005:
The Rest of the Story

*Nothing is concealed that will not be revealed,
and hidden that will not be known.*

Q 12:2

Contents

Preface xiii
Abbreviations xv
Introduction 1

1: THE NATURE OF THE UNIVERSE 13

§1 *The Biblical View of the Universe* 13
§2 *Is the Universe Just?* 15
§3 *Where does Evil Come from?* 17
§4 *Forces at Work in the Garden of the Lord* 20
§5 *How to Cast Out the Devil* 22
§6 *Halloween: Do the Dead walk?* 24
§7 *Natural Disasters, Acts of God, and the Bible* 26
§8 *Chance, Luck, Randomness, and the Being of God* 28
§9 *Does Anything Happen by Chance?* 30
§10 *Honey in the Rock, Water in the Stone, Better Wine in Stone Jars* 33
§11 *Will the Earth Abide?* 35

2: REASON AND FAITH 38

§12 *Are Religion and Science Incompatible?* 38
§13 *The Interface of Reason and Faith* 40
§14 *We Live by Fictions as Much as by Truths* 42
§15 *Pondering Confessions and Questions* 44
§16 *Faith Critically Examined* 46
§17 *The Nature of Religious Truth* 48
§18 *Does God Control the Wind?* 49
§19 *Does Mother Nature Control the Wind?* 51
§20 *Does the Wind Make Its Own Decisions?* 53

3: ON BEING HUMAN IN THE CONTEMPORARY WORLD 55

§21 *On Being Human 55*
§22 *From the Jesus Tradition: On Becoming and Being Human 57*
§23 *Why Am I Here? 58*
§24 *Intimations of Mortality 61*
§25 *The God Question 63*
§26 *What Does God Expect of Me? 65*
§27 *An Uncommonly Modern Question 68*
§28 *A Reason for Living 70*
§29 *Is Freedom an Illusion? 72*
§30 *Waiting for God/Waiting for Godot 74*
§31 *Human Suffering and Religious Faith 76*
§32 *What Is the Value of Religious Gestures? 78*
§33 *Living in the Old Country 80*
§34 *The Religious Experience 82*
§35 *Is God the Distant Creator or Your Intimate Soul Mate? 84*
§36 *My Lonely Brain and the Bible 85*

4: THE BIBLE 87

§37 *What Does the Term "Word of God" Mean as Applied to the Bible? 87*
§38 *When Did the Bible Become the "Word of God"? 90*
§39 *What about the Bible Gives It the Status "Word of God"? 92*
§40 *What Distinguishes the Bible from Other Collections of Holy Writ? 95*
§41 *Be There Dragons in the Bible? 97*
§42 *Legends in the Bible 99*
§43 *Living by the Bible Is Not Possible 101*
§44 *Should One Love God or Fear God? 103*
§45 *Dissenting Voices in a Text 104*
§46 *Does a Text "Mean" What the Author Intended? 106*
§47 *Satyrs or Wild Goats? The Politics of Translating the Bible 109*
§48 *Paul's Cross Gospel and First Thessalonians 113*
§49 *Jesus and Paul: A Lack of Continuity 115*
§50 *Did Jesus and Paul Believe in the Christian Heaven? 117*
§51 *Putting Paul in His Place 121*
§52 *Sex and Death: Paul's Arguments from Mythology 130*
§53 *An Allusion in Search of a Narrative: Betraying Jesus 131*
§54 *Narrative Realism in the Gospels 134*

§55 Did John Baptize Jesus? 135
§56 History, Historical Narrative, and Mark's Gospel 138
§57 The Problem of History in Mark 140
§58 Two Odd Locutions in the Gospel of Mark 142
§59 The Sibyl's Wish: A Mythical Encounter 144
§60 The Gospel of Mark Is Wrong—and other Quibbles! 146
§61 A Question of Identity 149
§62 The Gospel of John: A Revisionist Gospel 151
§63 Is John's Gospel History or Fiction? 154
§64 Memory in John and the Reshaping of Early Christian Tradition 156
§65 Historical Tradition in the Fourth Gospel 157
§66 Is the Gospel of John Historical Narrative? 159
§67 Does John know the difference between History and Faith? 161
§68 Why Does Jesus Not Use Parables in the Gospel of John? 163
§69 Was Peter Fishing Naked? Does it Matter? 165

5: THE NATURE OF GOD 168

§70 God does not "exist" 168
§71 From Where Does a Sense of the Divine Come? 170
§72 God the Spirit in a Material World 172
§73 Matter and Spirit: Making Sense of It All 174
§74 Is the Holy Spirit Part of a Trinity? 177
§75 Should We Always Trust Gods? 179
§76 Revelation: Did God Talk to Paul? 180
§77 Could God have a Character Flaw? 182
§78 Does God provide Signs that portend Future Events? 184
§79 Who Decides What Offends God? 185
§80 Does God Communicate in Dreams? 188
§81 Yahweh—the God Who Changed His Ways 190
§82 Ḥērem: God's Holy War 192
§83 What Does God Do? 194
§84 Consider a Universe without God 196

6: JESUS OF NAZARETH 199

§85 The Basic Problem of Historical Jesus Studies 199
§86 A Nearly Unknown Early Christian Title for Jesus 201
§87 The Beginning of Christology 203
§88 Was Jesus an Exorcist? 206

§89 "Scrubbing" the Early Jesus Traditions 208
§90 Parsing the Resurrection of the Christ 211
§91 Early Christian Confessions: An Inter-textual dialogue 213
§92 Will Christ Come Again? 217
§93 Reading Jesus' Mind 219
§94 Is Belief in the Divinity of Jesus Essential to Being Christian? 221
§95 Jesus was a Galilean Storyteller 233
§96 Why did Jesus Tell Parables? 236
§97 The Incarnation: Is Jesus God Incarnate? 237

7: TRADITIONAL CHRISTIAN BELIEFS 241

§98 Pondering the Origins of the Church 241
§99 Is the Trinity found in John's Gospel? 243
§100 Does Hell Exist? 245
§101 What Is Sin? 247
§102 Prophecy, Divination, and Fate 250
§103 Life is what you make it—or is it? 256
§104 Can the Church Grant Absolution for Sins? 258
§105 God's View of Marriage? 260
§106 Who Decides What Is "True Christianity"? 262
§107 Holiness Is a State of Mind 264
§108 How Did Moses Come by the Torah? 266
§109 How Relevant Is the Christian Worldview Today? 268
§110 The Church and Skeletons, Ghosts, Spirits, and Demons 270
§111 Prophecy Fulfilled, or Simply Creative Reading? 272
§112 Faith, Reason, and Mystery 274

8: ON BEING CHRISTIAN IN THE MODERN WORLD 281

§113 Learning to Live without Gods 281
§114 The Null Hypothesis, Epilepsy, and Evil Spirits 283
§115 Father George and the Sacred Mysteries of Faith 285
§116 On Wearing a Christian Label 287
§117 Is it Possible to Be Spiritual without Being Religious? 290
§118 Doing Right and Wrong 292
§119 Why Go to Church? 294
§120 End-of-Life Issues: Hospice, a Lingering Death, and Palliative Care 296
§121 An Impossible Situation: The Bishop versus the Nun 298
§122 On Dying Alone and Being Keepers of Sisters 299
§123 Sky Is Not Blue 301

Postscript 303
Bibliography 307
Index of Ancient Sources 323
Index of Modern Authors 349

Preface

Unmasking Biblical Faiths reflects the labor, and sometimes disappointing fruit,[1] of my early retirement years. At age seventy I retired from an academic career as professor of Religious Studies at Missouri State University, Springfield, Missouri, where from August of 1980 through December of 2004 I taught courses in New Testament and related literature and cultural backgrounds from a historical-critical perspective. In order to keep my mind active, and perhaps extend my life for some years, I purposed in the closing years of my life to analyze critically my own personal religious beliefs, and related matters, and to do it in a public manner online.[2]

The collection of short essays in this anthology[3] represents the results of ten years of critical reflection (2007–2017) on subjects related to religion, ethics, the Bible, the nature of the world, and human values; they have been later edited, revised, and annotated for publication in the present anthology. The essays are arranged topically in this volume, but the chronological date of the earlier online publication with reader comments is indicated at the end of each essay. Each essay considers things as they currently are on the basis of logic and reason rather than on what I have been taught or previously believed. The argument in each essay is complete in itself, but together the essays form the cumulative argument

---

1. I was disappointed that many of the fundamental ideas of my personal religious faith did not stand up to critical scrutiny.

2. The blog is titled *Wry Thoughts about Religion*. An archive of the essays is available online at the site.

3. Anthology, or florilegia, is an ancient literary form that continues to appear in modern publications in virtually every academic field of study. Chadwick, "Some Ancient Anthologies and Florilegia," xix. Two well-known anthologies of Jesus sayings are the Sermon on the Mount and the Gospel of Thomas.

that the Bible is only marginally relevant for contemporary religious faith, which is the thesis of this book.

I did not set out with a preformed plan of a particular set of ideas and issues to be analyzed for the project, but published every two weeks online an essay on a subject that interested me at the time or struck me as curious. The volume's present structure has been inductively drawn from the particular subjects of the essays themselves a considerable time after the fact of their original composition. As I look back over my earlier publications, it is apparent that the present volume was in my future. I had previously published two essays addressing my personal religious and academic journey, which lead directly to the essays in the present volume.[4]

---

4. Hedrick, "Out of the Enchanted Forest"; and Hedrick, "Excavating Museums."

Abbreviations

General

AD	*Anno Domini*, in the year of the Lord
BC	Before Christ
BCE	Before the Common Era
ca.	*circa*, about, approximately
CE	Common Era
cf.	*confer*, compare
chap.	chapter
comp.	compiler
ed.	editor, edition
e.g.	*exempli gratia*, for example
et al.	*et alii*, and others
i.e.	*id est*, that is
n.	note
no.	number
sic	so, thus, in this manner
s.v.	*sub verbo*, under the word
viz.	*videlicet*, namely
vol./vols.	volume/volumes

Ancient Sources

Ant.	*Jewish Antiquities*
1 Apol.	*First Apology*
Bar	Baruch
2 Bar	Second Baruch (Syriac Apocalypse)
1 Chr	First Chronicles
2 Chr	Second Chronicles
2 Clem.	Second Clement
Col	Colossians
1 Cor	First Corinthians
2 Cor	Second Corinthians
Descr.	*Description of Greece*
Deut	Deuteronomy
Dial.	*Dialogue with Trypho*
Did.	Didache
Diog.	Diognetus
Div.	*De divination*
Div. somn.	*De divination per somnum* (Prophesying by Dreams)
Eccl	Ecclesiastes
1 En.	First Enoch (Ethiopic Apocalypse)
Eph	Ephesians
Eph.	*To the Ephesians*
Ep. Pet. Phil.	VIII 2 Letter of Peter to Philip
2 Esd	Second Esdras
Esth	Esther
Exod	Exodus
Ezek	Ezekiel
Gal	Galatians
Gen	Genesis
Gos. Phil.	II 3 Gospel of Philip
Gos. Sav.	Gospel of the Savior
Gos. Thom.	II 2 Gospel of Thomas

Gos. Truth	1 3 Gospel of Truth
Hab	Habakkuk
Haer.	*Refutation of All Heresies*
Heb	Hebrews
Herm. Man.	Shepherd of Hermas, Mandates
Herm. Sim.	Shepherd of Hermas, Similitudes
Herm. Vis.	Shepherd of Hermas, Visions
Hist. eccl.	*Ecclesiastical History*
Hos	Hosea
Ig.	Ignatius
Isa	Isaiah
Jas	James
Jer	Jeremiah
Jdt	Judith
Jos.	Josephus
Josh	Joshua
Jub.	Jubilees
Judg	Judges
J.W.	*Jewish Wars*
1 Kgs	First Kings
2 Kgs	Second Kings
Lev	Leviticus
LXX	Septuagint (Greek translation of the Hebrew Bible)
2 Macc	Second Maccabees
Mag.	*To the Magnesians*
Mal	Malachi
Matt	Matthew
Mic	Micah
Mor.	*Moralia*
Neh	Nehemiah
Num	Numbers
Od.	*Odyssey*
Pan.	*Panarion (Adversus haereses)*

Phld.	*To the Philadelphians*
Phil.	*To the Philippians*
Pol.	Polycarp
Praescr.	*De praescriptione haereticorum*
Prov	Proverbs
Ps/Pss	Psalm/Psalms
1 Pet	First Peter
2 Pet	Second Peter
Phil	Philippians
Q	*Quelle* (hypothetical early sayings gospel used as a source by Matthew and Luke)
Rev	Revelation
Rom	Romans
1 Sam	First Samuel
2 Sam	Second Samuel
Sir	Sirach
Smyrn.	*To the Smyrnians*
Somn.	*De Somniis* (Dreams)
1 Thess	First Thessalonians
1 Tim	First Timothy
2 Tim	Second Timothy
Tit	Titus
Treat. Res.	I 4 Treatise on the Resurrection
Zech	Zechariah
Zeph	Zephaniah

Modern Sources

ABD	*Anchor Bible Dictionary*. Edited by David Noel Freedman. 6 vols. New York: Doubleday, 1992
ACW	Ancient Christian Writers
ANF	*Ante-Nicene Fathers*. Edited by Alexander Roberts and James Donaldson. 10 vols. Grand Rapids: Eerdmans, 1981–83

BRev	*Bible Review*
Berkeley Version	Gerrit Verkuyl, ed., *Holy Bible: The Berkeley Version in Modern English*. Grand Rapids: Zondervan, 1959
CEB	The Common English Bible Copyright © 2010, 2011 by Common English Bible.™ Used by permission. All rights reserved worldwide
DBib	John L. McKenzie, *Dictionary of the Bible*. New York, 1965
Douay	Douay Version
ForFasc	*Forum Fascicles*
Fourth R	*The Fourth R: An Advocate for Religious Literacy*
GNB	Good News Bible © 1994 published by the Bible Societies/HarperCollins Publishers Ltd UK, Good News Bible© American Bible Society 1966, 1971, 1976, 1992. Used with permission
IDB	*Interpreter's Dictionary of the Bible*. Edited by George A. Buttrick. 5 vols. New York: Abingdon, 1962–1976
JBL	*Journal of Biblical Literature*
JCoptS	*Journal of Coptic Studies*
JR	*Journal of Religion*
JSHJ	*Journal for the Study of the Historical Jesus*
LB	Living Bible © 1971. Used by permission of Tyndale House Publishers, Inc., Carol Stream, Illinois 60188. All rights reserved
LCL	Loeb Classical Library
MDB	*Mercer Dictionary of the Bible*. Edited by Watson E. Mills. Macon: Mercer University Press, 1990
Moffatt	*A New Translation of the Bible Containing the Old and New Testaments* by James Moffatt, copyright 1922, 1924, 1926, 1935 by Harper and Brothers
NABPR	National Association of Baptist Professors of Religion
NABPRSS	National Association of Baptist Professors of Religion Special Studies

NCB	New Century Bible
NEB	New English Bible copyright © Cambridge University Press and Oxford University Press 1961, 1970. All rights reserved
NHMS	Nag Hammadi and Manichean Studies
NICNT	New International Commentary on the New Testament
NIDB	*The New Interpreter's Dictionary of the Bible.* Edited by Katherine Doob Sakenfield. 5 vols. Nashville: Abingdon, 2006–2009
NIV	New International Version Copyright © 1973, 1978, 1984, 2011 by Biblica, Inc.® Used by permission. All rights reserved worldwide
NKJV	New King James Version
NPNF²	*The Nicene and Post-Nicene Fathers of the Christian Church.* Edited by Philip Schaff and Henry Wace. 2nd ser. 14 vols. Grand Rapids: Eerdmans, 1979–82
NRSV	New Revised Standard Version © 1989 National Council of the Churches of Christ in the United States of America. Used by permission. All rights reserved worldwide
NT	New Testament
OCD	*Oxford Classical Dictionary.* Edited by Simon Hornblower and Anthony Spawforth. 3rd ed. Oxford: Oxford University Press, 1999
OED	*Oxford English Dictionary* (1971)
OT	Old Testament
Phillips	*The New Testament in Modern English.* J. B. Phillips copyright © 1960, 1972 J. B. Phillips. Administered by the Archbishops' Council of the Church of England. Used by Permission
RSV	Revised Standard Version
SBC	Southern Baptist Convention
SBLBAC	Society of Biblical Literature The Bible and American Culture
SBLDS	Society of Biblical Literature Dissertation Series

SBLSymSer	Society of Biblical Literature Symposium Series
Smith-Goodspeed	*The Complete Bible. An American Translation.* OT translation by J. M. Powis Smith. Apocrypha and NT translation by Edgar J. Goodspeed ©1939 University of Chicago Press
SPCK	Society for Promoting Christian Knowledge
TDNT	*Theological Dictionary of the New Testament.* Edited by Gerhard Kittel and Gerhard Friedrich. Translated and Edited by Geoffrey W. Bromiley. 10 vols. Grand Rapids: Eerdmans, 1964–76
TEV	Today's English Version (= Good News Bible)
TUGAL	Texte und Untersuchungen zur Geschichte der altchristlichen Literatur
WIL	*The World in Literature Vol. 1.* Edited by Robert Warnock and George K. Anderson. 2 vols. in 1. Chicago: Scott Foresman, 1950

Introduction

Superstition, Faith, and the Marginal Relevance of the Bible

The Bible is well known, and rightly so, as a treasury of ancient religious wisdom and it is widely quoted approvingly by parents, judges, lawyers, teachers, ministers, poets, novelists, and so forth. Nevertheless it also has its faults and detractors, and rightly so, for it is also a repository of many harmful ideas, which must be avoided by those who use the Bible's treasury of positive religious wisdom. Hence touting the Bible as a positive guide for human life must be done very carefully, and proper cautions should be given about those ideas that cause harm.

The biblical texts[1] serve as the primary religious sources for the modern religions of Judaism and Christianity, in all their many forms. The historical significance of the Bible is that it sets forth the traditional origins of these two modern world religions. Jews and Christians accept the biblical texts as authoritative in varying degrees for many matters of religious faith and practice. In addition because of the influence of the Bible in Western culture through the centuries, it has played a role in

---

1. The generic name for the Bible in Judaism is *Tanak*, an acronym from the first letters of the words *Torah* (Law), *Neviim* (Prophets), and *Kethuvim* (Writings). Protestants, Orthodox, and Catholics include the Jewish collection in their Bibles, referring to it as the Old Testament. To these Jewish writings are added a smaller collection of Christian texts, called the New Testament books. The Protestant Old Testament does not have the same number of writings as the Catholic and Orthodox Bibles, since Catholic and Orthodox include a number of other books in the collection, which Protestants call Apocrypha (meaning "hidden"), but Catholic and Orthodox call these additional books deuterocanonical (meaning that they were added to the canon at a later time). See the brief description of these collections in Hayes, *Introduction*, 3–6.

shaping Western civilization, particularly with respect to religion, ethics, and social values in America.[2] Hence the two collections of ancient texts composing the Bible continue to be relevant, in varying degrees, to these groups, as well as to anyone else interested in American history and the progress of Western civilization.

The Bible, however, reflects in part cultural artifacts, social values, ethics, and religious practices, most of which no longer exist in living communities. It constitutes the traditions of two different ancient religious communities in the past, whose history is thought to extend roughly from the Israelite exodus (ca. 1250 BCE)[3] to the writing of 2 Peter (ca. 125 CE),[4] or for a period of about 1300 years plus or minus. The Hebrew Bible is a library of the written traditions of the ancient Israelite people, containing among other things their history and religious traditions along with their ancient laws, prophetic literature, hymnbook, wisdom literature, and so forth. Their traditions are thought to date from the thirteenth century BCE to about 400 BCE (the Second Temple period). The Apocrypha (or the deuterocanonical books) consists of additional Israelite religious texts written between 300 BCE and 70 CE.[5] The New Testament (ca. 50 CE to the early second century CE) contains among other things stories, personal correspondence, and theological essays.[6] Both Old and New Testaments came to be canonized in the Greco-Roman period,[7] and because of their antiquity these texts may be expected to be more susceptible to the influences of superstition and credulity, as would be expected in precritical societies.

Therefore modern groups that use the Bible as a basis to inform modern faith and practice are forced to deal with ideas in ancient texts of diverse cultural and religious influence covering some thirteen hundred years, or so, by ignoring much and adapting what they can for modern

2. Noll, "Bible and American Culture." Here are two titles in the SBL series The Bible in American Culture documenting more fully the role played by the Bible in American Culture: Phy, ed., *Bible and Popular Culture*; and Johnson, ed., *Bible in American Law*.

3. Kitchen, "Exodus, The," 703.

4. Elliott, "Peter, Second Epistle of," 287.

5. Charlesworth, "Apocrypha," 292.

6. See §39 below, p. 92, "What about the Bible Gives It the Status of Word of God?"

7. Eissfeldt (*Old Testament*, 560) finds that the canonization process of the Old Testament came to an end in the second century CE and the New Testament canon was established as a practical matter around the middle fourth century CE (McDonald, "Canon of the New Testament," 542).

life. One particularly challenging aspect of the antiquity of these texts for contemporary readers is the frequent clash between the primitive worldviews of these texts and mainstream modern worldviews, which have evolved as a result of the Enlightenment of the eighteenth century.[8] The clash between antiquity and modernity often forces a modern human being to make a willing suspension of disbelief when reading the Bible.[9] For example, when we read in the Hebrew Bible that a dead Israelite who was being buried in the grave of Elisha was revived and stood on his feet "as soon as he touched the bones of Elisha" (2 Kgs 13:20–21), it raises the specter of superstition, magic, and ancient fetishes.[10]

There is no word for superstition in biblical Hebrew, so arguably the concept did not exist as such among the ancient Israelites.[11] Nevertheless the recognition that human beings are superstitious creatures is an ancient idea. For example, in the fourth century BCE Theophrastus was well aware that human beings were incurably superstitious.[12] In his book, *Characters*, the sixteenth character that Theophrastus discusses is the superstitious person. He describes superstition as cowardice with respect to divinity (*to daimonion*), which seems to be an excessive fear of the gods. In the Greco-Roman period,[13] judging by how some authors[14] understood their own age, the time period in which the books of the New Testament were written and its collection canonized was an age characterized in large part by superstition and credulity. *Credulity* is defined as a belief, or a readiness to believe something, especially on slight

   8. Gay, "Introduction," 13–26; Randall, *Making of the Modern Mind*, 253–86.

   9. By a "willing suspension of disbelief" I mean to say that one suspends one's critical judgment, logic, and reason to "believe" something one recognizes as untrue or impossible.

   10. Frazer, *Golden Bough*, 12–52.

   11. Compare the lack of a concept of time among primitive cultures for example: Palmer, "Amondawa Tribe."

   12. See the different translations in Theophrastus, *Characters of Theophrastus* (trans. Edmonds), 106–13; and Theophrastus, *Theophrastus Characters* (trans. and ed. Rusten et al.) 106–13.

   13. The Greco-Roman period is usually conceived as beginning in the late fourth century BCE with the conquests of Alexander the Great, which extended Greek culture and thought throughout the Mediterranean basin. It extended throughout the Roman period to the collapse and disintegration of the Roman Empire (beginning 410 CE) and into the Christian period. See Hollister and Bennett, *Medieval Europe*, 5–7, as an example of this historical division.

   14. See, for example, Cicero, "On Divination," and "On the Nature of the Gods"; and Plutarch, "Superstition."

or uncertain evidence, and in the modern period credulity is associated with a willingness to ascribe a supernatural origin to both normal as well as uncanny phenomena, which are things that appear to go beyond what is considered normal, or things regarded as having a supernatural character or origin.

Today *superstition*[15] is defined as "a belief, conception, act, or practice resulting from ignorance, unreasoning fear of the unknown or mysterious scrupulosity, trust in magic or chance,"[16] or "*a belief affording the relief of an anxiety by means of an irrational notion.*"[17]

Superstition (Greek: *deisidaimonia*; Latin: *superstitio*) in the Greco-Roman period, however, is defined somewhat differently; it is "a free citizen's forgetting his dignity by throwing himself into the servitude of deities conceived as tyrants . . . Thus the superstitious were supposed to submit themselves to exaggerated rituals, to adhere in credulous fashion to prophecies and to allow themselves to be abused by charlatans."[18] Plutarch in contrasting the atheist and superstitious person wrote:

> Superstition . . . is an emotional idea, and an assumption productive of a fear which utterly humbles and crushes a man, for he thinks that there are gods, but that they are the cause of pain and injury. In fact, the atheist, apparently, is unmoved regarding the Divinity, whereas the superstitious man is moved as he ought not to be, and his mind is thus perverted.[19]

Cicero contrasted religion and superstition[20] in this way: superstition "implies a groundless fear of the gods," and religion "consists in piously worshipping them."[21] In the Roman period *superstition* (*superstitio*) also came to have the idea of "bad religion," a label by which a dominant religious group might libel a minority religious group.[22]

The term *superstition* (*deisidaimonia*) appears only twice in the New Testament (Acts 17:22; 25:19) and to judge from Greek lexicons it is a

---

15. One can find a few modern examples of superstition listed in Wikipedia, "List of Superstitions."

16. *Webster's Third New International Dictionary* (1961) s.v., superstition.

17. Planer, *Superstition*, 6; cf. 28.

18. Scheid, "Superstitio," *OCD*, 1456.

19. Plutarch, "Superstition," 456–57 (II.165 B–C).

20. Cicero offers some examples of superstition in "On the Nature of the Gods," 322–23 (III.xv.39).

21. Cicero, "On the Nature of the Gods," 112–13 (I.xlii. 117).

22. Versnel, "Deisidaimonia," 441.

general term for religion or excessive religious scrupulosity,[23] which generally agrees with the judgments of Greco-Roman writers. On the other hand, religious belief by modern definition is generally seen as something quite similar to superstition, differing only in a negative evaluation given to the latter and a positive evaluation given to the former. Today faith is generally defined as "belief and trust in and loyalty to God" or "a firm or unquestioning belief in something for which there is no proof."[24] Judging from their definitions, faith and superstition actually seem to function in a similar manner. What I conclude from the shades of meaning accorded the word *superstition* is that superstition and faith are not two qualitatively different kinds of belief. Rather they reflect a range of similar attitudes best represented by a spectrum with superstition at one end and religious belief at the other end.[25] They presumably meet somewhere around the middle, depending on who is describing the middle point. In short, what some define as acceptable religious belief, others will define as unacceptable superstition.

The modern definition of *superstition* casts doubt on much of what one finds in the Bible. For example, much of what one finds in the Bible demands a willing suspension of disbelief on the part of a twenty-first-century person. Educated persons will recognize that certain narratives reflect physical impossibilities and hence clash with the way things usually work in the world. For example, in the cycle of stories about the acts of Elisha in 2 Kings (chapters 2–13) one finds among other stories of the same sort the story of an iron ax-head that floated after falling into the Jordan River (6:1–7). Elisha, described as "the man of God," reputedly caused the ax-head to rise to the surface by tossing a stick into the water. The claim that the ax-head floated violates the buoyancy principle of Archimedes of Syracuse (third century BCE) that states, an object will float if its weight is equal to or less than the weight of the water it displaces. The weight of an iron ax-head is not equal to or less than the weight of the water it displaces and hence it will not float. And common sense tells

---

23. Bauer and Danker, eds., *Greek-English Lexicon*, 216; Moulton and Milligan, *Vocabulary of the Greek Testament*, 139.

24. *Webster's Third New International Dictionary*, s.v. "faith."

25. Others have noted the relationship between superstition and religious faith. For example, Rios, "Religion and Superstition through a Cognitive Perspective"; Cline, "Religion vs. Superstition." The temporal lobe of the human brain is the likely locus of both phenomena: Persinger, "Religious and Mystical Experiences." My thanks to Robert Conner for suggesting Persinger's article.

us that a stick tossed into the water would have no influence on what is essentially a law of modern physics.[26] In order to think that the narrative describes something that actually happened, readers must suspend disbelief.

Another narrative requiring a suspension of disbelief is the tradition of Joshua causing the sun to stand still in the sky to allow the Israelites to slay all their enemies, the Amorites, at Gibeon (Josh 10:6–14).

> And the sun stood still, and the moon stayed, until the nation took vengeance on their enemies. Is this not written in the Book of Jashar? The sun stayed in the midst of heaven, and did not hasten to go down for about a whole day. There has been no day like it before or since. (Josh 10:13–14, RSV)

The belief that the sun rises in the east, moves across the sky, and sets in the west, is an ancient superstition, shared by the biblical writers.[27] This belief was proven incorrect only in the sixteenth century CE. Until that time it was believed that the sun and the planets circled the earth, which held a position in the center of the solar system.[28] In other words they believed that the earth did not move, but today it is common knowledge that the earth makes an elliptical movement around the sun.

The New Testament also has narratives defying reason, logic, and explanation as actual historical events. For example, Jesus is represented as feeding five thousand people with five loaves and two fish; the account appears in all four canonical gospels (Mark 6:32–44; Matt 14:13–21; Luke 9:10–17; John 6:1–15). In the narrative everyone eats their fill and twelve baskets of food fragments are left over. The story depicts two logical impossibilities. While it is conceivable that five loaves and two fish could each be divided into amounts tiny enough to pass out to five thousand people, it is physically impossible that every person would be satiated from eating the tiny amount that they would have of necessity received (Mark 6:42; Matt 14:20; Luke 9:17; John 6:12), or that there would be twelve baskets full of fragments left over after the feeding (Mark 6:43; Matt 14:20; Luke 9:17; John 6:13).[29]

---

26. *Encyclopedia Britannica*, "Archimedes' Principle."

27. For example, Gen 15:12; Exod 17:12; Judg 14:18; 2 Chr 18:34; Matt 5:45; Mark 16:2; Eph 4:26.

28. Abell, *Exploration of the Universe*, 34–53.

29. Compare similar stories about Elijah and Elisha in 1 Kgs 17: 8–16 (the jar of meal and the cruse of oil) and 2 Kgs 4:1–7 (the jar of oil). Each story contrasts limited amounts at the beginning and the abundant residue at the end exceeding that with

Another narrative illustrating the presence of superstitious beliefs in the Bible is found in the Gospel of Matthew. At the very moment that Jesus died,[30] Matthew describes an earthquake apparently causing the opening of tombs in which were buried dead saints; their bodies "were raised" as a result of the earthquake; the saints who were raised then "went into the holy city and appeared to many" (Matt 27:53). The story is a logical impossibility, for decomposition of the human body begins around four minutes after death, and in twenty-four to seventy-two hours the internal organs of those deceased decompose.[31] Thus the story breaks with common human experience; those who are actually dead cannot return to a living state, for it would violate the physical law of the conservation of energy:[32]

> Energy cannot be created or destroyed, only converted from one form to another, and the amount of free energy always increases. In other words, things fall apart, converting their mass to energy while doing so. Decomposition is one final, morbid reminder that all matter in the universe must follow these fundamental laws. It breaks us down, equilibrating our bodily matter with its surroundings, and recycling it so that other living things can put it to use.[33]

An unusual statement in Acts 19:11–12 provides another example of superstition in the Bible; it is no more than a brief aside having little connection with the narrative in which it is embedded:

> And God did extraordinary miracles (*dunameis*) by the hands of Paul so that handkerchiefs or aprons were carried away from his body to the sick, and diseases left them and the evil spirits came out of them. (Acts 19:11–12, RSV)

The statement immediately plunges the reader into the occult world of ancient magic, superstition, and religious fetishes. The author, which

---

which the story began.

30. There is a discrepancy in the timing of the event. Although the story immediately follows the death of Jesus (Matt 27:50 plus 27:55–56), the narrative itself states the event occurred after the resurrection of Jesus (Matt 27:53). Note that the NIV translation replaces the opening words in the Greek text of 27:51 *kai idou* (and behold!) with a surprising English translation of "at that moment." The translation disagrees with the text, which claims the event took place "after the resurrection" (27:53).

31. *Aftermath*, "What Are the Four Stages of Human Decomposition?"; Costandi, "Life after Death."

32. Wikipedia, "Conservation of Energy."

33. Costandi, "Life after Death."

scholars call Luke,³⁴ describes God as working extraordinary deeds through the hands of Paul so that handkerchiefs (*soudaria*) or aprons (*simikinthia*) that touched his skin (*chrōtos*) were provided to the sick and demon possessed. As a result of contact with the cloth objects that had touched Paul, these people were healed and purged of evil spirits (Acts 19:12).

The principle involved in the account seems to be that of healing and exorcism from a distance by a power from the objects themselves rather than by the activity of an exorcist or healer. Thus it wasn't Paul himself who healed and exorcised. It was rather a power transferred from Paul's skin that came to reside in the cloths themselves that effectuated the cures and the exorcisms. The power in the cloths, which originated with God, had come to work through Paul, and was passed from Paul to the cloths. The healings and exorcisms are thus not described as healing acts performed directly by God or by Paul, but rather from what appear to have become religious fetishes having power in themselves. The principle involved in Acts 19:11–12 is similar to Frazer's idea of "contagious magic," which states that "things which have once been in contact with each other continue to act on each other at a distance after the physical contact has been severed."³⁵

The account in Acts 19 is similar to the woman's belief in Matt 9:20–21. The woman is described as believing that if she could only "touch the edge of [Jesus'] garment," she could be made well. That is to say, she is represented as thinking that the garment touching the body of Jesus possessed that same power by which Jesus is credited with performing his mighty deeds. In this same way the author of Acts appears to think that healing power also resided in things Paul touched.

The principle of healing from a distance and what Frazer called "contagious magic" also seems to be behind the odd statement in Acts 5:15 that the sick were laid out in the streets "that as Peter came by at least his shadow (*skia*) might fall on some of them." That is to say, that Luke represents certain people in Jerusalem as expecting a good result

---

34. This is because the author of Luke is believed to have written Acts.

35. Frazer, *Golden Bough*, 12 (12–14). Thus the magician "infers that whatever he does to a material object will affect equally the person with whom the object was once in contact whether it formed part of his body or not" (pp. 43–52). The principle at work in contagious magic is that things that have been conjoined "must remain ever afterwards" even when separated. Hence this narrative aside in Acts seems to reflect the principle of contagious magic: a sympathetic relationship is believed to continue existing between Paul and the cloth objects even when separated (p. 43).

from the "ministering" shadow of Peter.[36] Hence they brought the sick to a public place at the temple in hopes that Peter's powers of healing might be administered through his shadow.[37]

The transfer of power through objects and shadows is similar to Paul's idea that holiness can be transferred from a believing partner to an unbelieving partner in a marriage, so that the children of such a mixed marriage would not be "unclean" (1 Cor 7:13-14; compare 1 Cor 6:15-16 where the transference seems to work the other way).[38]

A kind of primitive power is apparently described as being at work in these incidents. Anthropologists have adopted the term *mana*, a Melanesian term (there are others),

> as a convenient designation for the widespread belief in occult force or indwelling power as such, independent of either persons or spirits . . . Taken together all such terms refer to the experienced presence of a powerful but silent force in things, especially any occult force which is believed to act of itself, as an addition to the forces naturally or usually present in a thing . . . It is a force that is thought to be transmissible from objects in nature to man, from one person to another, or again from persons to things.[39]

Broadly speaking the brief aside in Acts 19 suggests the operation of a kind of primitive magic in which objects taken from the body of Paul are themselves the source of a supernatural power that goes forth to cure diseases and drive out evil spirits.[40] *Magic* is defined as

> the use of means (as ceremonies, charms, spells) that are believed to have supernatural power to cause a supernatural being to produce or prevent a particular result (as rain, death, healing) considered not obtainable by natural means and that also contain the arts of divination, incantation, sympathetic magic, and thaumaturgy: control of natural forces by the typically direct

---

36. See Conner, "Shadow as a Magical Assistant."

37. The same primitive idea stands behind Luke 1:35, where "the power of the Most High will overshadow" (*episkiase*) Mary in order to effect her insemination. For an opposite view see Fitzmyer, *Gospel according to Luke*. 1:351.

38. See Hedrick, "Putting Paul in His Place," 7-8.

39. Noss, *Man's Religions*, 16. A belief in *mana* is one of fourteen common features of primitive religions (pp. 14-31).

40. Magic was pervasive in antiquity; see Betz, *Greek Magical Papyri*; and Meyer, et al., eds., *Ancient Christian Magic*.

action of rites, objects, materials or words considered supernaturally potent.[41]

This brief narrative aside appears to document the presence of a kind of primitive magic in early Jesus gatherings. If the early followers of Jesus did practice a kind of primitive magic, it should serve as a caution to modern readers of the Bible that all its ideas must be carefully evaluated before one acts on them. Ideas and events in the Bible, disallowed by logic and human reason, create the following problem for those who would take the Bible as a basis for life in the twenty-first century: how can one sort out in a formal way the Bible's reasonable ideas from the irrelevant and dangerous?

For example, the Bible's universal condemnation of human pride as "sinful" is clearly flawed. The Bible has virtually nothing positive to say about pride, and vigorously condemns it in every instance or virtually every instance (it depends on whether one uses the Protestant or Catholic Bible). In Hebrew Bible (the Christian Old Testament) a usual synonym for "pride" is "arrogance" (Prov 8:13; Isa 9:9, 13:11; 16:6; Jer 48:2) or "haughtiness" (Jer 48:29; Zeph 3:11). Its opposite is "humility" (Job 22:29; Prov 3:34; 29:23; 2 Chr 32:26), which God honors (Prov 22:4; 2 Chr 7:14, 12:7). I found only two positive statements about pride, both in the Catholic Old Testament (Jdt 15:9; Sir 50:1).

In the New Testament pride (*alazoneia*, 1 John 2:16)[42] is uniformly condemned, as is its synonym (*uperēphaneia*, Mark 7:22), which is defined in the lexicon as "a state of undue sense of one's importance bordering on insolence, *arrogance, haughtiness, pride.*"[43] These two words in the New Testament describe completely negative character traits (Luke 1:51; Rom 1:30; 2 Tim 3:2; Jas 4:6; 1 Pet 5:5).

A severely negative view of pride has persisted in Western culture without doubt because of the influence of the Bible. For example, near the end of the fourteenth century CE in the "Parson's Tale" Chaucer listed pride as the first of the seven deadly sins, and the root of all the others (pride, envy, wrath, sloth, greed, gluttony, and lust), noting that the only remedy for pride is humility or meekness, a virtue in which a person

---

41. *Webster's Third New International Dictionary*, s. v. "magic."

42. In Classical Greek *alazoneia* is translated as "pretension," "imposture," and "boastfulness": Liddell and Scott, *Greek-English Lexicon* (9th ed.), 59.

43. Bauer and Danker, eds., *Greek-English Lexicon*, 1033.

"considers himself worthy of no esteem nor dignity."[44] In the seventeenth century Milton traced the beginning of the woes of humankind to the pride of Satan.

> Th' infernal serpent, he it was, whose guile stirred up with envy and revenge, deceiv'd the mother of mankind, what time his pride had cast him out from Heav'n, with all his host of rebel angels, by whose aid aspiring to set himself in glory above his peers, he trusted to have equal'd the Most High."[45]

Keeping the biblical attitude toward pride in mind, it may be surprising to learn that self-respect is considered synonymous with pride. In fact, one definition of *pride* is "a sense of one's own worth and abhorrence of what is beneath or unworthy of oneself: lofty self-respect."[46] Here are a number of comments about pride that assess its character in a positive way (and even Paul seems to acknowledge pride's positive features in Gal 6:4, but without using the word "pride"), which most readers have heard at one time or another from parents, teachers, and others:

> Take pride in your work. A job well-done is a meaningful accomplishment / Take pride in your appearance. / Civic pride should be encouraged on the part of citizens of a state/ Pride is a personal commitment—it is an attitude that separates excellence from mediocrity. / There are two kinds of pride, both good and bad. "Good pride" represents our dignity and self-respect / Be proud of who you are instead of wishing you were someone else / Pride is holding your head up when everyone around you has theirs bowed—courage is what makes you do it.

Such statements ring true to a modern ear because they are true. Pride is not conceit or arrogance or haughtiness or pretension or hubris. Pride is an aspect of one's personal integrity and one of the better angels of human nature.[47] Viewed from the biblical perspective, however, pride, is firmly condemned by God. Nevertheless, from a secular common-sense perspective pride may well be an essential positive trait of what it means to become a successful human being. If pride, or being proud, can often be a positive concept, the biblical view of pride is thereby shown to

---

44. Chaucer, "Parson's Tale."
45. Milton, *Paradise Lost*, book 1, lines 34–40.
46. *Webster's Third International Dictionary Unabridged* (2002), 1799.
47. Estrada, "Pride—Sin or Incentive?"

be at the very least inadequate, but more likely it should be understood as flawed and misleading in that it masks the true nature of pride.[48]

Narratives (like those discussed above) requiring a suspension of disbelief on the part of most of us are nevertheless accepted as a normal part of modern reality by the deeply pious; they have a high degree of confidence in the Bible and simply dismiss the idea that the event could not have happened by asserting, *the Bible says it; I believe it; that settles it*—as if the story about how we came by Bible[49] has no impact on the relative value of its ideas. Others offer a slightly more sophisticated theory to explain away problems like these in the Bible: *God is in control of the universe; therefore God can do whatever God chooses in the universe.* This latter statement simply disregards how the universe is thought to work in secular society; those who live by this statement are simply changing "reality" to correspond to their religious faith. A third way of handling problems in biblical narratives requiring a suspension of disbelief rejects the "laws" of physics by arguing *the universe is not a closed system but rather an open system.* Hence the physical "laws" become general rules that are sometimes suspended, leaving open the possibility that "miracles" can occur.

The Bible is a selective collection of ancient texts whose ideas are, in part, simply out of place with what is known about how things work in the physical universe. Readers of the Bible should be cautious in accepting without challenge what it says. The Bible has played such an iconic role in Western culture, however, that it is difficult for an average person, unlettered in the critical approaches to biblical texts, to appreciate its foibles, blemishes, errors, and often insidiously captivating ideas. It has even been difficult for many of those specifically trained in the critical approaches to the Bible to specify its dangerous ideas. What follows in this book is an attempt to address specific instances of the vagaries of biblical faith in contemporary popular religion.

---

48. Azar, "The Faces of Pride."

49. The biblical text that one reads today is the product of the science of textual criticism. Textual criticism is basic to all other scientific approaches to the Bible. See the following short descriptions of the science of textual criticism: Fuller, "Text Criticism, OT," 529–34; Holmes, "Text Criticism, NT," 529–31.

1

The Nature of the Universe

§1 THE BIBLICAL VIEW OF THE UNIVERSE

The ancient Israelites had no single word for material space, such as "world" or "cosmos." The aspects of material space occupied by human beings were known simply as heaven and earth (Gen 1:1); heaven, earth, and sea (Exod 20:11); heaven, earth, and water under the earth (Exod 20:4); heaven, earth, sea, and the deep (Ps 135:6). The earth was like a saucer surrounded by water and resting upon water (Gen 1:1, 6–8) or foundational pillars (Prov 8:27–29). In short, there was a bit of firmament (the vault or arch of the sky) sheltering a flat earth from a surrounding watery chaos.

The material space of the world was created by God, who regarded it as "very good" (Gen 1:31). The biblical story about this space is marred by disobedience. Adam, the first man, created by God, breaks the creator's one rule (Gen 2:17), and as a result he and Eve, the first divinely created woman, are banished from the good life in the garden of Eden. Life outside the garden is difficult, threatening, and ends in death (Gen 3:16–19).

The apostle Paul used the banishment of Adam and Eve from the garden to explain why Adam and his descendants die. They die because of Adam's disobedience (Rom 5:12–14, 17). Perhaps even the physical creation was also affected by Adam's act, for Paul describes the creation as being in bondage to decay waiting for redemption (Rom 8:18–21). Today even the most ardent Bible believer should recognize that this primitive description of the universe is mythical because photographs have been taken from the moon of earth, a more-or-less spherical, planet surrounded by limitless space in a universe of billions of galaxies and planetary systems with not a drop of water around it.

The world into which Adam and Eve, the progenitors of humanity, were forced has a bizarre landscape. Things are not what they seem on the surface. Horrid demons lurk about (satyrs, Lev 17:7; the night demon Lilith, Isa 34:14; the noonday devil, Ps 91:6). For those sharing the biblical view of the world, a plethora of demonic entities and evil forces must be negotiated. For example, the Prince of the Power of the Air (Eph 2:2; John 14:30, 16:11) leads a consortium of demons and evil spirits that threaten harm to human beings.

> We denizens of the earth "are not contending against flesh and blood, but against the principalities, against the powers, against the world rulers of this present darkness, against the spiritual hosts of wickedness in the heavenly places (Eph 6:12 RSV).

Evil and unclean spirits fall upon humans unawares, possess them, and cause them to behave insanely (Mark 5:1–10); they infect them with deafness, muteness (Mark 9:25), infirmity (Luke 13:11), and epilepsy (Matt 17:15–18); they empower in them the black art of divination (Acts 16:16) and the performance of signs of coming evil days (Rev 16:13–14). They even cause prophets to lie (1 Kgs 22:21–23). Satan, the archenemy of God, can even transform himself into an angel of light (2 Cor 11:14), so that a person never knows if s/he deals with a good or evil force. There is also a cadre of good spirits and angels at work in the world; For example, a Great Spirit assigns angels to watch over "little ones" (Matt18:10).

Fortunately certain human beings, empowered by benevolent spirits can combat the evil forces. For example, Jesus gave his disciples authority to cast out unclean spirits (Matt 10:1) and in addition commissioned them "to heal the sick, raise the dead, cleanse lepers, cast out demons" (Matt 10:8). In other words the world is a place of constant struggle between the spiritual forces of good and evil, and the contested territory is precisely the mind, health, and behavior of human beings; at least that is what the Biblical writers seemed to believe.

Strange things happen in the biblical world: ax-heads float (2 Kgs 6:4–7), donkeys talk (Num 22:21–30), the dead won't stay dead (Matt 27:51–54), people defy gravity and walk on water (Mark 6:45–52), on command the earth stops rotating (Josh 10:12–14), snakes carry on conversations with people (Gen 3:1–5). There are magic cloths that heal diseases and drive out evil spirits (Acts 19:12; Mark 5:24–30).

I don't find the world I live in to be like it is described in the Bible. I have never personally encountered spirit forces. True, the world I live in is dangerous, but pretty bland when compared to the world seen through the eyes of the biblical writers. My life and welfare are always at risk from natural forces and even nature itself, but I have never been threatened with harm by evil spirits or demons. I have never met an angel. In the world, as I experience it, people who die stay dead, and day passes into night with amazing regularity.

Did a world such as it is described in the Bible ever actually exist? Or did it exist only in the imaginations of the ancient writers, and in the minds of those who choose to believe those ancient writers? My money is on the latter alternative. (2–21–16)

§2 IS THE UNIVERSE JUST?

I define *just* as acting or being in conformity with what is morally upright or good. This definition includes the idea of justice, which is an impartial administration of rewards and punishments; that is to say, if the universe is just, what you receive in common space and time should be balanced. By universe I mean the whole body of things and phenomena; the totality of material entities, conceived as an orderly and harmonious system.

How we humans have conceived the universe has changed through time. In antiquity it was a primitive three-tiered construct: earth in the center, the primordial waters beneath the earth, and the fixed luminaries in a domed structure that protected the earth from the waters above.[1] In biblical faith God is believed to have used weather, the elements, and historical events to reward and punish, although not always in a just way (for example, consider his treatment of the Amalekites, 1 Sam 15).

Until the twentieth century our view of the universe was limited. In the second century CE Ptolemy proposed a geocentric system for the movements of the heavenly bodies in what we now know as our solar system: the sun, moon, and five planets circulated around the earth below the (so-called) fixed stars, which were so distant they appeared never to move.[2] Dante Alighieri (1300s) draws on the theological system of the

---

1. Gaster, "Cosmogony," 702–6.
2. Sagan, *Cosmos*, 51–53.

Middle Ages in order to reflect the view of the universe at that time. With the earth at its center, the universe included both the various levels of hell as well as dwelling places for saints, angels, and the deity.[3]

In the 1600s, Copernicus proposed a heliocentric system: the sun was the center of our solar system. The earth rotated on its axis and circulated along with the planets around the sun. This explanation was resisted by the church until the nineteenth century, because an earth-centered universe was best harmonized with the Bible and Christian doctrine.[4]

Today we live on an insignificant planet on the outskirts of a galaxy of perhaps a hundred billion planetary systems in a universe of perhaps one hundred billion galaxies.[5] Our universe has no edge but is unbounded and expanding outwards toward some unknown destination.

The question with which I began (is the universe just?) assumes too much. Since the universe is not sentient, it could not be "just." The universe does not think or see, so there is no way that it could perceive an imbalance in justice—much less consider correcting it. The aggregate of existing stuff and entities that fill the void of space act more or less in accord with what physicists and astronomers (i.e., scientists: people who study the universe) call the laws of physics.

In short, the universe is inflexible. It blindly follows its own rules, some of which we know; most of which we do not. Do not expect the universe to balance out your allotment of good and bad in life. We only have to recall a few of our recent tragic encounters with the physical world on this blue and white planet to know that there is not an ounce of compassion in the universe over the loss of human life, unjustified suffering, and property damage caused by the physical elements such as the San Francisco earthquake (1989), the Indonesian tsunami (2004), Hurricane Katrina in New Orleans (2005), the Joplin tornado (2011), and Hurricane Sandy (2012).

What happens in the natural world is not the result of evil. Rattlesnakes and disease, for example, are not caused by the devil or by God. Rattlesnakes are true to their nature; disease is a natural phenomenon that human beings can cure, and control once the causations have been discovered. Chickenpox, diphtheria, and polio, for example, have been either cured or managed.

---

3. Alighieri, *Divine Comedy*, 2.160–201.

4. Sagan, *Cosmos*, 53; Copernicus, "Revolutions of the Heavenly Bodies," 499–503.

5 Sagan, *Cosmos*, 193, 212.

For these reasons I cannot seriously entertain the idea that "God" is a universal Spirit pervading all things in the universe with divine presence—a leaf, the sunrise, a drop of water, a gurgling brook, and so forth.⁶ The universe is simply too hostile toward human beings to think it reflects the character of benevolent Spirit. Nor can I seriously consider that God actively runs the universe in a benevolent hands-on way (Col 1:16–17), correcting, like Don Quixote, its excesses and imbalances.

We seem instinctively to know that the universe is not just, and recognize that a benevolent Deity is not controlling the universe in our interest. That is why a common feature of religion in general is to hope, believe, or expect that Deity will balance the books on our life in this world in the afterlife, if such there be. That is, that God will compensate us for any imbalance of good and bad we experienced in life. (3-19-15)

§3 WHERE DOES EVIL COME FROM?⁷

Every discussion of evil should begin with a definition of *evil*. What I mean by *evil* is an unethical, deliberately malicious, act that results in harm to human beings. By this definition, not everything harmful that happens to humans is evil. For example, an accident involving harm to another party is not an evil act, although it may maim someone or even result in someone's death. What is lacking in the accident is deliberate malicious intent, and the one causing the accident may be as grieved as the friends and family of the injured party.

Within this definition, nature does no evil, even though it is "red in tooth and claw."⁸ The destructive forces of nature (floods, tornados, hurricanes, disease, and so forth) are not acting with malicious intent; they are simply natural forces operating according to natural laws; that is, according to the usual observed patterns for such things in the universe. The natural world and the animal and plant worlds are therefore ethically neutral. When you get cancer, or when you are bitten by a poisonous snake, when you are maimed by a bear, or when your home is destroyed by a tornado or flood, those forces are not acting with malicious intent toward you; they are just being true to their nature.

---

6. As beautifully stated in Taussig, "Disparate Presence," 149–60.

7. This essay, here revised, subsequently appeared in the *Fourth R* 26/4 (July-August 2013) 15–16; used by permission.

8. Tennyson, *In Memoriam*," canto 56, line 15.

Unless, of course, you happen to subscribe to the belief that both the world of human beings and the world of nature fall under the influence of unseen mysterious, malicious, unethical forces that are able to co-opt for their own devious ends the usually benign forces of nature, as well as unsuspecting human beings. In this way of thinking Good and Evil are believed to be personified Spiritual Entities competing against one another in both natural and social worlds. These spiritual forces are popularly believed to harness the ethically neutral forces of the natural world and its living elements (flora and fauna) to their own ends, whether good or evil.

Traditionally in the Judeo-Christian West, God is regarded as the proponent for Good. But what can we say about evil? Here the picture is not so clear. In the Hebrew Bible before the fall of Judah to the Babylonians (587 BCE[9]) only one figure in Israel dispensed both good and evil in the world. Prior to the deportation of the Judeans to Babylon, God alone was believed to be the source of both good and evil (Job 2:10). Frequently one finds in the Hebrew Bible the repetitive expression "the LORD repented of the evil" he planned to do (Exod 32:14; Jer 26:13, 19; Jonah 3:10; 1 Kgs 14:10; 2 Sam 24:16), or "the LORD brings evil" against . . . (Josh 23:15; 1 Kgs 9:9; 2 Kgs 21:12; Ezek 5:13–17; 2 Sam 17:14; 2 Kgs 6:33; Neh 13:18; Job 42:11). Particularly impressive are the descriptions of God putting lying spirits in the mouths of his prophets to deceive (1 Kgs 22:13–23), or the idea that God uses evil spirits to do his bidding (Judg 9:23; 1 Sam 16:14–16, 23; 18:10; 19:9). Evil intentions and actions were, of course, always thought to lie within human beings (Gen 6:5; 8:21; 50:20).

After the Persian conquest of Babylon (539 BCE), Cyrus the Great, king of Persia, permitted the exiles to return to Judah (Ezra 1:1–11), and sometime after their restoration in the land of Judah (described in Ezra and Nehemiah) Satan gradually becomes the source of personified evil in Israel. This evil force was developed by the Judeans during their exposure to the Persian Zoroastrian religion where there were two competing spiritual forces in the universe, one Good and the other Evil. Initially Satan (a Hebrew word meaning "accuser" or "adversary") was described as a functionary of the divine court (at this point he is not yet the incarnation of evil, Zech 3:1–2); his principal activity appeared to be accusing or finding fault with human beings (Job 1:6–13; 2:1–6). The shift

---

9. The beginning date of the captivity of the people of Judah in Babylon, as noted in Kuntz, *People of Ancient Israel*, 356.

in theological thinking gradually coming after 539 BCE[10] is evident in a passage in 1 Chr 21:1 where Satan appears as the figure inciting David to commit the sin of counting the population of Israel. In the earlier parallel text (that is, prior to 587 BCE), which the Chronicler "borrowed" from 2 Sam 24:1, it is the LORD who incites David to count the people. This shift from the LORD to Satan as the inciter of evil is apparently due to changes in theological thinking in Israel.

In the Jewish Apocrypha the earliest reference to an evil competitor to God comes in the book of Jubilees (ca. 150 BCE[11]), where he appears as Mastema, chief of the unclean demons (Jub. 10:8). But as late as the beginning of the second century BCE, Sirach can trace to God the "evil" aspects of nature (vipers, teeth of wild beasts, hail, famine, and so forth, Sir 39:28-31).

In the New Testament period (after 50 CE), Satan and the devil are conceived as one figure (Rev 12:9; Mark 1:13, compare the substitution of "the devil" for Mark's "Satan" in Matt 4:1 and Luke 4:3). This figure, appearing as the chief opponent of God in the world, is known by a number of other names and designations: for example, Beelzebul (Matt 12:24); Belial (2 Cor 6:15); the prince of the power of the air (Eph 2:2); and ruler of this world (John 12:31; 14:30; 16:11). One statement by Jesus in Luke alludes to Satan's former association with God's heavenly court (Luke 10:18; but compare John 12:31). Revelation (12:7-12) describes a war in heaven in which Michael and his angels fight against the dragon "who is called the Devil and Satan." Michael wins the battle, and Satan is cast down to the earth, where he makes war on those who for a short time "keep the commandments of God and bear testimony to Jesus." A description of a battle among the stars appears in The Sibylline Oracles (book 5: at the beginning of the second century CE[12]), which features the Morning Star (*Lucifer*), popularly thought to be waging war in the heavens (lines 512-30).

Lucifer (a Latin word meaning "Light-bringer," or the Latin name for the Morning Star) is a special problem. Lucifer does not appear in the New Testament as an evil force, as such, although the equivalent term in Greek (*Phosphoros*) does appear in 2 Pet 1:19, where it is translated "morning star." However, in 2 Pet 1:19 it does not refer to an evil opponent

---

10. This is the date of release of the people of Judah from captivity in Babylon, as noted in Kuntz, *People of Ancient Israel*, 379-80.

11. VanderKam, "Jubilees," 1030.

12. Collins, "Sibylline Oracles," 4.

of God. The name or description also appears in the Hebrew Bible where the word is variously translated; in that context the word is applied to the king of Babylon (Isa 14:12–15). Later Christian writers (after the third century) associated Lucifer with Satan. Origen has been given credit with being the first specifically to argue that "Lucifer" is to be associated with Satan as the evil force in the world opposing God.[13]

This brief summary brings me to an important question: is there in actuality a malicious Spiritual Force in the world opposing God, or are we humans alone the source of deliberate malicious evil? It seems to me there are at least three responses:

(1) recognize nature as ethically neutral and human beings as the only source of deliberate malicious evil in the world;

(2) accept the idea that there is a God, and allow God to be the sole ruler of the world, and hence God is the source of both good and evil;

(3) admit that pagan thought was more insightful than Hebrew thought in recognizing that a "good" God simply could not be the source of evil—hence the need to invent another competitive unseen wicked power in the universe.

The third option creates a host of difficulties, not the least of which is whether any force actually controls the world, other than Mother Nature. (3–13–13)

§4 FORCES AT WORK IN THE GARDEN OF THE LORD

What "forces" are operating in the world? I don't refer to institutional forces, such as the rule of law or the Internal Revenue Service, or natural forces, like gravity, but rather to invisible supernatural forces that are not understood and cannot be controlled. Through time, a plethora of threatening or helpful spirit forces have been believed to be at work in the world. People sensed they needed to protect themselves from the hurtful forces and to petition the helpful for aid. In the ancient Greek and Roman traditions twelve traditional Gods and Goddesses needed to be appeased through animal sacrifices and other means, just as did the Israelite God. In the ancient world people believed that demons, some good and others

---

13. Origen, *De Principiis*, ANF, 4.259–60.

bad, affected human well-being. Such spirit forces are possibly indicated in Eph 6:12: we contend not against "flesh and blood" but against "the spiritual forces of wickedness in the heavenly places."

One impersonal force believed to be at play in the ancient world was destiny or "fate." Everyone including the gods had a personal destiny. The concept grew out of the Babylonian idea that our lives were written in the stars, and no one, not even the gods, could escape their inevitable destiny—their due apportionment. One's destiny cannot be predicted, changed, or understood, except in hindsight.

In the Greco-Roman world, following Alexander the Great, new deities and spirit forces emerged, such as Luck (i.e., *Tychē* or Fortune). Under *Tychē* nothing was determined; everything was always at risk. She was a fickle deity, who treated everyone capriciously; one never really knew how she would respond to entreaty.

Satan (the devil, or Beelzebub) was an evil opponent of God brought into Judaism from Zoroastrianism. Satan became the Yin to God's Yang, a personified evil entity against whom God competed in the world (Eph 2:2; Matt 25:41; Luke 11:14–20). Demonic evil forces were thought to cause sickness (Luke 11:14), insanity (Mark 5:1–20), epilepsy (Matt 17:14–21), spiritual failure (Eph 6:10–12), and more. Angels from God (or the devil: Matt 25:41; 2 Cor 11:14) helped (Acts 12:11) but sometimes harmed (Acts 12:23) human beings. An assortment of different spirits were thought to come from God to influence the human psyche, either for good (John 16:13) or for ill (Judg 9:23).

From the early Christian period through the Middle Ages an explosion of demons, angelic beings, and new greater-than-human powers threatened the human condition. They could be "managed," people believed during this period, by spells and other magical practices, even by reciting Christian spells or curses, and by wearing amulets for protection against the supernatural.

With the rise of modern scientific thought and reliance on human reason in the eighteenth century, the idea that the universe was inhabited by unseen spirit powers, forces, and deities was successfully challenged. Modern science was able to explain what was previously attributed to these forces as due to natural causes. For example, the scientific theory that unseen organisms (germs) caused disease led to a cure for tuberculosis and other diseases. Science, not prayer, had triumphed over what were regarded as disease-causing demons!

Where do things stand today? It depends. People who are heirs of Western secular education can live without fearing the spirit forces. They consult physicians rather than resorting to magic spells. They rely on human reason and the successes of modern science in explaining what was once attributed to the spirit forces. Nevertheless, even in Western culture some still live with a medieval mentality, and for them the spirit forces remain a practical and very real threat. This medieval mind-set is encouraged by religious institutions around the world through their use of ancient holy books that warn about the spirit forces at work in the world. Christianity's holy book, for example, originates in a primitive and naïve age, and bears the marks of its primitive and ancient culture; one indication of its culture is a belief in the existence of angels, demons, and spirits.

Truth be told, however, if any of these greater-than-human forces ever existed, they still do. How can any spirit force ever possibly be eliminated? The logical answer is this: Stop believing in evil spiritual forces, and that effectively neutralizes their influence and power. Zeus, for example, may still dwell on Mount Olympus, but since no one believes in Zeus any longer, he receives no sacrifices or libations and hence has no practical influence over anyone. Unseen supernatural spirit forces feed on fear and intimidation, and not believing in them effectively neutralizes their powers. (3–4–10)

§5 HOW TO CAST OUT THE DEVIL

An Associated Press release about Roman Catholic bishops holding a two-day training session in Baltimore on how to conduct exorcisms[14] is astonishing! According to the news story, major exorcisms can only be performed by a priest (not a layperson) with permission from a bishop, although every baptism in the Catholic Church involves a "minor exorcism." In this case an exorcism involves casting out the devil or demons by the intervention of a priest duly authorized to do so.

What are the signs of demon possession accepted by the Catholic Church? The article cites several: when a person is "writhing and screaming," is reacting violently "to holy water or anything holy," is speaking in a language the possessed person doesn't know," or is performing "abnormal displays of strength." It requires "discernment" by the exorcist to

---

14. Zoll, "Catholics: More Exorcists Needed"; Wikipedia, "Exorcism in the Catholic Church." See also Stanglin, "Demand for Exorcisms Is Up."

know when to attempt the rite, and the exorcist consults physicians and psychiatrists to ensure that the person does not suffer from some physical or mental illness. The Catholic Church even has an official handbook for the rite to guide the exorcist: *De exorcismis et supplicationibus quibusdam* (*Concerning Exorcisms and Certain Supplications*).

This practice on the part of Catholics and others raises serious questions about what is responsible behavior for religious people in the twenty-first century, and represents a frightening relapse to pre-Enlightenment thinking about the human psyche. No wonder (to quote the article) "skepticism about the rite persists in the American [Catholic] church." Those among us who are heirs of the Enlightenment share the American Catholic skepticism and therefore seriously question the competence of physicians and psychiatrists (not to mention church officials) who are a party to such a practice. One would think that a consultancy resulting in the approval of the rite would surely not be endorsed by the American Medical Association.

When the exorcism rite was updated in 1999, the church cautioned that "all must be done to avoid the perception that exorcism is magic or superstition." It is impossible, however, to escape the roots of superstition and magic that undergirds and empowers the rite of exorcism. Thinking that the world is inhabited by devils and demons belongs to our pre-critical and superstitious past, and has no place in the spiritual care of souls in the twenty-first century.

Let's take just one example. Holy water is water *believed to be* sanctified by a priest. Actually, nothing happens to the water; holy water is not a molecule different from unsanctified water. What has changed is how the water is viewed by those who believe that a priest has the (spiritual/magical) power to do such a thing. Put the same amount of plain tap water and sanctified tap water in two different glasses and show them later to the priest; and not even the priest will be able to tell the difference. So how would a demon know which is which?

Demons survive today only in the minds of those who have been unable to escape their superstitious past, and groups that practice rites of exorcism are reinforcing the worst aspects of a medieval mentality by pandering to human superstition. (11–14–10)

§6 HALLOWEEN: DO THE DEAD WALK?[15]

At the end of every October in these United States we observe one of the strangest folk celebrations of our annual calendar. Coming on October 31, as it does, the custom has become associated with All Saints' Day in the Catholic traditions. All Saints' Day, in the West falling on November 1, is a church celebration in honor of all the saints who have passed on; it is followed on November 2 by All Souls' Day, a day of solemn prayer for all the dead. These holy days in honor of the dead effectively render October 31 as All Hallows' Eve, from which we get the name Halloween.

The roots of Halloween have been associated with a number of ancient traditions: the ancient Roman celebration of *Pomona*, the goddess of fruits and seeds; the Roman festival of the dead, called *Parentalia*; and most closely with the Celtic festival of *Samhain*. The major focus of Halloween, as we know it, seems to have evolved out of the superstitious and dark side of the human soul; so costumes largely feature such mythical creatures as monsters, vampires, werewolves, zombies, ghosts, walking skeletons, witches, and devils. Today we relegate such supernatural creatures to the realm of fantasy, myth, fairy tale, and fiction—at least most of us do.

In the bright light of day it is easy to be a rational human being, but in a dark empty room in the late evening when the hair on the back of your neck stands up at a sudden sensation of an unseen nearby presence, we may have second thoughts. In the distant past, however, before critical thinking became widespread through public education, these creatures were regarded as real entities that could actually do harm, and people relied on certain protections against them, prayer being one. And today not everyone, even in America, possesses the liberating knowledge that these creatures are merely fictional characters, figments of our dark-side imagination.

The Bible is surely one reason that people are still uneasy about such mythical creatures, since it reinforces human superstition at many points. For example, the gospel writer we call Matthew apparently believed that dead people could come out of their graves and go on a walkabout (Matt 27:51–54). It is a strange story (appearing only in Matthew), but Matthew tells it graphically like an actual historical occurrence (as opposed to a symbolic or legendary story). Except for one phrase in 27:53 ("after his

---

15. This essay was subsequently published in the *Fourth R* 25/1 (January-February, 2012), 25–26; used by permission.

raising"), Matthew describes the incident as if it were happening simultaneously with the death of Jesus (27:50, 54). The phrase in Matt 27:53, however, effectively throws the event forward some three days or so (in Matthew's chronology) to a time following the resurrection of Jesus (Matt 28). The effect of this leap forward is that it associates the report with the Christian myth of the "harrowing of hell" or the "descent into Hades," when Jesus at his death descended into Hades to free those dead saints who had been in Hades awaiting release. Vestiges of the myth are found in the New Testament (Eph 4:8–9; 1 Pet 3:18–19), but it is fully developed in the post–New Testament period.[16] The phrase "after his raising" in Matt 27:53 may be due to a later editing of Matthew's Gospel, since the incident as a whole seems clearly to go with the death of Jesus and not with his resurrection. So what do we say about Matthew's sense of history as reflected in this story?

It appears to originate in a superstition that dead people can rise and walk about. A description similar to Matthew's story is found in Ezekiel's description of the people of Israel in the Valley of Dry Bones (Ezek 37:12–14). The Lord says, "I will open your graves . . . and bring you into the land of Israel." Matthew's description of tombs opening in an earthquake (27:51; compare Matt 28:1–2) and the bodies of dead saints being raised (27:52; compare Matt 28:9), and the saints coming out of the tombs and walking about in the holy city (27:53) is a very graphic account. Not even Paul, however, would describe the raising of Jesus as Matthew describes the raising of the saints. (In Paul's view Jesus rose with a "spiritual body," not a physical body [1 Cor 15:42–57].) Possibly Matthew's report could be an early Christian legend (a nonhistorical traditional story told for the purpose of encouraging faith). And that is exactly what Matthew's report did for the centurion and the soldiers (Matt 27:54); the "event" confirmed for them (and for Matthew) the identity of Jesus as "son of God." But the scenario of dead bodies actually coming out of their tombs and walking about Jerusalem around three o'clock in the afternoon (Matt 27:46) seriously strains credulity for a post-Enlightenment thinker. In order to think of the incident as "history" a twenty-first-century reader will have to "suspend disbelief," something we do with all ghost stories; in a sense, we simply ignore the incredulous aspects of the report. We know that the dead cannot come out of their tombs and wander about the city, no matter how serious the earthquake—or do we know that?

16. Bauckham, "Descent to the Underworld."

Has Matthew given us a kind of ghost story suitable only for telling around the campfire on a dark night, or is it an actual historical occurrence that confirms the identity of Jesus, or is it a legend that only the true believer can appreciate? As a post-Enlightenment thinker, I'd put my money on the ghost story. (10–16–11)

§7 NATURAL DISASTERS, ACTS OF GOD, AND THE BIBLE

A massive earthquake and devastating tsunami destroyed Sendai, Japan, and numerous other coastal villages on March 11, 2011. In May of 2015 Becky Oskin, a contributing writer for LiveScience, reported that 15,891 were confirmed dead as of April 10, 2015, and in May 2015 there were 2,500 still missing.[17]

Was this horrendous event a natural disaster or an act of God? Actually it will depend on whom you ask. The news media in this country reported it as a natural disaster, but, no doubt, conservative Christian clergy were already at work on sermons crediting God with the disaster because of the sins of the Japanese people. "Sin," of course, is always defined by such clergy as failing to follow their own ideas of being religious. That God caused the disaster may very well be right, however, because the Judeo-Christian God has a long history of such unconscionable acts—like ordering the Israelites to annihilate the ancient Amalekite people because of what they did to the Israelites (1 Sam 15:1–3); or personally destroying by his own hand, as it were, the entire city of Sodom and its inhabitants because of their sinful ways (Gen 19:24–25); or using the ancient Babylonians to destroy the temple at Jerusalem and deport all but the poorest people of the land into captivity in Babylon because of the sins of the Israelite people (2 Kgs 24:1–14). Many more such terrible acts by God are recorded in the Bible.

Yahweh is the personal name of Israel's God, and it appears to be in Yahweh's divine DNA to perpetrate such acts. If contemporary Jewish and Christian faith is to be believed, Yahweh not only controls the destiny of history but also controls whatever happens in nature. Jesus believed God controlled nature as well (Matt 5:44–45). If that is the case, then Yahweh is still up to his old ways today, and within recent memory destroyed New Orleans by flood, caused massive loss of life in Indonesia by

---

17 Oskin, "Japan Earthquake and Tsunami."

earthquake and tsunami, and caused massive loss of life by earthquakes in Russia, China, and Haiti—to mention only a few such disasters within recent memory.

Such aberrations in the regularly occurring benign cycles of nature pose the greatest challenge to both the existence of God and to the traditional Christian and Jewish belief that God controls nature. Such disasters have always "played the devil" with the belief that the Judeo-Christian God, who by most *definitions* is a gracious God, controls nature. This situation raises the following questions: If God controls nature and such unconscionable disasters occur in nature, how can God then be considered good? And if God is good, how can God either be responsible for such unconscionable disasters or permit such disasters to occur? It sounds like a proverbial catch-22.

Yet if Mother Nature is to be considered the cause of such events—that is to say, if such events are natural disasters—then the disasters make better sense. Mother Nature is ethically blind, and hence in an "act of nature" all suffer: the "wicked" along with the "righteous." On the other hand, the God of Christian and Jewish faith is supposed to behave in ethical ways—punishing the guilty, rewarding the just, and protecting the innocent, which is not what has happened in Japan. These disasters I have just mentioned are tantamount to killing a flea on your kitchen table with a hydrogen bomb; everyone and everything in the vicinity suffers: plant life, infrastructure, animals, innocent babies, the best of the populace, as well as the "wicked." So how can an ethical God be credited with destroying cities and their populations through acts of nature and still maintain an ethically divine character?

Hard-core conservative theologians will privilege traditional faith over common sense and claim no one is innocent before God—not even newborn babies still nursing. But they will stop just short of saying "they all deserved it," because they know how incredible it sounds. Another response is, God's ways are not our ways (compare the book of Job) as though there could ever be some rational way, which we cannot now conceive, to justify such egregious behavior on the part of God. Another response is, it will all eventually work out for the better (Rom 8:28), like a forest fire that clears out the old growth to make room for new growth. Such an idea would bring little comfort to the old growth, however. The disastrous fire was still a tragedy from the perspective of the trees, and should have been seen as such by a God with a conscience. Of course, we are not talking just about trees in the case of the tsunami in Japan; we are talking human lives.

For my part, I gave up blaming God for the weather and natural disasters years ago. Mother Nature is the real culprit here, and modern science has made great strides in understanding her, although I doubt that they will ever understand her completely. There are just too many variables. I admit that such a theological position is rather unorthodox, but I sleep better at night realizing that although we all live in a capricious universe, God can be trusted to do the best that s/he can—given Mother Nature's apparent capricious acts. God just cannot control or do everything (it's a big universe), and God is likely as grieved as we are for the foibles of Mother Nature. (3-17-11)

§8 CHANCE, LUCK, RANDOMNESS, AND THE BEING OF GOD

Does the presence of randomness in the universe negatively impact God's running of the universe? Or put another way, does God have absolute control over everything that goes on in the universe? In the final analysis what is at stake in the question is nothing less than the Being of God. If one accepts that a principle of randomness exists in the universe, one must also accept that God does not control everything, for some things simply happen "randomly"; that is, they are events lacking a regular plan, purpose, or pattern. God (if God there be) is likely as surprised by such events as we are. Randomness in the universe challenges anyone who believes in God to explain how s/he knows what events happen randomly and what events are planned and controlled by God. Failure to answer that question raises another: is God in control of anything? And then for some the ultimate question will arise: is there a God, after all? In this essay, however, I am only concerned with the issue of randomness in the universe.

Physical scientists recognize randomness in the behavior of light. Light can behave simultaneously as a particle and a wave. "This wave-particle duality is an unresolved dilemma of modern physics."[18] Another example of randomness is found in Darwin's views on natural selection and the survival of the fittest. His views are described as theory, but only by those who have never read objectively his *On the Origin of Species*.

---

18. Condon, "Two Theories of Light," 283.

The truth is, randomness, chance, and fortune determine who or what survives in nature—or not. For example, dinosaurs and similar creatures inhabited earth from the Jurassic period until the end of the Cretaceous period (200 to 66 million years ago) and then became extinct. Chance and genes, in part, explain why I am a living octogenarian rather than a deceased septuagenarian, like many of my high school classmates.

Oddly enough we find that some biblical authors acknowledge that chance and randomness play a part in everyday life. For example, one biblical author describes the Philistines devising a test to know whether a plague was caused by Yahweh, God of the Israelites (1 Sam 6:1–9), or whether it had happened to them "by chance" (1 Sam 6:9). In 2 Sam 1:1–10 the biblical author notes that the death of Saul at the hands of a young Amalekite happened "by chance" (2 Sam 1:6). In the law code attributed to Moses, the lawgiver describes how one should behave upon the chance finding of an occupied bird's nest (Deut 22:6–7). Koheleth (the "gatherer") observes that the same fate eventually comes upon good and bad people alike (Eccl 9:2–12), for "time and chance happen to them all" (Eccl 9:11). Even Paul describes a happenstance sowing of one sort of seed or another (1 Cor 15:37). In a parable of Jesus (Luke 10:29–35) Luke describes the three specific travelers passing by a severely wounded man lying beside the road as chance occurrences (Luke 10:31). In all of these texts there is a tacit acceptance of the principle of randomness and chance in human life. The conclusion is inevitable that even some biblical authors do not assume God controls everything.

Even though Jesus claimed that the very hairs of our heads are numbered (Matt 10:30; Luke 12:7), we seem instinctively to know that some things happen randomly. Hence we make room for luck in our view of events, and describe some things as good or bad luck—like accidents or misfortunes. Only the true believer describes the weather uniformly as an "act of God," as insurance companies describe floods, tornadoes, tsunamis, ice storms, and other catastrophes of nature. Accidents happen due to our carelessness or the carelessness of others. They cannot be predicted or guarded against; they are random and simply part of the natural order of things. Some conservative religious folk appeal to the permissive will of God to explain such phenomena:

> Because God is sovereign, nothing happens that is outside his will. But there is a difference between what he causes and what

he allows. By the permissive will of God things happen which
God does not cause to happen.[19]

Such a response has always perplexed me, since it impugns God's character, and ultimately makes God responsible for all the bad and tragic experiences of our lives—at least that must be so in the view of James, who wrote:

"Whoever knows to do good, yet does not do it, for him it is sin" (Jas 4:17).

The rationale works this way: God knows to do good; God can control what happens in the world; but God nevertheless allows bad things to happen. It seems to me that standing idly by and allowing bad things to happen when one could have prevented them, whatever one's reasons for doing so, is ethically wrong. (1–14–16)

§9 DOES ANYTHING HAPPEN BY CHANCE?

An expression in a parable attributed to Jesus may very well undermine the traditional Christian belief that God controls both the world and the affairs of human history. Christians prefer to believe that surely nothing could happen by chance in God's world, but that may not be the case. Virtually every churchgoer knows the parable of the good Samaritan (Luke 10:30–35). A traveler was set upon by bandits, who stripped and assaulted him, leaving him beside the road for dead. Subsequently three other travelers passed down that same road. The first traveler, a priest, is introduced in this way: "now by chance a certain priest was going down that road . . ." (Luke 10:31). The expression "by chance" immediately floods the story with randomness. The expression "by chance" informs readers that it was only a fortuitous accident that the first traveler happened to be a priest. It implies that anyone could have happened by after the assault. In other words, Jesus did not deliberately select a priest to play the role of the first traveler; that choice was simply a random event.

Lest you think this explanation of the status of the first traveler is misguided, the second traveler down the road, a Levite, is introduced by "so, likewise" (that is to say, in the same way); this expression signals that the Levite is "likewise" also a random selection as a character in the story. Hence, it appears that all the characters in the story are simply random

---

19. Slick, "Permissive Will."

picks. They were not deliberately cast in the roles they played but were simply the luck of the draw (a card game image) or the roll of the dice (a craps image). In other words the characters designated priest, Levite, Samaritan could have been anyone in any order. The expression "by chance" subverts the plot of the story, for it suggests that a priest or even a Roman soldier might have eventually tended the wounded man. The expression challenges any interpretation of the story that focuses on the named characters and incidentally ruins most modern interpretations of the story and likely a few sermons.[20]

The biblical view of reality is that everything happening in our world happens for a reason. However unclear or murky the situation may be, traditionally God is believed to be working within all things to bring about a good outcome (Rom 8:28), or if need be, to bring warranted punishment and suffering (2 Chr 7:13–14). A song writer of the nineteenth century, Maltbie Babcock, expressed this absolute Christian confidence in God's control of the world this way:

> This is my Father's world
> O let me ne'er forget
> That though the wrong
> Seems oft so strong
> God is the Ruler yet.[21]

That is to say, God is the Ruler of the universe, and nothing happens without his deliberate or permissive will.

People of faith tend to explain that things appearing to be glitches in the divine control of the world are likely not really glitches, because God frequently has unknown reasons, or reasons unclear to us, for what happens, "How unsearchable are his judgments and how inscrutable his ways" (Rom 11:33, RSV). That is to say, people of faith may not understand the whys and wherefores of what happens, but they can have absolute confidence that God, nevertheless, is in control.

How then should one understand the randomness introduced into this story by the word "chance"? As a part of the story attributed to Jesus, "chance" threatens the idea that Jesus even controls the plot of his own narrative, and in a similar way it threatens the idea that God controls the

---

20. See the discussion in Hedrick, *Poetic Fictions*, 93–116; and Hedrick, *Parabolic Figures or Narrative Fictions*, 219–28.
21. Babcock, "This Is My Father's World," 59 (third stanza).

world, for it demonstrates that not even in the Bible is everything under God's control. Some things just happen by chance.

The writer of Ecclesiastes also thinks that some things are chance occurrences; they accidentally, as it were, fall between the cracks and are not part of some grand design. The race is not always won by the swiftest, the writer says, and the strongest does not always win the battle, and it is not always the intelligent who accumulates the greatest wealth—for "time and chance happen to them all" (Eccl 9:11). Hence in Ecclesiastes all is subject both to the vicissitudes of time (aging) and the unpredictability of chance—concepts shared both by ancient and modern human beings alike. Other biblical writers also describe events occurring by happenstance rather than at the deliberate behest of God (Deut 22:6; 1 Sam 6:9; 2 Sam 1:6; 1 Cor 15:37).

No doubt many people of faith at one time or another have found themselves "between the cracks" with a growing sense of unease that matters are not under God's control—or worse, that to all appearances they have been abandoned. That is where Job found himself (Job 23:3–7; 30:17–21). Throughout the dark night of his soul Job had only his integrity, insisting that the disasters that had fallen on him were out of proportion to anything he may have done. He subscribed to the belief that both good and bad were dispensed by the hands of God, and did not think that chance played a role in life. But he did refuse to surrender his integrity (Job 27:3–6), and when his friends chided him with pious platitudes to confess his sins, Job embraced none of their easy answers. He said to his counselors: "I have heard many such things; miserable comforters are you all!" (Job 16:2–3 RSV). To have accepted the easy answers of traditional piety would have cost Job his integrity. Until the end of the book (Job 42:1–6) he steadfastly refused to admit that his suffering was commensurate with any sins he may have committed (Job 27:1–6).[22]

Job is the epitome of a modern human being who stubbornly clings to a questioning faith by refusing to surrender his personal integrity and repeat the tired shibboleths of traditional faith. At the last moment, however, Job capitulates. The writer of Ecclesiastes, on the other hand, evidently a person of nontraditional faith, was honest enough to admit that the world is a place of unsettling contingency. If the writer of Ecclesiastes is correct and a random contingency exists in the universe, how could anyone ever know for certain what was caused by chance, what

---

22. See the brief discussion of Job in Hedrick, *Wisdom of Jesus*, 66–69.

is fated, or what God makes happen. Random contingency pretty much undermines a benevolent oversight of the universe. (5–6–11)

§10 HONEY IN THE ROCK, WATER IN THE STONE, BETTER WINE IN STONE JARS

As Jesus entered Jerusalem a few days before his crucifixion, a large crowd of his disciples followed rejoicing, shouting loudly, and praising God. Jesus was told by the Pharisees to silence the crowd, and he replied: If they were silent, "the stones will cry out" (Luke 19:40; compare Hab 2:11). Is that possible? Does stone possess the intrinsic potential of changing its molecular structure so as to become or do something not in its nature, which is mute inanimate object? Of course, through intense heat rock can become molten lava; and, true, an artist can coax a great work of statuary out of the silent stone; Michelangelo's *David*, for example, is a great work of art created out of the marble, but the statue does not speak, at least not audibly. Would not speaking stones be like the proverbial leopard changing its spots?

Luke 19:40 is probably not a traditional saying of Jesus. It is too closely connected to Luke's narrative ever to have had an independent existence—at least as Luke quotes it. And in this story the statement seems to be only a case of exaggeration for effect, rather than a case of asserting the existential potentiality of rocks. In short, the Jesus character in the story is not serious about stones speaking—or is he?

Jesus is elsewhere represented as believing that stones have the potential to become human beings (Matt 3:9) should God so choose, and the devil seems to think that stones have the potential to become bread (Matt 4:3) should Jesus so choose. And Jesus himself is even credited with saying that stones possess the potential of becoming "servants" to the disciples of Jesus (Gos. Thom. 19). The apostle Thomas in a rather odd statement seemed to think stones could emit fire (Gos. Thom. 13); and why not?—so did the writer of Judges (6:21).

In general in the twenty-first century, however, people don't think of stones as anything but inanimate objects, although in our ancient past "scientists" called alchemists through the use of a legendary substance (called the philosophers stone[23]) believed they could actually turn base

---

23. Wikipedia., "Philosopher's Stone."

metals (e.g., lead or copper) into gold.[24] And in the Bible stones and rocks are believed to have the potential to be and do many things, and hence they are fit subjects for molecular change so as to live up to a "potential" that is out of character for rocks. Rock, for example, has the potential to produce water (Num 20:8–11; Neh 9:15; Pss 78:15–16, 20; 105:41; 114:8; Exod 17:6; Deut 8:15; Isa 48:21; 2 Esd 1:20; Wis 11:4) or honey (Deut 32:13; Ps 81:16) or even oil (oil for your lamp; not your car, Job 29:6).

In the Greek tradition after the great flood subsided, Deucalion disembarked from his ark, offered sacrifice to Zeus, and prayed at the shrine of Themis,[25] asking that humankind be allowed to repopulate the earth. His prayer was granted, and accomplished by Deucalion's picking up stones beside the river and tossing them behind him; the stones became human beings, replacing the drowned population of the planet.[26] In Matt 3:9 (see also Luke 3:8) Jesus is portrayed as believing that stones clearly have the potential to become people. To the Pharisees and Sadducees he says: "God is able from these stones to raise up children to Abraham" (Matt 3:9 = Luke 3:8).

The only instance in which Jesus is portrayed as manipulating molecular structure, however, is when he changed the water to wine at Cana (John 2:1–11). I suppose one could also make a case that Jesus manipulated the molecular structure of the dead son of a widow when he raised him (Luke 7:11–17), since the molecular structure of a corpse in process of decay is different from a living, breathing organism. The multiplication of the loaves and fish (Mark 8:1–9), however, would have been a creation ex nihilo ("out of nothing"), since Jesus is credited with creating more of something than was previously there.

My question at the beginning of this essay was, do rock and stone possess the intrinsic potential of molecular change? Or to put it crassly, can rocks become people? The throwaway answer of a true believer, no doubt, will be, God can do whatever s/he wants. Such an answer may work in Sunday school, but it works less well out of the cloister in the rough-and-tumble secularism of the twenty-first century. Not even devout church people go about actually running their nine-to-five lives by hoped-for exceptions to the way things usually work in the world, though all of us may be reduced at times of great stress to hoping for

---

24. Holmyard, *Alchemy*, 15.
25. That is, the Titaness; Graves, *Greek Myths*, 27 (1.d).
26. Ibid., 1.139.

exceptions to the inevitabilities of life. Scientific analysis of the natural world, however, has shown that the world works regularly (more or less), but, alas, with little oversight, as natural disasters unquestionably prove. In a world shaped by years of scientific inquiry and accomplishment, it is rather evident even to a ninth-grader that the Gods have never made people out of stone, nor could they have, given what we know of the way things work in our world.

Do you suppose that God could get blood out of a turnip? How you answer that question will determine the kind of world you think you live in: a first-century world or a twenty-first-century world. That is to say: is your view of the world determined by the Bible or by observation of the world around you? (4-27-11)

§11 WILL THE EARTH ABIDE?

Even to consider the question seriously starts the tectonic plates shifting beneath one's feet. If the earth passes away, it takes along with it human consciousness, history, and civilization. As unthinkable as it may be, the impermanence of the earth has been considered even by the biblical writers, even though at the act of creation God pronounced his creative act very good (Gen 1:31). The biblical myth, however, is that God once destroyed every living thing on the earth (Gen 7:4, 21-23), so apparently something had gone very wrong. The flood event, however, was not understood by the writers as a *destruction* of the earth, but (as we would say) a global destruction of life, which God promised never to do again by floods (Gen 9:11-17). God promised that the earth and earthly life cycles would continue "so long as the earth abides" (Gen 8:20-22), which is not quite a promise that the earth is permanent. Even this comment, however, does raise the specter of the earth's impermanence.

The threats of destruction involving the earth in Hebrew Bible are usually like the flood incident; they are threats against a particular people for a particular reason (e.g., Zeph 1:14-18; 3:1-8). The earth abides, but certain peoples are destroyed. Even the "Little Apocalypse" of Isa 24-27 (First Isaiah) predicts only a devastation of the earth and not its destruction. Isa 65:17-20 (Third Isaiah), however, foresees "a new heavens and a new earth" and asserts that "the former things shall not be remembered or brought to mind" (Isa 65:17).[27]

27. Kuntz, *People of Ancient Israel*, 290-93.

Paul's letters seem inconsistent. In one letter he suggests that even the (old) earth is anticipating redemption, because of its being in bondage to decay (Rom 8:19–23), which suggests that the present earth will continue after its redemption. Yet in another letter he writes that "the form of this world is passing away" (1 Cor 7:31). The writer in 2 Peter unambiguously announces the destruction of earth:

> The Day of the Lord will come like a thief, and then the heavens will pass away with a loud noise, and the elements will be dissolved with fire, and the earth and the works that are upon it will be burned up." (2 Pet 3:10 RSV)

The prophetic writer John echoes Third Isaiah in foreseeing the advent of a new heaven and a new earth, and echoes Paul in announcing the passing away of the first heaven and first earth (Rev 21:1–4).

Do you suppose that God's mind for some reason was changed about the creation being "very good," and as a result what began as good in God's judgment will end up in a fiery cataclysm? If so, why would God decide to destroy a "very good" and perfectly innocent creation? Animals, plants, and the "material stuff" of earth are not unrighteous, evil, or unethical, and scarcely deserve destruction. Such insentient things and creatures would scarcely even be able to appreciate that they were being punished. Perhaps the biblical writers are wrong in foreseeing the end of the world, for they cannot actually read God's mind. When it comes to God, all of us human beings are limited and see things only "indirectly as in a mirror" (1 Cor 13:12), and that includes even our religious professionals such as prophets, priests, preachers, and TV evangelists.

Nevertheless, that said, the transience of our currently habitable blue and white planet Earth has always been threatened by natural causes. A large enough wandering comet striking earth would cause catastrophic devastation. In 1908 a comet about the size of a football field, among other things, leveled two thousand square kilometers of forest in central Siberia.[28] Perhaps some other cosmic catastrophe might occur, such as a "super nova within ten or twenty light years of the solar system," an event that some conjecture was the cause of the passing away of the dinosaurs "some sixty-five million years ago."[29] Super novae are huge exploding stars.[30]

28. Sagan, *Cosmos*, 73–76.
29. Ibid., 283.
30. Ibid., 197.

Our sun is a star—or put another way, the stars you see in the night sky are suns. They have a limited life span. "Billions of years from now, there will be a last perfect day on earth. Thereafter the Sun will slowly become red and distended,"[31] on its way to becoming a red star, then degenerating to a white dwarf; ultimately it becomes a dark and dead black dwarf. Our earth would by then have long since become uninhabitable to life as we know it. Carl Sagan's description of the death of the earth echoes 2 Pet 3:10. Earth will "swelter even at the poles" and then,

> The Arctic and Antarctic icecaps will melt . . . Eventually the oceans will boil, the atmosphere melt away to space and a catastrophe of the most immense proportions will overtake our planet.[32]

Will we earth people be able to survive without our mother, the earth? We were spawned millions of years ago in an earthy primordial soup of dust from the stars and nourished at mother earth's breast on our way to becoming human beings. Perhaps, we will, but what might we become without her? (3-3-16)

---

31. Ibid., 231.

32. Sagen, *Cosmos*, 73-76 (comets); 230-32 (death of the sun); 283 (death of the dinosaurs); 30-31 (origins of life); 238-39 (super nova).

2

Reason and Faith

§12 ARE RELIGION AND SCIENCE INCOMPATIBLE?

Certainly not! Well, maybe. Perhaps! Probably! In the final analysis it will depend on who you ask, and what Science and Religion are about. (I capitalize the words to indicate their status in modern Western culture as iconic institutions.) *Science* comes from the Latin meaning "knowledge" (knowing), and *religion* also comes from the Latin meaning "piety" (fear of the gods). If I were to ask my question in terms of modern Western culture it might go something like this: is Athens (ultimately the original source of the scientific spirit in the West) incompatible with Jerusalem (ultimately the original source of religious piety in the Christian West)?[1]

Here are two helpful descriptions of Science and Religion from my perspective. They are necessarily broad.

> Science is a systematic enterprise that builds and organizes knowledge about the universe in the form of explanations that can be tested and from which theories about the universe may be developed.[2]

> On the other hand, Religion may be described as a set of variously organized beliefs about the relationship between the

---

1. An iconic statement contrasting competing alternatives first made by Tertullian in *Praescr.*, chapter 7 (*ANF* 3:246).

2. Young, "Editor's Note," 22–23.

REASON AND FAITH 39

natural and supernatural aspects of reality and the role of humans in this relationship.

Two other more narrowly framed descriptions from my own experience are these: Science raises questions about everything and answers them by experimentation; Religion provides answers to everything and subtly discourages questions. I realize that narrow definitions are easily challengeable, but from my experience these latter two catch up the spirit of what Religion and Science seem to be about. Here are several contrasting statements about Religion and Science.

1a On the basis of observable phenomena (viz. the universe is expanding) Science, in the main, attributes the origin of all things to the big bang but does not speculate about what preceded it.

1b Religion attributes the source of everything to God before the big bang.

2a Religion must affirm a nonphysical, spiritual world, because God is intangible Spirit and hence does not "exist" in time and space.

2b Science only investigates aspects of the physical universe.

3a Religion is prone to superstition and spiritual magic.

3b Science undermines any Religion prone to *superstition* (from the Latin meaning "unreasonable religious belief") and spiritual magic (viz. any manipulation of the physical world by spiritual means).

4a Religion demands faith.

4b Science demands experimentation and repeatability.

5a Science proceeds on the basis of natural cause and effect.

5b Religion in general posits God as the ultimate cause of whatever happens in the universe.

An example of a clash between Science and Religion was occasioned by Charles Darwin's book, *The Origin of Species* (1859). Darwin offered evidence that plant and animal life evolve from lower life-forms over time by means of natural selection. The default explanation for the origin of the species in the Christian West is that God created all things; in short human beings did not evolve from lower life-forms. Darwin offered physical evidence; Christianity cited the Bible in response. What counts in Science are reason, logic, and evidence. What counts in Religion in the

Christian West are obedience to God, following the Bible, and accepting church dogma. Christianity will eventually lose this debate, as it did the debate about the nature of the solar system.[3]

Christian belief in a spiritual world will not be engaged by Science, since Science investigates aspects of only the physical world. Christianity therefore wins this nondebate by default. Christianity's affirmation of the nature of spiritual reality is directly challenged, however, by the spiritual realities of other non-Christian religions. No scientific tests are available by which to prove which description of spiritual reality, if any, is an accurate description of the way things are in the spiritual universe. In the absence of objective evidence available to a neutral third party, settling whose view of the spiritual universe is accurate turns out to be "my opinion beats yours." Spiritual realities do not "exist" in the physical world, for by definition they are spirit. Spiritual realities are mental constructs in the minds of those who hold such beliefs and in sympathetic accounts in religious literature, which originally began as mental constructs in the mind of the ancient author. Thus, literary descriptions of spiritual universes do exist in time and space. (5–7–14)

§13 THE INTERFACE OF REASON AND FAITH

The devil may be in the details of the definitions I am using: reason is the mental power concerned with forming conclusions, judgments, or inferences; faith is a belief that is not based on proof. Reason proceeds on the basis of skepticism, critical inquiry, and logic; faith works on the basis of credulity, a priori premises, and confessions. In short, the two processes of thought are by definition two completely opposite ways of apprehending reality. For example, reason based on experience says that a person who is dead and not in some kind of deep coma remains dead; s/he does not return to a living state. Faith, on the other hand, argues— true; in general a person who is dead does not come back to a living state, but there is one exception. God "raised" Jesus of Nazareth from the dead. Behind this particular Christian response lies the a priori premise of an unseen divine being, and in the confession that Jesus was raised from the dead—both of which are evident only to a believer who shares that faith. Reason, on the other hand, demands that some rational proof be offered to justify this exception to the way of all flesh.

---

3. See "Pondering Confessions and Questions," §15 below p. 44.

Faith pleads an open universe where God has elbow room to make things deviate from the observed usual. But reason, willing even to accept the idea of an open universe where things may deviate from the usual, still demands proof that the deviation from the usual is based on natural cause and effect rather than on the basis of manipulation by an invisible hand outside the natural order of things.

At bottom, reason and faith are fundamentally two contradictory ways of viewing reality, but up to a point they can coexist and in some cases even exist cooperatively in the same mind. Where they part ways is in the deference given to the primary confessions of a given faith. These a priori premises of the faith are nonnegotiable: that is, without them, by definition, there is no faith. To join a given faith one must give assent to its confessions, and if one changes one's mind after joining, then one can be taken before some official body of the organization on heresy charges (and, yes, such trials did take place with some regularity even into the modern day[4]), and if convicted of heresy one either recants or is put out of the community of faith.

Apart from the primary confessions it is possible for a member of a given faith to practice a rational twenty-first-century existence as long as one does not make the mistake of thinking there is a one-to-one correlation between what one *believes* is so and what is *actually* so. Should one make that mistake, alibis will be required in order to accommodate the difference between belief and actuality. For example, faith asserts "this is my Fathers' world": i.e., God controls it, and can be expected to act in the best interest of the created order. Yet we also experience in the world pain, disease, natural disasters, and tragedy. How can that be reconciled with a benevolent God controlling the universe? When one comes to the point of recognizing that a disconnection exists between good God and dangerous creation, the disconnection must be bridged to enable one to hold both concepts at the same time.

One of the many alibis explaining away this phenomenon is as follows: The world was originally created as a benign place. We now, however, from the perspective of faith live in a fallen creation because of Adam's willful sin. The creation will, however, in the end be redeemed (Rom 8:18–23), but such a belief does not solve the problem of God's failure to render benevolent care to the creation and its creatures in the here and now. Here is another: Whatever bad happens to people is for their

---

4. Shriver, *Dictionary of Heresy Trials*.

benefit. The word "bad" used in this connection is really a misnomer; for the tragedies that come upon humans are frequently explained as part of God's refining process through which human beings grow and improve. So the "bad" is really a "good." Such a solution to the problem, however, turns God into a stern disciplinarian who shapes his creatures through pain and suffering—a far cry from a kind and caring "Father" (compare Luke 11:11–12).

When the alibis can no longer bridge the gap between benevolent deity and dangerous world, a fundamentally different way of viewing reality is required, and a gap appears in the confessional wall sheltering the faithful from the insistent voice of reason. We surrender items of personal religious belief with great difficulty, yet reason persistently continues its nagging and prodding. (9-15-14)

§14 WE LIVE BY FICTIONS AS MUCH AS BY TRUTHS

As a general rule we have little difficulty living by the fictions we ourselves invent. Fictions are things "made up." We recognize that they are not *actually* true, but we act *as if* they were. The difficulty, however, is that some fictions harden into myths.

For example, we sometimes fudge the truth by creating conscious fictions about ourselves to put things about ourselves in a better light rather than in the harsh light of actuality, and we think of them as only slight "exaggerations." Often we end up believing our own fictions, and even include them in our personal resumes. Thus have we consciously imposed a fictional pattern onto our personal reality, which becomes a datum in our own personal story. Over time some even forget that it was once only a fiction.

Society also creates fictions to live by. In the court case of *Sebelius vs. Hobby Lobby et al.*,[5] Justice Samuel Alito cited the dictionary as part of the justification for regarding corporations as "persons," when the U.S. Supreme Court concluded corporations can have religious beliefs. Corporations are fictional legal entities that can conduct business, acquire property, and sue or be sued. As legal entities they serve as shields for boards of directors. Even the most naïve among us, however, know that legal entities are not persons, because the first dictionary definition of *person* is "human being." Corporations do not have physical bodies and

---

5. *Mother Jones*, "Here Is the Supreme Court's Decision."

hence can neither make love nor perform other human bodily functions. They cannot think, feel, worship, or pray. Therefore corporations cannot have "personal" religious beliefs as people do, even though the members of a corporation's board of directors doubtless do have religious scruples. Nevertheless the fiction that corporations are "persons" is now the law that governs American society. The Supreme Court simply forgot that only Mother Nature can make a person. What mischief this legal fiction will lead to in the future remains to be seen.

Even scholars create fictions. A good example of a scholarly fiction is the collection of literary material shared by Matthew and Luke but not found in Mark. The source for this literary material in Matthew and Luke is believed to be a hypothetical (i.e., fictional) gospel source, which is called Q (i.e., *Quelle*—German for "Source").[6] Most New Testament scholars subscribe to the fiction that this collection of material originally came from an actual *written* text that is no longer extant. Degrees have been awarded, careers established, and money made on Q articles, commentaries, and theologies even though Q is only a convenient fiction for explaining gospel relationships.

Even church folk create religious fictions, forgetting in time that they are only fictions. In a brief newspaper essay Rev. Cliff Rawley argued that Scripture "if used correctly" is a "proven resource of positive transformation . . . a guide to a peaceful life."[7] Rawley recognizes, however, that the Bible contains both positive and negative ideas, and that used incorrectly it can be exploited for purposes detrimental and destructive to society. He offers a litany of many who have misused the Bible for destructive ends. But if the Bible is subject to exploitation by those who use it incorrectly, whence has come the idea that the Bible is an infallible guide? The answer is that the infallibility of the Bible is a church fiction that has become doctrinal truth. If the Bible can be misused by anyone who chooses to misuse it, then it cannot be "infallible," since it has an inherent potential for misuse.

Here is an example of a religious fiction turning into a myth. Pausanias (second century CE), a Greek tourist and geographer, wrote a description of Greece, noting religious customs and traditions. He described the beginning of the Hero cult of Theagenes of Thasos. Theagenes was actually a famous athlete—a boxer, wrestler, and runner

---

6. Hedrick, *When History and Faith Collide*, 95–109.
7. Rawley, "Scripture."

in fifth-century-BCE Greece—who won awards in the Olympic Games in 480 and 476 BCE. It was rumored by the Thasians that he was actually the son of the divine Herakles, rather than of the priest Timosthenes. By the second century BCE, however, Theagenes was credited with curing diseases, and receiving divine honors as a demigod at cult centers in different parts of Greece.[8] The fiction that great achievers in life have an affinity with the Gods, in time became the myth that the divine Theagenes cures diseases and deserves to be worshiped. (7–15–14)

§15 PONDERING CONFESSIONS AND QUESTIONS

Religious beliefs help us to order our lives and our world. They inform us about our place in the universe and provide us a rationale for being and living, and consolation in dying. Sometimes, however, certain beliefs (prime directives, really) in our traditional belief systems clash with personal experience, rational thought, or reason, which produces a crisis of personal faith. What does one do then?

One Sunday morning in a Bible study class at a local Baptist church this subject was broached when one of the class members said, "There are some things that I just take on faith," which I understood to mean that some things just don't make sense for whatever reason, and so he just accepted them without question. After a moment I raised my hand and asked this question: why do we accept things "on faith" without question? Shouldn't we challenge what we don't understand? The reaction from the class was defensive. We were, after all, talking about our Baptist confessional beliefs.

Religious confessions are not offers to dialogue, but statements demanding unconditional acceptance. And some beliefs are so basic to faith that even their challenge threatens to undermine "the faith that was once for all delivered to the saints" (Jude 3); some questions shake the very foundations of a personal faith that gives meaning and order to life. That morning what was an academic question for me, which I hoped might lead to a better understanding of how we think about faith, was seen by the class as an assault on faith, or so it seemed to them.

Religious confessions are holy things; for the confessor they are the very essence of absolute truth, and we defer to them as we do not to other secular beliefs we hold. Secular beliefs we change quite frequently,

---

8. Pausanias, *Guide to Greece*, 315–17 (book 6 [Elis II]. 11.1–9).

but circle the wagons in the face of a threat to basic religious beliefs. The fact is, however, that religious beliefs do change. What was gospel truth yesterday and today, tomorrow may very well be consigned to the dust bin of discarded religious belief.

Numerous examples arise of Christian "believers" who questioned beliefs and refused to take things "on faith." For example, that was precisely the case with Job. His friends told him that he was suffering because of his sins (it was the common view of Mediterranean antiquity that suffering is the result of sin[9]). That answer was not satisfying to Job. He was willing to admit that he may have sinned, but what he was suffering was out of all proportion to whatever sins he might have committed. He kept wrestling with a faith that affirmed the idea that sin always results in suffering; Job is suffering; therefore Job is a sinner. Job could not let the matter drop until he became convinced that God was powerful enough to do whatever God wanted, but Job never admitted that his suffering was the result of his sins (and of course readers know from reading the prologue to the poem that Job was right). In short Job never accepted the premise of his friends, even though he lost his one-sided argument with God. Because we have read the book of Job, we know that Job's friends wanted him to confess something that was not true.

Here is another belief that was once "gospel truth" in Christian churches. From the second century until the sixteenth century the standard view of the cosmos was that the earth was the center of the universe. A Polish scientist and churchman Nikolas Copernicus, however, in the early part of the sixteenth century proved that our solar system was heliocentric—meaning that the earth and all the planets in our solar system revolved around the sun. Fearing the inevitable conflict between his book and the church, Copernicus did not allow his book to be published until his death.[10] At the end of the sixteenth century Giordano Bruno, a monk-philosopher, believed Copernicus was right. Bruno was taken to court and given a chance to recant his heresy of the earth revolving around the sun. He refused to recant and was burned at the stake as a heretic.[11] Later Galileo Galilei, an Italian astronomer of the seventeenth century, was placed under house arrest by church authorities for agreeing with

---

9. Simundson, "Suffering."
10. Stimson, *Gradual Acceptance*, 28–29.
11. Ibid., 52.

Copernicus. In the end, however, he perjured himself and recanted.[12] The church was mistaken, the confession was wrong, and eventually it was quietly changed.[13] Today we all know that the earth is a planet in an out-of-the-way solar system at the edge of the Milky Way galaxy, and it circles around our sun. The religious belief that was once "gospel truth" for over a thousand years was replaced by a secular truth.

In short, confessions of faith are absolute truths only for those who accept them as such. It is my belief, however, that faith may not demand that I confess things I find questionable or untrue; for church confessions do not originate in the mind of God; they are temporary human formulas that are changed by vote or synod action. Or they are simply quietly changed over time. The historical Christian church is a conservative institution with a vested interest in its own survival with the least amount of change. Some things, however, will always be in need of change, and change begins with questions. (4-26-14)

§16 FAITH CRITICALLY EXAMINED

Believing a thing to be so does not make it so, regardless of how sincerely and firmly the belief is held. An example of a firmly held belief that turned out to be completely wrong is the sixteenth-century belief of the Catholic Church that the earth was the center of the universe. The church believed this item of faith because they believed the Bible affirmed it to be so.[14] Nikolas Copernicus, however, proved that the earth circled around the sun, which held a stationary position in the center of our solar system. The church's view was wrong, and the dogma was eventually changed, but not before the church burned the monk-philosopher Giordiano Bruno at the stake for refusing to accept the church's dogma.[15] The critical evidence presented by Copernicus could not be denied by a reasonable person.

An uncritical faith exposes one to the risk of being ensnared in the web of either a "true believer" or a religious charlatan, both of whom,

---

12. Ibid., 49-70.

13. It was not until 1835 that the works of Copernicus and Galileo were taken off the list of proscribed books for the Catholic Church: Stimson, *Gradual Acceptance*, 100

14. See the arguments that the earth is the center of the universe by Thomas Feyens (1619) in Stimson, *Gradual Acceptance*, 124-29.

15. See also §15, p. 44 above.

motivated for different reasons, aim to bring people under their influence, and the influence of their views of faith. In conservative Christianity both of them use the Bible successfully to exert influence over the unknowledgeable, incautious, and unwary. One assertion that is now almost a byword within some conservative religious groups is, "if the Bible says it, I believe it, and that settles it." Any faith that demands such unquestioning trust in an ancient collection of documents is essentially an uncritical faith.

On the other hand, persons who exercise critical judgment will not allow faith to demand that they affirm something they find to be patently untrue. How might that work, for example? A critical faith may be willing to affirm that Jesus healed people, on the grounds that their ailments were psychosomatic (physical illness induced by psychological causes), and their own faith was the trigger that accomplished their self-healing (Mark 5:34; 10:52). But those who actually observed any putative healing would not be able to make such fine modern distinctions, and to them it would appear that Jesus had performed the healing. But incidents in which Jesus is represented as manipulating the natural world (usually referred to as "nature miracles" by biblical scholars) a person of critical faith would find patently impossible on the basis that the world, as we now know it, does not work by magic-like manipulation. So such things as restoring a withered hand to its former vigor (Mark 3:1–5) or changing water to wine at Cana (John 2:1–11) as they are described in the gospels a person of critical faith would decline to affirm as historical events. A person of critical faith would likely not be persuaded by the belief that because Jesus was divine (or God) he could manipulate the natural world, since such claims were also made for others in the ancient world.[16] Persons of critical faith do not allow religious dogma to determine for them either the nature of reality or the character of historical event.

A critical faith is not unlike that of Job. The Job of the poetic sections of the book (Job 3:1—42:6) remains almost to the end a questioner. He does not settle for traditional answers, rejects the easy answers of his well-intentioned friends, and continues to pressure God to explain himself. But in the end Job eventually capitulates before a barrage of perplexing, unanswerable questions (Job 38–39) and returns to traditional faith (42:1–6), at least this is the suggestion of the romantic narrative conclusion that ends the main poetic section of the book (Job 42:7–17).

16. Cartlidge and Dungan, eds., *Documents*, 151–61.

I suspect, however, that in reality a modern critical thinker, having escaped the ancient worldview supporting the creeds and confessions of the church, will never be able to return to the confines of traditional or populist faith. (3-4-12)

§17 THE NATURE OF RELIGIOUS TRUTH

Truth is a slippery concept, even though the word is generally used with complete confidence. A working definition of *truth* is, a verified or indisputable fact, proposition, principle, or the like. But *truth* also has an ontological (i.e., metaphysical) association; that is to say, truth is an ideal or fundamental reality transcending perceived experience; it is always and eternally true. While one may wonder whether any such ethical value in the universe deserves such an accolade, it is certainly the case that religious truth is not to be equated with "always and eternally true." The history of religions in Western culture confirms two axioms about religion: On the one hand, believing something is true does not make it true. But, on the other hand, if you believe something is true, so it is—*for you*. What follows from these two axioms is that truth is not always true, and sometimes an untruth is true. Or put another way, all religious truth is relative.

Here is how it works: believing a thing to be so does not make it so. For example in the sixteenth century the Catholic Church took the second-century Ptolemaic view of the universe virtually as an item of faith: the sun, moon, and planets circled the earth, which then was regarded as the center of the universe.[17] Such a view fitted and supported the stories of creation in Genesis. God created the earth for human beings, and it was on the earth that God's plan of redemption took place. To lessen the earth's position in the universe was perceived as an attack upon the Church, the Bible, and Christian faith. Such a view was contrary to Scripture, so the church reasoned and believed deeply. When Nikolas Copernicus proved that the earth rotated about the sun, the religious authorities suppressed his views, which Copernicus wisely had not allowed to be published till his death in 1543. The religious authorities took a dim view of anyone who thought differently and around 1600 burned Gordiano Bruno at the stake for refusing to recant the views of Copernicus.[18]

---

17. Rogers, "Triumph of a Theory," 125-29; Stimson, *Gradual Acceptance*, 85-94.
18. See §15, p. 44 above.

The church's belief was "religious truth" in the sixteenth century, even though it was not actually true.[19]

Religious doctrine is the easiest place to see these axioms at work. Baptists believe that the Lord's Supper is purely symbolical; it is *for them* a memorial of the death of Jesus, which the church practices to commemorate the "sacrifice" of Jesus. Catholics, on the other hand, believe the wine and "host" (i.e., the bread) are transformed at a certain point in the Mass into the actual blood and body of the Lord. Hence, for Catholics participation in the Eucharist is participation in the actual body and blood of the Lord; it is *for them* a means of receiving grace from God. Each of these beliefs, though contradictory, is true for those who believe it to be so. In this way religious truth is true for those who believe it to be so, but not true for those who do not.

Religious truth is affirmed by value-laden, or "opinion" language. It is like saying "I like ice cream"; or, "Apple pie is better than turnip greens!" Religious truth is like appreciating beauty, which, as we all know, lies in the eye of the beholder. One person's destructive "act of God" is another person's natural occurrence or misfortune. There is no universal standard. Religious truth is not like a mathematical formula (2 x 2=4, for example). This latter statement actually is an eternal truth in our universe. But the statement that "the Bible is the Word of God," or that "the Word of our God abides forever" (Isa 40:8) is in all universes only true for the person who believes. To regard any deeply held religious belief as having eternal certitude overlooks the obvious relative and contradictory nature of religious truth. (4-15-10)

§18 DOES GOD CONTROL THE WIND?

With one exception the Bible seems pretty clear on this issue: God controls the wind. The biblical writers believed God used wind to cause the waters of the great flood to subside (Gen 8:1); he fed the wandering Israelites with quail, which he brought to their camp by wind (Num 11:31). The LORD parted the waters of the sea by a strong east wind to facilitate the Israelites' escape from Egypt (Exod 14:21), and sent wind to cause the sea to cover over and drown the pursuing Egyptian armies (Exod 15:10). It is well attested that the biblical writers believed that God controls the

---

19. Stimson, *Gradual Acceptance*, 28–52.

winds (Pss 135:7; 148:7–8; Isa 11:15; Jer 10:13; 49:36; Jonah 1:4), and everything else as well.

Oddly, however, the writer of the Gospel of John has Jesus remark that the wind obeys no commands: "The wind blows where it wishes, and you hear its sound, but don't know whence it comes or whither it goes" (John 3:8). In other words, the wind is a free agent, under no controls. But Matthew (8:26–27), Mark (4:39, 41) and Luke (8:24–25) in one shared story portray even Jesus controlling the wind.

The statement in John attributed to Jesus about the wind's independence approximates the modern popular view that wind blows hither and thither at random, but neither Jesus nor the popular modern view is quite accurate. Scientific study shows that wind does have some set directions. Wind

> is caused by the difference in pressure from one point on the earth's surface to another. The air moving from the area of higher pressure to the area of lower pressure is called wind. The air does not move directly from the point of highest pressure to the point of lowest pressure. The earth's rotation affects the air flow by deflecting it to the right. This effect is called the Coriolis Effect. In the Northern Hemisphere, this [effect] causes air to flow clockwise around high pressure areas and counter-clockwise around low pressure areas.

The directions are reversed in the Southern Hemisphere. Generally, the difference in pressure across the globe is caused by the uneven heating of the earth's surface by the sun.[20]

If one believes that God controls *everything*, including wind, one would have to assume on the basis of scientific observations that God has established a set pattern for winds to follow, for they do function according to an observable pattern, more or less with regularity. Apparently God only gets involved in wind movements when he wants to reward or punish. But if that is true, then God is involved with wind movement only now and then. God's established system normally directs the usual course of the winds by the heating and cooling of the earth from day to day. But this logic leads to the conclusion that God is not always hands-on (as it were), personally directing the movement of wind twenty-four/seven. And if this rationale is applied to everything in the universe, then God, it appears, *normally* runs things in the natural world by set programs

20. Dave, "What Causes the Wind?"

that do not require continual personal oversight. In other words the wind desk of the universe is generally automatically controlled.

Of course, it is possible that God personally "mans" (as it were) the wind desk of the universe at all times, and every gentle summer breeze or frosty "nor'easter" is under God's direct control. But such logic raises the disturbing question of divine ethics. Devastation and subsequent death caused by strong winds and tornados seem a lot more like a case of someone falling asleep on duty, or a case of disproportionate treatment, rather than anything approximating justice. Job complained about, among other things, a similar use of wind (Job 1:18–19). But, then, who knows for sure what goes on in an omniscient divine brain (so to speak)?

For my part, I simply cannot imagine that God is personally directing the course of every wind that blows in the universe, because we would then have to imagine God personally playing around with water spouts and dust devils. These wind-produced phenomena are smaller cousins to tornadoes, and the smaller ones are not particularly dangerous. If God is controlling everything, then we would have to imagine God, perhaps, amusing himself, at innocuous wind-play—what with having too much time on his hands (as it were), because normally the set programs do most of the work.

Perhaps that is what happened in 2011. At the end of April devastating winds and tornadoes ripped through the South, causing extensive property damage and the deaths of approximately three hundred people.[21] Were these winds divine justice or natural phenomena, or was God perhaps preoccupied with wind-play on Mars or in Arizona, while the devastating winds on earth simply escaped his notice? For people of traditional faith such disturbing questions have the character of a catch-22: they can't really be answered without raising other disturbing questions. (5-19-11)

§19 DOES MOTHER NATURE CONTROL THE WIND?

The answer given by the Bible and orthodox Christian and Jewish theology is an unequivocal no! God directs the affairs of human history and regulates the course of the natural world—although Jesus did once say that "the wind blows where it wants to" (John 3:7), ultimately suggesting that there is no control over the natural order. In the light of the

21. Tanglao and Forer, "Tornadoes and Storms."

devastating tornado in Joplin, Missouri, this question about the wind is really about theodicy—or in plain language, why does God do what s/he does? Or, how is God evidenced, if at all, in the natural world? Here is the issue simply stated: was the tornado in Joplin, Missouri, on May 22, 2011, "the costliest single tornado in U. S. history," an "act of God" or a "natural disaster"? Who destroyed 25 percent of Joplin, killed 158 people, and caused millions of dollars in property damage, God or Mother Nature?[22]

Those among us who consider ourselves people of faith and at the same time post-Enlightenment human beings, who tend to think of the world in scientific categories rather than theological categories, will simply reject out of hand the notion that God is responsible for the disaster in Joplin, Missouri. But, quite frankly, we have difficulty explaining how God is related, if at all, to the natural world.

This difficulty is caused by the excesses of nature, of which the EF 5 winds in Joplin are but one instance. Nature is both benign and deadly. On the one hand, she blesses us with bounties of field and orchard, but on the other hand, she is "red in tooth and claw."[23] Nature has always been dangerous, capricious, and ethically blind. In recent memory in the twenty-first century Mother Nature, or God, destroyed New Orleans by hurricane and flood (August 28, 2005), caused massive loss of life in Indonesia (26 December 2004) and in Japan by earthquake and tsunami (11 March 2011), as well as massive loss of life by earthquakes in Russia, China, Haiti, and by tornados and winds in Alabama, and Georgia, and now in Joplin, Missouri. It is not possible in a single sentence to enumerate all the "natural disasters," or "acts of God," occurring in recent memory.

Nature does not reflect the character of a God I would care to associate myself with, assuming it is true that God controls nature. Such aberrations in the regularly occurring benign cycles of nature pose the greatest challenge to both the traditional understanding of God and to the traditional Christian and Jewish belief that God personally regulates nature. Such disasters have always played the devil (so to speak) with the belief that the Judeo-Christian God, who by most accounts is gracious, controls nature. If God controls nature and such unconscionable disasters occur, how can God be considered good? On the other hand, if Mother Nature regulates the world, disasters make better sense. Mother

22. Wikipedia, "2011 Joplin Tornado."
23. Tennyson, *In Memoriam*, canto 56, line 15.

Nature is ethically blind, and in a natural disaster the righteous suffering along with the wicked is understandable. Mother Nature is the real culprit here. But this solution leaves unanswered exactly how God is related to the world. Traditional answers are simply inadequate. (6-6-11)

§20 DOES THE WIND MAKE ITS OWN DECISIONS?

Is it possible that, for some reason, God has abandoned the natural world? Things do seem, pretty much routinely, to run themselves without observable direct interference from powers higher than the natural order of the universe. In many ways the thought is frightening, but nonetheless if we are honest, it appears to accord with our experience. We must make our way in the universe with no help except from ourselves. If we insist that God is good, then we must logically conclude that for some reason the natural world is, or has become, impervious to God, because nature can, from our perspective, be both good and bad. The one area of our experience that seems to be pervious to divine initiatives is our human state, as flawed as it may be.

The Bible, one ancient religious collection of writings that has most influenced our Judeo-Christian culture, reflects many ideas of questionable value, but 1 Kgs 19:1–18 may suggest an approach to the problem of God and the natural world. The prophet Elijah had fled from Queen Jezebel, who wanted to take his life. For forty days and forty nights he put as much space between himself and Jezebel as he could, and he finally took refuge in a cave on Mount Horeb.

The word of the LORD came to him! In those days people apparently believed that God communicated audibly. In our day, however, the audible voice of God has fallen silent, and usually we institutionalize people who claim to hear audible voices coming from out of nowhere. God asked, what are you doing in this cave Elijah? Elijah complained that he was the only faithful Israelite left in the land, and now his life was threatened. So God told him to go to the front of the cave:

> And behold, the LORD passed by, and a great and strong wind rent the mountains, and broke in pieces the rocks before the LORD, *but the LORD was not in the wind*; and after the wind an earthquake, *but the LORD was not in the earthquake*; and after the earthquake a fire, *but the LORD was not in the fire*; and after the fire a still, small voice. (1 Kgs 19:11–12 RSV; italics added)

This is a remarkably novel idea in the ancient world: God was not to be equated with the forces of nature.

The human species has shown itself throughout its existence to be incurably religious. The question is, will we grow out of our religious attitudes as our species matures, or is our propensity to religion of some sort indelibly imprinted in our genes? No one can answer this question definitively, but certainly the human psyche has demonstrated itself pervious to what it regards as divine initiatives, which are thought to come from outside ourselves. That is to say, we claim to experience divinity. Often the divine communication (if such it be) is garbled, if we judge by our competing religious ideas as a people. Here is the reason: there is as much of us as there is of the divine in our reception of what we take to be divine communication. Our problem has become sorting the wheat from the chaff. (6–20–11)

3

On Being Human in the Contemporary World

§21 ON BEING HUMAN

What are we—we creatures that rule over the earth? Our scientific designation is *Homo sapiens* (the sagacious primate); we are the surviving species of the genus *Homo* ("man") of the primate family. We are mammals, and hence broadly speaking animals. In polite company we generally refer to ourselves as human beings. We tout ourselves as "made in the image of God" (Gen 1:26), and when ambitious as a "little less than God" (Ps 8:4–8); we believe that we have, or are, an "eternal soul." On the other hand, some of us are capable of unimaginable inhumane atrocities. Two questions arise in my mind: what exactly, besides our brains, distinguishes us knowledgeable primates from the rest of the animal kingdom? What distinguishes our better self from the egregious, evil aspects of our own nature? Or putting the second question another way, could it be that some *Homo sapiens* are actually less than human?

One way to begin is by asking, what distinguishes the species *Homo sapiens* from other mammals? Here are a few distinguishing features of our species. Perhaps in some slight degree some of these traits have been recognized in other mammals as well; nevertheless, it is only *Homo sapiens* that is characterized by things such as these:

Discovery and use of fire, invention of language, invention of writing and reading, abstract thought, curiosity, problem solving, inventiveness, pursuit of science, inventors of the family and the state, respectful disposition of our dead, mathematics; inventors of the family and state, geometry, poetry, music, and pioneers in space travel, etc.[1]

The word *human* comes from a Latin adjective: *humanus*: that is, characterizing "man." The word is primarily used of the finer aspects of our nature: we can be humane, philanthropic, gentle, obliging, polite; of good education, well-informed, refined, civilized. The word and its use suggest that someone can be *Homo sapiens* and yet be less than what we characterize as humanity at its finest. The trajectory of our species from our animal origins to our current passion for knowledge suggests that there are likely degrees to being human. Apparently not all members of our species have either the capacity or the inclination to achieve in the various areas noted in the quotation above.

The accomplishments of *Homo sapiens* have generally benefitted our species. And that feature (i.e., benefitting the common good) might be considered one standard for distinguishing the human among us from those whom we might characterize as "less human." In other words some *Homo sapiens* are more controlled by the animal aspects of their nature than by their humane aspects. While all of us are *Homo sapiens*, not all of us are human in the sense of behavior embodying, or aiming to embody, the higher aspects of our nature. Hence, an ethical distinction exists between the members of the species *Homo sapiens*. Some are clearly human in that they behave according to the higher aspects of their nature; others are less human because they do not; and still others may be said to be only marginally human because they behave in accord with the worst animal aspects of their nature.

If these observations have any merit, they raise questions about how we educate and provide treatment for those in society who live by the laws of the jungle. (6-20-14)

1. Bronowski, *Ascent of Man*, 20.

§22 FROM THE JESUS TRADITION: ON BECOMING AND BEING HUMAN

All of us are special, even those of us who are not. We belong to the animal species *Homo sapiens* (intelligent man), a thinking animal capable of abstract thought and logical analysis. Anthropologists tell us there have been several iterations of the genus *Homo* that preceded our species, apparently without our mental capability and potential; here are the names of those closest to us in the genus *Homo: heidelbergensis, neanderthalensis, erectus, floresiensis*.[2] They are now extinct.

As a species of the animal kingdom, our kind (*Homo sapiens*) often exhibits an insensitive, brutish behavior that unfortunately reflects a destructive aspect of our nature. Nevertheless, the higher aspects of our nature enable us to contribute to the enhancement of civilization and life in community through the arts, philosophy, science, and so forth. This dissonance in the nature of the species *Homo sapiens* between the lower and higher aspects of our nature—or perhaps better, between the animalistic and the humanistic aspects of our nature—raises the following question: what is the quintessential characteristic of human nature? That is to say: what is best in the nature of our species?

I suggest that what is best in our nature is a kind of liberal humanitarianism grounded in the concept of altruistic and unconditional love. Altruistic love is an unselfish concern for and devotion to the welfare of other human beings without regard for personal benefit or personal cost. In a sense it is a self-denying love for other members of our species of whatever ethnic background.

This kind of love is first met in the ancient world in the Jesus tradition. The Israelite tradition of "love your neighbor as yourself" (Deut 15:1–3) is essentially a tribal ethic, since a neighbor was one of your own tribe; that is to say, your fellow Israelite. And love was also extended to the stranger sojourning in the Israelite community (Lev 19:33–34), a custom grounded in the hospitality codes of the ancient Near East (e.g., Gen 19:1–3; Jdg 19:21).

Through the Jesus tradition love for the neighbor passes over into the Christian communities (Rom 13:8–10) where the neighbor is not a fellow human being of whatever ethnic background but another Christian in the community (as in Rom 15:1–2; Gal 5:14). James 2:1–13, however, does seem to shade over into a universal humanitarian code of care and

2. Potts and Sloan, *What Does It Mean to Be Human?*, 32–33.

concern for fellow human beings of whatever ethnic background because concern and care is extended to any poor, shabbily dressed person who wanders into a Christian assembly. So it is not necessarily at bottom a religious community ethic but seems grounded in a kind of humanitarian concern for other human beings.

One of the clearer expressions of a kind of secular altruistic love as a quality in human life is found in 1 Cor 13:1–13. In this chapter love is not motivated by religious belief or empowered by divine sanction. Here love has more value than religious acts and knowledge (13:1–2) and other forms of charity (13:3). It puts others before self (13:4–7), and epitomizes what it means to be a mature human being (13:11–12). Hence, love has greater value than even religious faith or hope (13:13). There is no mention in the chapter of God or Christ, but love is apparently an altruistic human response to the human other. For these reasons some scholars of the Jesus tradition do not regard chapter 13 as composed by Paul but as borrowed from the Greco-Roman tradition.[3]

The clearest expression of an altruistic unconditional love is the challenge of Jesus to "love your enemies" (Luke 6:27b; Matt 5:44). Matthew and Luke each try to domesticate the saying by suggesting practical actions one can perform that do not involve one in actually loving an enemy: that is to say, do favors for those who hate you, bless those who curse you, pray for your abusers (Luke 6:27–31; Matt 5:43–44)—all of which one can do without actually *loving* an enemy.

When our behavior displays altruistic love, we are quintessentially human; when our behavior is brutish and uncaring, we are marginally human. Being human is not an accident of birth but a matter of behavior. (6-5-17)

§23 WHY AM I HERE?

This is not a question asked by octogenarians who, upon entering a room, wonder what brought them there. It is a question about human existence; that is to say: does life have a purpose beyond simply the living of it? That question is not the same for everyone. It is suitable only for those on the front end of life. For those of us on the back end of life the question becomes, why was I there? Only the young have the luxury of asking the

---

3. Conzelmann, *1 Corinthians*, 217–31.

question in the present tense. The question has two foci: first, what is the purpose of all life; and second, what is my individual purpose in life?

The first focus is a wide-eyed wondering that anything at all exists, and hence in part the question asks about origins. Depending on your personal commitments, however, that question may or may not be answerable. If you are a creationist, you doubtless believe that God originated all you see about you. Various religious traditions offer a number of different answers to the question, but all would consider creation as an act of God. The ancient Israelites answered the question, why am I here? as follows. Your purpose as a human being is to

> Be fruitful and multiply, and fill the earth and subdue it; and have dominion over the fish of the sea and over the birds of the air and over every living thing that moves upon the earth. (Gen 1:28, RSV)

Hence in this view the chief aim of humanity is to manage the earth and all its life processes. The answer that comes out of the Christian Puritan and Reformation traditions is that human beings are here to serve and glorify God (e.g., 1 Pet 4:11; 1 Cor 10:31).

On the other hand, if you are an evolutionist, the origin of life was not a purposeful act. Life simply happened quite by accident over time around "4.0 billion years ago in the ponds and oceans of primitive earth."[4] Hence the answer to the origins question, why am I here? for an evolutionist is, there no reason; you just happened along in the course of things.

There is, however, a second aspect to the question, why am I here? It is this: what am I supposed to do with my life now that I am here? In many ways it is a quotidian question. That is to say, how should I occupy my time throughout the day? It is also a serious existential query, however, and prompts the question, what is my purpose in life? We usually bump up against this aspect of the question when we think about occupation, but it also has a more narrow focus: how should I act in a particular situation?

A good example of this latter significance of the question is that faced by Esther. Hadassah (Esther), a Jewess, had become the queen of the Persian Empire. Her uncle Mordecai learned of a plot to annihilate all the Jews in the empire and sought help from Esther with these words: "Who knows whether you have not come to the kingdom for such a time

---

4. Sagan, *Cosmos*, 30-31.

as this?" (Esth 4:14, RSV). In other words: this is your moment; time to step up to the plate!

Creationists have already answered the origins question by projecting a creator behind the cosmos. For creationists, human beings are here to obey the will of the creator in all things. The evolutionist, on the other hand, finds no need to pander to the will of a supposed deity mediated through imperfect and contradictory interpreters. The evolutionist is free (to a point) to decide what to do in life and with life. It is both exhilarating and terrifying to realize that what I do with my life is my personal choice; or in the words of the poet:

> Out of the night that covers me,
> Black as the Pit from pole to pole,
> I thank whatever gods may be
> For my unconquerable soul.
>
> . . .
>
> It matters not how strait the gate,
> How charged with punishments the scroll,
> I am the master of my fate;
> I am the captain of my soul.[5]

From the perspective of the creationist, however, the child of the creator replies to the evolutionist's arrogant assertion with the following: true freedom can only be found in complete submission to the creator, for only where the Spirit of the Lord is does true freedom exist (2 Cor 3:17). Everyone is enslaved by their sin, and only the Son brings freedom from sin (John 8:31–37; Rom 6:17–28 and 8:2). Or in the words of the hymnist,

> Free to be me, God, I really am free.
> Free to become what you want me to be.
> Free to decide whether I should be Lord
> or be your slave and obey your word.[6] (1–27–16)

---

5. Henley, "Invictus," lines 1–4, 13–16. The poem was originally untitled.
6. Woolley, "Free to Be Me," first stanza.

§24 INTIMATIONS OF MORTALITY

The ancient Israelites believed in Sheol, and the ancient Greeks believed in Hades; both were gray places of departed spirits.[7] Both postmortem locations are characterized as places of shades or shadows, and by the absence of vibrant life. Later the Israelites anticipated a resurrection of the physical body,[8] but the Greeks had also looked forward to the Elysian Fields (or the Isles of the Blessed) as a place of reward for the heroes, sons of the Gods, and those who lived noble lives.[9] In Christianity, hell is the eternal fate of the damned, while the righteous will enter the blessed state of heaven. Beliefs are not "intimations of immortality."[10] Intimations are indirect hints or suggestions of a future lying beyond the realm of the physical senses, which cannot be directly experienced. In our day a hint of a postmortem future comes generally from surgery patients who claim to have seen a bright light at the end of a long dark tunnel, and simultaneously having experienced feelings of peacefulness and reassurance from deceased friends and family who have "passed on."[11] Many such intimations that life continues beyond the grave can be found on the internet and in print media.

In Israelite and Hellenistic antiquity there were also intimations of postmortem survival. For example, Odysseus sailed to Hades, the place of departed spirits, in the *Odyssey* (book 11), where the dead were described as shadows flitting about—not a very pleasant prospect, but a clearly a survival of sorts.[12] On a brighter note there were a number of heavenly journeys, similar to the light at the end of the tunnel.[13] Paul's trip to paradise in 2 Cor 12:1–4 is the only firsthand reported ascent in the New Testament, but alas Paul tells us nothing he experienced there (2 Cor 12:4).

What strikes me about all these supposed hints that something lies beyond the grave is that the unknown future is generally described from the perspective of the contemporary cultural and religious experience of the individual bringing the report.

---

7. Lewis, "Dead, Abode of."
8. Nickelsburg, "Resurrection," 684–88.
9. Kearns, "Elysium," 521.
10. Wordsworth, "Ode."
11. Wikipedia, "Near-death Experience."
12. Homer, *Od*, 10.495; Rieu, *Odyssey*, 168.
13. Tabor, "Heaven," 93.

While I am neither a seer nor the son of a seer, I have on two occasions had what I will describe as "intimations of mortality" (with apologies to Wordsworth). The first occurred in the 1970s during a long transatlantic flight. While I was in a semiconscious state (neither awake nor asleep), a poem called itself forth in my head. That is, it "came to me"; I did not consciously create and craft it:

> The land is long and empty;
> And we dance through it;
> Aging moths
> Before flickering candles
> Casting no shadows.

I am not sure I understand the poem, and I do not particularly like my interpretation of it. The long narrow land, empty and shrouded in darkness, struck me as an utterly alien place devoid of life. The moths, the only living things in the poem, are insects (the poem's "we"), which portray human life as fragile and ephemeral. The fascination of the moths for the open flame and their macabre "dance" bringing them increasingly closer to self-immolation suggests their inevitable demise; the absence of shadow in a land dominated by candles suggests abject nothingness—not even shadows of the moths survive the dance. The poem is dismal, evoking a sense of complete hopelessness. I am not normally given to such pessimism, and have always been surprised the poem came out of my head.

The second intimation came on the Greek island of Corfu in 2002:

> I awoke from a sound sleep in a clammy sweat, anxious and profoundly disturbed, the sounds of the Ionian Sea faint but distinct beyond the closed shutters of the room. My vaguely remembered dream replaying itself in my mind only increased my agitation. I had dreamed that the fabric of reality suddenly split down the side directly in front of me, and for a few seconds I stared into an empty void beyond. In the second I realized that absolutely nothing lay beyond, I knew my own personal mortality, not intellectually but viscerally.[14]

I did not at the time consider this dream a supernatural premonition or a warning from God. Rather I explained it as a wake-up call from

---

14. Hedrick, *House of Faith*, 60.

my inner biological clock; it was a reasonable inference considering my advancing years.

Both experiences are rather pessimistic hints of a postmortem future. Considering my religious background, I do not think that I can easily dismiss these experiences as the result of my cultural and religious experience, as I suggested above was the case with the "lights at the end of the tunnel." My cultural and religious experiences are heavily invested in traditional Christian faith, so I should have expected something a bit more optimistic. At the very least, however, these two experiences likely are subconscious indications of my repressed fears of a postmortem future. I was in control of neither the poem nor the dream, so I must assume each was evoked in some way from within my subconscious.

What can be said about intimations of immortality (i.e., the lights at the end of the tunnel) and intimations of mortality (i.e., the empty void beyond)? Which experience provides a reliable hint of our common but hidden future, if either one? Another question suggests itself: why should my intimations of mortality be merely an expression of a repressed subconscious fear, but the more popular intimations of immortality be regarded as objective proof of life after death? Why are not both subconscious responses that tell us about only ourselves? (3-28-13)

§25 THE GOD QUESTION

Human beings are incurably religious! Even in the basically secularized scientific West most of us still ponder in our more reflective moments the ultimate God question: what is it that God (if God there be) expects of me? This question has many permutations depending on your stage and situation in life. At bottom, however, the question is intensely personal and concerns the viability of what traditionally religious people think of as the soul (i.e., that is, some eternal aspect of ourselves)—what can we do to ensure that at our inevitable end God will have been pleased enough with us to issue an invitation as appears in a story of Jesus: "well done, good and faithful slave ... enter into the joy of your Master" (Matt 25:21, 23)?

Those who find the Judeo-Christian writings helpful for answering religious questions (i.e., both those writings affirmed by the synagogue and church, as well as the writings they rejected) also find that the literature is contradictory. Even in the Bible there are contradictory answers to the question, what does God expect of me? For example, the ancient Israelites were a cultic, priestly society. Their life was regulated by laws mandating temple sacrifices and laws that identified what was and what was not acceptable human behavior. According to the divine law (Torah), among other things, sin (i.e., what displeases God) was forgiven by blood sacrifices (Lev 4:1–6:7); it seems the God of the ancient Israelites enjoyed "the pleasing odor" of burning flesh (Gen 8:20–22). My point here is that the ancient Israelites trusted and generally followed the law in order to receive God's "well done." Psalms 1 and 119 reflect a deep appreciation for the law.

Israel's ethical prophets, however, did not agree, and argued instead that God hated the temple cult and paid no attention to it (Amos 5:21–23; Mic 6:6–8). What God actually wanted was justice and righteousness and not temple sacrifices (Amos 5:24): the Lord requires the doing of justice, the loving of kindness, and a humble walk with God (Mic 6:8). The prophets believed that the way of justice and righteousness was the exclusive way to please God and regarded the temple cult as misguided.

In the New Testament Paul rejected the Jewish law as incapable of producing lives that pleased God, even though he had a profound respect for the law (Rom 7:7–12; Gal 3:19–29). Paul concluded that faith alone was the answer to the ultimate God question (Rom 4:1–5:2): "if you confess with your lips that Jesus is Lord and believe in your heart that God raised him from the dead, you will be saved" (Rom 10:9, RSV). One is not justified by performing works of the law, but through the faith of Jesus Christ (Gal 2:16).[15]

The writer of the book of James, however, disagrees with Paul's idea that faith alone is the answer to the ultimate God question. According to James, God expects ethical behavior (Jas 2:14–26) in addition to faith: "religion that is pure and undefiled before God and the Father is this: to visit orphans and widows in their affliction, and to keep oneself unstained from the world" (Jas 1:27 RSV). Citing the example of Abraham, James wrote, "You see that a person is justified by works and not by faith alone" (Jas 2:24).

Every Christian group has a way of resolving these conflicting answers to the God question. For example, the populist Baptist response to the disagreement between Paul and James is that they are supplementary: a person of faith will naturally perform ethical deeds. Paul and James, so

---

15. Dewey, et al., *Authentic Letters*, 65–66.

the populist response goes, are focusing on complementary aspects of the same answer. At bottom, however, the reason the obvious contradiction between the views of Paul and James is ignored is that the Bible *must* be consistent; otherwise the Bible's status as "Word of God" is threatened. Disagreements in the Bible would make it an imperfect instrument, and hence untrustworthy.

When I was in a Baptist seminary in the early sixties,[16] the conservative theological solution to such disagreements in the Bible was to argue a kind of "progressive revelation": God's self revelation was progressively made as people were prepared to receive it.[17] The difficulty is that the Bible itself is simply inconsistent. A historical explanation is far more reasonable: religious ideas and practices evolve out of a flawed human condition, and people come to different conclusions depending on their situation in life. Change is the way the world works, and it is no less true with religion; we humans invent our gods and religions, and modify them as seems best to us at the time.

We must each answer the God question for ourselves, using the most responsible and balanced information we can find, evaluating it with the best judgment of which we are capable. The answer is far too important to be left to religious professionals, who will insist on their own doctrinaire answers. If I must live and die by the answer I give to the question, it should at least make sense to me. As the poet William Henley put it: "I am the master of my fate: I am the captain of my soul."[18] Paul puts it more appropriately: "work out your own salvation with fear and trembling" (Phil 2:12). (7-9-12)

§26 WHAT DOES GOD EXPECT OF ME?

When I first raised this question in the previous essay on July 9, 2012, a reader was disappointed that I did not answer the question. The reader averred that I should have put all my cards face up on the table, as it were, and answer the question I posed. I am not certain that my answer would work for anyone else, since in my view everyone must answer this question for himself or herself. My answer to the question (for me only) has become how I make sense of life.

---

16. Golden Gate Southern Baptist Theological Seminary, Mill Valley, California.
17. Dodd, *Authority of the Bible*, 269-85.
18. Henley, "Invictus," lines 13-16.

Some years earlier I had published a longer essay on this issue.[19] That essay was written from the perspective of a nontraditional Baptist "Christian" who was trying to make sense of the religious traditions that had nourished his personal thinking from childhood; in other words it reflected my views as someone who continued with difficulty inside the community of faith. Looking back over that essay today, I find little reason to change it.

In this shorter essay I am writing from the perspective of a twenty-first-century human being, an heir of the fourth-century Christian creeds and biblical canon, who today finds himself principally indebted to the eighteenth-century Enlightenment[20] and modern scientific thought. My formal education in the Western academic tradition from the earliest years has been thoroughly secular, principally drawing on logic, critical methodology, and human reason to answer questions that before the eighteenth century were the strict purview of religion. In short, in this essay below I set out five very personal conclusions about how I see my place in the world.

One: I believe in God, although I admit I have no personal knowledge of God. I only know what others have written or told me. I hold this belief only because I cannot explain why it is not the case that there is nothing at all, or as the German philosopher Martin Heidegger put it: the fundamental question of metaphysics is, "Why are there beings at all instead of nothing?"[21] I hasten to add, however, I did not come to this observation through metaphysical philosophy or prayer, but rather through general reading, observation, and personal pondering. The universe exists and that neither scientists nor religionists can adequately explain why that is so brings me eventually to a belief in God.

Two: No matter what we are told, no one knows, or can know, the mind of God. Even Paul and Isaiah shared that thought (1 Cor 2:16 = Isa 40:13 LXX). People of faith have always found God's ways to be inscrutable (Rom 11:33–34; similar to 2 Bar [Syriac] 8:14). Hence the answer to the question is this: I have no idea what it is that God expects of humankind in general or of me in particular. I cannot even read the minds of human beings who are personally close to me, much less the mind of God. I cannot take the pronouncements of religious professionals seriously when

---

19. Hedrick, "Out of the Enchanted Forest."
20. Hedrick, "Introduction," xvi–xvii.
21. Heidegger, *Metaphysics*, 1.

they tell me that they know what God expects of me, since they disagree between themselves. For the most part they are usually well-meaning but claim to know more than is humanly possible.

Three: I alone am responsible for making my way in an increasingly complex world and must be dependent on my own judgment in making moral decisions in a modern world where knowing right and wrong has increasingly become a question of choosing between dirty shades of grey. For a thoughtful person an ethical decision in the modern world frequently can be both right and wrong simultaneously. I am often called upon to choose between the lesser of what I consider two less-than-moral options, and upon finding myself in such a situation, I must accept the responsibility for doing harm while aiming to act in love.

Four: All ethical decisions are by definition situational.[22] This means that right and wrong take their character from the situation. There are few absolute rights or wrongs. In some cases an act usually judged right in one situation is completely wrong in another. I would describe my rule of thumb for decision-making and ethical action as a beneficent or empathetic humanism, informed in particular by the best in the Judeo-Christian tradition broadly conceived; meaning that the tradition is both broader and longer than the fourth-century canon and Christian orthodoxy.

Five: I am hopeful that my physical death will not result in an ultimate loss of personal consciousness. Hope is not the same thing as faith, confidence, and certitude, as Paul noted: "Now hope that is seen is not hope. For who hopes for what he sees? But if we hope for what we do not see, we wait for it with patience" (Rom 8:24–25 RSV). So like everyone else I am waiting to see if my hope is realized. From my perspective, however, God shows an apparent disinterest in the world specifically with reference to natural disasters, and disease.[23] I do not live in fear of God in the present or in fear of personal judgment in the future. In spite of compelling evidence to the contrary (disease and natural disasters), I continue to hope that God, who may or may not be in control of the considerable powers of the universe, will in the divine economy not consign my consciousness to oblivion. (1–11–13)

---

22. Fletcher, *Situation Ethics*.
23. See, for example, §§18–20, pp. 49–54 above.

§27 AN UNCOMMONLY MODERN QUESTION

For the first time in history retired folk of the working class are pondering this question: how should I spend my time? After the Social Security Act of 1935, and the economic boom of World War II in America, when jobs were plentiful and salaries on the increase, many of the working class found they could retire and live comfortably without being forced to supplement their retirement income, a situation that formerly appertained only to the independently wealthy. Today my wife and I are flexible enough to begin the day with the question, "Well, what are you doing today?" Less than a hundred years ago such a question would have been unimaginable for members of the working class. The aged, having no pension or other means of support, would still be scrambling to eke out a daily living.

I recently thought about this question while struggling with the Greek prologue to a turn-of-the-previous-century novel. The novel (*H Phonissa, The Murderess*) was written by Aleksandros Papadiamantis in 1903. The prologue (1971) by Giannis Katzinis is written in rather turgid and inflated Greek (my apologies to Mr. Katzinis). Some might consider such a pedantic exercise an extravagant and wasteful use of personal time (about four hours each week) and wonder why I am not doing something more beneficial for society, the church, or humanity, with my time. Such a question leads me in turn to the bigger question: exactly what should one do with one's time, when paid employment is no longer necessary?

I am well aware of the numerous appeals from charitable, educational, public, and religious groups for money and volunteers to support their causes—actually more in the recent past than I can ever remember. These appeals for money and volunteers prompt for me a more specific and personal question: should appeals from charities for gifts and volunteer service, and solicitations from educational institutions for "payback" take precedence over individual activities of personal interest with regard to flexible time and disposable income? It seems to me that there are four broad but basic reasons why people in reasonably good health spend their time and money as they do: personal necessity, personal interest, humanitarian and religious reasons, and public welfare concerns.

If the Jesus tradition and the Christian tradition (they are not the same thing[24]) are drawn upon for help in making sense of things in life,

---

24. The early Jesus tradition was Israelite; the Christian tradition began in the fourth century with the creeds of the church.

little practical guidance will be found to help resolve the question as to how flexible time and disposable income should be spent. I know of nothing specifically on point in the early Christian tradition that helps the retired working class practically to balance the numerous appeals for their time and resources by charitable groups. Two stories and several sayings in the Jesus tradition (as critically assessed), however, at least relate to this issue.

To the man who asked Jesus what must he do to inherit eternal life Jesus said, sell what you have, give to the poor, and follow me (Mark 10:17-22). The gospels represent Jesus as a kind of wandering mendicant, or at least he was someone who depended solely on God (a cynic might interpret this as depending on the kindness of others) for his daily needs (Matt 6:25-33).[25] This story suggests that there are no such concepts as disposable funds and discretionary time; rather one must be fully engaged with Jesus in homeless mendicancy.

Here is a saying from the Gospel of Thomas (69b) that probably originated with Jesus, which reflects a similar attitude as the passage in Mark: "Those who go hungry to fill the starving belly of another are blessed." In other words, all your resources are placed at the disposal of the needy. The saying simply does not address the needs of the one who is "blessed." So exactly how long must one go hungry before one tends to one's own very practical needs?[26]

Paul, however, is more practical in soliciting funds as an offering from his "gatherings of saints" for the poor "saints" in Jerusalem (1 Cor 16:1-4; 2 Cor 8-9; Gal 2:10; Rom 15:25-29). His principle seems to be proportionate giving based on what a person has (2 Cor 12-13). Even though he encouraged a liberal attitude in giving (2 Cor 8:3-4), he specifically did not encourage the Corinthians to exhaust their own resources (2 Cor 8:13), and he left it up to the individual to decide what should be his/her part in the offering (2 Cor 9:7; 1 Cor 16:2). He was, however, convinced that the Gentile gatherings of saints at Rome had an obligation to assist the poor saints in Jerusalem (Rom 15:27).

If one follows Jesus and the choice offered to the man in the gospel story, the result will be that the candle of one's charity will flame rather brilliantly for a moment, but eventually it dies. If one takes the attitude, "I have mine; you get yours," and turns a deaf ear to the evident need all around, the result eventually will be that the world becomes a jungle in

---

25. Hock, "Cynics," 1223-24.
26. Hedrick, *Wisdom of Jesus*, 89.

which only the fittest and the most ruthless survive. The responsible answer seems to lie somewhere between these two alternatives, and where that point lies is the individual's choice.

For my part, at least for the moment, I will continue reading the Papadiamantis novel and consider life changes tomorrow. (2-8-13)

§28 A REASON FOR LIVING

What gets you up each morning and keeps you going through the day? I have in mind those things that add spice and meaning to life, rather than those daily humdrum, quotidian tasks we all must endure. On one occasion I caught the tail end of a TV commercial, which concluded with the question, what are you living for? That question was on my mind for several days. As an about-to-be octogenarian, I found it an interesting question to ponder because getting out of bed had become much more difficult. In the abstract the question was perplexing. I didn't think it could have referred to health; that is to say, the question related to, why am I still alive? There is a perfectly good generic answer to the question if it addresses health: in my case I am still alive because of fairly good genes; I exercise regularly, eat healthy, have a good health plan, and admit to being a bit lucky. On the other hand, I did not regard it as a politically incorrect question about a deliberate termination of life: that is say, I didn't think the question related to me taking my own life in view of death's inevitably. At my stage of life it should be no surprise that such a fleeting possibility about the question crossed my mind.

Quite logically, that left me with a purpose question to consider: what is my purpose in life; perhaps it is better stated this way: what gets me up every morning and keeps me going through the day? I immediately wondered, however, why I should need a purpose for living; why can't I just live and enjoy being alive? I don't know why, but it appears that in general people do seem to need some kind of a larger purpose other than just "hanging out and doing the living thing." For example, Dustin Hoffman's character Rizzo in the movie *Midnight Cowboy* lived off the grid and had to scrabble out a meager existence on the streets of New York. What sustained him through that difficult existence, however, was a larger dream about finding a way into the Florida sunshine—something he never achieved.

Lack of a larger purpose may even have something to do with the "alarming suicide numbers" among "young veterans just out of the service receiving health care from the government." Among those in this group suicide is "nearly three times the rate of active duty troops."[27] Human beings seem to need a purpose larger and more meaningful than "just living."

No one single answer suffices to the question about what gets one up each morning and sustains one. The answer is unique to each one of us. An individual may have several purposes in life at the same time, and these may change over time. It is a good guess, however, that what sustains many of us would likely be related in some way to family, work, or faith, or perhaps any number of other things.

The prophet Micah suggested that what sustained him was doing what the Lord required: doing justice, loving kindness, and walking humbly with God (Mic 6:8). For Koheleth, the rationalistic author of Ecclesiastes, the sustaining purpose of life was rather secular: What is good and fitting is to eat and drink and find enjoyment in life's few days of toil; it is the gift of God (Eccl 5:18–19), so eat your bread with enjoyment and drink your wine with a merry heart (Eccl 9:7). Enjoy life with the wife whom you love all the days of your vain life (Eccl 9:9). For Paul, the rather intolerant apostle of Christ, the purpose was deeply religious:

> For me, to live is Christ and to die is profit. And if it is to be life in the flesh that would mean for me fruitful labor; yet which I shall choose I do not know. (Phil 1:21–22)

Using these three statements (Micah, Koheleth, and Paul) as points of reference, I discover that I am not motivated by the spiritual humanism I find reflected in the statement of Micah, however worthy it may be, or by the edgy sectarian religiosity I find reflected in the statement of Paul. I am surprised to find that my ideas at this stage of life are more akin to the mildly religious secularism of Koheleth. Specifically, what gets me up in the morning is the prospect of engaging new ideas, and what sustains me through the day is the opportunity of articulating them in a well-turned phrase. My purpose in living does not need to be some grand ideal, like "tilting at windmills," for example; I just need something that gets me up, adds zest to a daily grind, and keeps me engaged in life. (1–15–14)

---

27. Zoroya, "Young Veterans," 2A.

§29 IS FREEDOM AN ILLUSION?

I do not have in mind political freedom, which is always limited. Fortunately in a representative democracy (a republic), however, the citizen has a voice in setting the limits and deciding how free "freedom" should be. Political freedom is not absolute. Ideally laws are drafted to give all groups the greatest amount of freedom possible under the law in a way that does not unnecessarily abridge the freedom of others who share minority views. So in a representative democracy all give a little to get a little.

In this essay, however, I have in mind the ability of individuals to make decisions that have not been influenced, whether overtly or subtly, by others and their environment. From the earliest moments in life no one can independently envision their course of life. You cannot pick your parents, their social and economic status, or their prospects. You take what chance decrees for you. You cannot pick where you are born. Your birthplace is chosen by your mother or by chance. You cannot pick your native language, your skin color, or nationality. All these things happen by chance. Your religion or nonreligion in the early years is the choice of your parents, whom you did not pick. You are indoctrinated by their religious views, or lack thereof. You do not choose in the lower grades your educational institutions. Schooling hinges on where you live or on your parents' economic circumstances, or both. So the attitudes, values, quality and kind of instruction, inductively learned prejudices in the region where you live, and the acquired knowledge (both formal and cultural), which subtly mold and shape you, are also not of your own choosing. Your socialization happens almost by osmosis. By the time you think you have gained control over the dominant powers in your life (parents, local educational and political systems, religious institutions, regional cultural mores, and so forth) you have already become something that may not be able to be changed, even if the thought occurred to you to do so. Your future choices have already been influenced by the powers outside your control in the past. Thus people are free only to the extent that they can escape their own pasts.

In later life you find yourself immersed in a culture whose expectations, moral values, and ideals demand compliance if you are to live peacefully and successfully in society. The compliant are rewarded with status in the community, and those who resist are marginalized. In later years you marry and become focused on job and advancement; each economic institution has its own rules that must be mastered. Children must be tended, a home kept up to community standards, taxes paid, medical bills met, the children's future considered, and retirement planned for. The demands are such that you have little time to give to abstract things such as thinking about becoming something—and anyway you have already "become" by buying into or resisting the culture and its expectations. You simply meet the requirements, without thinking, or challenge the expectations. In any case you are simply too far into life to make radical changes.

Nearing the age of retirement, some do find time for reflecting on where life has brought them, or—perhaps better—for reflecting on what their past and present have made of them. In retrospect, they look back over their lives searching for the turning points that shaped them.

Religion is part of the problem rather than the solution. All religions claim to possess Truth, particularly the missionary religions in their traditional forms: Judaism, Christianity, and Islam. All three of these have attached themselves to certain cultures sympathetic to their religious systems. They reciprocate symbiotically by helping to reinforce the cultural norms in the societies in which they find themselves. This has always been the case with Christianity, for example. In the first century, Paul is reckoned to have urged his churches to be subject to the governing authorities: "There is no authority except from God and those that exist have been put in place by God" (Rom 13:1)—and this was said this about the Roman Empire, no less! The author of Revelation, whose time and situation were different, disagreed, calling the Roman Empire Babylon the Great, a dwelling place of demons, a haunt of every foul spirit (Rev 18:2). Rome is the mother of harlots and earth's abominations (Rev 17:5). Paul, a Roman citizen, found in the Roman Empire a symbiotic partner; the writer of Revelation did not.

Christianity in America thinks of its gospel as "freeing." Jesus said to those Judeans who believed in him, "you will know the truth and the truth shall make you free" (John 8:32). And Paul wrote: "Christ has liberated us (to live) in freedom; therefore stand firm and do not again be subject to a yoke of slavery" (Gal 5:1). He was of course talking about freedom from the Israelite Torah. But Christianity in general has assimilated to American culture and to its political system to such an extent that "Americanism" has become a synonym for "Christian." The American flag is displayed in churches, the pledge of allegiance is taught to children in church schools, and patriotic songs are sung in worship. The religious

74 UNMASKING BIBLICAL FAITHS

instruction and preaching in mainstream reformation-era churches aim to produce good Christian citizens who reflect American societal norms, so that their lives reflect well on the church, something the early churches were concerned to do as well (1 Thess 4:10–12; Tit 3:1–2; 1 Pet 2:13–15). The early churches rejected the radical ethics of Jesus[28] (if they happened to remember them) and turned to the ethical values (called "household codes") that governed private life in the early Roman Empire (see, for example, Col 3:18–4:1).[29]

Growing up in a lower middle class family in the Mississippi Delta in the 1940s and 50s leaves me wondering just how free I really was. (5-31-13)

§30 WAITING FOR GOD/WAITING FOR GODOT

Waiting for God was a British sitcom (1990–94) about the residents of a retirement community in England.[30] Life in the home was anything but boring. Every week residential life was depicted full of zany activities, with rare moments of pathos; it was after all a comedy! In real life, however, I suspect the situation is much different.

Except for the idle rich, figuring out what to do with life is a problem that under the best of circumstances primarily concerns young adults and the very aged. In our youth there are many options, but in advanced old age options are severely reduced. Because of health issues, life in very old age can even border on the tedium, somewhat like the situation depicted in Samuel Beckett's strange play in two acts (*Waiting for Godot*, 1953), featuring two characters, Vladimir and Estragon, waiting on a road beside a tree for someone called Godot, who never comes. Things happen in the play, true enough, but there seems little point to it all, and at the end of the play the two protagonists are left, still waiting for Godot, whom they are told "will surely come tomorrow." The playwright once claimed that his play was about symbiosis, but interpreters have been encouraged to seek allegorical meanings. The play has left audiences pondering what sense to make of the absurdity of it all.[31]

Sitting beside the road, absurdly waiting is where many in advanced old age find themselves, pondering what to make of their situation. They

28. Hedrick, *Wisdom of Jesus*, 85–90.
29. Ibid., 42–42.
30. Wikipedia, "*Waiting for God.*"
31. Wikipedia. "*Waiting for Godot.*"

are in the world but no longer of it, in the sense that they are no longer contributing to the principal structures of society. The primary option left open to them, health permitting, is that of "helper." More often than not, in the case of many, they are simply marking time and wondering when life's last great adventure will begin.

Like the mammals we are, human beings are biologically hardwired for survival and for active participation in life as protagonists or actors. Human beings are not wired to be consigned to last season's sets stored away when the play is done. We are naturally curious and motivated to aspire rather than to despair. Self-survival, curiosity, and aspiration may very well be among the primary features that make us human.

Alas, another feature of our humanity is mortality, so many of us will not make it into advanced old age. Those of us who do, if we are fortunate enough to avoid the "Big C" in the spinning down of their lives, will still experience unexpected health issues with which we are unprepared to cope: loss of independence, restricted mobility, lack of energy, hearing loss, failing eyesight, inability to focus, imbalance, short-term memory loss, forgetfulness, arthritis, dementia, Alzheimer's, the shrinking of one's world and one's prospects in it—to mention only a few. Under such conditions we are apt to forget that we humans come from a long tribe of explorers and world adventurers who have found cures for smallpox and tuberculosis, have overcome superstition through education, have left footprints on the moon, and have done much more. At this stage of life, however, it is small consolation to be reminded that we are fortunate enough to be at this point in life only because of the accomplishments of our tribe! At this point the struggle commences between the nobler aspects of our humanity and its baser character.

Remembering we belong to a proud species, we take each day as it comes, accepting what it brings but always aiming higher, even if it is only to take just one step more than the previous day. The opening stanza of a poem by Dylan Thomas expresses in my estimation the essence of what it means to be human in advanced old age:

> Do not go gentle into that good night,
> Old age should burn and rave at close of day;
> Rage, rage against the dying of the light.[32]

To do less diminishes humanity to its baser elements. (11–19–13)

---

32. Thomas, *Collected Poems*, 128 ("Do not Go Gentle," first stanza).

§31 HUMAN SUFFERING AND RELIGIOUS FAITH

When suffering comes, as it does to all, the one who suffers wonders why s/he has been singled out for such an experience. The classic work on human suffering and religious faith still remains the book of Job. The characters in this ancient drama provide several perplexing answers to the question: why me, God? The protagonist in the book (Job) is initially extolled by God as the quintessential "righteous man" (1:8), but in the prose prologue (1:1—2:13) Job is afflicted with unimaginable suffering, caused by Satan with the expressed permission of God. Satan wants to test Job's faith: "Take away Job's blessings," Satan urges God, "and Job will curse you" (1:9–11). Job is completely unaware of this dialogue between God and Satan.

Job's three friends in the central poetic section—Eliphaz, Bildad, and Zophar—tell Job that his suffering is due to his sins. Such was the general view in antiquity: sin causes suffering; Job is suffering; therefore, Job is a sinner (4:7; 8:1–6; 11:4–6). Job dismisses their views as full of hot air, and calls them "miserable comforters" (16:2–3). Job admits he may have sinned but continues to insist that his suffering is out of proportion to whatever his guilt may be (6:24-30; 9:20–21; 10:5–7; 12:4; 13:2–5; 16;2–3; 19:4; 23:3–7; 27:2–6). The chapters featuring Elihu (32:6—37:24) are a later addition to the book,[33] but Elihu adds a further reason for human suffering: God refines or disciplines the human being through suffering (36:8–12).

God's response (38:1—43:6) does not answer Job's questions (23:3-7; 6:24-25), but simply intimidates Job with God's awesome power and superior knowledge (chapters 38–41). Readers of the book, however, having read the prologue, know that Job is suffering because of the capricious backroom bargain struck between God and Satan (2:1–6), which is not something God is apparently willing to admit in the poetic section. In the end Job simply capitulates (40:1–5), accepting that he will never know why he is suffering (42:1–6). The book as a whole affirms that "no theoretical solution to the problem of suffering is possible."[34]

It is perplexing to me that those who suffer persist in thinking that they have been singled out to suffer by an invisible power for some particular reason. The universe for all its regularity is still full of randomness. For example, a desiccated brown leaf falls in front of you as you walk

---

33. Kuntz, *People of Ancient Israel*, 469–70.
34. Eissfeldt, *Old Testament*, 457.

into the back yard. It is not an unusual event—in a sense it is a nonevent, meaningless unless you decide to assign some particular significance to it. Here is another example: even though your car is the only one in the lot to suffer the indignity of bird droppings, few of us would ask, why me, God? but would shrug it off as the random act it is. In spite of the regularity of the universe (meaning that things usually work a certain way), deviations from regularity in the physical world do not have religious significance, unless we decide that they do.

Many think, however, that God micromanages the universe, and is therefore responsible for everyday tiny details, such as thinning your hair and clogging your shower drain (cf. Matt 10:30). They will imbue with religious significance even the most banal events in the most insignificant pedestrian day. Hair loss, however, is a perfectly natural occurrence; your thinning hair is likely due to genetics or perhaps a diet deficiency. The truth is we live in a dangerous universe and are subject to any number of debilitating diseases. The state of our health depends on our genetics, our physical condition, our diet, the quality of our medical care, and, unfortunately, on our ability to pay for medical services. "Mother Nature" is a more likely cause of your suffering; another is the lack of progressive health and human welfare programs in your community, for which our political leaders share the heaviest load of blame.

People who suffer do not in the first instance turn to God for help with their physical pain. Physicians do the better job of helping us manage our physical pain. A faith in God, on the other hand, may do better with helping us manage mental and emotional suffering, although some illnesses in this area also require medication and God is reduced to playing a supportive role. Many testify that faith in God brings spiritual comfort and emotional peace in suffering. Such faith in many ways is a spiritual elixir, bringing palliative psychological and emotional comfort to the sufferer. Such "spiritual therapy" cannot be measured in a test tube, but for believers what it produces is just as real as aspirin for a headache.

The why me? question, however, completely stumps true believers, even though they may find spiritual strength to bear the indignities of severe disease. The answer of the author of Job is surprising: people suffer, and there is no theoretical explanation. In the prose epilogue God chides Job's three friends for not telling the truth about God with their orthodox answers (Job 42:7–9), but God commends Job for "speaking of me what is right" (Job 42:7). Job never learns why he has suffered, but he refuses to accept the easy orthodox counsel of his friends. The only thing of which Job seems sure was that God was not punishing him because of his sins. (7-13-13)

§32 WHAT IS THE VALUE OF RELIGIOUS GESTURES?

Why do people make religious gestures? I define a *gesture* broadly as any action, courtesy, or communication intended for effect or as a formality. For example, an offering taken during public worship is a religious gesture, which the church teaches is an expression of stewardship, by which we return to God a part of what God has given us. This is a seriously flawed idea, however; God doesn't need money! A former seminary professor with whom I studied in the past saw the flaw and described monetary gifts to the church as support for what he called the "gospel enterprise." Personally I have come to think of money contributed to the church as "paying my church dues." The value of such a gesture, however defined, certainly benefits the church by keeping its doors open, but it only indirectly benefits those who contribute. In many cases paying church dues strains their budget, and to that extent the contributor is harmed, unless one believes they receive some intangible credit with God for the gesture.

Prayers, both individual and congregational, are religious gestures by which people "reach out" to God for a particular reason. Congregational prayers are clearly ceremonial, formal, and conventional; that is to say, prayers are an act expected in religious services. They may occasionally be comforting or inspiring, but more often they are perfunctory and propagandizing. An individual gestures toward God for personal reasons by means of prayer, but even individual prayer can become a charade, if it is used by a "spiritual advisor" to develop piety in others. Nevertheless in both situations the gesture is always one-sided. No conversation occurs between the individual and God, however comforting the gesture may seem. God never addresses the one who prays (people who hear voices in their heads even in prayer need professional help).

Words are also gestures. For example, at a time of great sorrow in one's life someone may say "I am deeply sorry for your loss." At its best the statement is a gesture of genuine sympathy and caring; at its worst it is a perfunctory act performed to meet the requirements of social convention; we expect such gestures in times of crisis. The verbal expression "God bless you" is odd. It is hard to know the significance of the expression. For the one who gestures, it could mean something like, (it is my prayer that) God bless you, or (may) God bless you. That is to say: I sense that you may need emotional support. On the other hand, the individual may be arrogant enough to think that their utterance actually confers God's favor, such as occurred in the laying on of hands (ordination), a gesture in the early church that was believed to confer the Spirit of God (Acts 19:6, 8:17–18; 1 Tim 4:14; 2 Tim 1:6–7). Religious sentiments printed on tee-shirts may be little more than church advertising, or a means of parading idiosyncratic beliefs. Perhaps the wearing of the crucifix serves the same purpose, unless it is worn as a religious charm for personal protection.

A digital gesture, such as making the sign of the cross, is a learned gesture, and may have no meaning beyond the idea that "by this act I fulfilled the obligation required under such circumstances." Pointing skyward at an individual's standout moment ostensibly to give God (or Jesus?) credit may be conceived as a personal religious thank you, but it also elevates an individual's piety in the public eye and is dangerously close to an ostentatious religious act. Such digital gestures always run the risk of shallow religious show, for which Jesus is credited with saying no one receives any credit with God (Matt 6:1).

In fact all such public religious gestures are disparaged by Jesus in Matthew's opinion (Matt 6:1–8, 16–8). Jesus is thought to have said, "Take care that you do not perform your righteousness before people to be seen by them; otherwise you have no compensation from your father in heaven" (Matt 6:1). Hence the motivation for performing religious gestures is crucial for determining their value.

Does God ever reward individuals for their religious gestures? Some seem to think so. Here is a case on point: Jesus said "unless you eat the flesh of the Son of man and drink his blood, you have no life in you" (John 6:53); this is likely a reference to the sacred meal of the church (1 Cor 11:23–32), which Ignatius (ca. 110 CE) thought of as the "medicine of immortality, the antidote preventing death," which led to "life in Jesus Christ forever" (*Eph.* 20.2). Even earlier than Ignatius Paul suggested that baptism benefited one by bringing a kind of union with Christ: "as many as were baptized into Christ Jesus were baptized into his death" (Rom 6:3).

Are religious gestures empty acts, or does God, if God there be, actually post in his Divine Ledger a spiritual credit to the account of those who perform them? (7-3-14)

§33 LIVING IN THE OLD COUNTRY

When I was younger, I perceived my future bright with prospects and promise. On waxing old and being full of days, however, I have discovered my interests now are more about retrospect than prospect. We elderly live in another country, and even though like Moses we may be permitted to view the prospects of a New Year's promised land (Deut 34:4), we are fated to remain in the land of Moab, in our own country and time (Deut 34:5-6). In the late autumn of our years and with the onrush of winter our vengeful enemy, time, has taken a terrible toll: sagging skin, thinning hair, diminishing life force, failing eyesight, lapsing memory, other assorted aches and pains, and physical impairments. Few of us octogenarians are like Moses, of whom it was fabled, "his eyes were undimmed and his vigor unabated" (Deut 34:7). Nevertheless we elderly have "eternity in our minds" (Eccl 3:11) and seem to think we should live forever.

I prefer to think of aging and my eventual physical demise as the natural course of things. A prime axiom of the universe is obsolescence; things just wear out and become obsolete and disappear. Or put another way, they die out and pass out of existence. We instinctively know it is true—whether of nations, neighborhoods, sump pumps, or, alas, people. Such is the way of all life and things in the universe as we know it.

I could, of course, be wrong. Paul turned what in my view is a natural occurrence into a theological dogma. Based on the Israelite myth of creation, he argued that because the first human being sinned (Gen 2:17) the human potential for death entered the world and passed onto all human beings, in that all have sinned (Rom 5:12, 17; 1 Cor 15:21). Apparently Adam's sin even affected the universe, as it too is under bondage to decay (Rom 8:20-23) and obsolescence (1 Cor 7:31). So, in part, Paul and I are of the same mind—except that he thinks theologically, and my statements are made on the basis of observable evidence. It must be said, however, that the universe is expanding at a rapid rate and as yet shows little sign of diminishing energy.[35]

The psalmist seems to regard a limited life span as a natural phenomenon: "The years of our life are threescore and ten, or even by reason of strength fourscore; yet their span is but toil and trouble; they are soon gone, and we fly away" (Ps 90:10 RSV). There is no talk here of our life span being reduced by God's judgment because of sin. The situation

---

35. Sagan, *Cosmos*, 254-57, 259; Gamow, "Toward the Limits," 395, 397; Sloan Digital Sky Survey / Sky Server, "Expanding Universe."

seems to be that the psalmist has observed only the natural way of life in the universe. The human life span is only so long because of the prime axiom of the universe: obsolescence. It is likewise the view of Koheleth (Eccl 1:1), who philosophizes about those things he "has seen under the sun" (Eccl 1:14; 2:17; 3:16, 22; 4:1, 7; 5:13: 6:1; 7:15; 8:9, 17; 9:11, 13; 10:5). No appeal is made here to divine revelation; rather Kohleth appeals to human experience in a similar way that a proverb appeals to human wisdom.

For those who have lived into their yellow leaf, a New Year is not about resolutions but rather reminiscences. We near the twilight of life are poised on the threshold of one of life's greatest adventures, and what matters now is not the coming year and its prospects, but what lies behind, along with our regrets and personal satisfactions. Perhaps that is why I don't have a bucket list. These days I think about those things I have left undone, the roads never taken, the questions never asked, the books never read, old friends with whom I have lost contact, the essays never finished. Have I left a deep enough footprint in the sand that the first high tide will not erase? I suppose in the long term it does not matter. Very few things endure the ravages of time.

Is there a lesson in all this introspection? In the last chapter of Ecclesiastes (12:1-14) a later editor has concluded, "The end of the matter; all has been heard. Fear God and keep his commandments; for this is the whole duty of man" (Eccl 12:13 RSV). I prefer thinking on the views of the principal author of Ecclesiastes: these I regard as the "intellectually honest ponderings of a man who looked at the world primarily from a rational perspective rather than through the eyes of faith. He struggled with the question: what is the point of life and found no satisfactory answer."[36] But the point is, he continued struggling with the questions, and in the final analysis gave up on neither life nor God. His struggles with the dichotomy between the answers of traditional religion and what he sees going on in the world around him have led him to be satisfied with the simple pleasures of life (Eccl 2:24; 10:19).

So a New Year comes! Yet the first day of a New Year, after all the fuss, is just another day to be followed seriatim by many others. Those of us fortunate enough to see its dawning should rejoice and be glad in it (Ps 118:24). Koheleth would appreciate that sentiment; he thought of life as a great gift—hope is only for the living. Or as he put it: "a live dog is better than a dead lion" (Eccl 9:4).

36. Hedrick, *Wisdom of Jesus*, 72.

For my tribe, you elderly: may your New Year's Day be full of happy memories that bring smiles to your faces rather than blushes to your cheeks. For those who are younger: may your new country be full of bright prospects. (12-31-15)

§34 THE RELIGIOUS EXPERIENCE

The author of the book of Acts (whom scholars call Luke) portrays in novelistic fashion his impressions of early Christian religious experience. The author wants readers to think that the description of religious faith in Acts is the normative way Christians should experience God. In the main, he does not portray their experience of God as ecstatic,[37] although he does use the word "ecstasy" (*ekstasis*) a number of times, which is translated in various ways (3:10 ["amazement"], 10:10 ["trance"], 11:5 ["trance"], 22:17 ["trance"]) to describe certain ecstatic experiences. Ecstatic experiences in Acts, however, are something out of the ordinary rather than routine or typical.

The normative religious experience in Acts is also not mystical,[38] for God is described as the creator, "who made the world and everything in it," the "Lord of heaven and earth," "who does not live in shrines made by man" (Acts 17:24 RSV). Nevertheless, "God is not far from each one of us" (Acts 17:27-28 RSV), for the earth is his footstool, although his throne is in heaven (Acts 7:49). Compare the following references that suggest God's ascendant position in the universe (Acts 2:33; 7:32-34; 7:55-56). Believers in Acts do not have a direct and intimate consciousness of the Divine Presence, and must therefore reach out to God through prayer in order to overcome the distance that separates them (see, for example, Acts 1:14, 24; 2:42; 3:1; 10:4; 12:5, 12; 22:17).

From my perspective the normative religious experience in Acts is best described as *charismatic*, a word that does not appear in the New Testament. A charisma (*charisma*) is usually translated by the English

---

37. See Harkness, *Mysticism*, 32. Ecstatic religious experience is an intense "state in which the mind is carried from the body; a state in which the functions of the senses are suspended by the contemplation of some extraordinary or supernatural object. It is a kind of 'out of this world' rapture . . ."

38. See Harkness, *Mysticism*, 20. Mystical religious experience is "the *type of religion which puts the emphasis on immediate awareness of relation with God, on direct and intimate consciousness of the Divine Presence. It is religion in its most acute, intense and living stage*" (italics original).

word "gift." *Charisma* does not appear in Acts, but a synonym does. In Acts the gift (*dōrea*) of God (Acts 2:38) is the Holy Spirit/Spirit (Acts 5:32), who fills (Acts 4:31; 9:17; 13:9) and empowers (Acts 1:8) believers for mighty works, wonders, and signs (Acts 2:43, 4:30, 5:12, 6:8); the Spirit enables them to prophesy, see visions, and have dreams (Acts 2:16–18, 10:9–19, 11:4–5, 12:6–11); empowers them to perform healings and drive out evil spirits (Acts 8:6–8, 14:8–10, 16:16–18, 19:11–12), to raise the dead (Acts 9:36–41), and miraculously be understood by speakers of a different language (Acts 2:7–8); and to speak with tongues and prophesy (Acts 19:6, compare 1 Cor 14:26–33). The Holy Spirit is given spontaneously (Acts 2:4, 10:44–48) or by the laying on of the hands by those who have received the Spirit (Acts 8:14–18, 9:17, 19:1–6). The Holy Spirit only comes to those who obey God (Acts 5:32), who have been saved by believing in Jesus Christ (Acts 2:38; 5:30–32; 13:29–39) and in his resurrection (Acts 16:28–31; 17:2–4). Salvation brings with it the forgiveness of sins (Acts 2:37–38; 10:43; 26:18) and the empowerment by the Holy Spirit to perform these evidences of the Spirit. Such was the normative religious experience in Acts.

Fast-forward to the present day: except within one segment of Christianity's very wide tent, these kinds of religious phenomena are no longer experienced as normative among those churches emerging from the Reformation of the sixteenth century. For these churches originating in Europe the charismatic evidences of the Spirit in Acts are a thing of the distant past, relegated to what they refer to as the apostolic age. Nevertheless, among churches described under the broad rubric Pentecostal (deriving from Acts 2:1–21) the evidences of Holy Spirit possession found in Acts are very much alive.

In an odd turn of events, however, the Holy Spirit/Spirit does not empower anyone in the final third of the book (Acts 19:21—28:30). In these final chapters the tone of the writing is different, and the Spirit's role is basically reduced to that of advisor to Paul (Spirit is only mentioned seven times: Acts 19:21, 20:22, 23, 27; 21:4, 11; 28:25), and the one clear allusion to an act by the Spirit refers to an event that had happened much earlier (Acts 20:27), and that is not even described in the book of Acts. These latter references to the Spirit correspond generally to the way the Spirit is usually regarded in the churches of mainstream Protestantism in America; the Spirit is reduced to an idea and only has as much power as a person allows the idea to have over him or her.

There is no such thing as a normative religious experience. That is to say, there is not one definitive religious experience against which one may measure all other claims of religious experience. While some religious experiences may be harmful, no generally accepted standards exist by which one may describe a given religious experience as illegitimate. (6–12–16)

§35 IS GOD THE DISTANT CREATOR—OR YOUR INTIMATE SOUL MATE?

Acts 16 describes an incident that creates a problem for anyone who thinks that all worshipers of the Christ had a personal, heartfelt religious experience. At Philippi (a Roman colony, Acts 16:12) the jailer asks, "Sirs, what must I do to be saved?" Paul and Silas reply (in unison?) "Believe (second-person singular imperative) in the Lord Jesus and you (singular) will be saved—you (singular) and your household" (Acts 16:31). In other words apparently the jailer's faith in Jesus saved not only the jailer but also his entire household (family and slaves), and the members of the jailer's household were baptized along with him (Acts 16:33)—even though Acts states only that the jailer believed Paul and Silas (Acts 16:34). The same circumstances apply earlier in the chapter (Acts 16:14–15): Lydia opened her heart to what Paul said, and then *she* was baptized, along with her whole household. The situation is very different in Acts 18:8, however, where Crispus, his household, and many others in the city believed Paul, and they were all baptized along with Crispus (see also Acts 11:13–18; John 4:53).

The temptation is to assume that Luke was simply a careless or imprecise writer, and that he really intended that these two incidents at Philippi in Acts 16 (the jailer's conversion and baptism, and his household's baptism) should be read in the light of the incident in Acts 18, which unambiguously states that the members of Crispus's household actually did believe, and hence (one assumes) had a personal religious experience, although that is not what the text says. But what if Luke was being very precise in Acts 16, and the jailer, as paterfamilias (head of a Roman household), had introduced a new deity (i.e., Jesus) to his family's household Gods? Hence the jailer's family and slaves would also join in worship of the jailer's new household deity. "The *pater familias* [sic] was the priest of the household, and those subject to his *potestas* [authority] assisted in the prayers and offerings [of] the *sacra familiaria* [family rites]."[39] From this perspective the jailer's family and all his household, slaves were required to participate in an exercise of Christian (?) worship, even though they may not have shared in the jailer's religious belief.

That is not unlike the situation in contemporary Christian worship where we find elaborate ritual and liturgy at one end of a wide spectrum of beliefs and worship styles, and a charismatic type of worship at the other end. Think of that wide spectrum as the distance between Paul's charismatic and spirit-led Christianity (the Pauline letters) at its one end, and the institutional religion of the Pastoral Epistles (1 and 2 Timothy and Titus) at its other end.

Assuming that readers have not abandoned participation in formal Christian worship altogether, where might they fall on a spectrum between a keen sense of personal union with the deity and a somewhat perfunctory participation in a ritual, the underlying beliefs of which they no longer share? Or put another way: does God's Spirit dwell within to the extent that one is conscious of an intimate sharing in the divine presence, or is it simply the case that God is in his heaven while worshipers at a distance "experience" God only as ritual, liturgy, and Eucharist (or Mass) in formalized worship? (5-31-16)

§36 MY LONELY BRAIN AND THE BIBLE

I think of my brain as a quite lonely little muscle that is basically a thinking data control center. It stores memory, assesses data, and sends and receives signals as appropriate throughout my physical system. I describe it as lonely for it has no direct connection with anything outside of I-me-myself separated as it is by a thin layer of bone, skin, and (at one time) hair. As capable as it is, however, it must depend on signals from other parts of my anatomy for outside information: sight, smell, sense, taste, and hearing. It receives inside information through my nervous system. On the basis of this information I-me-myself (I am more than sinew, gristle, bone, and brain, or so I think) can override what brain reports. Let's call this center of judgment (i.e., I-me-myself) mind.

Because the outside receptors are limited in ability, brain and mind are always processing suspect and incomplete data. For example, the brain will sometimes interpret incorrectly what the eyes see, and other

---

39. Johnston, *Private Life of the Romans*, 29.

data from my several outside receptors are all often contradictory, and this compromises the rational analysis of both brain and mind.

Here is one literary example from the New Testament of outside receptors being mistaken. (There are others: for example, Acts 12:9 and 12:15.) In Mark 6:45–50 Jesus comes toward the disciples "walking on the water." The disciples are all terrified (Mark 6:49–50) because they think they see a *phantasma* (a phantom; translated in RSV as "ghost"). Matthew 14:26 follows Mark; Luke omits the entire narrative, and John 6:16–21 eliminates any reference to a *phantasma*. So the earliest source (Mark) describes *all* the disciples seeing something simultaneously, which they all take to be a phantom, and believe strongly enough in such apparitions that they all react in the same way—with terror! In my reading of the text it portrays the situation as follows: erroneous information from the physical senses has been relayed to the brain, and the mind accepts the report without challenge, at least momentarily. Accordingly, the mind calls up the fight or flight response.

So here I am in the early twenty-first century asking my mind to reach a responsible judgment on the historicity of Mark's narrative on the basis of incomplete and imperfect information, a judgment that mind and brain regard as logically and reasonably impossible based on information at hand; hence only a provisional judgment based on too many assumptions is possible.

This essay begs a question about faith, because most readers of Mark simply assume that the incident in some form derives from an actual historical event. In this essay only physical stimuli available to the brain have been considered. My analysis has been rational, based on reason. Is there not, however, another inner source available to the brain that should have been considered? Should faith be thought of as a responsible source that can inform the brain about an actual event behind the narrative? If so, then faith can either replace or work alongside reason, although the obvious question is whether faith is capable of giving any information at all on historical issues. But if it can, then when and for what reasons should faith outweigh and replace analysis and reason? (9-22-12)

4

The Bible

§37 WHAT DOES THE TERM "WORD OF GOD" SIGNIFY WHEN APPLIED TO THE BIBLE?[1]

The word *Bible* means simply "books." The term is applied to a Jewish collection of books (*ta Biblia*) in the ancient Greek Septuagint translation of Dan 9:2. The books mentioned in this passage included Jeremiah, which was treated as a prophetic book with special hidden meanings.

In the early first century the contents of the Jewish Bible were debated. All people of Israelite faith accepted the Torah (the first five books of the Bible) as word of God. The Pharisees also included a section called Prophets, as well as another collection called Writings in their Bible, but Samaritans and Sadducees did not. When Jerusalem and the temple were destroyed in 70 CE by the Romans, in the postwar reconstruction of Judean religion led by the Pharisees, the Hebrew Bible came to include three divisions: Law, Prophets, and Writings.[2] These books were regarded as divinely inspired.

Early Christians used the Jewish Bible in Greek translation (i.e., the Septuagint) as their Scripture. The Septuagint also included certain other texts not in the Hebrew-language collection. Christians referred to the

---

1. This essay subsequently appeared as part of a dialogue "Is the Bible the Word of God?" in the *Fourth R* 29/3 (May-June, 2016), 3–4; used by permission.
2. Goodspeed, *How Came the Bible?*, 9–47; Hayes, *Introduction*, 3–13.

Greek collection with its additional writings added as the sacred Scriptures (2 Tim 3:15–16), which were inspired by God.

Early Christians associated these books with the "old" covenants that God had made with ancient Israel. They conceived of themselves, however, as a people with whom God had established a new covenant (Heb 8:8–12, quoting Jer 31:31–34). On the basis of their interpretation of Jeremiah's "prophecy" Christians regarded the old covenants as obsolete, inadequate for the new covenant people of God. Nevertheless they retained the Old Covenant books (i.e., the Old Testament), since they considered them inspired, reading them from a Christian perspective. Eventually a new collection of Scripture emerged for the Christians; it included the Old Testament books plus a smaller collection of new covenant books (i.e., the New Testament). The New Testament books known today were first listed by Athanasius in 367 CE. The Old Testament collection of the Protestant Bible was brought into accord with the Hebrew Jewish Bible by Martin Luther in his 1534 German translation. Collecting the non-Hebrew-language texts in the Old Testament at the end he designated them Apocrypha ("hidden), a designation Jerome had used.[3]

Hence the Bible is composed of three parts—Law, Prophets, and Writings—if you are referring to the Jewish Bible. The Protestant Bible is composed of two parts—Old Testament (which is the same as the Jewish Bible) and the New Testament. The Catholic Bible is also composed of two parts—an expanded Old Testament (which includes the books of the Apocrypha) and the New Testament. What Protestants refer to as the Apocrypha was declared to be inspired in all its parts at the Catholic Council of Trent in 1560.[4] Today Protestants do not include the Apocrypha in their Scriptures, although it was part of the Old Testament in the first edition of the King James Version of 1611.

The expression "word of God" appears in the New Testament, although it is unclear in many instances what the phrase signifies. In the instances that are clear "word of God" refers to a number of things: to something preached (Acts 4:31; 11:1; 13:5, 46; 1 Thess 2:13; Heb 13:7; 1 Pet 1:23–25), to the word God spoke in creating the world (2 Pet 3:5–7), to the resurrected Christ (Rev 19:11–18), to God's son Jesus (Heb 1:1–4), and to the Torah (Mark 7:13).

---

3. Goodspeed, *How Came the Bible?* 59–86.
4. Westcott, *Bible in the Church*, 255–58.

The earliest explicit applications of terms relating "word of God" to the Bible date from the fourteenth century. In *The Love of Books* Richard Aungerville, bishop of Durham (1287–1345) refers to "Scripture given us by inspiration of God" and to the "Word of God."[5] In his introduction to the 1382 English translation of the Bible, John Wycliffe referred to the Bible as the "Word of Truth," and in the later version of 1388 as "Holy Writ." William Tyndale in 1534 refers to his translation of the New Testament as "Scripture" and "the word of God." The Coverdale Bible of 1535 on its title page refers to the Bible as "the word of God." The introduction to the King James Version of 1611 and 1769 says that the Bible "contains the word of God, nay is the word of God," but also seems to regard the act of "preaching" as the "sacred word." Another statement suggests the idea that the Scripture communicates the word of God, apparently meaning that the Scripture in some way contains the "word of God."

During the Reformation of the sixteenth century, the reformers (Luther and Calvin) referred to the Bible as the Word of God, but they did not mean that the book and the revelation were the same. The authority of the Bible as the Word of God derives from its content. "There was no acceptance of the Bible simply as 'sacred book.'"[6] To put it differently, the word of God is contained in the biblical content; the Bible is not a written icon.

This hasty and incomplete survey of Christian history suggests that the phrase "word of God" can refer to a number of things: writings containing the word of God, an act of preaching, Jesus, the word God spoke at the act of creation, the resurrected Christ, or the Torah. In the Judeo-Christian tradition the term "Holy Scripture" or "inspired Scripture" is applied in one tradition exclusively to the Jewish Bible, in another exclusively to the Jewish Bible and New Testament, and in another exclusively to the Jewish Bible, Apocrypha, and New Testament.

It appears that the phrase "Word of God" can be applied to whatever one wants. If you believe that *it* (whatever *it* is) is the word of God, then so it is. As applied to a collection of books, the phrase "word of God" carries with it a claim that books so designated are special religious literature, having an unspecified divine authority. (1–12–15)

---

5. Aungerville, *Love of Books*, chapters 2 and 6.
6. Dillenberger and Welch, *Protestant Christianity*, 45–46.

§38 WHEN DID THE BIBLE BECOME THE WORD OF GOD?[7]

In the previous essay I argued that when the Bible becomes the Word of God depends on which Bible one is talking about: Jewish, Protestant, or Catholic.

The Jewish Bible

The discovery of the book of the law in the temple suggests there was no special religiously authoritative book in Israel before 621 BCE (2 Kgs 22–23; compare 2 Chr 33–34). Based on the reforms instituted in Israel by Josiah, it is clear that this book of the law (generally thought to be Deuteronomy) held a special religious authority, for people determined to govern their lives by it.

The phrase "word of God" is little used in the Jewish Bible (for example: 1 Sam 9:27; 1 Kgs 12:22; 1 Chr 17:3, 25:5; Ezra 9:4; Prov 30:5; Isa 40:8). Generally the "word of the LORD" is used instead. Most of these references to the "word of the LORD" refer to an oral communication by God through a particular human intermediary, but in several instances the word of the LORD is associated with written texts: Moses writes the words of the LORD in the Book of the Covenant (Exod 24:1–7); Jeremiah sends a letter of the words of the Lord to the exiles in Babylon (Jer 29:1–4); Jeremiah dictates words of the LORD in a letter against Israel and Judah (Jer 36:1–4); Jeremiah dictates to Baruch sayings of the LORD against Israel, Judah, and the nations to be written on a scroll (Jer 45:1–5).

In the books of the Jewish Apocrypha (first and second centuries BCE), however, it becomes clear that special religious authority has been conferred upon the twenty-four books of the Jewish Bible, which were thought to be the revelation of God (2 Esd 14:44–48; Sirach, Prologue, and 24:23). The phrase "word of God" is not used to refer to this collection, however.

---

7. This essay subsequently appeared as part of a dialogue "Is the Bible the Word of God?" in the *Fourth R* 29.3 (May–June 2016), 8–10; used by permission.

The Early Christian Bible

The Bible used by the early Christians is the Septuagint (the Greek translation of the Hebrew Jewish Bible; it includes books of the Apocrypha along with the contents of the Jewish Bible). The legendary account (from the second century BCE) of the Jewish Bible's translation into Greek for use by Jews in the diaspora confers the status of inspired upon the translation as well. The story goes like this: a number of scholars were brought together for the translation project, put into different cubicles, and each in seventy-two days under inspiration produced the exact same translation.[8] This "miraculous" result was taken as proof that the Septuagint was an inspired translation.

It was this translation that early Christians used and regarded as sacred Scriptures (2 Tim 3:15–16). By 367 CE in Egypt, however, the books of the Apocrypha were not considered part of the canonical Scriptures. Bishop Athanasius of Alexandria described the books of the Old Testament (the Jewish Scriptures not including Esther) and the books of the New Testament, as we know them today in the following way: they are "included in the Canon, and handed down, and credited as divine." These books are "fountains of salvation that they who thirst may be satisfied with the living words they contain." Athanasius describes a number of other books that although not included in the canon, are "appointed by the Fathers to be read by those . . . who wish for instruction in the word of godliness." These books are Wisdom of Solomon, Wisdom of Sirach, Esther, Judith, and Tobit; and two books of the apostolic fathers, the Didache and the Shepherd of Hermas.[9] There must have been some fluidity throughout the churches as to what books were and were not considered canonical, for in the oldest Bibles from the fourth and fifth centuries (Codex Alexandrinus, Codex Sinaiticus, and Codex Claromontanus) the canonical books are being used along with books that were not on the canonical list, such as the Epistle of Barnabas, the Shepherd of Hermas, 4 Maccabees, two Epistles of Clement, the Psalms of Solomon, the Acts of Paul, and the Apocalypse of Peter.

---

8. Barrett, *New Testament Background*, 208–13.
9. Athanasius, "Letter XXXIX," 552.

The Catholic Bible

The Catholic Church had long used the Jewish Apocrypha, which it calls the deuterocanonical books ("added to the canon at a later time"), along with the books of the Hebrew Bible and the New Testament. In 1560 the Council of Trent removed any question about the status of these books by declaring them all to be inspired. So by the sixteenth century the various parts of the Bible (the Jewish Bible, the Apocrypha, New Testament) used as Scripture in the English-speaking world had been accorded the status of divinely inspired Scripture. As far as I can see, it was not until the sixteenth century that the appellation "word of God" came to be applied to the Bible (see section §37, above).

The following are the kinds of expressions by which the Bible has been described in order to set it apart as special religious literature from just any old books: Scripture, Holy Writ, sacred, inspired by God, the Word of Truth, the Word of God, the Revelation of God, Divine, and the like. I consider these expressions to be heightened, poetic, or figurative language, which expresses a religious *belief* about the texts so described. The elevated language puts the texts into a special category. These terms used to describe the books, however, say nothing about their essential nature; the terms describe only what the one using the language believes about the books, or the regard in which one holds the books. Is the Bible (of whichever community) the "Word of God"? It is if one believes it is; but that confession says nothing about the content of the texts. (1–26–15)

§39 WHAT ABOUT THE BIBLE GIVES IT THE STATUS WORD OF GOD?[10]

If I was correct in the previous essay (§38, above) that the phrase "Word of God" is heightened language to express an opinion about a particular collection of books, then it follows that the sacredness of those books does not derive from their essential nature but derives from what people think about the books. In other words, like beauty, the Bible's character as "Word of God" lies in the eye of the beholder! The one poetic term that seems to undergird and support the other figurative terms is the claim

---

10. This essay subsequently appeared as part of a dialogue "Is the Bible the Word of God?" in the *Fourth R* 29/4 (July-August 2016), 15–16, 19–20; used by permission.

that the Bible (whichever version) is *inspired* by God. This expression seems to be the principal claim from which other descriptions derive.

Divine inspiration of individuals was a common idea in Greco-Roman antiquity; the inspired ecstatic utterances of certain figures were commonly treated as oracles (i.e., utterances of the God). The God spoke through an inspired host. One of the best known oracular sanctuaries was the shrine of the God Apollo, located at Delphi in central Greece, where individuals throughout the ancient world would go for answers to personal, political, and religious questions. A priestess known as the Pythia received the questions. She was believed to be possessed by the God when she spoke the oracle, and her reply was considered "the Word of the God."[11]

This situation was similar to that of the ancient prophets of Israel; the words they spoke at the LORD's behest were treated as the very words of Yahweh, the God of Israel (for example, Jer 1:1–10). Both situations are likely part of the deep historical background behind the modern appellation "Word of God" applied to the Bible. The legendary story of the translation of the Bible into Greek clearly reinforces the idea of the Bible's inspiration: the translators who were put in separate cubicles make *exactly* the same translation from Hebrew into Greek without consulting the work of one another.[12] The story reinforces the idea that the Greek translation was as inspired as the Hebrew.

The Roman state consulted the Sibylline Oracles, a collection of ancient Greek oracles that had been gathered from women thought to be inspired by the God. These books were brought out and consulted for guidance at times of national crisis. Some of the books show the influence of Jewish and Christian thought.[13]

The need for a "word from God" in the Jewish, Christian, and ancient Roman traditions originates in the human psyche, where a similar need for divine guidance was felt in facing the uncertainties of life. The shift from the oracular utterance to the written word was likely occasioned by skepticism and the decline of oracular centers in the ancient world. Plutarch, a priest of the God Apollo at Delphi (late first century CE), for example, wrote two essays in the late first century CE on the

---

11. Potter, "Oracles," 1071–72.
12. See §38 above.
13. Collins, "Sibylline Oracles."

decline of oracles.¹⁴ As confidence decreased that the Gods continued to speak audibly through inspired individuals, divine authority transferred to the fixed written collections. What had once been a continuing viable word from God had become fixed, static, and an out-of-date collection of written words.

The early Christians treated the Jewish Bible like prophetic oracles that proved the truth of Christianity. They did not use the literal sense of the statements in the Bible as words from God, but insisted that the Bible's oracles were veiled prophecies attesting to Christ (see, for example, Gal 3:16; 1 Cor 10:1-4; Rom 10:5-11): they argued that the truth of the "Christ centered nature" of the Jewish Bible was clear to anyone who read it with the eyes of faith (for example, 2 Cor 3:13-16; 4:3-6). Already by the time of Paul, the literal sense of the words of the Jewish Bible had generally ceased to be meaningful for Christian experience (1 Cor 9:9-12; Gal 4:22-31), and that led to the eventual development of a new set of holy books that became authoritative in Christian communities for interpreting the old "obsolete" Jewish books.

The Jewish Bible, the Jewish Apocrypha, and the New Testament constitute the traditional remains of two different religious communities, which extended from the Israelite exodus to the writing of 2 Peter. These texts reveal different social, cultural, ethical, and religious traditions covering around 1,300 years. The Jewish Bible is a library of traditional ancient Israelite writings, containing among other things the history of the people told from a religious perspective, along with its ancient laws, prophetic literature, hymnbook, wisdom literature, and so forth, from the thirteenth century BCE to roughly 400 BCE. The Apocrypha consists of additional Jewish religious texts written between 300 BCE and 70 CE. The New Testament (50 CE to the early second century) contains among other things stories, personal correspondence and theological essays.

These collections are quite diverse and clearly reflect their ancient origins. How can one today recognize a valid Word of God within them? Indeed, how would anyone know a word of God if they saw it? The texts are written in different social contexts at different times, and thereby contain the seeds of their own irrelevancy. To maintain relevance the ethical and religious values of each book must constantly be prioritized and reinterpreted for every new generation. However, some instructions in the books are clearly not the words of an ethical God (for example,

---

14. See Babbitt, trans., *Plutarch's Moralia*, 256-501. The essays are "The Oracles at Delphi No Longer Given in Verse" and "The Obsolescence of Oracles."

Deut 17:2–5; 21:18–21; 1 Tim 2:8–15). If there was once a justification for such things as managing slaves, executing rebellious children, or subordinating women, no justification can be offered for such practices in modern society. In short, the Bible is out-of-date as a book for faith and practice—at least in part. (2–3–15)

§40 WHAT DISTINGUISHES THE BIBLE FROM OTHER COLLECTIONS OF HOLY WRIT?[15]

The term *Holy Writ*, as used here, refers to Scriptures used by a religious community. The term is figurative. It claims a special religious authority for the Scriptures, so designated. Any collection so designated would be considered authoritative for faith and practice by the community using it. Any collection of literature purporting to give readers clarity of insight into the divine will and to serve as a guide for life in this world, or for a world to come, is Holy Writ. The Bible can be distinguished from other collections of Holy Writ by its content but not by the claim that it is an exclusive supreme revelation. Each collection is touted by its adherents as the supreme authority from God.

Claims for authority in religious texts are often supported by claims of special origin. For example, the Bible is the Word of God because it is thought to be inspired (2 Tim 3:15–16). The Book of Mormon, the sacred Scripture of the Latter-day Saints, was written on golden tablets, and their hidden location was revealed to Joseph Smith by the angel Moroni. The Jewish Torah was written by God himself and given to Moses (Deut 9:9–10; 10:1–5), or it came from God to Moses through the agency of angels (Acts 7:38; Gal 3:19; Heb 2:2; Josephus, *Ant.* 15.5.3 [§136]).

In the contemporary world a number of Holy Scriptures are imbued with the same authority as the Bible. A few of those collections that currently compete with the Bible include the Rig-Veda (Hinduism), the Avesta (Zoroastrianism), the Quran (Islam), the Tao Te Ching (Taoism), and the Tripitaka (Buddhism).

The existence of multiple sets of Scripture claiming to be the supreme religious authority does not necessarily disprove the claim that "my Scripture is true but others are not," since that claim only represents *my* opinion. The existence of multiple sets of authoritative Holy Scripture,

---

15. This essay subsequently appeared as part of a dialogue with Lee M. McDonald, "Is the Bible the Word of God?" in *Fourth R* 29.5 (2016) 9–12; used by permission.

however, does raise theoretical questions about one's own religion, in light of the fact that others claim the same exclusive authority for their Scripture.

1. The existence of multiple sets of Holy Scripture refutes the claim of uniqueness for any one set. Although each set may be unique in content, no test exists to demonstrate that its content is revealed truth. True, some sets of Holy Scripture may be more ethical or more historical or more rational or more ancient than others. These features, however, do not measure that mysterious, innate, but ultimately vaporous, quality of "sacred revelation," claimed somehow to reside in all Holy Writings. In other words, content alone is not what transforms a collection of texts into revealed truth.

2. The fact that multiple sets of Holy Scripture exist raises the question of the "there-ness" of all Gods. Gods are not "mortal beings" like humans, existing in space and time. Gods are believed to be immortal; they are not limited by time, and do not exist in space. Nevertheless we think of them as "there" somewhere, but do not define "there" as a place within the physical universe. Competing sets of Holy Scripture challenge the "there-ness" of any God in the following way: If the claim for the innate essence of revelation or holiness for any set of Holy Writings cannot be quantified or identified in its particulars but is due merely to individual or group opinion, then God becomes an unnecessary postulate. Gods may be "there," but the sacredness of the Scriptures does not originate with them.

3. Multiple sets of Holy Scripture argue against the idea that one God is responsible for their multiple contradictory revelations. The supreme authority claimed for each set renders that idea impossible, as is suggested by the difficulty later Gentile followers of Jesus had with the Jewish Scriptures. They inherited the Jewish Scriptures as divinely inspired (2 Tim 3:15–16), but the church held a different faith from that of the Israelites and later Jews. Christians resolved the disconnect between the old faiths and the new faith by prophetic interpretation of the Old Testament, which allowed them to disregard a literal understanding in favor of a figurative understanding, as well as to pick and choose certain ethical concepts while ignoring others. Thus they were able to claim the revelation of one God behind the obsolete Old Testament (Heb 8:8–13) and their new books of faith. Not all embraced that solution, however. Marcion, for example, rejected the Old Testament as Scripture.[16] Many

---

16. Clabeaux, "Marcion," 515–16.

critical scholars have long recognized that the adoption of Jewish Scriptures as part of a Christian canon is a non sequitur. Hence, multiple sets of Holy Scripture imply multiple Gods.

4. Affirmation of the religious truth of any set of Holy Scripture is generally due to geographical happenstance and cultural conditioning. Had I been reared in Greek culture rather than in the Mississippi Bible Belt, I would probably have been baptized Greek Orthodox, and my Scriptures would have been a modern Greek translation of the ancient Greek Septuagint.[17] Had I been reared in ancient Persia, I would no doubt have been Zoroastrian and the Avesta would have been my Holy Scriptures. Had I been born in modern Iran, I would surely have been Muslim and the Quran would have been my Holy Scriptures. In the absence of any critical thinking skills I would have held to the truth of each of those Scriptures as avowedly as I affirmed the Bible in my youth. In short, belief in the inspiration and authority of any set of Scriptures is the result of cultural conditioning and what we are taught. (2–10–15)

§41 BE THERE DRAGONS IN THE BIBLE?[18]

How could there be? Dragons are mythical or legendary creatures. They constitute the stuff of fantasy and fiction and are certainly not the material on which history and revealed religion are based—at least that is the prevailing view today. The dragon has a long and widespread tradition in the world.[19]

Answering the question of whether there are there dragons in the Bible is more complicated than one might suppose, however. It is complicated because translators practice their art differently in rendering ancient words into what they take to be a modern equivalent, and because we must work in two ancient languages Hebrew and Greek. The two most authoritative Hebrew lexicons agree in the translation of "land-serpent, dragon" as appropriate for the following passages: Deut 32:33; Ps 91:13; Exod 7:9, 10, 12; Jer 51:34; Neh 2:13.[20]

I checked seven English translations and found that they sometimes do and sometimes do not use "dragon" in translating the verses listed

17. Ware, *Orthodox Church*, 208.
18. *Fourth R* (forthcoming).
19. See, for example, Wikipedia, "Dragon."
20. Gesenius and Robinson, trans., *Hebrew and English Lexicon*; and Brown, et al., *Hebrew-English Lexicon*.

above. And some of the seven translations use "dragon" in other verses not mentioned by the lexicons as places where "dragon" would be appropriate (Ps 74:13; Isa 27:1, 51:9). For some of the passages referenced above, the Septuagint and the Vulgate (ancient Greek and Latin translations of the Hebrew Bible) use *drakōn* (Greek) and *draco* (Latin), words that mean "dragon" or "serpent" and that are obviously sources for our English word *dragon*.

The word *dragon* (*drakōn*) appears in the following New Testament passages: Rev 12:3, 4, 7, 9, 13, 17, 17; 13:2, 4, 11; 16:13; 20:2. In two of these verses the dragon is also identified as an *ophis*, which the Greek lexicon terms a "snake, serpent" (Rev 12:9; 20:2). The Latin translation of the Greek text uses *draco*, which the lexicon identifies as "a sort of serpent, a dragon."

Is the mythical or fantasy dragon actually described in the Bible? The answer is yes, and dragons were part of the landscape of nature in antiquity, at least to judge from the writings by some of the best-known names in our classical and Greco-Roman past; these names include Aristotle, Herodotus, and Pliny, as well as others. Their reports on the nature of the creature, however, were not uniform. The description of the dragon in Philostratus (second century CE), the author of *The Life of Apollonius of Tyana*,[21] is most similar to what we have come to know as the mythical creature. These ancient writers, however, describe creatures they claim to know; sometimes they are serpent-like and at other times dragon-like. The description of the creature in Revelation, however, is actually something more than simply a snake or a serpent. What is described is a species of reptile with a tail; snakes do not have tails. And this creature "stood on the sand of the sea" (Rev 12:18). Serpents do not have legs, and hence cannot "stand." In describing another monster the author of Revelation says that "it spoke like a dragon" (Rev 13:11), which suggests that the author and his ancient audience presumed to know what dragons sounded like.

What do we learn from this information? The lexicographers really didn't know the species of the creature on which they offered translation advice. The ancient, classical writers are confident that they are describing actual existing creatures. And there actually are dragons described in the Bible.

---

21. Conybeare, trans., *Philostratus*, 1:242–247 (chapters 6–8).

THE BIBLE 99

As Oliver Hardy said to the second of the famed comic duo, his partner Stan Laurel, "Well, here's another nice mess you've gotten me into!" The Christian and Jewish Bibles, that are thought to report ancient history and are confessed popularly in conservative Christianity as "the Word of God," attest to the actual existence of what we today regard as a mythical and fantasy creature. Archaeologists and geologists, on the other hand, have given us the pterodactyl and pterosaur, flying reptiles that actually lived during the late Jurassic period (to judge from their petrified skeletons). These creatures, which actually did exist at one time, are not a part of the biblical record.

So the "Word of God" (if I may call it that) leads us to a fantasy creature that never existed, but modern scientific study of the earth gives us historical dragon-like creatures that actually existed. (8-12-16)

§42 LEGENDS IN THE BIBLE

Every culture has legends. Readers will recall the legends about Paul Bunyan and his blue ox, Babe; John Henry the railroad pile-driving man; the headless horseman of Sleepy Hollow; and George Washington's cherry tree; among others. A current dictionary definition of a *legend* is: a story coming down from the past, especially one popularly regarded as historical, although its historicity cannot be verified.

Biblical scholars have found that certain narratives in the Bible are also legends, stories popularly regarded as describing historical events, whose historicity cannot be verified. In his magisterial work on the Old Testament Otto Eissfeldt, for example, identifies the story of David's victory over Goliath (1 Sam 17:40–50) as a legend.[22] According to Eissfeldt, a biblical legend is a poetic narrative "intended to give pleasure and entertain, and not really to adhere to the recalling of what has happened, nor to instruct."[23] In this legend the force of the story is not really on the man David, but rather on the divine power that controls him (1 Sam 17:47).

Here is another definition of *legend*: Legends are stories about holy people and religious heroes that are read for inspiration, religious

---

22. Eissfeldt, *Old Testament*, 42.
23. Ibid., 34–35.

instruction, and spiritual benefit.²⁴ By this definition the story of Jesus besting the devil in a debate is a legend (Matt 4:1–11; Luke 4:1–13).

Generally people want to know if a historical event actually happened at all as described in legend. The answer is no. Legends are not history. In form the legend is thought to be fictional, although there may be a historical element at the base of it. For example, with regard to the temptation narrative: it is surely plausible that Jesus may have experienced an inner personal struggle at some point in his career, as, for example, the much simpler statement in Mark 1:12–13 suggests; but even Mark's brief statement, as it appears, is legendary in character. The details of biblical legends, if dependent on oral tradition, are enhanced in the oral transmission of the stories and appear at the time of their first inscription. In the case of the temptation narrative, the story is enhanced further in Matthew and Luke.

Mark's narrative about Jesus' personal struggle at Gethsemane before the crucifixion (Mark 14:32–42) could be either a pious fiction invented by Mark or possibly a legendary account based on a historical datum that in considering his death Jesus did indeed struggle through his own "dark night of the soul." There is in fact a similar tradition in Heb 5:7 (RSV):

> In the days of his flesh Jesus offered up prayers and supplications, with loud cries and tears, to him who was able to save him from death, and he was heard for his godly fear.

Even this brief report, however, has a legendary character ("and he was heard for his godly fear"). Scholars are divided on whether the brief report in Hebrews is to be related to the more developed narrative account in Mark.²⁵ But in light of the fact that Hebrews shows no obvious influence from the Synoptic Gospels, this brief description of a personal struggle of Jesus in the face of death could possibly have a historical basis. In light of the courage of the Johannine Christ in facing his death (John 12:27–33), one is inclined to see in John a reaction to a tradition about Jesus' torturous personal struggle in facing death (John 12:27–33), one is inclined to see in John a reaction to a tradition about a tortuous personal struggle of Jesus in facing his own death.

---

24. Nickle, *Synoptic Gospels*, 28.

25. Attridge, *Hebrews*, 148–52n144; Nicoll, et al., eds., *Expositor's Greek Testament*, 4:288–89.

The romanticizing of the traditions about Jesus in the gospels has obscured for the most part the historical details of Jesus' humanity and personal history. The Jesus Seminar in its second report on the deeds of Jesus found that only 16 percent of the 176 events they considered in early Christian literature had credibility as actual historical events.[26] (8-1-16)

§43 LIVING BY THE BIBLE IS NOT POSSIBLE

It is a bit of flimflam on the part of pastors or Bible teachers when they encourage us to "live by the Bible," or else they simply do not know the biblical literature. Trying to live a life obedient to what the Bible says will drive a person bananas! "Living biblically" means trying to do what the Bible says. But people who aim to govern their behavior by the Bible's teaching are never able to succeed at it. Here is why. The Protestant Bible is different from the Roman Catholic and Jewish Bibles.[27] The Jewish Bible is composed of the religious texts of ancient Israel, whose ethics and values are markedly different from those met in the New Testament because they record the values and culture of a different historical period. And the ethics and values of the New Testament books are equally different from those of modern Christianity.

We read the Bible in the context of a community tradition. What I mean is this: Baptists read the Bible from a Baptist perspective, which differs from the perspectives of other religious groups. Each religious community has a way of resolving those texts that do not fit its traditional understanding of the Bible. In general, a community will repeatedly celebrate passages from the Bible reflecting its core religious values, but will ignore others. Community leaders usually have perfected theoretical rationales for explaining passages conflicting with the community view. In the final analysis, even the understanding of God is shaped by the community's view.

Here are some examples of dissonance in the biblical texts. Christians and Jews ignore what the Bible says about how to worship. In the Hebrew Bible/Old Testament (in Lev 7-10, for example), the nature of corporate worship is specifically defined in terms of ceremonies and animal sacrifice. But today since there is no "tent of meeting" or Jewish

---

26. Funk and the Jesus Seminar, *Acts of Jesus*, 1.
27. Hayes, *Introduction*, 3-6.

temple where such sacrifices are performed, all of these instructions for ritual and sacrifice are simply ignored as literal obligations by Jews and Christians alike. Few, if any persons, in the Jewish and Christian traditions today offer animal sacrifices as a sin offering, and, what is more, they have no intention of doing so! Christians appeal to the ancient Christian view that the death of Jesus satisfied the legal and ritual requirements of the Jewish Torah once and for all (Heb 8–10). This idea discards large parts of the Torah as no longer valid for Christians; therefore some parts of the Bible are not included in the injunction to live biblically. And this raises the question of whether or not there are other parts I can ignore. How does the Bible believer handle the ancient ethical commands of Torah, which are not accommodated by the argument in Hebrews? For example, many (most?) conservative Christians regard the Ten Commandments (Exod 20:2–17; Deut 5:7–21) as part of a "Christian" ethical code; some even want to mandate the Ten Commandments as the basis for the legal system in America. On the other hand, other ethical directives of the Hebrew Bible/Old Testament are simply ignored: for example, that adultery should be punishable by death (Lev 20:10); that stubborn and rebellious sons should be stoned to death (Deut 21:18–21); and that daughters found not to be virgins are also stoned to death (Deut 22:13–21).

Here are two conflicting directives between the Hebrew Bible/Old Testament and the New Testament: how should one reconcile the clash between "Be fruitful and multiply" (Gen 1:27–28) and Paul's advice that Christians should remain single (1 Cor 7:8)? How should one reconcile the order from God to his prophet Samuel to utterly annihilate the Amalekites (1 Sam 15) and Jesus' directive to "Love your enemies" (Matt 5:44; Luke 6:27)?

One must pick and choose between directions for ethical behavior between texts even in the New Testament. For example, is a man permitted to divorce his wife when she has been unfaithful (Matt 19:9), or is divorce absolutely forbidden (Mark 10:10)? Is it mandatory that Christian bishops and deacons be married, as the Pastor says (1 Tim 3:1–13), or should we listen to Paul again, who had a rather low view of marriage (1 Cor 7:1–9)? Was Paul correct that salvation is by faith alone (Gal 2:15–16), or was James right that faith without works is dead (Jas 2:21–26)? (1–6–10)

THE BIBLE 103

§44 SHOULD ONE LOVE GOD OR FEAR GOD?

The Bible is scarcely consistent, even in some of its most basic dicta. There is of course a good reason for that, which is unfortunately lost on the most devout believers in revealed religion, who regard the Bible as originating in the mind of God. Here is the reason: the Bible's texts are written at different times in various cultural locations by human authors, who quite naturally have different views. For example, in one of its most basic pronouncements, regarding how believers should relate to God, the biblical texts have a range of responses. The basic guidance is that believers should "fear the Lord." Paul, for example, condemned people whom he regarded as being under the power of sin because "there is no fear of God before their eyes" (Ps 35:1 LXX; Rom 3:18). "The fear of the LORD" is the classic expression for being a pious servant of Yahweh in Israelite religion (Exod 20:20; Deut 6:2; Job 28:28; Prov 1:7; 3:7; compare Acts 10:34–35; 1 Pet 2:17; Rev 14:7); and appropriately enough pious non-Israelites, who worshiped in synagogues, were called Godfearers" (Acts 10:2, 22; 13:16).

Jesus tells a story (Luke 18:2–5) about a judge hearing a case in which the plaintiff is a widow who badgers the judge to rule in her favor. The judge, however, prides himself on his integrity as a judge who calls cases on their merits. He says of himself, "I neither fear God nor regard man" (18:4). The narrator actually introduces him that way, as a judge who doesn't fear God or show deference in his judgments (18:2). "Fearing God" would signal the traditional religious deference a pious person would render to God through traditional religious beliefs; "regarding man" would reflect deference one would pay to influential and powerful persons in the community. In neither assertion does love play a role.[28]

Nevertheless alongside this typical expression for piety in Israel (i.e., the fear of the LORD) are found injunctions to love God (Deut 10:12; 6:2; 6:5). In Sirach these two responses (fearing and loving) are paralleled as two sides of the same emotion (Sir 2:15–16). The two emotions strike me, however, as inconsistent responses, and the author of 1 John had a similar response: "For fear involves punishment, and the one who fears is not perfected in love" (1 John 4:18; compare 4:13–17). A relationship based on fear would produce anxiety, which contains the seeds of uncertainty, doubt, and mistrust. It is scarcely a wholesome relationship (Matt 28:4; Mark 16:8; Heb 12:18–21).

28. Hedrick, *Parables as Poetic Fictions*, 187–207.

A relationship based on fear prompts obedience because of what the dominant, controlling party can impose on the lesser party; such a relationship is one between a slave and the slave's owner (Eph 6:5). Occasionally a modern translator will render the Greek word "fear" (*phobos*) as "awe," which doesn't help, since "awe" suggests dread or terror (Mark 4:41; Rom 11:20). Sometimes "awe" as a translation does not do justice to the Greek text; for example in Mark 4:41 the Greek is "feared greatly."

The lexicographers who survey how words are used in the New Testament and by writers elsewhere in antiquity tell us that the verbal forms of "fear" (*phobeo*) carry the idea of "reverence" or "respect for." Nevertheless, reverence, honor, deference, veneration, and the like still contain the idea of fearful obeisance and awe. At least it is something very different from what I understand as love: "Love puts up with all things, believes all things, hopes all things, endures all things" (1 Cor 13:7); "Love is patient and kind" (1 Cor 13:4). "Love does not insist on its own way" (1 Cor 13:5). "Faith, hope, love abide, these three; but the greatest of these is love" (1 Cor 13:13). The dominant way God is understood in Hebrew Bible does not include much emphasis on love.

Perhaps the problem, however, is not God's character, about which we actually know very little. We only know what others have told us and that includes the testimonies of the authors of the biblical texts. The problem is the manifold ways that we humans view God. In a sense God is always subject to what we think about God. And we frequently must choose between contradictory views, as in this case: do we love God or fear God? How is it possible truly to love someone before whom you must always be terribly afraid? (11-27-16)

§45 DISSENTING VOICES IN A TEXT

This essay is not about history; that is to say, it is not about what actually happened in the past. It is an essay about how we create the past. Every text contains the seeds of its own destruction; that is to say, every text contains points at which the integrity of the text breaks down and undermines itself. In short, these points of breakdown render the text ambiguous, leaving a perplexed reader to ask, what's going on here?

Here are several examples; some are well known and others are not so well known. John 4:2 is perhaps the best known since a dissenting voice (John 4:2) interrupts the statement of another voice (John 4:1 and 4:3).

THE BIBLE 105

> Now when the Lord knew that the Pharisees had heard that Jesus was making and baptizing more disciples than John (although Jesus himself did not baptize, but only his disciples), he left Judea and departed again to Galilee. (John 4:1–3 RSV)

In John 4:1 a first voice informs the reader that it was common knowledge that Jesus was making and baptizing more disciples than John the Baptizer. In 4:2 a dissenting voice emerges dividing the sentence that begins in 4:1 (a subordinate clause) and concludes in 4:3 (the main clause). Clearly the inserted dissenting voice disagrees with the voice that began the sentence. The dissenting voice asserts that Jesus himself did not personally perform any baptisms, but the voice that began the sentence, equally assertively, insists that he did perform baptisms, and that it was common knowledge that he did. Note that translators of the text recognize the disagreement, and place John 4:2 in parentheses. Who should the reader believe: the first narrative voice (John 4:1 and 4:3) or the dissenting voice (John 4:2) that corrects the first voice?

By my count there are at least 121 of these "clarifications" in the text of John.[29] Another example is found in the narrative of the feeding of the five thousand (John 6:5–14). The reader is told that the healings Jesus performed (the narrator calls them "signs") created a sensation, and as a result a great crowd followed him (John 6:2), which the reader later discovers numbered five thousand (John 6:10). Jesus takes five barley loaves and two fish and feeds this huge crowd and has five baskets of fragments left over from the barley loaves (John 6:13). The narrator's positive climax to the feeding story is that "when the people saw the sign," they confessed Jesus as "the prophet who is to come into the world" (John 6:14). Imagine a reader's surprise to learn a little later that the Jesus character in the narrative disagrees with the narrator's judgment: "Jesus answered them ... you seek me not because you saw signs, but because you ate your fill of the loaves" (John 6:26). Should we believe the narrator of the incident or the Jesus character? Was the crowd persuaded by the sign they had witnessed, or was it because their bellies were full (John 6:12)?

In John 7:22 again a dissenting voice interrupts a compound sentence by the Jesus character in the narrative: Jesus asserts to his interlocutors in the temple (the Judahites), "Moses gave you circumcision ..., and you circumcise a person on the Sabbath." Translators put the dissenting statement that follows in parentheses, after the word *circumcision*, to show that it is not part of what Jesus said to the Judahites, but rather it is

29. Hedrick, "Authorial Presence and Narrator."

an aside directly addressing the reader of the gospel. The dissenting voice (in a translator's parentheses) corrects the assertion of Jesus by saying, "(not that it is from Moses but from the fathers)." Those who prepared the critical Greek text found the dissenting voice so disruptive that they set the dissenting statement off with dashes (which are not found in the Greek manuscripts), as they also did in John 4:2. Who should a reader of John think has provided the correct response: the Jesus character or the dissenting voice?

The phenomenon is not limited to the Gospel of John; another interesting disagreement is found in Mark 5:22–24, 35–43. A synagogue ruler (Jairus) implores Jesus to come heal his twelve-year-old daughter, who at that moment was at the point of death (5:23). Jesus goes with him (5:24), but he is delayed by another healing (5:25–34). At that moment Jairus receives word that his daughter in the meanwhile has died (5:35), but Jesus ignores the report, urging the synagogue ruler only to believe (5:36). When they arrive at Jairus's home, loud lamentations are in progress because of the child's death (5:38). Before he even sees the child, Jesus asserts to the mourners that "the child is not dead but sleeping" (5:39 RSV), and the mourners laugh at him (5:40). When they go into the building, Jesus takes the child by the hand and says, "Arise," and immediately the girl got up (5:41–42). Was the Jesus character correct and the girl was only sleeping, or were the mourners correct and the girl was dead? In short the problem is this: is this narrative a story about the resuscitation of a dead child (i.e., the mourners were right), or is the story about the healing of a sick child (i.e., the Jesus character was right)?

The raw data of history are often contradictory, forcing historians to choose between the more probable and the less probable. What eventually becomes history in these judgmental situations is what a preponderance of historians decides to call history. In the segment from Mark above the historical issue is, what is the nature of the story, a healing narrative or a story about the resurrection of a dead girl? In the Gospel of John the issue is, which voice is the final authority for reading John: the narrator's voice or the dissenting voice? (4-1-15)

§46 DOES A TEXT MEAN WHAT THE AUTHOR INTENDED?

In a letter to the editor of a local newspaper a writer gently chides a young woman who (unknowingly) gave an interpretation of a poem authored by the writer in a speech tournament at which the writer was one of the judges. It seems that the speaker offered a reading of his poem that described "what the author had meant," and he lamented that her view was "not even close to [his own] real intent."[30]

This incident is a perfect example of the poem (or creative essay) as an artistic object. Once an author has written and published a poem, he (or she) no longer controls it. The issue is not what authors *intend* to do, but what they *actually* do. In other words the published poem or essay is autonomous and has an existence totally apart from the creative artist's intentions.[31] In short, the author himself or herself becomes only one more interpreter of the poem or essay, and not even the authoritative interpreter. It really doesn't matter what the author intended; what matters is what the essay is. The creative piece exists apart from the author's intentions; it draws attention to itself and "speaks" to the reader, or the viewer in the case of objects of art such as paintings and sculptures. Thus authors may learn something new from others about what they have actually accomplished in the artistic object. The poet Wallace Stevens once wrote:

> It is not a question of what an author meant to say but of what he has said. In the case of a competent critic the author may well have a great deal to find out about himself and his work. This goes to the extent of saying that it would be legitimate for a critic to make statements respecting the purpose of an author's work that were altogether contrary to the intentions of the author.[32]

In short, language is ambiguous even on an author's best days, as any poet well knows. For example, Miguel de Cervantes in his seventeenth-century novel *The Ingenious Gentleman Don Quixote of La Mancha* described an insane man who fancied himself a knight errant on a quest to restore chivalry and bring justice to the world He jousted (tilted) and fought with imaginary foes (windmills and giants), which were real to him in his insanity. Cervantes's novel inspired a book (by Dale Wasserman) and a Broadway musical, *Man of La Mancha*. In the musical the signature song, "The Impossible Dream," describes a man on a quest fighting "unbeatable foes," righting "unrightable wrongs," fighting "for the

---

30. Krause, "Interpreting God's Word," 7E.

31. See the arguments on the intentional and affective fallacies in Wimsatt, *Verbal Icon*, 3–39.

32. Stevens, *Letters*, 346 (letter #396).

right," and walking "through hell on a heavenly cause." The protagonist of the musical is certainly inspired by Cervantes's mad hero Don Quixote de La Mancha, but in the interpretation by the musical lyricist (Joe Darion) Don Quixote has become a symbol of the idealistic person who dares to dream impossible dreams, including establishing a just social order.[33] What might Cervantes have thought of the use made of his novel?

The situation is similar with respect to biblical texts, which were written by human authors. They are not God's words, as Mr. Krause claimed in his letter, but the words of human authors written in behalf of a particular understanding of God. Krause's affirmation of faith completely ignores the human authors of these ancient writings, who themselves were conditioned by their situations in life; they crafted what they wrote from vastly different perspectives, with different intentions and opinions. Letting God interpret these words, as Mr. Krause advises, is only Krause's faith speaking again. Readers, not God, interpret texts, in the nexus between how they read the text and the life experiences they bring to the text. God has nothing to do with it.

If you doubt the ambiguity of language, just ask a Baptist, Lutheran, and Roman Catholic about their understanding of the Eucharist. They come to very different understandings from their understandings of the Bible. The classic example of reading the same biblical text and arriving at different conclusions is found in how differently Paul (Gal 3:6–14) and James (2:18–26) understand the biblical story of Abraham (Gen 22:1–18): Paul's view is that God requires faith alone (Gal 3:8–11); James's view is that God requires both faith and works (Jas 2:24).

Galatians 2:16 provides another example of the slippery nature of language, and how the personal life experience one brings to a reading of biblical texts influences what we read in the text. Paul writes, "A person is not justified by works of the law, but through the faith *of* Jesus Christ"; that is through a confidence in God like that of Jesus. And so the passage was translated in the English Bibles of the sixteenth and seventeenth centuries. At the end of the nineteenth century and the beginning of the twentieth the translation changed, and became: "a person is not justified by works of the law but through faith *in* Jesus Christ."[34] Alas, not even the Gods (if Gods there be) can control a reader's interpretation of the divine pronouncements of the Gods. (12–12–14)

33. Wikipedia, "*Man of La Mancha.*"
34. Dewey, et al., trans., *Authentic Letters*, 65–66.

§47 SATYRS OR WILD GOATS? THE POLITICS OF TRANSLATING THE BIBLE[35]

The God Pan, a lesser deity in ancient Greek religion, was born in the region of Arcadia (in the central Peloponnese) with the upper body of a man and lower body of a goat; he had horns, a beard, a tail, and goat hind legs with hooves. He was a god of the woodlands who lived in caves and wandered through mountains and valleys. In appearance he resembled Greek satyrs and Roman fauns, who were similarly portrayed in early art. Small ancient statuettes have been found in Arcadia portraying demonic figures with a human body and goat features.[36] Today in Western culture, however, we regard Pan, satyrs, and fauns as mythical. But were they? In the latter part of the nineteenth century, satyrs and other greater-than-human figures survived in popular belief in the Greek islands of the central Aegean Sea.[37]

Satyrs even appear in some Bibles. Certain words in the Hebrew Bible are translated by the English word "satyr" (from *satyros* in Greek). Passages that mention these figures are

- Isa 13:21: Satyrs dance among ruined cities.
- Isa 34:14: Satyrs cry out to each other.
- 2 Chr 11:15: Jeroboam appoints priests to serve satyrs, along with the "high places" of worship and calves he had made.
- Lev 17:7 the Israelites are forbidden any longer to sacrifice to satyrs.

The Hebrew word *saʿir*, rendered sometimes as "satyr," receives a range of translations. Some of the ways it is translated are "satyr," "wild goat," "he-goat," "shaggy goat," "field spirit," "demon," "goat-demon," "devil," and "goat idol." Such a wide array of translations, suggesting different figures, does not seem justified by Hebrew lexicons, which uniformly identify this figure as a satyr. The 1810 German-Hebrew lexicon of Wilhelm Gesenius identifies *saʿir* in Lev 17:7 and 2 Chr 11:15 as a he-goat that is the object of worship for the Israelites, while Isa 13:21 and 34:14 describe *saʿirim* (the plural of *saʿir*) as he-goat figures dwelling "in desert places, that dance and call out to one another." This goat-shaped forest

---

35. This essay subsequently appeared in the *Fourth R* 25/6 (November–December 2012), 21–22, 24; used by permission.

36. Jost, "Pan"; and Jost, "Arcadian Cults."

37. Bent, *Aegean Islands*, 360, 361–62, for example.

figure (similar to a satyr or a faun) appears in legend or fairy tales. In the Gesenius German edition of 1921, the entry is much shorter: the *saʻir* is described as a goat-shaped demon or satyr living in the wilderness. In Gesenius's Latin version of his Hebrew lexicon (1829) these desert creatures are associated with Greek satyrs or Roman fauns. They are fabled figures, part human and part he-goat. Gesenius gives the translation as "he-goat" or "buck," which relates to a satyr or a faun. In Edward Robinson's English translation (1868) of Gesenius's Latin-Hebrew lexicon, *saʻir* is rendered as "he-goat" or "buck," which he associates with satyrs or wood demons living in desert places. In the current standard Hebrew lexicon Brown, Driver, and Briggs (1968), based in part on Robinson's English edition of Gesenius's Latin-Hebrew lexicon, the Hebrew is rendered as "satyr, demon (with he-goat's form or feet)." On the other hand, the 1998 Hebrew-English concordance by Kohlenberger and Swanson follows the New International Version translation of the Bible and renders *saʻir* in the Isaiah passages as "goat idol." The same word in Leviticus and 2 Chronicles is translated "wild goat."

The ancient Greek Septuagint translates *saʻir* in Isa 13:21 and 34:14 as a compound word, *onokentauros* (combining *onos*, "donkey," and *kentauros*, "centaur")—a "donkey-like" centaur. Centaurs in Greek antiquity were creatures with the lower body of a horse, including a tail and the upper torso of a man, similar to a satyr but a completely different mythical species.[38] The second-century author Aelian describes an *onokentauros* as a centaur and distinguishes it from the satyr.[39] The Septuagint renders *saʻir* in 2 Chr 11:15 as "idols" and in Lev 17:7 as "vain things."

Jerome's Latin Vulgate translates *saʻir* in Isa 13:21 as *pilosus* (a hairy shaggy creature, especially a satyr), but renders Isa 34:14 as *onocentauros*, a "donkey-centaur." The Vulgate renders *saʻir* in 2 Chr 11:15 and Lev 17:7 as "demon." In commenting on these figures Jerome says these shaggy creatures, who dance among the ruins, are *incubones* (the demon incubus, or another spirit), or satyrs or fauns or certain figures regarded as deities of the fields or forests.[40]

Martin Luther renders *saʻir* as "field spirit," and the translation by Smith-Goodspeed (1964) renders it as "satyr," as does the Bible of the Jewish Publication Society of 1945. The New International Version

---

38. Griffiths, "Centaurs."
39. Aelian, *On the Characteristics of Animals* 16:15, 18; 19:9.
40. Jerome, "Commentary on Isaiah," 232–33.

(1970) renders both Isaiah passages as "wild goats" and Leviticus and 2 Chronicles with "goat idols." The New American Bible (1970) translates the text in all four cases as "satyr," with a note to Isa 13:21 that reads "Satyrs: in the popular mind, demons of goatlike form dwelling in ruins, symbols of immorality." The New English Bible (1970) renders both Isaiah passages as "he-goat" and Leviticus and 2 Chronicles as "demon" (with a note: "or satyrs"). The New Revised Standard Version (1991) renders all four passages as "goat-demons." The Greek Orthodox translation (2003), which uses the Septuagint as its Holy Scriptures, renders the Isaiah passages with "goat shaped demons," the 2 Chronicles passage with "the goat shaped," and Lev 17:7 with "demon."

So how should *saʿir* be translated? The root idea of the word is hairy or shaggy, and because the contexts in which the word appears suggest that these figures are human-like but other than human. That is to say, they are not simply wild animals. The Hebrew lexicons have quite reasonably associated *saʿir* with the widespread ancient belief in satyrs. Apparently some modern translators, however, prefer to avoid attributing a mythical character to the biblical text and render *saʿir* as "he-goat," "wild goat," "shaggy goat" or "goat idol" or "demon," or both. The translation "demon" or "goat idol" fits well with the Bible's general depiction of demons and idols as the opponents of the faithful believer, and hence of God. Translating the text in this way avoids having the Bible affirm the existence of Greek and Roman mythical figures.

T. H. Gaster explained that the proper understanding of *saʿirim* is simply "hairy ones." This term, he thinks, refers to a particular class of genies or sprites analogous to the hairy or shaggy demons with which Arab popular imagination fills desert places and ruins. Gaster argued against translating the text with "satyrs," however, because in Isa 34:14 and 13:21 *saʿir* is linked with "ostriches, wild beasts, and hyenas," which, he says, are simply wild animals, although he also notes that the mythical night demon Lilith is also linked with the *saʿirim*; so even by his reading there are at least two mythical creatures in the Isaiah passage.[41] The question then becomes, why not another? J. K. Kuemmerlin-McLean calls the *saʿirim* simply "hairy demons, satyrs."[42]

Not everyone thinks that all the other animals mentioned with *saʿirim* in the Isaiah passages are simply wild creatures of the forest.

---

41. Gaster, "Demon," 1:818.
42. Kuemmerlin-McLean, "Demons (Old Testament)," 2:139.

Smith-Goodspeed translates the series in Isa 34:14 as "Desert demons will join goblins, and satyrs will meet one another; there will the night hag repose and find herself a place of rest," apparently regarding the presence of two mythical creatures in the passage as justification for taking a closer look at the other creatures. And in Isa 13:21–22 the translation is, "But there desert demons will make their lair, and the house will be full of jackals; there ostriches will dwell and satyrs will dance there; goblins will howl in her palaces . . ."

The issue raised by *sa'ir* is not whether figures of Greek mythology ever existed. They did not, and neither did demons! The issue raised by these observations is the politics of translating the Bible. Unless modern readers of the Bible know the ancient languages, they are always at the mercy of translators; that is, they are at the mercy of the translators' prejudices and abilities (or lack therof), as well as their faith presuppositions (or lack thereof). In this case, until recently, virtually all lexicographers recognized the *sa'irim* as greater-than-human goat-like figures worshiped at one point by the Israelites. The lexicographers found a ready parallel for these figures in similar goat-like greater-than-human figures well-known in antiquity: the satyrs and the fauns. Similar mythical figures were known in Arab mythology. There was even a shrine dedicated to the Greek god Pan in northern Israel at Paneas at the base of Mount Hermon. Pan came to the area sometime after Alexander the Great's march into Egypt (after 334 BCE). Around that time Pan merged with a local Canaanite God to whom the shrine was originally dedicated.[43]

In the case of satyrs some translators have, at the very least, simply disregarded the uniform rationale of the lexicographers without calling attention to the problem posed by *sa'ir*. These translations, while giving the biblical text a modern character, are ill suited to its ancient roots—at least according to the judgment of Hebrew lexicographers.

The Bible is a very "human" book. It is always at the mercy of its many users—whether scribes who recopy and inevitably change the texts by error or deliberately, or lexicographers who rescue the vocabulary of its ancient languages, or translators who convert the ancient text into modern linguistic equivalents, or ministers who purport to explain the meaning of the ancient texts. Anyone who knows the Bible only in a modern translation doesn't really know it. They only know what the translator wants them to know. The ambiguity of ancient languages leaves

---

43. Wilson, *Caesarea Philippi*, 2–4.

room for great variety in translation, and how they are translated depends on the skill and bias (both admitted and unrecognized) of translators. English-only readers are best advised to read several translations, which may reveal problems that reliance on a single translation may conceal, either inadvertently or deliberately. (3–30–10)

§48 PAUL'S CROSS GOSPEL AND 1 THESSALONIANS

In antiquity crucifixion was a popular way of punishing enemies of the state and criminals; even Judean officials (Alexander Janneus) crucified fellow Judeans.[44] There was a religious reason for crucifixion in Israelite texts: executed idolaters and blasphemers were hanged on a tree to show they were accursed by God (Deut 21:22–23). So it seems odd that the crucifixion of Jesus and the cross became central elements of Pauline theology:

- "For Christ did not send me to baptize but to preach the gospel, and not with eloquent wisdom, lest the cross of Christ be emptied of its power." (1 Cor 1:17 RSV; see in particular 1:17–22)
- "For I decided to know nothing among you except Jesus Christ and him crucified." (1 Cor 2:2 RSV)
- "May I not boast except in the cross of our Lord Jesus Christ, by which the world has been crucified to me, and I to the world." (Gal 6:14)

Nevertheless only three of his seven letters specifically mention the word "cross" (1 Corinthians, Galatians, Philippians); four do not (2 Corinthians, Romans, 1 Thessalonians, Philemon). On the other hand, four of his seven letters mention crucifixion, and three do not (1 Thessalonians, Philippians, Philemon). And of those that mention crucifixion, Romans mentions it only once (Rom 6:6).

The two letters that mention neither the cross nor crucifixion are 1 Thessalonians and Philemon. The absence of these two motifs from Philemon is understandable. Philemon is a familiar letter of recommendation, a well-known literary form in the Greek world,[45] in which Paul is trying to secure from a slave owner certain personal considerations for

---

44. Josephus, *Ant.* 13.14.2 (§§380–383); Josephus, *J.W.* 1.4.6 (§§97–98).
45. Kim, *Form and Structure.*

a runaway slave. It is a delicate situation and his language is accordingly sensitive to and appropriate for the situation.

But 1 Thessalonians is another matter. By general agreement, 1 Thessalonians is the earliest of Paul's letters (ca. 50 or 51), and the earliest writing in the New Testament. In a number of ways this letter reflects a Paul at the beginning of an apostolic career, not yet aware of what eventually became his characteristic apostolic message. For example, one does not find in 1 Thessalonians Paul's emphasis on justification by faith, or the role of the law in Christian faith (but compare 4:18), or reliance on the Hebrew Bible in argumentation; there are no quotes here from the Hebrew Bible. His idea that the Judeans are "enemies of the whole human race" (1 Thess 2:15) is scarcely typical of Paul in the later letters (compare Rom 11–13). And his idea that God's wrath has come upon the Judeans "at last" (1 Thess 2:16) is contradicted later by Rom 11:25–26 where "all Israel will be saved."

Most significant, however, is the absence of Paul's cross gospel and the theological significance of the crucifixion of Christ, which seems to suggest that he has not yet made the cross gospel central to his theology. For example, in 1 Thessalonians Jesus is not crucified but "killed," and Paul blames the Judeans for his death (1 Thess 2:14–16), while Mark blames the Romans (Mark 15; cf. Matt 27:25 where the Judeans accept responsibility for his death). In 1 Thessalonians Paul proclaims the gospel of God (2:9; cf. Mark 1:14) or the gospel of Christ (1 Thess 3:2); the content of his gospel in 1 Thessalonians seems to be: that Jesus died for us (5:9–10), that God raised him from the dead (1:10), and that he is coming again in Paul's own lifetime (1 Thess 4:13–18).

There is no developed thinking in 1 Thessalonians about the cross or the crucifixion and its role in the Christian experience, such as we find in Paul's later writings (e.g., Rom 6:6; 1 Cor 1:18; Gal 2:20, 5:24, 6:14). In 1 Thessalonians Paul had not yet developed the concept that believers (1:7; 2:1, 13) or "brothers" (as he usually referred to them) in the community gatherings (e.g. 1:4; 3:1, 7) were saints (i.e. "holy ones"). In 1 Thessalonians the term "saint" is reserved for those coming with Jesus at his appearing (*parousia*, 3:13, or perhaps it refers to holy angels, Zech 14:5 LXX). The word "saint" is a usual locution for those in Paul's community gatherings in the later letters (Rom 15:25–26; 1 Cor 14:33; 2 Cor 1:1, 13:13; Phil 1:1, 4:21–22). The reason for the difference is perhaps because Paul had not yet discovered (1 Thess 4:3) that the Holy Spirit had sanctified (i.e. "made holy") those in Christ (Rom 15:16; 1 Cor 1:2, 6:11).

If these observations are correct, 1 Thessalonians gives us a remarkable window into the mind of a not-quite-ready-for-prime-time apostle before he developed his characteristic theological thinking that shaped Christianity for around two thousand years. Apparently Paul matured in his thinking, as all of us do. His theology of justification by faith based on the crucifixion of Jesus did not come to him in a blinding flash of divine inspiration (in spite of what he claimed, Gal 1:11–12), but it was a case of human creative thinking that needed to be developed over time.

And where does that leave a church that uses his letter as "inspired Scripture," even though Paul likely might no longer regard 1 Thessalonians as reflecting his best thinking? First Thessalonians is clearly deficient in the sense that it does not reflect Paul's mature thought. If this assessment of 1 Thessalonians has merit, should 1 Timothy also be regarded as ethically deficient because of its misogyny (1 Tim 2:8–15)? (11–13–15)

§49 JESUS AND PAUL: A LACK OF CONTINUITY[46]

Scholars working in the early twentieth century knew very well that there is a virtual lack of continuity between the Pauline tradition and the synoptic tradition. In short, Paul is completely unaware of the Jesus tradition as represented in the master narrative of the Synoptic Gospels. The discussion of this lack of continuity between Jesus and Paul goes back at least to 1858.[47] Rudolf Bultmann, perhaps the most influential New Testament scholar of the twentieth century, summarized Paul's knowledge of Jesus in this way: "his letters barely show traces of the influence of Palestinian tradition concerning the history and preaching of Jesus. All that is important for him in the story of Jesus is the fact that Jesus was born a Jew and lived under the law (Gal. 4:4) and that he had been crucified (Gal. 3:1; I Cor. 2:2; Phil. 2:5ff., etc.)."[48] To be sure, Paul knows an oral tradition of Jesus sayings. He cites three explicit sayings that have parallels attributed to Jesus in the Synoptic Gospels (1 Cor 7:10–11; 9:14; 11:23–26), as well as two sayings that do not have parallels in the Synoptic Gospels (1 Cor 14:37; 1 Thess 4:15–17). First Corinthians 7:25 seems

---

46. The information in this essay was later made a part of Hedrick, "Baptism of Jesus."

47. Scott, "Jesus and Paul," 331.

48. Bultmann, *Theology*, 1:188.

to suggest that Paul was aware of a number of Jesus sayings but knew no saying that addressed the issue of "virgins": this signals that he may even have had a list of Jesus sayings. Everyone would acknowledge that at least eight "echoes" of Jesus sayings known from the Synoptic Gospels appear in the Pauline letters; a larger number of disputed "echoes" occur.[49]

Earlier discussion of the continuity, or lack thereof, between Jesus and Paul focused on the question of who was the founder of Christianity—Jesus or Paul. If Paul had only a smattering of knowledge about the teachings of Jesus, then it would appear that Christianity ultimately is founded on Paul and his idea of the resurrected Christ, rather than on what Jesus, the Galilean teacher, said and did.

In this brief essay, however, I am only concerned with Paul's knowledge of the synoptic master narrative: that is to say, the story of the career of Jesus as it is shared between the Synoptic Gospels. Knowing an oral tradition of a few Jesus sayings is not the same as knowing the later master narrative about Jesus shared in common between the Synoptic Gospels. The current dominant theory about gospel origins is that all three writers used oral tradition, while Matthew and Luke independently used two written sources, Mark and Q. Hence Paul could have known some of the same oral sayings that are used in the Synoptic Gospels without having known their later narratives about Jesus.

What is the evidence that Paul could have known the synoptic master narrative about Jesus in some incipient oral form? What is at stake in the answer to this question is how much information from the shared synoptic narratives may be assumed to be extant in Paul's day. For example, should we assume that Paul knows the synoptic tradition of the baptism of Jesus by John, the Baptizer? The question is important because Jesus' baptism by John is today regarded as a virtually *certain* historical event in the life of Jesus,[50] even though Paul gives no indication that he knows of a baptism of Jesus.

Paul does practice baptism as a community rite, but it was not a major focus for him, and he even specifically denied that it was a part of his commission from Christ (1 Cor 1:13-17; i.e., the resurrected Christ, not the Palestinian man). He regarded the significance of the rite as a mystical participation in the death and resurrection of Christ (Rom 6:3-4; Gal 3:27; compare 1 Cor 10:2; 12:13), and not something done in

---

49. Hedrick, *Wisdom of Jesus*, 25-29.
50. For example, Hartmann, "Baptism," 584.

obedience to the commission of Jesus (cf. Matt 28:18–20). Baptism seems to be part of the community lore he inherited, such as the practice of the Lord's Supper (1 Cor 11:20–34), a rite Paul appears to modify in focus and practice.

There are four reference points for dating how early the shared synoptic master narrative about Jesus may have been known:

1. Second Peter (1:16–18), whose date is usually given as early second century, appears to know the story of the transfiguration (Matt 17:2–5).
2. The earliest manuscript evidence for the baptism of Jesus is second/third century: P^{64}, having the text of Matt 3:13–17, is dated around 200; P^4 and P^{75}, having the text of Luke 3:21–22, are dated third century; P^{104}, dated second century, has fragments of the Gospel of Matthew.
3. P^{52}, early second century, is a fragment of the Gospel of John.
4. The bishop of Smyrna, Polycarp (Letter to the Philippians), who was martyred middle second century, probably knew the written Gospels of Matthew and Luke.[51]

Hence the earliest that a general knowledge of the synoptic story about Jesus may reasonably be argued is early second century. Why, then, should we think that a Palestinian tradition of the baptism of Jesus by John is "historically certain"? No evidence of the baptism story is attested before early second century. The church's embarrassment at having to admit that the Christ had once been a follower of John is the primary argument for regarding the baptism as historical. (11–17–14)

§50 DID JESUS AND PAUL BELIEVE IN THE CHRISTIAN HEAVEN?

I cannot read minds much less the mental state of paper characters invented by others; that is to say, the synoptic evangelists of whom virtually nothing personal is known for certain. Here is a prolegomenon addressing the question in the title. The Greek word for "heaven" (*ouranos*) according to the lexicographers is used three ways in the New Testament: 1. referring to a part of the ancient universe, hence firmament or sky; 2.

---

51. Koester, *Ancient Christian Gospels*, 14–20.

referring to a transcendental abode, hence not part of the universe; 3. as a circumlocution for God, hence not a location.

I limit my inquiry about Jesus to the testimony of the Gospel of Mark and the hypothetical gospel Q. In Mark there are 17 uses of *ouranos*. I would describe the uses of *ouranos* in Mark to refer to the following: firmament or sky (1:10–11; 4:32; 6:41; 7:34; 13:25 [twice]; 13:27; 13:31; 14:56); a circumlocution for God (8:11; 11:30–31); a transcendental abode (10:21; 11:25; 12:25; 13:32).

The question now becomes, do the four "heaven-is-a-transcendental-abode" sayings attributed to Jesus in Mark survive the scalpel of critical scholarship? The report of the Jesus Seminar[52] is the most critical sifting of the Jesus tradition to date. All but one of the heavenly abode sayings attributed to Jesus by Mark are colored gray, meaning that in the judgment of the seminar there has been some mistake in attributing the saying to Jesus, although the ideas expressed are (likely/possibly/probably) close to his own.[53] Hence, the sayings on heaven as a transcendental abode in the Gospel of Mark are likely later Christian traditions attributed to Jesus. Apparently Jesus himself did not share the later Christian view of an eternal heavenly abode of the righteous soul/spirit, or at least no such clearly reliable information has been preserved by the tradition reflecting such an idea.

The hypothetical early Christian gospel Q (*Quelle*: that is, "source"), which no longer exists but is reconstructed by scholars from close verbal parallels between Matthew and Luke, is thought to be earlier than Mark. It is dated by some as early as 50 CE.[54] Reconstructions of Q include seven sayings on heaven, four of which appear to be referring to heaven as a transcendental abode: Q (Luke) 6:23; 11:13; 12:33; 15:7. One saying can either be a transcendental abode or a circumlocution (Q 10:15). One refers to heaven as part of the firmament (Q 16:17), and the last is a circumlocution (Q 17:29).

The Jesus Seminar scholars regard four of these Q sayings as highly questionable; hence, they are colored gray: Q 6:23; 11:13; 12:33; 16:17; and three of them they regarded as definitely not spoken by Jesus; hence, they are colored black; Q 10:15; 15:7; 17:29. Such is the judgment of the

---

52. Funk et al., *Five Gospels*.
53. Ibid., 36–37.
54. Robinson et al., *Critical Edition of Q*, lv.

critical scholarship of the Jesus Seminar on Jesus' sayings in Mark and Q about heaven as a transcendental abode of departed spirits/souls.

When the earliest sources about Jesus (Mark and Q) are read critically, it appears from the extant material that Jesus did not share the later Christian hope of heaven as a transcendental abode to which the Christian soul journeys after death. Jesus did, however, anticipate the imminent coming of what he called the "imperial rule of God" (Mark: 10:14, 23, 25; Q: Matt 6:10a/Luke 11:2b; Matt 12:28/Luke 11:20). All of these Markan and Q sayings, when evaluated critically, are affirmed by the Jesus Seminar as originating with Jesus. The imperial rule of God, however, does not appear to be a transcendental abode but rather a reign or rule, in the sense of God's sphere of influence over human life, whether future or present.

It is a naïve mistake to assume that what the church believes is what Jesus believed. Basically people must decide if they will live by the uncritical faith that the New Testament gospels are historically correct in all particulars, or live by an informed reason and logic and make use of the results of nearly 250 years of historical-critical studies of the biblical text.[55] Critical scholars are not always right—true enough! But neither are they always wrong. One must look at the evidence and make informed judgments.

Fortunately we do not have to wonder about the uncertainties of what Paul may have believed; his views can be described from what he himself wrote. How Paul used the word "heaven" (*ouranos*) shows that he clearly understood heaven as a divine realm, the abode of God, Christ, and the angels (Rom 1:18; 10:6; 1 Cor 8:5; 15:47; Gal 1:8; 1 Thess 1:10; 4:16). The view as expressed in these passages is identical to that of the ancient Greek world where heaven or Mount Olympus (or both) was seen as the abode of the Gods.[56] In Paul's view this heavenly abiding place of the divine appears to have been permeable (2 Cor 12:2–4), so perhaps we must think of heaven's lower regions as being open to visitation by other travelers on heavenly journeys as well as by Paul.[57]

Paul described those who shared his religious views as citizens of the commonwealth of heaven (Phil 3:20–21), which is their ultimate eternal home (2 Cor 5:1–4) where they will always be with the Lord (2 Cor

---

55. Schweitzer (*Quest*, 13–26) dates the beginning of critical studies of the historical Jesus from the work of Hermann Samuel Reimarus in 1778.

56. Traub, "οὐρανός," in *TDNT*, 500.

57. Tabor, "Heaven, Ascent to," in *ABD* 3:91–94.

5:6–8; 1 Thess 4:16–17). With respect to the imperial rule of God, in five instances the concept appears to be something that will be realized in the future (1 Cor 6:9; 15:24, 50; Gal 5:21; 1 Thess 2:12), but in two instances it appears to be something related to the present (Rom 14:17; 1 Cor 4:20).

One way Paul's understanding may have differed from popular contemporary views of the Christian heaven is on the state in which the departed soul would experience heaven. The Christian view of heaven today seems to be more Greek than that hope anticipated by Paul. Today, in general, the popular imagination thinks of a person's soul in terms of a disembodied state; the soul is the essential spiritual essence of a person that survives after its body has been discarded. This view is essentially an ancient Greek concept.[58] Paul, however, being Israelite, was more influenced by the Israelite myth of the first human (Adam), who was created as a unified living being (Gen 2:7); hence for Paul a disembodied soul was apparently a strange concept. In Paul's view a person was essentially a living being, and not an embodied spirit/soul. He argued that the dead will again be embodied with an imperishable "spiritual body" (1 Cor 15:35–50; 2 Cor 5:1–5; Phil 3:21), and in that state, one must presume, the believer would experience an eternal home in the heavens.

Another concept in Paul strange to Christian ears today is Paul's association of the hereafter with the liberation of the physical creation (Rom 8:19–23) from its futility (Rom 8:20) and bondage to decay (Rom 8:21), perhaps occasioned mythically by God cursing the ground when Adam and Eve were cast out of the garden (Gen 3:17). Rom 8:19–23 reflects a kind of restoration or renewal of the physical universe, perhaps to its original "very good" state (Gen 1:31).[59] The idea of a "new heavens and a new earth" (Isa 65:17) is shared by other early Christians (2 Pet 3:13; Rev 21:1). Paul, however, has specifically associated this restoration of the physical universe with a discussion of believers awaiting the "redemption of their bodies" (Rom 8:22–23), as the universe awaited its own renewal. The situation of believers who were still alive and consciously awaiting the redemption of their bodies may be equivalent to that of those who have died and were "sleeping" while awaiting the appearance of the Lord (1 Thess 4:13–17). For both the living and the dead awaiting their "glorious bodies" (Phil 3:21) is a kind of interim state between their present reality and the future full realization and completion of their redemption.

58 Rowe, "Soul," in *OCD*, 1428.

59. But compare Michaels, "Redemption of Our Body," who takes *ktisis* to be "creature" rather than "creation."

That timetable does not take into consideration Paul's simplistic statement about being "away from the body and at home with the Lord" (2 Cor 5:8) or the necessity of Christians at some point having to "appear before the judgment seat of Christ" (2 Cor 5:10), but then no one has ever accused Paul of being a consistent thinker. Nevertheless, I am not at all sure what role a restored *physical* universe would play in the completely *spiritual* reality of heaven. But Paul did not elaborate.

In sum, Paul anticipates that at some point after death the believer will be with the Lord in heaven; that experience, however, does not appear to be quite identical to popular ideas of the Christian heaven. (5-10-17; 5-22-17)

§51 PUTTING PAUL IN HIS PLACE[60]

How Christians live out their faith today differs greatly from the earliest communal gatherings to which the modern Christian church traces its roots. The earliest sources providing a clear window into the faith and behavior of the forerunners of the modern church reflect many ideas that seem strange to those whose worldview has been shaped by the Enlightenment, an eighteenth-century current of thought that developed the critical method, rejected the hegemony of Christian belief, and relied on human reason for explaining humanity's place in the universe.

Those of us who from our earliest years have grown up in the traditional Reformation Christianity that established and nourished the growth of Christianity in America have tended to give Paul too much credit as a responsible, creative thinker. This tendency is due to Paul's literary influence in the first-century New Testament canon of Scripture. What the synoptic writers, the author of John, and others did not do, Paul did by conceiving an early institutional framework and conceptual rationale for the Jesus movements, which eventually produced through his later disciples a workable institutional understanding of Jesus the Galilean wisdom teacher. In a sense Paul is the founder of institutional Christianity, although not of the earlier, more freewheeling Jesus movements. My statement about Paul should not be taken to ignore the diversity of the

---

60. This essay first appeared as three separate essays on *Wry Thoughts about Religion*, 5-6-12, 5-22-12, and 6-12-12; they were combined under the present title, and later subsequently published in the *Fourth R* 51/1 (January-February 2018) 5-8, 22; used by permission.

earliest period, but simply to credit Paul for that conceptual foundation for the church that, for good or ill, has survived into the modern period.

Paul knew only a few details of the life of Jesus the Judean man on whom, as the resurrected Christ, he developed his gospel. Nevertheless his linkage of the death of Jesus to the Israelite sacrificial system produced an appealing theological explanation for the death of Jesus that has generally worked well for the church's outreach. For these reasons, at a minimum, readers tend to overlook some of Paul's other less-than-plausible ideas. Paul lived in a prescientific age and could not help being influenced by its antique way of thinking.

The primary sources for the earliest religious gatherings of the Jesus movements are Paul's letters. The letter most revealing of the differences between modern perspectives and Paul's ancient one is his first letter to the "gathering of saints" at Corinth, which is generally dated around 50 CE. In this letter Paul tried to influence their behavior and beliefs with arguments that fitted well into the mythical worldview of the first century, but that sound quite odd in the post-Enlightenment twenty-first century. Here are three examples from 1 Corinthians.

Judging Angels

> When one of you has a grievance against a brother, does he dare go to law before the unrighteous instead of the saints? Do you not know that the saints will judge the world? And if the world is to be judged by you, are you incompetent to try trivial cases? Do you not know that we are to judge angels? How much more matters pertaining to this life! If then you have such cases, why do you lay them before those who are least esteemed by the church? I say this to your shame. Can it be that there is no man among you wise enough to decide among members of the brotherhood, but brother goes to law against brother and that before unbelievers? To have lawsuits at all with one another is defeat for you. Why not suffer wrong? Why not rather be defrauded? But you yourselves wrong and defraud, and that even your own brethren. (1 Cor 6:1–8 RSV)

In this passage Paul is scandalized that members of the community are suing one another in civil courts. In Paul's view this amounts to allowing their cases to be judged by the "unrighteous," rather than bringing their disputes before the members of the community themselves (who were the *agioi*, that is, "holy ones" or saints, 1 Cor 1:2). His rationale is that the holy ones will soon be judging the world; therefore, they are surely competent to try trivial matters, such as personal disputes within the community. Furthermore, they will also judge angels (1 Cor 6:3). And if members of the community are capable of judging supernatural entities like angels, surely they can resolve disputes over ordinary matters of human life. Paul argues that members of the community should not engage in lawsuits with one another at all, and if they cannot resolve their disagreements, they should simply let themselves be defrauded.

The scenario Paul describes in which the world and angels are judged by the Corinthian saints is clearly not an event in normal time and space; it is part of some final end-time drama. So Paul's rationale for shaping the behavior of the Corinthians is based on his own idiosyncratic view of what happens after the world ends. His argument can persuade only those who think he has some unique insight into what will happen at the end of common time and space. (And since Paul was confident that the End would come during his own lifetime [1 Cor 7:29–31], we have every right to be skeptical about his power of prophecy.) But even if one believes what Paul says about angels, the impracticality in the twenty-first century of avoiding civil courts for some sort of "church" tribunal is obvious, as are the personal hazards of subjecting oneself to a religious court. Paul has a higher degree of confidence in the members of the Corinthian fellowship than is warranted, to judge by their behavior reflected in his letter.

Angels are supernatural entities that apparently make up a middle category of sentient beings between humans and Gods. We humans seem to have always believed in such supernatural creatures of a third estate, although with the advent of critical thinking the numbers of people who do are being steadily reduced. In the modern world many of these creatures are recognized as mythical or legendary, meaning that they never really existed except in the dark recesses of our minds. Hundreds of such creatures have been endemic to every culture through time. Here are a few familiar examples: elves, fairies, angels, demons, trolls, gnomes, ogres, water sprites, witches, vampires, satyrs, sileni, unicorns, goblins, pixies, leprechauns, sirens, centaurs, and nymphs. Basically, we invented them to explain what we did not understand. A great number of these supernatural entities are still considered "real," but the truth is that angels, as is the case with demons, can influence your life only if you believe in them.

But if angels do exist, how exactly would one go about judging them? What behavioral criteria apply to supernatural creatures? What constitutes proper and improper behavior for angels? What judicial procedures might govern the court hearings: who prosecutes, who defends, who regulates the course of the trial? I know very little about angels, but I know they are both earlier and later than the Jewish and early Christian period. In the thirteenth century, for example, angels permeated Christian medieval society, and still today in many conservative Christian colleges, angelology is part of the academic curriculum. Belief in angels thrives among those who take the Bible to be literally true.

I am not persuaded by Paul's argument for church tribunals. For one reason, my world is not populated by angels, satyrs, dragons, and unicorns, despite the fact that the Bible describes them as real. For another reason, church tribunals do not offer the same legal protections that are enjoyed in the "pagan" courts.

Spirit Travel or Astral Projection?

> It is actually reported that there is immorality among you, and of a kind that is not found even among pagans; for a man is living with his father's wife. And you are arrogant! Ought you not rather to mourn? Let him who has done this thing be removed from among you. For though absent in body I am present in spirit, and as if present, I have already pronounced judgment in the name of the Lord Jesus on the man who has done such a thing. When you are assembled, and my spirit is present, with the power of our Lord Jesus, you are to deliver this man to Satan for the destruction of the flesh that his spirit may be saved in the day of the Lord Jesus. (1 Cor 5:1–5 RSV)

In this passage Paul addresses what he regards as outrageous immorality in the Corinthian community: a man is cohabiting with his father's wife and the Corinthians are tolerating the arrangement. Paul considers their tolerance an egregious scandal. We are given no further information about the persons involved, who were, of course, well known to the Corinthians, but I note that Paul did not say that the lady was the man's mother, so likely she was a stepmother. It is also likely that the man's father was dead, for if he were alive Paul would surely accuse the man of adultery. The community clearly tolerates the relationship, but Paul considers it a moral outrage. Why? Most likely because Paul's moral sensitivities are grounded in the Torah, which prohibits a man from marrying a woman who had formerly been his father's wife (Lev 18:8). Paul urges the community to expel the man.

Paul says (1 Cor 5:3): "For though absent in body I am present in spirit, and as present [not "*as if* present"] I have already pronounced judgment." (Compare this to a similar statement that does not create the same difficulties: "Though I am absent in body, yet I am with you in spirit" [Col 2:5].) Paul directed that when the community was assembled "and my spirit is present with the power of our Lord Jesus," the man should be delivered "to Satan for the destruction of the flesh so that his spirit may be saved" (1 Cor 5:4-5). This latter statement clearly presupposes that human beings are comprised of a separate spirit/soul inhabiting a physical body, a quintessential Greek concept.[61] Conventional scholarship, however, maintains that Paul thought of humans the way the Hebrew Bible does: as unified living beings (see Gen 2:7).[62]

How might Paul have conceived of his own spirit "being present" although his body was absent? He says it twice (5:3-4). The temptation is to think that Paul has just been careless in his language, and that he meant to say something like the following: when you assemble and think like me about this situation (i.e., in this way I am psychologically present in spirit), you will pass judgment on this fellow (as I have already done), and deliver him over to Satan—an odd way of stating (what he probably means) that the man should be expelled from the community. The New International Version and Today's English Version ignore the difficulty posed by the Greek text, and make Paul's statement completely innocuous: "Even though I am not physically present, I am with you in spirit, and have already passed judgment ... just as if I were present." The Scholars Version also avoids the problem by translating what in Greek literally means "I am present in spirit" as "I am truly present."

One respected commentator, however, recognizes the oddity of the Greek text and thinks Paul's presence in spirit has to do with unity in the Spirit: that is to say, the belief that when the community is assembled, the Holy Spirit is present among them. "For Paul that means that he too is present among them by that same Spirit" (which is still an odd idea).[63] Gordon Fee cautions, however, "We must nonetheless not try to make

---

61. Annas, "Plato," in *OCD*, 1192-93.
62. Sumney, "Anthropology, NT Theological," in *NIDB*, 169-70.
63. Fee, *First Epistle to the Corinthians*, 205.

Paul think or talk like us." An excellent caveat! No one really knows what Paul thought. Paul's statement on its surface actually sounds like some kind of spirit travel.

Spirit travel was a familiar concept in antiquity, and Paul clearly refers to it in 2 Cor 12:1–4: "I know a person . . . who was caught up into the third heaven" (three heavens?—how odd!). Heavenly journeys are amply attested in ancient texts.[64] Here are a few references in the Bible related to the odd idea of spirit travel.

- John was "in the Spirit on the Lord's Day" (Rev 1:10; 4:1–2), and he says that an angel "carried me away in the Spirit" (17:3; 21:10).
- Ezekiel also was carried away by the Spirit from Babylon to Jerusalem (Ezek 2:12–15 and 8:3; see also 11:24–25; 37:1; 40:2).
- After the baptism of the Ethiopian eunuch, the Spirit caught up the apostle Philip (physically?) and transported him several miles to the city of Azotus (Act 8:39–40).
- Spirit travel is also referred to in 1 Kgs 18:12, when Elijah tells a friend, "As soon as I have gone from you, the spirit of Yahweh will carry you I know not where."
- In Bel and the Dragon verses 33–36 (which Jews and Protestants do not consider canonical), an angel takes the prophet Habakkuk by the hair and carries him to Babylon, in order to deliver food to Daniel in the lion's den.

These observations on 1 Corinthians chapter 5 have taken an odd turn by evoking such ideas as astral projection and out-of-body experiences. I am more than skeptical about such things, although a great deal has been written about them. It is difficult to know what to make of Paul's statements in 1 Cor 5:3–4. Is he thinking of an ecstatic experience, like John's in the Apocalypse, or perhaps more substantively like Ezekiel's? Did Paul think perhaps that he could be present with the Corinthians when he was in an ecstatic state? Or did he think of a divided spirit, part of which travels and part of which inhabits his body? (I assume that the body needs its spirit/soul force in order to remain alive.) But if part of one's spirit does travel, neither the spirit particle in transit nor the deficient part left behind can be thought of as an individual's complete spirit; a divided spirit is something other than the usual condition of one's spirit

---

64. Tabor, "Heaven, Ascent to."

at rest in the body, it seems to me. Perhaps Paul is thinking of a "spirit twin" that could be projected at will?

This passage requires a strange way of thinking in a post-Enlightenment world, and it is little wonder that twenty-first-century folk, who are heirs of the Enlightenment, might have difficulty with the odd ideas in it.

Are Holiness and Unholiness Contagious?

In discussing the problem of interfaith marriage with the Corinthians Paul expresses another rather strange idea: "The unbelieving husband is made holy through his [believing] wife and the unbelieving wife is made holy through her [believing] husband. Otherwise your children would be unclean, but as it is they are holy" (1 Cor 7:14). To "make something holy" is technical language normally used in discussions of ritual requirements, where it means to render something suitable for ritual purposes. Paul uses the same language describing his gathering of saints at Corinth; they are made holy, or sanctified (1 Cor 1:2; 6:11) and hence are "holy ones," set apart for the Lord's service.

The word "unclean" describes something that renders one unsuitable to stand before the presence of God or to be a part of the covenant community (see Num 19). Moses sets forth purity codes enumerating things and people that are considered unclean (see Lev 15; Mark 7:14–23; Acts 10:9–35). This formal language of ritual impurity or uncleanness is carried over into the ethical sphere, where sin renders one unclean before God, and hence disqualifies the sinner from serving God (see Isa 7:1–10; Ps 24:3–4).

Paul's statement affirms that parents pass to their children the condition of either unholiness or holiness. A child born to an interfaith couple is rendered holy because the holiness of the believing parent trumps the unholiness of the unbelieving parent, and the child is born undefiled or "clean." Hence Paul seems to conceive of some kind of religious contagion, an essence of holiness or unholiness that is actually transmitted from parent to child. In the case of interfaith marriage, holiness is more powerful than unholiness (see also Rom 11:16).

Compare this to the opposite argument about interfaith marriage in 2 Cor 6:14—7:1. (This segment is probably a non-Pauline insertion into the letter.[65]) This passage rejects interfaith marriage out of hand and

---

65. Dewey, et al., trans., *Authentic Letters*, 148.

suggests that marriage to unbelievers will defile the holy character of the believer. In this passage the unholiness of the unbelieving partner compromises the holiness of the believer.

Paul applies the same logic when addressing the case of male members of the Corinthian community who visit prostitutes (1 Cor 6:15–20). He argues that coitus with a prostitute compromises a brother's holiness; for sexual intercourse with a prostitute makes them both "one body," and defiles the believer's body, which is an extension of Christ (1 Cor 6:15). In other words the contagion passes from the prostitute and corrupts the holiness of the brother. In the case of coitus with a prostitute unholiness is more powerful than holiness (1 Cor 5:6–7).

Ritual defilement, the idea that a state of holiness or unholiness can be communicated to things or people, is an ancient idea that survives in the modern Western world in only rare instances. Hence, the tendency seems to be for translators to select translation language for this verse that does not readily betray the blatant ritual defilement language that comes across so strongly in the Greek text. Their translations attempt to domesticate the ancient worldview reflected in what Paul wrote. For the most part modern human beings in the Western world do not function in their daily lives with the idea that religious defilement can be inherited or transmitted by physical contact with persons or things. But Paul apparently did.

Here are a few modern translations showing how translators handled the offensive ritual defilement language in 1 Cor 7:14:

- The unbelieving spouse "is consecrated" through the believing one, otherwise the children would be "unclean," but now they are "holy" (RSV).

- The unbelieving spouse is "made holy" through the believing one, otherwise the children would be "unclean," but now they are "holy" (NRSV).

- The unbelieving spouse "is consecrated" through the believing one, otherwise the children would be "unblest," but now they are "are consecrated" (Smith-Goodspeed).

- The unbelieving spouse "is consecrated" through the believing one, otherwise the children would be "unholy," but now they are "consecrated to God" (Moffatt).

- The unbelieving spouse "is sanctified" through the believing one, otherwise the children would be "unclean," but now they are "holy" (NIV).
- The "Heathen" spouse "now belongs to God through" the "Christian" spouse, otherwise the children "would not belong to God, whereas in fact they do" (NEB).
- The unbelieving spouse "is made acceptable to God" through the believing one, otherwise the children would be "pagan," but "as it is, they are acceptable to God" (GNB).
- The "non-believing" spouse "is dedicated" through the believing one, otherwise the children would be "unholy," but now "they are dedicated" (Berkeley Version).
- The unbelieving spouse "is, in a sense, consecrated" through the believing one; "if this is not so, children would bear stains of paganism whereas they are actually consecrated to God" (Phillips).
- The "non-Christian" spouse "may become Christian with help of Christian spouse"; otherwise "if family separates, the children might never come to know the Lord." "A united family may, in God's plan, result in the children's salvation" (LB).
- The non-believing spouse "has been spiritually set apart from the world" because of the believing spouse. "Otherwise your children would be contaminated by the world, but now they are spiritually set apart" (CEB).

Clearly many things may be inherited from parents or transmitted from prostitutes, but religious defilement is not one of them. Paul's ideas are survivals of a prescientific way of thinking that engaged the natural world in terms of unseen spirit realities. Having lived as he did some fifteen centuries before the advent of modern science, he could not help sharing the ancient worldview of his day.

It is not surprising that some of Paul's ideas sound strange to those of us who have lived into the twenty-first century. They belong to a pre-critical worldview, and serve as vivid reminders that the Bible does not belong to our age. One may use the Bible for ethical, moral, and religious guidance should one choose, but the task of interpreting the Bible for guidance demands that one must always respect its integrity as an ancient text, and not conceal features that do not conform to a modern worldview. Truth be told: Paul's place lies in our past as the innovator of a new faith not in the present as an arbiter of ethical behavior. (5–6–12; 5–22–12; 6–12–12)

§52 SEX AND DEATH: PAUL'S ARGUMENTS FROM MYTHOLOGY

Despite the extremely negative associations of the term *myth* in the New Testament, early followers of Jesus, like virtually all people who try to make sense of their religious beliefs, made use of the accepted myths of their culture as they worked to understand how their new faith affected their lives. Here are two instances of Paul drawing on the Mediterranean myth of an original man who was fashioned by God, a myth that crystallized for Israelites in the story in Gen 2–3.

In Rom 5:12–21 Paul asserts that all people are sinners because the sin of the original man (Gen 3:1–13) passed onto the entire human race, which is the reason that all people die (Gen 2:17; 3:19; Rom 5:12). The notion that Adam passed his sin on to his descendants seems to be Paul's application of the principle set in Torah that God held descendants culpable for the sins of their father to the third and fourth generation (Exod 20:5). Hence, an act in mythical space and time before the beginning of historical time explains why people are sinners and why they die.

In a second example (1 Cor 6:12–20) Paul again draws on the Mediterranean myth of the first man, arguing that an act of coitus with a prostitute establishes an essential physical relationship with her; they in fact become "one body." To support his rationale he again quotes scripture appealing to the myth of the first man and his consort (Gen 2:23–24) of whom it is written "they shall become one flesh." In other words, as it happened in mythical space and time between the first couple Adam and Eve, so it is in historical space and time between a man and a prostitute. Coitus is not simply a casual physical moment between men and women; it is a deed that effectively alters the physical composition of the male body/flesh, for the female prostitute is incorporated as part of the male body (Gen 2:23), and the two are essentially one; so Paul argues. It is important to note that Paul's argument is not based on "Scripture," which only informs him of the myth. His argument turns on what putatively "happened" in the case of the mythical man Adam. It was the "event" (so to speak) and not the later writing about it that is authoritative for Paul's argument. The mythical man, Adam, was fashioned by the divine creator as male/female and then s/he was divided into different genders (Gen 2:18-23). Subsequently the "union" between a man and his mate restores the original state of the first man, Adam (Gen 2:24): the two become one flesh. (11-15-16)

§53 AN ALLUSION IN SEARCH OF A NARRATIVE: BETRAYING JESUS

The tradition about Judas Iscariot, the betrayer of Jesus, may be a simple case of early Christian creative fiction. The earliest mention of a betrayal of Jesus comes in a liturgical text from Paul's letters associating "the night on which [Jesus] was betrayed" with the Eucharistic celebration (1 Cor 11:23-25). No further description is given, and no betrayer is named. Paul did not know the stories about Judas's betrayal of Jesus in the early Christian gospels, which in his day had not yet been written. Paul's passing allusion to a cryptic betrayal was a mystery in search of a narrative to clarify it.

A generation or so later (around 70 CE), Mark's Passion Narrative (chaps. 14-16) begins with a plot by the chief priests and scribes to arrest Jesus "by stealth" for they were afraid of starting a riot (Mark 14:1-2). One assumes their fear derived from the popularity of Jesus with the crowds (Mark 11:18-19). Judas Iscariot is portrayed as an insider in Jesus' circle who offered "to betray him," and the chief priests offered him an unstated amount of money for the service (Mark 14:10-12). What was being betrayed is unclear. One assumes that Judas promised to disclose a place where Jesus could be arrested away from the crowds, for it happened that way (Mark 14:32-50). Judas came with a rabble organized "by the chief priests, scribes and elders," to Gethsemane and betrayed Jesus with a kiss. Jesus, however, was a public figure, and his whereabouts were clearly known (Mark 11:15—13:1), as Jesus himself complained at his arrest (Mark 14:49), alluding mysteriously to an unnamed "scripture" being "fulfilled." It strains credulity to think that Jesus' whereabouts out of the public eye could not easily have been known by the authorities without the aid of an informer. Judas's motives are unknown. He asked for nothing, although the priests on their initiative promised him an unspecified amount of money. What happened to Judas is also unknown. Mark apparently lost interest in continuing that aspect of his story.

Sometime after Mark was written, the Judas tradition underwent significant developments. In Matthew the chief priests and elders plot to apprehend Jesus "and kill him" (Matt 26:3-4). Judas volunteers to betray Jesus, asking for an unspecified consideration in return: "What will you give me if I deliver him to you?" (Matt 26:14-15), and they pay him "thirty pieces of silver." Matthew, prompted by what he regarded as a "prophecy," has turned Mark's unstated amount of money into "thirty pieces of silver" (Zech 11:12; cf. Exod 21:32), as the "prophecy" foretold. Judas comes with a rabble organized by the chief priests and elders to Gethsemane, and betrays Jesus with a kiss (Matt 26:47-50). Later, conscience-stricken, Judas repents, returns the thirty pieces of silver to the temple, and hangs himself (Matt 27:3-5). The chief priests, regarding the thirty pieces of silver as "blood money," purchase a potter's field, which according to Matthew, fulfills a prophecy (Matt 27:7-10) in Zech 11:13 (not in Jeremiah, as Matthew states). In linking the figure of Judas to the Zechariah passage, Matthew makes an unfortunate association between Judas the betrayer of Jesus and the good shepherd of Zech 11.

Sometime later, unaware of Matthew's narrative, Luke described Judas as the "pawn" of Satan. Under the influence of an evil power, Judas did not come to the chief priests and scribes seeking money (Matt 22:3-6) but simply offered to betray Jesus because Satan had "entered into" him (Luke 22:3). He was given money, but that was not his motive (Luke 22:4-6). His motive was not rational; rather it was demon inspired. Judas then led the crowd to the Mount of Olives, and among them were officers of the temple, chief priests, and elders (Luke 22:39, 47-54). Luke completes the story of Judas in his second volume (Acts). Under the influence of what Luke regards as "prophecies" (Pss 69:26; 109:8), he describes the death of Judas (Acts 1:16-20) as falling, "bursting open in the middle," so that his bowels gushed out.

At the end of the first century in John's story about Jesus there is no mention of money changing hands for information. Judas has become the helpless puppet of the devil; Jesus knew ahead of time what Judas would do (John 13:11) and described him as a devil (John 6:70-71), not simply "demon possessed," as Luke does. John cites a "prophecy" about a specific act of betrayal (Ps 41:10), apparently unknown to the other evangelists. The character of Judas is castigated as only pretending to be interested in the plight of the poor, for he was a thief (John 12:4-8) who betrayed his friends by taking money from the group's money box (John 12:6; 13:29). Twice it is said of Judas that the devil put it into his heart to betray Jesus (John 13:2, 27). While the chief priests and Pharisees wanted to kill Jesus (John 11:47–53), there was no collusion between Judas and the priests to accomplish it. Judas, prompted by Jesus (John 13:27), procures a "band of soldiers" (John 18:2–3) and leads the band of soldiers with their captain and officers of the Judeans to a garden to seize Jesus (John 18:1–12). Judas's eventual fate is not described in John.

The Pauline allusion to an ambiguous betrayal had found four different narratives in a half century:

1. a dubious idea that an insider provided unnecessary information in exchange for financial considerations, shaped by figurative readings of unstated "scriptures" (Mark)
2. an enhancement of Mark's narrative, shaped by figurative interpretations ("prophecies") of the Hebrew Bible (Matthew)
3. an enhancement of Mark's narrative, attributing the betrayal to demonic possession and shaped by figurative interpretations ("prophecies") of the Hebrew Bible (Luke)
4. a mythical narrative of the transmogrification of Judas into a devil, shaped by figurative interpretations ("prophecies") of the Hebrew Bible (John)

Where is the history in these imaginative fictions? All four are clearly shaped by early Christian hermeneutic. In Luke and John the betrayal is accomplished by the superstition (the ancient prescientific worldview) that the world is inhabited by demons. Mark's depiction of Jesus as a public figure is a serious obstacle to the idea that an informer is even necessary. (11-1-13)

§54 NARRATIVE REALISM IN THE GOSPELS

Reality, that is to say the way things are "out there all around us," is not directly apprehended by the mind. Things "out there" are communicated to the mind indirectly through the senses (seeing, hearing, touching, tasting, and smelling). The mind processes what information the senses provide and deduces the situation "out there" as best it can from the data it receives. Thus, the reality that each individual perceives "out there" in society and nature is unique to the individual.

Narratives also reflect a "narrative realism," which is the reality effect authors produce for readers, whether they intend it or not. At least five kinds of narrative realism have been used in Western literature; they are fantasy realism, mythical realism, romantic realism, fictional realism, and historical realism.

Romantic realism describes the activities of superhuman beings in a supernatural world. It portrays characters like us, only much better than we are in every way, in a space similar to ours, in a time of marvels.[66] In such a world the ordinary rules of nature are suspended, and the extraordinary regularly occurs. The early Christian gospels reflect similar features. They portray a narrative realism that is akin to the King Arthur legends and Harry Potter tales, and hence fit better into the category of romantic realism than into the category of historical realism. Historical realism, on the other hand, portrays what has actually happened in common space and time, as it can be reconstructed on the basis of empirical evidence. The subject of historical narrative is real people and actual events portrayed in terms of natural cause and effect.[67]

That the early Christian gospels correspond to a realism best described as romantic implies that their realism is due to how the evangelists actually perceived reality or chose to portray it, which is the case with any author. The circumstances of Jesus' career, however, are not necessarily identical with the evangelists' perceptions of it. For example, Mark, Matthew, and Luke portray Jesus performing exorcisms, but John does not perceive Jesus as an exorcist, and has no exorcisms. It is true that historical narrative is whatever historians and literary critics say it is, but that statement is actually a caveat, a warning to historians that they should not be overly confident in their reconstructions of history, since it is only a reconstruction, and others may reconstruct things differently.

The early Christian gospels are not "history" in the sense of what was actually lived; they are only particular reconstructions of history. History itself is the aggregate of the lived past; that is to say, history is composed of all the billions of things that have ever happened in the past—significant and insignificant, public and private, natural and arranged, remembered and forgotten, personal and impersonal, seemly and unseemly. Narratives about the lived past (or selected aspects of it), on the other hand, are attempts at reconstructing the lived past, never in its aggregate totality

---

66. Hedrick, "Realism in Western Narrative," 352–53.
67. Ibid., 354–55.

but in what the historian considers the more significant moments or aspects of it. Hence history is different from historical narrative. The reality that was the moment as it was actually lived can never be recaptured, but its scattered bones (individual artifacts and memories) can be gathered, catalogued, and analyzed. From these vestiges of the past the historian aims to revive a given "lived moment" by making connections between the bits of data and imagining how things might have played themselves out given the data at the historian's disposal. Thus the historian attempts to codify the lived past into a reconstructed historical narrative. But a reconstructed historical narrative is no more "history" than a corpse is a human being.[68]

Thinking of history as lived past and historical narrative as later reconstruction may actually free us from the idea that Jesus' "lived past" is what the evangelists said it was. The widely differing reconstructions of Jesus by modern scholars graphically illustrate the shortcomings of the early Christian gospels as historical sources.[69] It is not simply a case of one is right and the others wrong; but that the sources themselves are simply flawed and cannot be trusted.[70] (4-15-14)

§55 DID JOHN BAPTIZE JESUS?[71]

The clear consensus of contemporary scholarship is that the baptism of Jesus by John is virtually historically certain! The Jesus Seminar printed Mark 1:9 in dramatic red in *The Acts of Jesus*, with the comment that few Fellows of the Jesus Seminar doubted that John baptized Jesus.[72] Here are some comments by a few scholars expressing the confidence they feel in the baptism of Jesus by John as historical event: "historically certain" (Lars Hartman);[73] "one should not doubt the baptism" (Dale Allison);[74]

---

68. See §56, below.
69. For example, see the discussion in Hedrick, *Wisdom of Jesus*, 164–78.
70. This essay is slightly adapted from Hedrick, *Wisdom of Jesus*, 195–96, used by permission.
71. See §49, above, for a related discussion.
72. The color "red indicates that the Fellows had a relatively high level of confidence that the event actually took place" (Funk and the Jesus Seminar, *Acts of Jesus*, 1 and 54).
73. Hartmann, "Baptism," 584.
74. Allison, "Jesus Christ," 271.

"one of the firmest elements of the Jesus story" (Craig Evans);[75] "as historically certain as anything in the gospels" (Bart Ehrman);[76] "almost beyond dispute" (E. P. Sanders);[77] "a basic historical fact" (Gerd Theissen).[78] One finds many similar statements in critical literature.

Of course, not everyone agrees. The baptism of Jesus by John is described as myth by Burton Mack[79] and Martin Dibelius.[80] (Myths are stories about Gods in a time and place not recognizable as our own time; hence they are not critical history.) Rudolf Bultmann, probably the most influential New Testament scholar in the twentieth century, described it as a Christian legend about Jesus that emerged in the later Hellenistic church.[81] (A legend is a story about holy people and religious heroes intended to be read for inspiration, instruction, and spiritual edification; hence it is not critical history.) One can understand their reluctance to regard the story as a historical event. Mark 1:9-11 clearly has the trappings of myth, legend, or both: Jesus saw the heavens split asunder, and he saw the Spirit descending; and a voice came out of heaven addressing him, "you are my beloved son." Was it a vision and only available to Jesus? (Compare Matt 3:17 where the voice addresses the bystanders.) Did such events actually occur? In truth, these kinds of happenings are not part of our common, everyday world.

What is the evidence for John baptizing Jesus? Those who regard the baptism as historically certain are most persuaded by the criterion of embarrassment: that is to say, since it would cause the church a great deal of embarrassment to admit that Jesus was once the disciple of John the Baptist, it is hardly something that the church would have invented. Those who doubt that the baptism is historically certain raise a number of objections to its historicity. The obvious mythical/legendary character of Mark 1:9-11 for one. For another, the baptism of Jesus appears indisputably in only one late source (i.e., after 70 CE): Mark 1:9-11. In Matthew John has some discomfort with the idea that he baptize Jesus, and Matthew never in so many words describes John as baptizing Jesus

---

75. Evans, "John," 349.
76. Ehrman, *Jesus*, 100-101.
77. Sanders, *Historical Figure of Jesus*, 10-11.
78. Theissen and Merz, *Historical Jesus*, 207.
79. Mack, *Myth*, 54-55.
80. Dibelius, *Tradition to Gospel*, 271, 274.
81. Bultmann, *History of the Synoptic Tradition*, 244-53.

(Matt 3:13-17). In Luke John is put in prison before Jesus is baptized (Luke 3:18-22), and the baptism is not described specifically as a baptism by John; in the Gospel of John, the Baptist only *observes* a spirit baptism of Jesus (that is, it is not a water baptism, John 1:29-34). The reluctance of Matthew, Luke, and John to depict Jesus as being baptized by John upon the confession of his sins is seen as evidence for the criterion of embarrassment (Mark 1:4-5). But that criterion works as easily for the church in the later first century as it has been claimed for the early first century.

There is no evidence, however, that Paul knew of the baptism of Jesus by John, and early Christian baptism is not linked to the baptism of Jesus. The baptism of Jesus, according to Q scholars, is not found in Q (a sayings collection thought to have been used by Matthew and Luke as a source for their gospels), and Josephus does not know a tradition of John baptizing Jesus. Only one source in the latter half of the first century attests to the event: Mark 1:9-11.

Whence then comes the supreme confidence that contemporary scholars have that John's baptism of Jesus is historically certain? Likely they must be assuming that an incipient oral pre-Pauline Palestinian tradition of Mark 1:9-11 existed in some form prior to 70 CE. That might possibly have been true, but there is no evidence of such a tradition, and hence such a "hail Mary" argument is not probable, much less certain.

Bultmann did not address whether or not a kernel of history lies behind the legend of Mark 1:9-11. But in describing it as a Christian legend that arose in the Hellenistic church, and in ruling out any chance that the legend was already circulating in the Palestinian church, Bultmann seems to have made a de facto decision, which is that the baptism of Jesus by John as Mark 1:9-11 presents it is clearly not historically certain; perhaps it never even happened.[82] (7-8-15)

§56 HISTORY, HISTORICAL NARRATIVE, AND MARK'S GOSPEL

I begin at the beginning: what is the definition of *history*? The definitions of *history* in the *Random House College Dictionary* read as follows: history is:

1. "the branch of knowledge dealing with past events";

---

82. I have subsequently discussed the subject addressed here and in §49, above, in the following essay: "Is the Baptism of Jesus by John Historically Certain?," 311-22.

2. "a continuous systematic narrative of past events as relating to a particular people, country, period, person, etc., usually written in chronological order";
3. "the aggregate of past events"; and
4. "the record of past events, especially in connection with the human race."

Basically these definitions break down into three ways of viewing history: it is a branch of scientific inquiry; it is everything that happened in the past; it is a narrative reconstructing what happened in the past. Webster's *Third International Dictionary* (unabridged) agrees with these three ways of defining *history* but in its listing of options gives precedence to the idea that history is a narrative of events or a systematic written account comprising a chronological record. In my view the idea that history is principally a narrative of past events can threaten the independent reality of the lived past.

At a recent conference of the Society of Biblical Literature one panel speaker claimed: "History is only available in narrative." I objected, claiming that history is a reality in its own right completely apart from all historical narratives. Narratives change as new information and insights become available, but the lived reality that was history is what it was, whether we can recover it or not.

History is all the millions and billions of things that have ever happened in the past—significant and insignificant, public and private, natural and arranged, remembered and forgotten, personal and impersonal, seemly and unseemly. Narratives about that aggregate of the lived past are attempts to reconstruct it—not in its aggregate totality but in what the historian considers its more significant aspects.[83]

Bits and pieces of the aggregate that was the historical past actually survive apart from the historical narrative in the residue, artifacts, residua, and relics of the past. These odds and ends are the residue of the raw data of history, remainders of a lived past before it was codified into the Master Narrative of a particular reconstructed history. For example, remainders of the lived past of the Battle of Gettysburg survive in such things as official lists of the dead and wounded, anecdotal reports of the battle from observers or participants, military dispatches, photos, maps, prisoner lists, scattered equipment from the battlefield, and so forth.

---

83. See §54, above.

Historians rely on these bits and pieces of the lived past as well as on their imaginations to fill in gaps in the data.

History itself is something far different from historical narrative. History consists in billions of events themselves as played out at the time. They are momentarily present but then immediately become part of the lived past. The reality that was the living moment as it was actually lived can never be recaptured, but its scattered bones (artifacts and memories) can be gathered, catalogued, and analyzed. The historian aims to revive a given living moment by making connections between bits of data and imagining how things might have played themselves out given the data at the historian's disposal. Thus the historian codifies the lived past into historical narrative. But a given historical narrative is no more "history" than a corpse is a human being.

A narrative cannot be historical if it is not informed by the residua of the lived past. And hence a historical narrative cannot be "history" as such, but it is only an attempt at reconstructing the lived past through its residua. A narrative about the lived past is historically reliable as a reconstruction only to the extent that it conforms to the residua of the lived past, and only to the extent that the historian's imagination corresponds to a critical sense of what is actually real.

This way of looking at history and historical narrative has significant implications for the historical character of the Gospel of Mark, our earliest gospel in the view of a majority of modern scholars. No residua of the lived past informs Mark's narrative except unconfirmed oral reports, which scholars assume that Mark had at hand when composing the narrative. Mark's imaginative composition of the story, however, does not conform to a modern critical sense of what is real, or even to that represented by the finest history writing of the ancient past, such as is represented, for example, by Thucydides in his *History of the Peloponnesian War* (fifth century BCE). Mark's narrative turns out to be pious historical fiction written for the purpose of informing readers about the origins of the gospel (Mark 1:1) preached by the Markan community in the latter half of the first century.

Many contemporary scholars, however, routinely treat Mark as if the narrative and the lived past are as Mark imagined it; in other words what Mark says happened—actually happened that way. Thinking of history as lived past and historical narrative as an attempt to reconstruct that lived past puts Mark in its place as a questionable reconstruction of the events of the lived past of Galilee and Judea in the first third of the first century. (12–22–13)

§57 THE PROBLEM OF HISTORY IN MARK

One hallmark of narrative fiction, which distinguishes the writing of fiction from the writing of history, is the novelist's ability to move in and out of a character's mind and to tell readers what a character is thinking. This shift in a reader's point of view from seeing events from the narrator's perspective to seeing the situation from within a paper-character's mind is a primary feature of the rhetoric of fiction by which a flesh-and-blood author develops characters and furthers the plot of a novel.[84] Modern historians, on the other hand, work with theories of what constitutes the chronology of past events; in doing so they are obligated to reconstruct their historical plan by a plausible cause-and-effect sequence. They do not have the luxury of appealing to what a participant in an event was thinking at the time in order to further their reconstruction of events. Historians cannot read the minds of flesh-and-blood people who were involved in past historical events; it is easy, on the other hand, for novelists to read the minds of the characters they invent.

The author of the Gospel of Mark makes extensive use of interior views of a character's thoughts; two of Mark's characters even read the thoughts of other paper-characters in the narrative: Jesus (2:5, 8; 12:15); Pilate (15:10).

A technique the author uses repeatedly throughout the narrative is the feature of characters or groups of characters registering "astonishment" at the presence of Jesus, at something he has said, or at something he has done (1:27; 2:12; 5:42; 6:51; 7:37; 9:15; 10:26, 32; 11:18; 12:17). Mark also employs this technique with the young man at the empty tomb (16:5, 8). When one is astonished, one is struck with sudden great wonder and surprise. Astonishment is an inner emotional response to some exterior element and reveals what is going on in the mind of the character. Providing interior views of characters is more prevalent among primitive storytellers, but modern fiction writers are artistically more self-conscious and use a variety of techniques.[85]

---

84. Booth, *Rhetoric of Fiction*, 16–20.
85. Arp and Johnson, *Perrine's Literature*, 238.

Mark uses the technique excessively, providing access to the inner thoughts of individuals and groups throughout the narrative: Jesus (1:41; 5:30; 6:6, 34; 8:12; 10:14, 21; 11:12; 12:15; 14:33), the scribes (2:6), the disciples (4:41; 6:51–52; 10:41), minor characters (5:29; 14:4; 16:8), Herod (6:20, 26); Peter (9:6; 11:21; 14:72); chief priests and scribes (11:18); chief priests, priests, scribes and elders (11:32; 12:12), David (12:36), Pilate (15:5, 15, 44), Joseph (15:43).

The most extensive instance of the use of an interior view is in the case of Jesus' tortured prayer in Gethsemane (14:34–36) in which he seeks a reprieve from the crucifixion. It is possibly the most realistic moment in the narrative, but oddly it was not information available to Mark from an outside source.

These interior views Mark provides to readers are not traditional lore passed forward over time to the author orally by participants in the actual events. How could anyone have known, for example, what Herod "felt" (6:20, fear; 6:26, sorrow) unless Herod specifically told them? And the prayer of Jesus in Gethsemane may have even been an audible prayer, but Mark clearly rules out the possibility that it was overheard; Jesus was alone, and Peter, James, and John were asleep (14:34–41); hence it becomes an interior view. The interior views can only be accounted for as Mark's literary creations. It might very well be true, for example, that Joseph "gathered his courage" (i.e., had mental or moral strength) in going to Pilate (16:43), but it is not historical data. The observation only represents how Mark wanted readers to regard his paper-character Joseph in the situation presented in the story.

What should one then say about the Gospel of Mark as historical narration, in light of the fact that Mark uses the conventions and literary techniques of novelistic fiction? Several years ago, I argued that Mark's realism (i.e., how Mark views objective reality) is more akin to literary works portraying a romantic realism (i.e., to works relatively free of realistic verisimilitude) than it is to historical realism.[86] Mark's pronounced tendency to inform readers what characters are thinking in his narrative lacks verisimilitude (i.e., lacks in the appearance of truth), because no one can actually read minds, and know precisely what others are thinking—except omniscient narrators who invent characters and have absolute control of events in the novel. Mark appears to be such an omniscient

---

86. Hedrick, "Realism in Western Narrative."

narrator. That is, Mark knows everything, even what his characters in the narrative are thinking.

How should a reader then regard Mark's reconstruction of the dialogue in the scene where Jesus appears before the High Priest (14:55–65)? Should the dialogue be regarded as what was actually said? Or did Mark, the omniscient narrator, create it as dialogue that readers might expect in that situation? Mark's use of the rhetorical features of narrative fiction does not encourage one to regard the scene as history. (10–1–16)

§58 TWO ODD LOCUTIONS IN THE GOSPEL OF MARK

There are other statements in Mark's Gospel that strike me as odd (that is: peculiar, strange, or unexpected), but these two locutions are markedly so. New Testament scholars in general have come to rely on Mark as the earliest gospel; at least that Matthew and Luke wrote their gospels relying on Mark as a source seems to be the general consensus. Luke even noted many had tried their hand at "compiling a narrative" of the doings and sayings of Jesus; if so s/he apparently accepted Mark's narrative as the most acceptable of the "many" who wrote (Luke 1:1), and yet Luke frequently edits out and changes much of Mark's narrative.

The first locution is Mark's obvious exaggeration about John the Baptizer's success with the population of Judea. An exaggeration is a political statement; it is not a historical statement:

> And there were going out to him all the region of Judea, and all the people of Jerusalem; and they were being baptized by him in the river Jordan confessing their sins (Mark 1:5; see also 1:28, 33).

In the time of Jesus the "region/country" of Judea incorporated the area around Jerusalem extending northward to about the valley of Aijalon and southward to Masada, and included eight to ten villages. The population of the city of Jerusalem during the time of Jesus has been estimated at an upper limit of around twenty-five thousand to thirty thousand.[87] Even if the population of Jerusalem were only half this number, it is simply not credible that *every single person* in the city and all the villages in the region of Judea were going out, and eventually being baptized by John. Luke eliminates Mark 1:5, but Matthew (3:5) repeats the exaggeration with a slight modification.

87. Jeremias, *Jerusalem*, 84.

Mark borders on another unfortunate exaggeration when he writes: "And [Jesus] could do no mighty work there," but avoids the exaggeration by adding: "except that he laid his hands upon a few sick people and healed them" (6:5; see Matt 13:58 for a more carefully worded statement).

Several translators have completely removed Mark's exaggeration (1:5) in their translations:

- From all Judea and Jerusalem crowds of people went to John (TEV)
- And they flocked to him from the whole Judean country-side and the city of Jerusalem (NEB)
- People from Jerusalem and from all over Judea traveled out into the Judean waste-lands to see and hear John (LB)

A second locution is found in Mark 4:36. The sentence is ambiguous, rendering it difficult to translate. To illustrate the problem, here is my literal translation, which follows the Greek word order, with the unclear statement in italics; it is followed by several other translations:

- And leaving the crowd they take him *as he was* in the boat (Hedrick)
- And leaving the crowd, they took him with them in the boat, *just as he was* (RSV)
- So leaving the crowd, they took him (*just as he was*) in the boat (Moffatt)
- Leaving the crowd behind, they took him along, *just as he was*, in the boat (NIV)
- So they left the crowd and took him with them in the boat where he had been sitting (NEB)
- So they left the crowd and took him away in the boat in which he was sitting (Smith-Goodspeed)
- And when they had sent away the multitude, they took Him along in the boat *as He was* (NKJ)
- And sending away the multitude, they take him *even as he was* in the ship (Douay)
- So they left the crowd, and his disciples started across the lake with him in the boat (TEV)

Translators have taken the odd locution to refer either to Jesus already being in the boat (see Mark 4:2), or to the appearance or condition of Jesus (*as he was*: NKJ; or *just/even as he was*: NIV, Moffatt, Douay). Smith-Goodspeed and NEB use words other than Mark's in their translation. And TEV simply eliminates the obscure phrase. Both Luke and Matthew resolve Mark's lack of clarity by having Jesus get into the boat with the disciples when they leave, and thus eliminate the obscure phrase *as he was* (Matt 8:23; Luke 8:22).

The larger issue raised by these two odd locutions is the ethics of Bible translation.[88] Does the interpreter/translator allow Mark's problematic locutions to remain, or does the interpreter/translator change Mark's text in order to resolve the ambiguity in the interests of maintaining a text suitable for worship, since public reading of the Bible should not raise questions in the minds of the worshipers? To put the matter differently, does the interpreter/translator serve the interests of the church, or serve a sense of history that always demands complete transparency? (10–14–16)

§59 THE SIBYL'S WISH: A MYTHICAL ENCOUNTER[89]

T. S. Eliot prefaces his famous poem "The Waste Land" with an epigraph from the *Satiricon* of Petronius (first century CE):[90]

> I saw with my own eyes the Sibyl of Cumae hanging in a jar and when the boys said to her, "Sibyl, what do you want?" She replied, "I want to die."[91]

For the rest of the story we must look to the Roman poet Ovid in his poem *Metamorphoses* (first century CE), collections of tales from classical and Near Eastern myth and legend. He tells a story about the famous Sibyl of Cumae (a Greek colony on the eastern coast of Italy). The Sibyl, a prophetess who channeled the oracles of the God, was offered eternal, endless life by the Greek God Apollo if she would consent to sacrifice her virgin "modesty" and make love with Apollo. She pointed to a mound of sand and asked for "as many years of life as there were sand-grains in the pile." But she forgot to ask that she would be perpetually young for

---

88. Hedrick, "Satyrs or Wild Goats?"

89. My thanks to Charles W. Hedrick Jr., who made the suggestion that led to this essay.

90. Eliot, "Waste Land." For the epigram see under "structure."

91. Petronius, *Satiricon* 48:8 (my translation). The text of the *Satiricon* is taken from Sage and Gilleland, *Petronius the Satiricon*, 36.

those years. Through seven hundred years of life she continued to shrink and fade away until the time would come some three hundred years in the future that she, a tiny thing, consumed by age, would shrink to a feather's weight, and at the end she would only be known by her voice.[92] Of course it is only a mythical account; the God Phoebus Apollo and the Sibyl did not actually have such a conversation or liaison, and the Sibyl did not live for a thousand years. Such mythical stories do not inform us about ancient history, although they may serve a didactic purpose. In this case the "moral" of the account is perhaps something like, be careful what you wish; for your wish may be granted. So we may benefit from mythical narratives as long as we do not insist on their historicity; that is to say, as long as we recognize them for what they are: made up stories. If we insist that a mythical account is really history, we confuse two very distinct types of narrative, and, what is worse, we mislead people about past history.

Much of the biblical narrative is mired in myth (stories about Gods in a time and place not recognizable as our own). For example, Mark's account of the baptism of Jesus by John (1:9–11) is mythical (viz. the heavens open up, Spirit descends on Jesus, and a voice from heaven: "my beloved son"). And so is the story about the transfiguration of Jesus (Mark 9:2–8: his garments became glistening intensely white as no fuller on earth could bleach them; Jesus was joined on the mountain by the dead heroes of Israelite faith, Elijah and Moses; a voice comes out of a cloud overshadowing them: "my beloved son").

There are other definitions of myth, and no one definition satisfies all. Here are a few others that I have heard:

- Myth is a story that interprets natural events in terms of the supernatural.
- Myth is a means by which a people legitimize a secular ideology by projecting social patterns onto the supernatural realm.
- Myth is a narrative expression of an idea foundational to human existence which can be known, experienced, and appropriated repeatedly by means of recitation and ritual.
- Myth is a traditional story of ostensibly historical events that serves to unfold part of the worldview of a people.

---

92. Ovid, *Metamorphoses* xiv. 130–53: Miller and Goold, trans., *Metamorphoses*, 4:309–11.

The early Greeks used the term in a neutral way as simply stories about the Gods; later, however, the stories about the Gods were recognized as fictional. Plato, for example, describes some stories from the past as true, but others are fictitious (*pseudos*), and those in Homer, and particularly Hesiod's stories "taken as a whole are false (*pseudos*), but there is truth in them also."[93] Hence Plato refers to myth (*mythos*) as "something not wholly lacking in truth, but for the most part [it is] fictional."[94] And for that reason in *The Republic* (Plato's description of the ideal state) Plato (fifth/fourth century BCE) virtually banned telling children the stories of Greek poets such as Homer and Hesiod and others, who told "false" stories about the Gods. The reason was that such stories misrepresent the Gods, in spite of the little truth in them.[95]

Is there harm, do you suppose, in telling children mythical Bible stories and letting them think they are historical narratives? I have in mind such negative stories as narratives portraying God ordering the complete annihilation of a people (the Amalikites: 1 Sam 15:1–35), or a story that portrays God attempting to kill Moses after sending him to tell Pharaoh to release the Israelites (Exod 4:24–26), or a narrative about Baalam's talking ass (Num 22:15–35), or about the sun standing still at Joshua's command while the Israelites took vengeance on their enemies (Josh 10:12–14), or about Jesus' bodily ascent into the clouds of heaven (Luke 24:36–42; Acts 1:6–11. (6-26-15)

§60 THE GOSPEL OF MARK IS WRONG— AND OTHER QUIBBLES!

Perhaps I should say Mark is clearly incorrect in at least two places, and that fact has been known since the late second century. Jerome (fourth/fifth century) in a letter (57.9) cites the writings of early critics of Christianity (Celsus, *On the True Doctrine* [late second century]; Porphyry, *Against the Christians* [third/fourth century]; and Julian, *Against the Galilaeans* [fourth century]) on a number of errors, which according to Jerome these critics of Mark called "falsifications."[96] Likely many readers

---

93. Plato, *Republic*, II.376E–377A: Shorey, trans., *Republic*, 174–75.
94. Cuddon and Preston, *Penguin Dictionary of Literary Terms*, 525.
95. Plato, *Republic*, II.377A–383E: Shorey, trans., *Republic*, 174–99.
96. Fremantle et al., trans., "Letter LVII," 116–17.

will be unfamiliar with the two errors I describe here, but they are well known to most historians of Christian origins.

Jerome calls Celsus, Porphyry, and Julian "impious men," but he does not deny the errors. One well-known error is Mark's citation (Mark 1:1–3) of a passage supposedly from Isaiah, but which turns out to be a blending of Mal 3:1 and Isa 40:3. A second error is even more glaring. In Mark 2:25–26 Jesus cites the actions of David who "entered the house of God when Abiathar was high priest." When this event supposedly happened, however, Ahimelech was actually high priest (1 Sam 21:1–6); Abiathar was his son and met David only after the bread incident in the house of God (1 Sam 22:20–23).

Jerome in response to the first error simply solicits the indulgence of the reader for Mark's error, and for the second he argues that the evangelists were more concerned with the sense of Old Testament passages than with giving the literal words (Letter 57.9). Matthew and Luke correct Mark's errors in the following ways: Matthew (3:3) and Luke (3:4–6) correct Mark by eliminating the words of Malachi and then the reference to Isaiah (40:3) is correct. Luke also adds more material (Isa 40:3–5) to the Isaiah quotation. Both Matthew and Luke also correct Mark's historical error in naming the wrong high priest by simply eliminating Mark's erroneous phrase: "when Abiathar was high priest" (Matt 12:4; Luke 6:3).

Strictly speaking, the ascription of Mark 1:1–3 to Isaiah is wrong, for the passage contains statements from both Malachi and Isaiah. Strictly speaking, David took the dedicated bread from the altar when Ahimelech was high priest; so from existing evidence Mark was wrong when he says the incident took place when Abiathar was high priest.

What do these obvious errors suggest about Mark's reporting in a narrative about the public career of Jesus? Perhaps nothing! But since we have no way of verifying most of Mark's narrative and its details, when Mark is caught in an error it should be taken very seriously. These obvious errors suggest that the gospel should be read very closely and Mark should not be given a pass when other questionable statements are reported in the account. For example, Mark egregiously exaggerates in reporting that John, the baptizer, baptized "all the county of Judea and all the people of Jerusalem" (Mark 1:5) and exaggerates again at Mark 1:33 in reporting that the "whole city was gathered at the door." Mark is simply not writing responsibly in these instances. Accuracy in historical detail is not in itself a signature of historical narrative, but inaccuracy in historical detail is a clear warning of the possible historical unreliability of a narrative.

Questions can also be raised about some of the sources of the narratives Mark reports: specifically with respect to how Mark knows about things he reports. Here are two narratives that are clearly challengeable as historical narration. How does Mark know the precise words of the conversation he reports in the story of Jesus in the high priest's home (Mark 14:53–72)? His only likely source is Peter, who was not present but is portrayed as being out in the courtyard of the high priest's home, and not privy to what was happening inside the house (Mark 14:54, 66).

In Mark's story about the beheading of John the Baptist (Mark 6:14–29) Mark has used the narrative technique of time compression to create the fanciful story about the dance of Herodias's daughter and her dramatic request for the head of the Baptist in front of Herod's guests (Mark 6:24–25). Mark situates the narrative in the Galilee area (Mark 6:1, 14, 21, 45); so the banquet for "his courtiers, officers, and leading men of Galilee" must have taken place at his palace in Tiberias. According to Josephus, however, John the Baptist was imprisoned and beheaded in the fortress at Machaerus, located in modern Jordan (at that time in Nabatea), a number of miles east of the Dead Sea and at a level near its midpoint.[97] Mark's compression of time (6:25–27: "with haste," "at once," "immediately") forces readers to understand that John the Baptist was near at hand, and hence his beheading takes place while the dinner party was continuing; it is a much more dramatic story than sending a soldier of the guard on a long trip to Machaerus for the head! And, of course, there is always the question of how Mark knew the precise words of the conversations during the party. Was it actually oral tradition or simply Mark's imaginative re-creation, or simply whole cloth invention?

Such problems suggest that Mark is not technically early Christian history; rather his gospel has all the earmarks of historical fiction; that is to say, much of the gospel is due to Mark's imagination and inventive re-creation. (10–16–13)

§61 A QUESTION OF IDENTITY

We know of over thirty-four gospels from the early Christian period. Some are complete whereas for others only a few pages survive; fragments

---

97. Josephus, *Ant.* 18.5.2 (§§116–119).

of others survive; some are attested only in quotes by other ancient authors, and some we know only by title or name.[98] Complete versions of the canonical gospels are all late exemplars (fourth century and later). The earliest versions of the canonical gospels exist merely as scattered fragments. But the striking thing is that these gospel texts do not present a uniform description of Jesus of Nazareth in the details of his public career, his teaching, and his deeds. It is impossible to harmonize them convincingly. For example, the Markan Jesus refuses to give a sign (Mark 8:11–13); the Jesus portrayed in Matthew and Luke, however, offers a single sign, the sign of Jonah (Matt 16:1–4; Luke 11:29), while the Gospel of John has two numbered signs, and neither of them is the sign of Jonah (John 2:11; 4:54).

Such differences are not a problem for those of us who grew up in church; we have a learned image of Jesus that exists alongside the gospels as yet another understanding of Jesus. This learned image does not derive from the contradictory portraits of the early gospels but rather from the faith of the church in which we learned the Christian basics, for we were taught about Jesus from selected texts in the canonical gospels. And we continually reinforce that learned image of Jesus by the selective way we read the canonical gospels. Naturally, we ignore the other noncanonical gospels, even though there are reliable, inexpensive translations available.

But every now and then we stumble across a saying attributed to Jesus in the canonical gospels that brings us up short: the saying simply does not fit our learned image of Jesus, but there the saying is in one or more of the canonical gospels and unambiguously attributed to Jesus! Such sayings are usually referred to as "hard sayings" precisely because they do not fit our learned image of Jesus.

One of the more problematical is Mark 4:11–12: "To you has been given the secret of the kingdom of God, but for those outside everything is in parables; so that they may indeed see but not perceive, and may indeed hear but not understand; lest they should turn again, and be forgiven" (RSV). The saying asserts that Jesus used parables to keep outsiders from understanding about the kingdom of God, lest they should repent and be forgiven; at least so Mark appears to have thought (Matthew and Luke drop the offensive phrase: "lest they should turn again and be forgiven"). If Jesus made this statement that Mark attributes to him, then he is not

---

98. Hedrick, "34 Gospels."

announcing the good news of God's kingdom, and calling on all to repent, as Mark portrays him doing in Mark 1:14–15.

A number of such hard sayings run counter to the traditional view of who Jesus was in the gospels and raise the question, whose words are these that have mistakenly been attributed to Jesus? For example, recall the callous saying attributed to Jesus in response to the Syrophoenician woman. When she implored him to cast an unclean spirit out of her daughter, he said, "Let the children be fed first, for it is not right to take the children's bread and throw it to the dogs" (Mark 7:27). Surely there has been some mistake here! Whose words are these that run counter to everything we have been taught about Jesus?

On the other hand, we also find a number of extremely radical statements attributed to Jesus in the gospels, which make unrealistic demands. These statements are dangerous. One of the best known is Matt 5:39 "Do not resist the evil (one)" (or one who is evil), and another is, "Love your enemies" (Matt 5:44; Luke 6:27). If you followed either saying literally, your life, the lives of your loved ones, and the lives of your friends would likely be endangered.

Here is another remarkably imprecise and demanding saying: "Blessed are those who go hungry to feed the starving belly of another" (Gos.Thom. 69B). This saying expresses a very high ethical sentiment; it calls for the feeding of the starving up to a point where your own sustenance is exhausted. You continue feeding those who are starving till your own belly begins to growl! And what then, one is prompted to ask? Should I continue feeding every hungry person I meet until I myself am forced to join the ranks of the starving? Is there no reasonable compromise, no middle ground? But the saying is unequivocal—feed the starving till you reach the point of starving![99]

Such hard sayings force the question of the speaker's identity upon us; whose words are these that do not fit our learned image of Jesus? Do they actually originate with Jesus of Nazareth? Considering how the canonical gospels came into being, it should not be surprising that other voices are sometimes erroneously attributed to Jesus. The authors of the gospels drew upon oral traditions passed along for a generation or more, and also used the works of earlier writers. And of course they themselves were authors, and their own creative ideas gave their narratives a focus, a plan. They shaped the character of their hero according to their own

---

99. Hedrick, *Wisdom of Jesus*, 89.

views. So statements and ideas attributed to Jesus in the gospels may not have originated with Jesus. For example, Luke 4:23, "Physician heal yourself," a saying attributed to Jesus, was composed much earlier than Jesus; it appears in a fragment of a lost play by the fifth-century-BC Greek writer of tragedies, Euripides ("doctor to others; full of sores yourself," the saying goes).[100] How should followers of Jesus handle these remarkably difficult sayings that Jesus may or may not have spoken?

People who like to think of themselves as followers of Jesus are faced with a bewildering array of Jesus figures who say contradictory things in the gospels. Here are the options: a person can choose between the contradictory faith portraits of the first-century gospels or accept the fourth-century orthodox ecclesiastical understanding or return to the Jesus that they learned in Sunday school or embrace the Jesus of TV evangelists, or they can analyze the raw historical data made available by the Jesus Seminar report,[101] which sorts out the multiple voices in the gospels in terms of voice-prints, and from that evidence develop their own understanding of Jesus. (10-31-12)

§62 THE GOSPEL OF JOHN: A REVISIONIST GOSPEL

John has been described as the spiritual gospel and the maverick gospel, but because John has (either deliberately or inadvertently) revised the gospel tradition, it should be regarded as a revisionist gospel. As Matthew and Luke freely change and revise Mark's narrative (compare Mark 8:11-12 with Matt 12:38-42 and Luke 11:29-32 about whether or not Jesus gave a sign to validate himself), in a similar manner John revises the Synoptic Gospel tradition represented by Mark's text.

Here are some brief data on the Gospel of John:

Today the composition of John is dated to the last decade of the first century,[102] because of an early papyrus fragment of John (P^{52}) containing part of John 18:31-33, 37-38. In the ancient past, however, some believed it to have been written by the second-century writer Cerinthus.[103]

Mark, the earliest gospel (dating around 70), and John, the latest of the canonical four, share very little common material, but what they

---

100. Ibid., 103. The comments about Mark 2:17 are in reference to Luke 4:23.
101. Funk et al., *Five Gospels*.
102. Feine et al., *Introduction*,175.
103. Epiphanius, *Pan*. 51.3.6.

do share appears in the same order in each gospel, yet with remarkable differences. For example, compare:

- Healing the paralyzed man (Mark 2:1–12 = John 5:1–9)
- Feeding the five thousand (Mark 6:32–44 = John 6:1–15)
- Walking on the water (Mark 6:45–52 = John 6:16–21)
- Being anointed at Bethany (Mark 14:3–9 = John 12:1–8)

Striking differences appear between the narratives of Mark and John. In fact, truth be told, Mark and John are more unlike than alike. The differences prompt the question, what actually happened in the public career of Jesus? Here are just a few of the differences:

- Was Jesus baptized by water (Mark 1:9–11) or the spirit (John 1:29–34)? There is no water baptism of Jesus described in the Gospel of John.
- Does Jesus' public career overlap the public career of John the Baptist (John 3:22–30) or not (Mark 1:14–15)? In John's Gospel Jesus and John the Baptizer are competitors, making and baptizing followers at the same time, but in Mark John is put in jail before Jesus launches his public career.
- Did Jesus "cleanse" the Jewish temple at the beginning (John 2:25–30) or end of his public career (Mark 11:15–19)?
- Did Jesus perform exorcisms—that is, did Jesus drive out evil spirits (Mark 3:21–27; Luke 11:20 = Matt 12:28) or not (John)? No record of exorcisms is found in the Gospel of John.
- Was Jesus' public career one year, plus or minus (Mark has one Passover: see Mark 14), or three years, plus or minus (John has three Passovers: see John 2:13; 11:55; 18:28)?
- Did Jesus make only one trip to Jerusalem during his career (Mark 10:1, 17, 32; 11:1, 15), or five trips (John 2:13, 23; 5:1; 7:10; 11:7, 18; 12:12)?
- Was Jesus' last meal with his disciples a traditional Passover celebration (Mark 14:12, 22–25) or not (John 13:1–20)? In John Jesus is crucified before the Passover celebration (see John 19:14, 31, 42).

- Does Jesus give a sign to validate his authority? Jesus' public career in John is accompanied by numerous signs (2:1—12:50; cf. 2:1–22; 4:46–54), but in Mark Jesus refuses to give a sign (8:11–13).
- In Mark, Jesus' major opponents were Pharisees and Sadducees, but in John his major opponents are described as a group called "the Jews" (sometimes translated Judahites or Judeans). Mention of such a group is not found in Mark.

Two significant shifts from Markan theology are evident in John:

1. What was Jesus like? In Mark Jesus is portrayed as a Judean man from Nazareth; his debates with scribes and Pharisees are Jewish family arguments. In John he is only a Jewish man in appearance; he actually originated with God and came from God (John 1:1–18).

2. Why did Jesus have to die? Mark agrees with Paul: In Mark Jesus died in order to give his life as a ransom for many (Mark 10:45; see Rom 5:8–11). In John, on the other hand, Jesus' death is his supreme moment of glorification in which the world ruler is cast out (John 12:27–36; 13:31–32). What brings salvation in John is the illumination that Jesus brings from the Father (John 8:12; 12:35–36). Believing in him as the witness to the Father brings eternal life (John 11:25–26).

Mark and John, as the bookends of the canonical gospels, are different on most everything, but they do agree on at least one thing: that a story about the virgin birth of Jesus was not significant for explaining who Jesus was.

The remarkable differences between the canonical gospels are seldom seen by an average church reader, because such a reader encounters the gospels selectively under the influence of an ecclesiastical Master Narrative about Jesus, a legacy from fourth-century Christian orthodoxy. That Master Narrative goes something like this:

> Jesus was the Jewish Messiah and Son of God. He was born of the Holy Spirit and the Virgin Mary, and was attested by God with mighty works and wonders and signs. He was crucified under Pontius Pilate and was buried, and on the third day rose from the dead ascending into heaven, where he sits on the right hand of the Father. He will come again to judge the living and the dead.

This story is not told by any of the canonical gospels. In fact this Master Narrative does not exist as such in any one early Christian gospel. The gospel writers show no evidence that they knew it. The ecclesiastical Master Narrative exists alongside the four canonical gospels as yet a fifth way of understanding the story about Jesus. Since the fourth century, it has remained the preferred and popular story about Jesus that most of us unconsciously absorb in Sunday school, catechism classes, and sermons. Escaping from the influence of the Master Narrative is only possible by reading the gospels comparatively. (12-6-12)

§63 IS JOHN'S GOSPEL HISTORY OR FICTION?

Three types of literature are closely related in form and style: fiction, history, and gospel. They all are narrative; that is to say, they all tell a story. The character of two of these genres is well known: Fiction, by definition, is about things that never happened, but if it is realistic historical fiction one would have to add the following to the definition: although these things never occurred, they could have happened (in the sense that the realistic action approximates conventional reality). History on the other hand, by definition, is about things that did actually occur.

Gospel literature, according to critical scholarship, falls somewhere between the two definitions above: it is neither history nor fiction; or perhaps better, it is both history and fiction. Gospel literature is unapologetically propaganda literature, which is enough to compromise its reliability as unbiased history if one pauses to think about it. Of course what we usually think of as history and fiction can also be propagandistic. In fact they often are, and are thereby rendered unreliable for the same reason. The historical character of the canonical gospels is more akin to Eusebius's *Life of Constantine*, which is a fourth-century encomium or eulogy written in praise of the first Christian emperor, extolling his role in establishing fourth-century orthodoxy. The encomium is not critical history but principally pietistic propaganda.[104]

In many ways gospel narratives appear to have more in common with fiction than history, in that gospel and fiction share many of the same techniques and conventions. For example, ancient Greek novels frequently digress into vivid description. In handbooks of rhetoric of the second century and later this phenomenon is called *ekphrasis*,

---

104. Eusebius, *Life of Constantine*.

"description." Depending on who is explaining the reason for the feature, *ekphrasis* either digresses from the story to enhance reader enjoyment (to make the narrative more vivid) or furthers the plot in some way.[105] Historical narrative, on the other hand, should not enhance data with the goal of increasing the reader's enjoyment, or aiding the historian's argument in some way. If it introduces description that is not actually part of the events themselves in order to enrich the reading experience, to that extent the historical reporting is compromised as critical historical narrative.

In making a story more vivid a fiction writer often uses sensory words; that is, words that appeal to the five senses: hearing, seeing, touching, tasting, and smelling. In the Gospel of John one finds only a few meager instances of enhancing description by appealing to a physical sense: seeing (4:35—white), (5:35—burning and shining), (20:5-7—purple), (21:7—naked; translations vary considerably[106]). With respect to the Gospel of Mark, however, such meager description was likely due to the author's inadvertence; it was just the way the author conceived what was being written that caused him to compose as he did; the author simply wrote what was in the mind's eye, so to speak. Mark's use of descriptive language appears to be inadvertent because Mark has simply missed too many chances to enhance the reader's enjoyment with deliberate vivid language for his few descriptions using colors in Mark to be considered deliberate.[107] With the exception of one other instance in John, author inadvertence may explain the few instances in John noted above. In John 12:3, however, the author deliberately passes over into descriptive language that enhances the vividness of the narrative. The entire verse is laced with vivid, sensuous language: "Mary took *a pound of costly ointment* of *pure* nard and *anointed the feet* of Jesus and wiped his feet *with her hair; and the house was filled with the fragrance of the ointment*" (RSV). In this instance the author of the gospel has evidentially utilized a technique of the fiction writer and appealed to readers' physical senses of smell and touch, as well as to an economic sense by emphasizing the quality, high cost, and amount of the ointment. The more that the gospel writers can be shown to use the techniques of narrative fiction, the longer

---

105. Hedrick, "Conceiving the Narrative."
106. See §69 below.
107. Hedrick, "Conceiving the Narrative," 184–86.

will be the shadow of doubt cast over the gospels as historical narratives. (1-25-14)

§64 MEMORY IN JOHN AND THE RESHAPING OF EARLY CHRISTIAN TRADITION

The early Christian gospels are ultimately based in part on the memories of the survivors of the crucifixion. What gets passed down orally, eventually to the writers of the gospels, originates with the survivors and their competing memories. Everything depends on what they think they heard, saw, understood, and accurately reported. This datum raises the question, how reliable and consistent were their memories? The accuracy of their memories cannot be verified, but we know from our own experiences how contradictory and flawed memory can be. We have all experienced both short-term and particularly long-term memory failure, or have simply misremembered and misunderstood events, conversations, and statements. The results for us can sometimes be embarrassing, inconvenient, or disastrous. In the case of the survivors of the crucifixion, their faulty or religiously shaped memories would have resulted in a faulty misrepresentation of their own experiences.

Even at the written stage of the gospels there are several indications that multiple generations of oral Jesus tradition were less than perfect, and at times the actual circumstances of the past were piously misrepresented. In John 21:20–23 at least two generational levels of the tradition are portrayed. The earliest level (the situation of the disciples immediately following the crucifixion) is represented in John 21:20–22. Jesus had just given Peter some kind of authoritative role in subsequent events (John 21:15–19: feed my lambs; tend my sheep; feed my sheep). Peter looks over at the beloved disciple and inquires: what about this man? (21:20–21). Jesus replies, "If I want him to remain till I come, what is that to you? Follow me."

The later level (the situation of the Johannine narrator, writing around the end of the first century) is represented in 21:23. The early saying of Jesus, urging Peter to follow him and ignore the situation of the beloved disciple, was later interpreted and repeated among the "brethren" (that is, between the events following the crucifixion and the later situation of the Johannine narrator) as a saying about the immortality of the beloved disciple. In John 21:23 the later narrator of the Gospel of

John corrects what he regards as a misrepresentation of the earlier tradition, but without explaining the original saying in John 21:22.

Several other passages in John suggest that the memories of the early Jesus followers were compromised by their beliefs about Jesus and their use of the Hebrew Bible in Greek translation to shape how they remembered events. Two of these passages occur in the Judean temple incident (John 2:13–22). Jesus says, "Take these things away" [i.e., the pigeons]; "you shall not make my Father's house a house of trade" (2:16). The Johannine narrator explains that sometime after the resurrection the disciples "remembered" the incident and at that later time associated it with Ps 69:9 as a scriptural prediction of what brought about the death of Jesus (John 2:17).

In this same passage occurs another shaping of the remembered tradition by the later faith of the church. To the Judeans who asked him for a sign to confirm his authority for doing what he did in the temple (2:18) Jesus replies: "Destroy this temple and in three days I will raise it up" (2:19). The Judeans in the Johannine narrative are portrayed, quite understandably, regarding the statement as a reference to the destruction of the Judean temple, since that was the issue at hand (2:20). But the later Johannine narrator overrides the earlier report and explains that Jesus "spoke of the temple of his body" rather than the Judean temple (2:21). The narrator further explains that after Jesus' resurrection the disciples recalled the event and the saying; and "believing the Scripture" they came to believe that the saying was actually a prophecy of the resurrection (2:22). No particular Scripture is quoted, but the statement likely refers to the Hebrew Scriptures as a whole, a custom of the later apostolic church (see 1 Cor 15:3–4).

Another instance of the shaping of early Christian memory by the use of Scripture occurs on the occasion of the triumphal entry of Jesus into Jerusalem (John 12:12–19). Jesus mounts a young ass to enter Jerusalem (12:14). The later Johannine narrator then quotes an abridged version of Zech 9:9 (12:15) and explains that the disciples at the time of the incident did not understand why Jesus was riding on an ass's colt (12:16). But sometime later after the crucifixion ("when Jesus was glorified"),"they then remembered that this had been written of him and had been done to him" (12:16). The Johannine narrator's portrayals of the reshaping of the memories of the crucifixion's earliest survivors further call into question the reliability of the gospels as historical narratives. (3–20–14)

§65 HISTORICAL TRADITION IN THE FOURTH GOSPEL

The Fourth Gospel (John) is the latest of the four canonical gospels. Its tone (i.e., its ideas, style, and manner of expression throughout the text) is remarkably different from the earliest gospel, Mark. Compared to Mark, John breathes the rarified air of a high Christology and a religious tradition completely different from Mark, Matthew, and Luke. Mark's and John's narratives rarely overlap in content, and on the rare occasions that they do, John's version has little in common with the Markan narrative and its characterization of Jesus. For example, compare the healing of the lame man (Mark 2:1–12 and John 5:2–18), where John tells a very different story, which has few similarities to Mark; this is also the case in the story of Jesus walking on the water (Mark 6:45–52 and John 6:16–21), where John's version is much shorter and only superficially similar.

John 1:1–18 is confessional language, and it is also unabashed mythical (not historical) language (compare it to the christological statement in Phil 2:5–11), which sets the theological tone for the Gospel of John. In general myth is a story about gods and heroes in a time and place not recognizable as our own. Myth is about creation and origins that attempt to explain such things as creation, divinity, and religion. History is about what actually happened in the past, and historical description is based on evidence available to a neutral third party. The event described in chapter 1, opening the Gospel of John, is not historical in the sense that it takes place in common space and time; it occurs for the most part in the primordial past: that is, it describes earliest origins and events taking place before the world and time began. The first event described in the Gospel of John depends on the faith of the gospel writer. Plato, however, regarded all the Greek myths told by the Greek poets as "made up" stories; hence they were things that never happened in the past.[108]

The character of John's Gospel is such that critical historians attempt to rehabilitate its history by appealing to its rare similarities with the Synoptic Gospels, and in this way arguing that it is possible that "within the material shared by John and the synoptic gospels" the author of John had access to an "independent and primitive tradition" about Jesus.[109] It is virtually impossible to harmonize the linguistic interests of the Judean Jesus of Mark with the language of John's Jesus. For example, the striking dualisms in John—light/darkness (1:5), truth/falsehood (8:44–45),

---

108. See §59 above.
109. Brown, *John*, 1:xlviii.

Spirit/flesh (3:6), above/below (8:23)—do not fit the language world of Mark's Judean Jesus, even though John's language is, in part, shared with the Dead Sea Scrolls, which overlapped the time of Jesus.[110]

Nevertheless John is not without historical value, even though critical scholarship generally recognizes that it tells us virtually nothing about Jesus, the Judean man who lived more than a generation before the writing of John. Its value lies in the fact that the Gospel of John attests a very different type of Christianity (at the end of the first century CE) from what we find portrayed in the Synoptic Gospels at least a generation, earlier; John represents a type of Christianity that draws on different traditions—some of which are likely as early as the synoptic tradition. John demonstrates that a wide breadth of responses to the Judean man, and ideas about him, continued to proliferate. The Jesus traditions in the first century were pluralistic, rich, complex, and contradictory—and all of them claimed exclusivity for what was reported.

Remarkable differences between John and the Synoptic Gospels make it impossible to describe who Jesus actually was when John is read along with the Synoptic Gospels.[111] In short, one must make an either/or decision between Mark and John. As Albert Schweitzer saw at the beginning of the twentieth century, one must choose either the Jesus of Mark (which Schweitzer incorrectly regarded as history) or the Jesus of John's Gospel.[112] A middle path of harmonizing the two is not a historical solution. Hence, since the beginning of the twentieth century the Gospel of John has been discredited as a historical source for Jesus, the Judean man who lived at the end of the first third of the first century.[113] (9–30–15)

§66 IS THE GOSPEL OF JOHN HISTORICAL NARRATIVE?

The answer would, in part, depend on the reliability of the sources used by the author. John, however, is the latest gospel, dating around the end of the first century and some sixty years after the crucifixion of Jesus, which is considerably past the time of the eyewitnesses who participated in the events narrated in the gospel. What is more compromising for John as

---

110. Cross, *Ancient Library*, 206–16.
111. See §62 above.
112. Schweitzer, *Quest*, xiv–xvi, 6.
113. Hedrick, "Introduction," 3–4.

historical narrative, however, is the matter that the author writes like a theologian rather than a historian. The principal theological concerns of John's community are, in part, Christology (e.g. John 1:1–51) and soteriology (doctrine of salvation: see, e.g., John 3:1–21). The author simply does not seem concerned about the historical aspects of the narrative. Hence, the gospel appears to be narrated theology rather than historical narrative.

Historical writing portrays life realistically, which is to say that historical writing is the opposite of idealistic or romantic writing. Realism presents readers with "a serious representation of contemporary everyday social reality against the background of a constant historical movement."[114]

The author of the Gospel of John has no real interest in the passage of time and chronology, which is what I take Auerbach to mean by "constant historical movement." Chronology is the sequence in which events occur. A historian is principally interested in the exact order in which events take place; defining an accurate sequence of events helps the historian to understand the causes and effects of those events. In short, there is no historical narration without accurate chronology.

One does find a chronological segment in John 11:55—20:29, where events appear to be loosely arranged on a sequential frame surrounding the Passover (11:55; 12:1, 12; 13:1; 19:14; 19:21; 20:1; 20:19; 20:26). It may only be an artifice, however, for the real purpose of the arrangement is to provide a framework for a series of minispeeches and the crucifixion/resurrection account. In John 14:31 at the conclusion of one series of minispeeches (13:31—14:31) Jesus says, "Rise, let us go hence." Jesus and the disciples were reclining (13:2, 12, 23, 25) at a meal when he began (13:31) the series of speeches that culminated in the command to rise and go (14:31). No one moves, however, and Jesus continues to make speeches (15:1—18:1).

The first half of the gospel (1:1—11:54) makes no attempt at producing a genuine chronological account. It consists of a series of literary vignettes strung together by a limited series of connectives intended to suggest a chronology. Here is a list of some of the author's faux chronological connectives. They give an illusion of chronology but are only literary connectives:

---

114. Auerbach, *Mimesis*, 518.

> The next day (1:29, 35, 39, 43); the third day (2:1); the sixth hour (4:6); after two days (4:43); that day a Sabbath (5:9); a Passover (5:9); a Passover was at hand (6:4); When evening came (6:16); on the next day (6:22); feast of Tabernacles (7:2, 14, 37); early in the morning (8:2); feast of Dedication, it was winter (10:22); it was night (13:30); stayed two days (11:6).
>
> Most of the connectives are mere transitions, however:
>
> After these things (3:22; 5:1; 6:1; 7:1; 19:38; 21:1); after this thing (2:12; 6:66;11:7; 19:28); now (2:23; 3:1; 5:2; 5:9; 11:1, 5, 17, 55; 12:20; 13:1; 18:25); therefore/then (3:25; 4:1, 44; 6:52; 11:17; 18:28; 19:1); again (4:44; 8:12, 21; 10:7, 19); meanwhile (4:1).

Events in the gospel narrative are fated, and the inevitable ending is controlled from the beginning. Jesus tells his mother, "My hour has not yet come" (2:4). This anticipation of the critical moment of the gospel is repeated throughout the narrative (7:5, 8; 5:25, 28; 8:20; 12:23, 31–33; 13:1, 31; 16:25, 32; 17:1). Jesus is "not from this world" (8:23; 17:14, 16) but has been sent (5:30, 37, 38; 6:29, 38, 44; 7:16. 28, 8:16, 42) into it for the purposes of judgment (9:39), which is the casting out of the ruler of this world (12:31–33).

Historical narrative, on the other hand, reflects a natural cause-and-effect system where events are not fated or preplanned but are spontaneous and randomly occurring. The author of John, however, organizes details and writes narrative and speeches from the perspective of a particular faith. The author's faith perspective and how s/he understands "history" to proceed is clearly reflected in John 2:14-22; 12:12-16, and 20:3-9: in these segments events in the career of Jesus are, the author believes, controlled by scriptural prophecy.

In life historical events are not controlled by means of prophecy. Describing historical events as controlled by prophecy involves arbitrarily imposing a religious plot on time and results in a theological interpretation of history. (9–10-15)

§67 DOES JOHN KNOW THE DIFFERENCE BETWEEN HISTORY AND FAITH?

Does the flesh-and-blood author of the Gospel of John respect the difference between historical information and personal religious confession?

Or put another way, is the author aware when s/he shifts from historical description into a confession of faith?

I am not proposing that we read John's mind. The implied author of the gospel that readers know is a mental construct that they develop in their own minds in response to reading the text.[115] What I am asking with this question is whether there are any literary features in the text suggesting that the actual flesh-and-blood author either was not aware of the crucial difference between historical information and confessional rhetoric or did not regard the distinction as relevant.

The answer, like everything in the history-of-Jesus research, depends on who you ask. For example, the Jesus Seminar found that only one *saying* in John probably originated with Jesus (John 4:42).[116] With regard to the *deeds* of Jesus, the seminar found that only a few features (in John 7:15; 18:12–13, 28; 19:1, 6, 18) suggested a rather superficial knowledge of aspects of the historical career of Jesus. That is a vastly different judgment from that of Craig S. Keener, for example, who argued that all four gospels are "historical biography."[117]

From my perspective John's narrative frequently sacrifices history in the interest of confessional rhetoric. For example, according to the Jesus Seminar, the cleansing of the temple in Mark 11:15–19 reflects, in part, aspects of an actual historical incident,[118] but the seminar found that the account of the same incident in John 2:13–22 was not grounded in history; in other words, in John's narrative, theology trumps history.[119] Scholars generally regard the cleansing of the temple as a historical event, and Mark reported aspects of it in a more or less historical way. Yet even the barest historical outlines of the incident are lost in John's religious rhetoric, at least according to the Jesus Seminar.

Apparently John is more interested in right faith than in describing the career of Jesus from a historical perspective. For example, John 1:1–18 is clearly a confessional statement. The only bit of historical data in the section is the mention of John (the baptizer), the Judean prophet, whom the author of John co-opts as a Christian witness (1:6–8, 15), as also was the case in Matt 11:12–15, where he is not part of the Israelite

---

115. Holman and Harmon, *Handbook*, 243; Booth, *Rhetoric of Fiction*, 71–76.
116. Funk et al., *Five Gospels*, 412.
117. Keener, *Gospel of John*, 1:33.
118. Funk and the Jesus Seminar, *Acts of Jesus*, 121–22.
119. Ibid., 373–74.

old order, but part of the new (compare the parallel in Luke 16:16, where he is part of the old order). John chapter 1 uses confessional language rather heavily (1:9–13, 15, 19, 20, 29, 32, 34).

The author interrupts the story about Jesus with confessional rhetoric in spite of the fact that it threatens the integrity of the narrative. For example, in John 3:11 in the middle of the dialogue between Jesus and Nicodemus the author suddenly breaks into confessional rhetoric: John 3:11 begins as a part of Jesus' comment to Nicodemus but then shifts into an accusation against those who do not "receive *our* witness."

> Truly, truly I say to you [singular; to Nicodemus] that *we* [the evangelist and his community] speak of what *we* know and you [plural; to his opponents] do not receive *our* witness. (John 3:11)

In John 3:12 the evangelist assumes the persona of speaker to continue the criticism of his opponents: "If I (the evangelist) have told you (plural) earthly things, and you (plural) do not believe, how will you (plural) believe if I tell you (plural) heavenly things?" Immediately following, John 3:13–21 (which refers to Jesus in the third person) is spoken by the evangelist reciting the confession of the community. At this point the conversation between Jesus and Nicodemus (3:1–10) has been completely forgotten.

Once again in John 3:31–36 the evangelist shifts into confession, leaving behind John's answer to his disciples about Jesus baptizing beyond the Jordan (John 3:25–30). In these two instances the evangelist overrides description with confession.

Another similar instance is John 4:22–24. The evangelist intersperses a community confession (4:22–24) between two dangling ends of the discussion between Jesus and the Samaritan woman (i.e., 4:21/25)—as s/he does at John 7:22 where the evangelist intrudes into a statement by Jesus in order to correct what Jesus says (this latter phenomenon is part of a much larger problem in the Gospel of John).[120]

Judging from these few instances, it appears that the flesh-and-blood author of John was more interested in confessional rhetoric than in historical description. (9–21-15)

---

120. Hedrick, "Authorial Presence."

§68 WHY DOES JESUS NOT USE PARABLES IN THE GOSPEL OF JOHN?

The word "parable" (*parabole*) does not even appear in the Gospel of John, and neither does the brief story form, which is what scholars usually describe as the classic form of the parable.[121] Instead John uses the word *paroimia* to describe an aspect of the discourse of Jesus. The figurative image of the sheepfold in John 10:1-5 is not a story and is not described as "parable," but rather as *paroimia* (10:6). Scholars provide several translations for *paroimia*: "pithy saying," "proverb," "maxim," or "hidden, obscure speech." Its only other occurrences in the New Testament are translated as "figure" (John 16:25, 29) and "proverb" (2 Pet 2:22). The kind of language to which it refers is indirect language (i.e., not directly related to the issue at hand) or language that paints a picture.

John 16:16-29 deliberately contrasts *paroimia* (16:25, 29) with clear speech (16:29): *paroimia* is conceived as obscure, unclear, inscrutable, and mysterious language; in other words it is not plain speech but rather obscure — speech whose significance is open to question. In this section (John 16:16-29) there really is no "figurative" language to perplex the disciples. They quite plainly state that what confuses them is Jesus' statement "a little while, and you will see me no more; again a little while, and you will see me" (16:16-19). Jesus calls his explanation to the disciples over their perplexity (16:20-28) "*paroimian* language" (i.e., unclear, 16:25). And they accept his explanation of what they regard as an obscure saying, as plain or clear language (16:29-30). In short, the narrator in John 16:16-29 seems to misunderstand *paroimia*; at least, one may say that what the disciples are confused about does not have the character of a figure, pithy saying, proverb, or maxim.

The image in John 10:1-5 (and presumably also in John 10:7-18) is described as a paroimia (John 10:6). And it certainly is, without a doubt, a figure that paints an image of the situation with a sheepfold and the door to the sheepfold, and that identifies the one who has legitimate access to the sheep and to the fold. This image (unlike the saying in John 16:16-29), however, does not confuse; it only succeeds in angering the

---

121. Brown, *John*, 1:385-86. Brown finds that *paroima* and *parabole* are used synonymously in Sir 47:17. Thus he concludes there is no difference in the two literary forms. But in this matter he is clearly incorrect. It appears that the author of Sirach has listed a series of different forms in Sir 47:17.

audience of Judeans (10:19), who apparently are not confused about the image, but who are confused over the person of Jesus.

The reason for the correct usage of *paroimia* in one instance and the incorrect usage of *paroimia* in the other is that John 10:6 is a "narrative aside," written from a perspective different than that held by the principal narrative voice of the Gospel of John, which in this case is represented by John 16:16–29.[122]

The Jesus of the Gospel of John does not use parables simply because the flesh-and-blood author does not know the tradition that Jesus told brief stories the synoptic evangelists dubbed parables. Nevertheless, both the authors of the Synoptic Gospels and the author of John agree that the language of Jesus was cryptic and in need of explanation, which is very interesting in the light of their almost complete disagreement on everything else. Their lack of understanding of the nature of parable arises from their erroneous idea that Jesus the early first-century Israelite believed the same things they did. But he was a Judean Israelite and they, coming along later, were Greek Christians. Little wonder that they found his language strange, arcane, and in need of explanation. (1–8–17)

§69 WAS PETER FISHING NAKED? DOES IT MATTER?

John 21:7 has posed problems for both Bible translators and commentary writers. Here is the situation. Peter and the other disciples are fishing on the Lake of Galilee and Jesus calls to them from the shore. The beloved disciple recognizes his voice. "It is the Lord," he says, and Peter, hearing that statement, "girded an outer garment about him, for he was naked . . ." (author's translation). Modern translators in general avoid the use of the bare word "naked" and cover it up with a variety of euphemisms apparently in order to avoid the issue of Peter's nakedness.

- RSV: "he put on his clothes, for he was stripped for work."
- Smith-Goodspeed: "he put on his clothes, for he had taken them off."
- Jesus Seminar: "he tied his cloak around him, since he was stripped for work."
- NEB: "he wrapped his coat about him (for he had stripped)."

---

122. Hedrick, "Authorial Presence."

- TEV: "he wrapped his outer garment around him (for he had taken his clothes off)."
- LB: "Peter put on his tunic (for he was stripped to the waist)."
- NKJ: "he put on his outer garment (for he was wearing only an undergarment)."

Older translators, on the other hand, do not seem to be bothered by the use of "naked."

- King James: "he girt his fisher's coat unto him (for he was naked)."
- Douay: "Peter girt his coat about him (for he was naked)."
- Martin Luther: "he girt his shirt [*hemd*] around him (for he was naked [*nackt*])."
- Latin: "he girded himself with an undergarment [*tunica*] (for he was naked [*nudus*])."
- French (1615 edition): "Peter put on his garment [*habit*], because he was naked [*nud*]."

Lexicographers agree that there are subtleties to how the word "naked' is used in Greek literature. All agree, however, that the basic or literal sense of the word is naked, nude, bare, uncovered, and the like. But in some contexts the lexicographers assert that the word carries the idea that an individual is only improperly or poorly clothed (for example, Jas 2:15 [naked]; but cf. Jas 2:2 [filthy clothing]), or wearing only an undergarment (for example, 1 Sam 19:24 and Isa 20:2, both from the Septuagint, not the Hebrew). As these latter two examples show, however, the parallel passages used to support "wearing an undergarment" must be carefully checked, since lexicographers assume that a writer is speaking of literal nakedness, when nothing else in the context suggests the wearing of an undergarment. (I only checked parallels from biblical literature.)

Two highly regarded authors of commentaries on John (Raymond E. Brown[123] and Barnabas Lindars[124]) in commenting on John 21:7 explain that Peter was fishing in a loincloth or a small undergarment and girded his outer garment around himself (because total nudity would offend Jewish sensibilities) before swimming to shore. Without introducing the idea of an undergarment, however, the text seems to suggest that Peter

123. Brown, *John*, 2:1072.
124. Lindars, *John*, 628.

was literally naked and girded (secured) his outer garment around him so that when he reached shore he could cover his nakedness.

In the final analysis, however, the image created in the reader's mind upon reading this passage (in the Greek text) may not matter. What does matter, however, is that translators and interpreters of biblical texts influence the public's perception of the Bible when they resolve its ambiguities and other difficulties in the translation rather than in a note. If ambiguities and awkward passages are resolved by translators, the biblical text becomes more polished and acceptable to modern sensibilities, or at least it is less offensive than it might be when "unimproved." That is to say, texts glossed by a modern translator's sense of decency will raise few questions in a reader's mind.

Such difficulties or awkward turns of expression as presented by John 21:7 are better left unresolved in the translation and discussed in a note. What we moderns may regard as defects in the texts of one sort or another constitute signatures of the ancient authors or editors, and they serve to remind us that our biblical texts share in the deficiencies of the human condition.

Another case on point is 1 Sam 19:24 (Septuagint) where Saul prophesies before Samuel: "he stripped off his clothes . . . and lay naked all that day and all that night" (RSV). But in the NIV the translation reads: "he stripped off his robes . . . He lay that way all day and night." Hence it would appear that the word "naked" does not always mean "naked." (2-4-14)

5

The Nature of God

§70 GOD DOES NOT "EXIST"

If God is spirit, as must be the case (John 4:24), then God is not an entity existing in space and time, as we human beings are. We humans do exist; that is, we are bound in space and time during our brief lives. God, on the other hand, appears to be a concept, an invention of the human imagination, whose nature and character changes with the confessions of each religious group or individual, or both. Hence, it appears that God, however conceived, has no independent existence, which exactly corresponds to the many ideations of the human mind.

The rationale for this surprising statement is self-evident when viewed from the perspective of the history of world religions. Each religion (and there have been a lot of religions through human history) conceives God differently, yet the adherents of this or that religion believe that God is just like what they conceive God to be. In short, they believe their view is the only accurate and true view that captures the essence of God. But, alas, different understandings of God exist in other religions, and the adherents of those other religions likewise think that their understanding of God is actually how God is.

For example, there is no one biblical understanding of God. There are various views of God in Christian and Jewish Bibles. One can be confident in describing each of these ways of understanding God as different, since it is based on the recognition that the Bible is a collection of diverse texts representing the historical evolution of two different religions—Israelite and Christian. The authors of texts in the Bible can only be held responsible for the concepts of those texts they composed. This idea may be difficult to accept because modern users of the Bible tend to treat the Bible as a homogeneous whole rather than as what it is: a collection of largely originally unrelated texts. Treating the Bible as a unified and homogeneous text, readers tend to develop in their own minds composite images of God (which themselves are to be distinguished from the various images of God in the Bible).

Here then, necessarily briefly, are three different ways God is represented in the biblical texts.

1. *God the Giver of Tribal Laws*: Principally, this view is reflected in the Mosaic covenant, which is found in Exod 19-23 and Leviticus. Ancient Israel is directed to keep the laws that have been given by God through Moses. The obligations to which each party is committed are stated in Lev 26: The commitments of the tribe of Israelites are given in Lev 26:3-5; and the commitments made by Yahweh are given in Lev 26:6-13. If Israel breaks any of these laws, there is a penalty: Lev 26:14-33. Would anyone doubt that the God given credit for promulgating the tribal laws takes obedience to his commands completely seriously?

2. *God the Merciful and Compassionate*: The book of Hosea is permeated by the theme of divine compassion. The narrative is at one and the same time a story of Yahweh's steadfast love for Israel, and Hosea's love for the prostitute Gomer, whom he married at God's direction (Hos 1:1-2). She bore three children (Hos 1:4-8) of whom Hosea was presumably not the father (Hos 2:4-5). Gomer abandoned the family to take up again a life of prostitution, and Hosea at God's direction bought her back (Hos 3:1-5), just as Yahweh refuses to abandon his people Israel (Hos 11:1-12). The dominant image that emerges from the book is the love and faithfulness of Yahweh in the face of Israel's unfaithfulness and abandonment of Yahweh (Hos 4:1-19).

3. *God the Capricious and Unjust*: The book of Job comes in two parts: a prose prologue (Job 1:1—2:13) and epilogue (Job 42:7-17), and a central poetic section (Job 3:1—42:6). The central section is concerned with showing that not all suffering is the result of sin. The prologue, however, casts God as a capricious eastern potentate who allows Satan to submit Job to every kind of suffering short of taking his own life—even though God knows that Job is a righteous and blameless man (Job 1:1). The only reason for Job's suffering was to settle a casual dispute between

170 UNMASKING BIBLICAL FAITHS

God and Satan concerning whether Job served God in his own self interest (Job 1:8–12; 2:3–6).

In each of these "types" I have described what seems to be the essential tone of how that particular writer views God's character. Vestiges of other views may still be seen in each text, however. For example, the major chord of Ecclesiastes seems to be *God the Distant and Disinterested Creator*. The view of this writer is that although God is the creator of all, God has little to do with the creation. Nevertheless, one does still find in Ecclesiastes vestiges of a kind of secular view of God (Eccl 3:17–18; 7:18; 8:12–13), and even a bit of traditional piety (Eccl 12:13–14). For this author God is not really a major concern in human life, and the ponderings of the author bring him virtually to the edge of despair.

My point in this essay is this: God is who we think or believe God to be. If there is a deity apart from the inventions of our minds, how would we ever come to the knowledge of that apparently completely unknown figure? Does one pick the God with which one is most comfortable and claim that figure as true God? Or does one simply stay with the understanding of the God of one's personal childhood? (5–17–16)

§71 FROM WHERE DOES A SENSE OF THE DIVINE COME?

The Bible and modern Christian faith generally describe the Judeo-Christian God as something like "tangible essence" existing somewhere in space and time as part of our universe. In short God is essentially an entity of the cosmos. The modern Christian church perpetuates that concept of God in its hymns, sermons, liturgy, prayers, and so forth. In most ethical biblical concepts of God, however, God is far less like we are; that is to say, God is not just another inhabitant of our physical universe. At least three concepts of God are found in the Bible that mostly bypass the general view that God is like us but more powerful. In 1 Kgs 19:12 God is conceived as sound, "a gentle whisper" (Smith-Goodspeed); in John 4:24 God is described as "spirit," and in 1 John 1:8 God is described as attitude: "God is love."

Spirit may still be tangible, however; depending on how it is conceived. If spirit is conceived as an entity that takes up space, like visible steam from a tea kettle, or the nearly invisible vapor arising from a heated substance, or the taste left in the rum cake when the "spirits" have evaporated, then it would follow that spirit is tangible. But if spirit is not left-over taste or vaporous mist or something barely visible to the eye, or if spirit does not leave an image on the retina of the eye, then what is it?

I would suppose that God, as intangible spirit, is likely conceived as denizen of a parallel spirit(ual) universe, a complex that does not occupy space and time. If this is the case, then God is not part of the physical universe but is "over there" in the spirit(ual) universe—along with other invisible spirits (good, evil, and unclean); along with demons and devils; along with Satan and other spiritual forces such as angels; along with principalities, powers, rulers, and authorities (see, e.g., Rom 8:38; Eph 2:2; 3:10; 6:12).

I prefer the description in 1 Kgs 19:12 or 1 John 4:8. These descriptions reject the crass physical manifestations of God, such as wind, seismic convulsions, and fire (1 Kgs 19:9–13). God is conceived, for good or ill, as no more or less than a particular sense or an awareness or attitude, whether in the mind or vibrating on the eardrum. It is once stated that Elijah "heard" the voice (1 Kgs 19:13), but people "hear" voices and even carry on conversations in the mind, in dreams, in "visions" without the voices resonating on the eardrum. Twice the voice is not "heard" but is simply "there" (1 Kgs 19:12), "and a voice came to him" (1 Kgs 19:13)—that is to say, "an awareness" of a voice. When the Divine is sensed, the sensing is always incomplete and imperfect. What is sensed does not exist over against the one who senses it, but can, perhaps, arise from within.

It is obvious that people who claim to sense the Divine do so in different ways; whether the awareness is a divine righteousness that must be appeased (as sensed by Paul) or a divine emptiness (as sensed by the author of Ecclesiastes) or a divine legalism (as sensed by "Moses") or a divine capriciousness (as sensed by Job) or the sense of the sacredness of all life (as sensed by Albert Schweitzer[1]). In sensing and experiencing the Divine, we do not each have the same sense or experience. Consider the differences in sensing the Divine that are projected in the mystical Orthodox tradition or the philosophical Roman Catholic tradition, or in the charismatic Assemblies of God tradition, or in the emotional fundamentalist Baptist tradition. The difference of religious experience is most marked when the various international religions of the world are considered; Buddhist, Shinto, Hindu, Taoist, and Islamic traditions provide striking testimony as to how diverse religious experiences can be.

1. Meyer, "Affirming Reverence for Life"; Schweitzer, *Out of My Life and Thought*, 102–18, 254–83.

Whence have come those fleeting impulses that have led out into such startlingly different religious experiences? Are they "sent" to us from "out there"? That is, have they come from a parallel invisible universe of the Spirit? There is no definitive critical answer to this question.[2] All the evidence is anecdotal and testimonial. It consists only of the experiences claimed by those who believe in and attest to the parallel spirit universe. There is nothing to analyze except their confessions and anecdotal experiences—not even a fleeting image on the eye's retina.

Is it possible that our various senses of the Divine arise from within each of us? That is, the impulses come not from "out there" but from somewhere in the cortex of the human brain, or they are built into our DNA. If that is the case, some of us would seem to be hardwired either to receive Divine impulses or, more probably, to create a sense of the Divine.

In the final analysis, the question of whence originates the sense of the Divine is unanswerable, but then the answer may not matter at all. In the long run, human beings are better for having sensed the Divine—however imperfectly so. The difficulty lies in vetting what people claim to experience as the Divine. Paul thought Satan could "disguise himself as an angel of light" (2 Cor 11:13–15). The warning is inevitable: be wary of those who confidently claim to have an absolute knowledge of the Divine. (8-2-15)

§72 GOD THE SPIRIT IN A MATERIAL WORLD

In the Christian tradition God is conceived as invisible Spirit (Col 1:15; John 4:24) and not as matter or stuff occupying space and time; that is to say, God does not exist materially and hence is not substantial, but rather simply *is* (if at all) in a way that cannot be apprehended by any of the physical senses; that is, by seeing, touching, tasting, hearing, smelling. This inability to access God directly makes any description of God completely subjective. A God composed of substance would be subject to the change, dissolution, and decay of the cosmos, as all cosmic stuff is, and hence could scarcely be God.

God's immateriality makes it rather difficult for one to describe God with any degree of accuracy or reliability. Hence a responsible description of God is simply impossible, a logical fact that renders all descriptions of God inadequate and misleading. Therefore in communities of faith, for

---

2. See the discussion at §72 and §73, p. 174, below.

THE NATURE OF GOD   173

the most part, believers in God are only describing what they have been taught about God's character and activities.

Such a state of affairs forces the question, how is God present, if at all? Does divine Spirit simply permeate matter like leaven does flour, for example? A little leaven mixed into flour and water and kneaded becomes dough, which rises in the oven (Matt 13:33), changing the compound into something different.

One theological explanation for the relationship between Spirit and matter is called "panentheism": God as Spirit permeates all matter in the universe but is not to be identified with any one thing;[3] that is to say, God the Spirit is infused throughout the universe but without mingling with matter. Apparently the mingling of divine Spirit and matter would be necessary to "enhance" or "raise" matter to a higher level, as leaven in flour does. We are still bothered with the problems of a dangerous universe, however: disease, flood, drought, famine, natural disaster, and so forth. Our natural world does not seem "enhanced" by an infusion of Spirit throughout matter but remains clearly flawed, as Paul seemed to recognize when he anticipated that "the creation itself will be set free from its bondage to decay" (Rom 8:19–21).

Perhaps God as Spirit simply interfaces with matter only periodically here and there, and is not engaged in its day-to-day operations. The general regularity of the universe seems to eliminate this possibility, if the regularity of the universe is conceived as the result of God's being in control.

On the other hand, perhaps the general regularity of the universe is caused by God as Spirit enabling the universe. But if that is the case, why then are there so many "glitches" in the smooth operation of the universe? Perhaps God as Spirit simply hovers over the universe in a way similar to Gen 1:2 and is not directly involved with the universe at all. Religious groups in the early years of the Christian period argued for a sharp divide between the cosmos and God. Thus the highest deity had nothing to do with the creation of the cosmos; some attributed the cosmos to the work of a lesser God in the divine realm.[4] In such systems of thought the matter of the cosmos was seen as flawed and evil.

My colleagues would describe my question about the interface of God the Spirit and matter as a fool's errand. My religiously conservative

3. Robinson, *Exploration into God*, 86–96.
4. Rudolph, *Gnosis*, 67–87.

friends would say, accept on faith that God the Spirit is involved with matter, even if how Spirit and matter are related cannot be quantified. My critically inclined friends would also counsel me to abandon the question on the basis that Spirit itself falls outside the parameters of any kind of objective proof. Perhaps they are correct, but if there is no way logically to explain how Spirit and matter are related, Christianity is left open to the charge of superstition and self-delusion on a grand scale. And that means it is the case that human beings through time have simply convinced themselves that there is a parallel spiritual universe of Gods and other spirits; and Christianity is merely another in a long line of inadequate religious views of reality, continuing the formally pagan but now Christian view of a belief in a real world of spiritual realities *out there somewhere*—within, alongside, or parallel to the material cosmos. (10-7-13)

§73 MATTER AND SPIRIT: MAKING SENSE OF IT ALL

There is no way to examine God directly, and hence we must rely on secondary evidence to talk about God. We can (1) examine the temples and ruins of temples human beings have built in honor of a good and great Invisible Spirit, (2) examine the testimonies of those who claim to have experienced the great Invisible Spirit or some other divine personage, (3) examine their responses as to what they think the character of God's Spirit is, (4) examine their fearful responses to what they perceive to be evil Spirits, (5) or examine their written confessions about both good and evil Spirits. The bottom line, however, is that we cannot examine God directly. It is only possible to examine human responses to what they claim is God; that is, to examine human archaeology, anthropology, psychology, and theology. Hence I must begin with the material universe to inquire into God, and here is how I personally make sense of matter and spirit.

Observation #1: If the universe is not eternal, it had a beginning. If it is eternal,[5] it is our "Alpha and Omega," a claim put on God's lips (so to speak) in the Apocalypse (Rev 1:8).

---

5. While not claiming that the universe is eternal, the steady-state theory for explaining the universe contends that it extends to an infinite time in the past; see Lovell, "Origin of the Universe," 419-20.

Observation #2: It does not appear that the universe is eternal, however, since it is expanding at a rapid rate. This expansion is an indication of remarkable change (hence, the universe is not eternal because it changes; even stars are born and die[6]). This datum (i.e., the expansion of the universe) makes the idea of the known universe originating in a big bang a plausible theory.[7] But from whence came the elements necessary to produce a big bang, and what ignited it? The igniter and matter-from-nothing become the basis of all that possesses the quality or state of existence and constitute the Ground of Being, since from the other side of the big bang they have brought an end to nothingness or nonbeing. But both igniter and matter-from-nothing are invisible, unknown, and unknowable, since they are precedent to and not immediately tangential (even touching lightly) to our present cosmos. If they were tangent to or part of the cosmos, then possibly the universe has simply perpetuated itself (see *Observation #1*). Hence I conclude that there is an Unknown, Unknowable preceding the big bang.

Observation #3: In theological thinking God is thought of as the Ground of Being in the sense that God is the ground or matrix that lets all things in our cosmos come to be.[8] Accordingly the Ground of all Being is thought of as "God." But the Ground of Being from my perspective is not part of the physical universe or even involved with the universe, a fact that is verified for me by observation of the known natural and social worlds. The survival of the fittest (i.e., Mr. Darwin's more plausible theory of the *Origin of the Species by Natural Selection*[9]) rules out from my perspective any master plan for the universe and its denizens, and it seems to be the case with social organisms as well, for they succeed or fail based on human ingenuity, energy, and money, and one must suppose, that also includes the social organism called church. In short, no overall supernatural guidance or care appears to exist for things as they are. The universe and human beings have simply emerged into existence in the cosmos. We are left to our own devices and must do the best we can. In short, human fate hinges on good genes, lady luck, and natural selection.

Observation #4: Human beings are, however, universally "religious." To judge by our universal preoccupation with religion, religious-like

6. Sagan, *Cosmos*, 246–67; Bragg, "Universe of Light," 290–91; Gamow, "Limits of the Unknown," 395.

7. Gamow, "Limits of the Unknown," 380–81.

8. Tillich, *Systematic Theology*, 1:235–38.

9. Darwin, *Origin of the Species*, 76–144.

gestures are endemic virtually to all human cultures. Hence humans seem to have in some way come by a concept of a Divine Other, and seem to have a vague sense, awareness or impression of a Divine Other, or they claim to. The limitations and imperfections in our sense of a Divine Other account for the contrasting varieties of human religious expression: we sense in part and imperfectly so. Because of the universality of the religious preoccupation, however, our "sensing" a Divine Other seems plausible; so where does the concept of a Divine Other come from, or does it arise from within us; that is to say, are we taught it, or is the concept of a Divine Other simply latent in the material stuff of the universe,[10] the human gene, and/or DNA?

Observation #5: Certainly it is possible that we each generate the concept of a Divine Other from within ourselves, or perhaps it is generated by a few and learned by others.

Observation #6: Possibly concepts of a Divine Other arise from the Ground of Being, that is, from "the other side" of the Big Bang. How might that occur, if the Ground of Being is not, and never was, a part of our experienced reality (see *Observation #2*)? Astrophysics suggests a possible parallel in the material world for how that might happen. Scientists discover unseen planets that orbit stars (those tiny pinpricks of light in the night sky) in distant solar systems by watching for the gravitational effect of an invisible planet on a visible star: "when the star has a planet orbiting around it, the star wiggles slightly from the gravitational attraction of the planet."[11] There may also be a similar effect from an "attraction" between the Ground of Being and human beings that prompts the universal religious responses. (The truth of the matter is that human beings seem to be hardwired for religion and must learn how to live without recourse to Gods.)

The scientist sees nothing except the effect of the gravitational pull (i.e., the wiggle of the star) and does not actually see the planet or the gravitational attraction. Claims of "sensing" a Divine Other may be based on a similar "wiggle" effect between human psyches and the Unknown Unknowable. The only evidence of gravity between the star and the postulated invisible planet is the "wiggle"; the only evidences of the influence

---

10. Basing this idea on the theory that religiosity may be as much an "evolutionary inevitability" as intelligence is Morris, "Evolution," 154–65.

11. Sagan, *Cosmos*, 210–12; it is what Nick Cohen calls "the radical velocity method" of identifying planets in other solar systems: "Various Methods used to identify Planets in other Solar Systems."

of a Divine Other on humanity are the religious responses, as imperfect and different as they are. (8-14-15)

§74 IS THE HOLY SPIRIT PART OF A TRINITY?

The Nicene Creed describes the third person in the Trinity this way:

> [We believe] . . . in the Holy Spirit, the Lord and Life-giver, that proceedeth from the Father, who with the Father and Son is worshipped together and glorified together, who spoke through the prophets.[12]

Thus in contemporary orthodox faith the Holy Spirit is believed to be a persona of a Divine Godhead: Father, Son, and Holy Spirit; "God in three persons, blessed Trinity," so the hymn goes.[13]

The confession in creed and hymn sounds plausible, but when one goes to the biblical texts to confirm that the earliest Christians actually shared this fourth/fifth-century belief in a Triune Godhead, there is a significant problem. The Trinity (i.e., belief in a three-in-one God), as such, is not in the Bible—at least not in so many words, although all three of these figures are mentioned together in 2 Cor 13:14 (except that the earliest Greek manuscript, P[46], omits the word *holy*), where they appear side by side in a benediction that does not claim these three figures as the Trinity of orthodox faith.

In the earliest Christian literature (the Pauline letters) Paul maintains a healthy distance between God and Jesus Christ (1 Cor 15:27-28; 8:4-6; Phil 3:3); Paul clearly conceives God as one (i.e. as a singular unity: e.g. 1 Cor 8:4, 6; Rom 3:30; Gal 3:19-20). His emphasis on the unity of God ultimately derives from the Israelite faith (see the Shema, Deut 6:4-5).

Paul is a writer of letters; he does not write religious handbooks, and does not usually express himself systematically, which means that ideas must be tracked here and there throughout his letters. When Paul calls God "spirit," he is describing the essential nature of God. Spirit is not an appendage of God so that one may distinguish it as an entity independent from God. God *is* spirit. That seems clear from Paul's appeal to Exod 34:25-35 when arguing for the new covenant in Christ (2 Cor

---

12. Bettenson and Maunder, eds., *Documents* (3rd ed.), 29
13. Heber, "Holy, Holy, Holy," first and fourth stanzas.

3:4–18). "The Lord [i.e., Yahweh, God of Israel] is the spirit" [2 Cor 3:17a] to whom people turn [2 Cor 3:16–18] to have the veil removed from their minds when the books of Moses are read:

> And we all with unveiled face, beholding the glory of the Lord, are being changed into his likeness from one degree of glory to another [as happened to Moses, Exod 34:29–30, 35]; for this comes from the Lord who is the spirit (2 Cor 3:18 RSV).

God as spirit is described by Paul in various ways: "the spirit" and "his spirit" (Rom 8:11), "the spirit of God" (Rom 8:9), "the spirit of holiness" (Rom 1:4), "the spirit of the living God" (2 Cor 3:3), "his holy spirit" (1 Thess 4:8), the "holy spirit" (Rom 5:5). Spirit and holy spirit are used interchangeably in 1 Cor 12:3. He even uses the expression "spirit of Christ" interchangeably with the "spirit of God" (Rom 8:9–11; Gal 4:6–7).

Here is how I make sense of the interchangeableness of God's spirit and the spirit of Christ in the Pauline letters. Jesus was a human being *appointed* son of God "by the spirit of holiness" at the moment God raised him from the dead (Rom 1:3–4; Acts 17:31). He, the human being, was the "first fruit of those who have fallen asleep" (1 Cor 15:20; 1 Thess 4:23), and as the first fruit he became the means through whom God "was reconciling the world to himself" (2 Cor 5:19). Thus, he is the "precursor" whose spirit, having been first transformed by the spirit of holiness, enabled other human beings to share that experience (1 Thess 4:8). Through the transformed spirit of this human being (Jesus), other human beings become sons of God (Gal 4:4–7; Rom 8:9–11) by sharing in the divine spirit; yet the divine spirit remains a singularity and undivided, is how Paul's reasoning must have gone (cf. 1 Cor 8:6; 12:4–13), even though he is hardly clear in his expression and terminology.

God's "Anointed" (i.e., Christ), as precursor, became the conduit through whom the blessings of the divine spirit are shared (1 Cor 8:6; compare Heb 6:20, where a later writer uses the term "precursor"): grace (Rom 5:2, 21; 1 Cor 1:4); peace (Rom 5:1), reconciliation (Rom 5:11; 2 Cor 6:18), deliverance (Rom 7:24–25), sanctification (1 Cor 1:2), victory (1 Cor 15:57), all God's promises (2 Cor 1:20), justification (Gal 2:16), righteousness (Phil 1:11), salvation (1 Thess 5:9)—all come through Christ.

It does not appear to me that Paul conceived God as a Trinity, as later orthodoxy did. But then, to judge by his letters Paul was scarcely an orthodox Christian in the sense of the later creeds, as some already suggested in the second century (2 Pet 3:14–17). Might this present essay also have been construed by the writer of 2 Peter as a twisting of Paul's words? (11-25-15)

§75 SHOULD WE ALWAYS TRUST GODS?[14]

Can humans really trust the Gods always to treat us with integrity, when on our better days we appear to have a sharper sense of morality than they do on their worse days? We assume Gods will always act with integrity; after all, they are divine. We expect wicked behavior from demons, but not from Gods. The record, however, is flawed. For instance, in Homer's epic poem *The Iliad* Zeus deceives Agamemnon with a lying dream—to the hurt and detriment of Achilles (2.1–35). And even Yahweh, the God of the Israelites, sent a lying spirit to deceive King Ahab of Israel so he would be defeated in battle. Later he placed lying spirits in the mouths of all the prophets of Israel (1 Kgs 22:19–23). On another occasion, he sent an evil spirit to torment King Saul (1 Sam 16:14–15). These are certainly strange behaviors for Gods! Such behavior by the Gods recalls Homer's description of Zeus's father, Cronus, as the God "of the crooked ways" (*Iliad* 2.205).

Humans believe it is not ethical behavior when one deceives or mistreats others. And that is one reason the serious misconduct and loss of a sense of moral value by American soldiers in the Abu Ghraib prison during the Iraqi war was so reprehensible. The soldiers were held accountable for their actions, but apparently Gods can act as they wish—and with impunity! We explain their occasionally shocking ways by arguing that Gods obviously must know the big picture. Since they are Gods, we assume they must know what is best for us in the long term. Our human view of things is finite; we see matters dimly and then only in the short term. So we conclude: an event appearing tragic to us must only be so from our limited perspective, for surely the Gods always act justly. For that reason, we tend to think that our personal tragedies must somehow be for the best. This solution, however, leaves honest folk with a nagging ethical question: how can bringing anyone harm ever be considered "good"? Is it possible that Gods do not *always* know best after all, and humans invented that idea to cover up divine misbehavior? Or is it, perhaps,

---

14. An earlier version of this essay appeared in Hedrick, *House of Faith*, 12–13; used by permission.

possible that the writers of our religious texts have mistakenly misled us? For example, did Jesus really instruct his disciples to take up the sword? (Luke 22:36).

The biblical book of Job is one of the clearest examples of divine misbehavior in the literature. Job simply could not understand why tragedy struck his life. When his "friends" told him that God punished him because of his sins, Job was perplexed. He was willing to admit that he was not perfect, but he knew his suffering was not proportionate to whatever sins he may have committed. And Job actually was correct: God *permitted* Job's unconscionable suffering to see if he would commit a greater sin, as the text makes plain (Job 1–2).

"The ends never justify the means" is clearly an idealistic sentiment, and not uncommonly most of us on our worst days do not quite measure up to what would be considered ethical behavior. In cases of expediency, we frequently find our ends justifying our means, like at Abu Ghraib, for example. Nevertheless, when we privilege ends over means, we at least know we are traveling down a lower road. And if we finite humans *sometimes* know the difference between high roads and low roads, shouldn't Gods *always* know the difference? (4-7-16)

§76 REVELATION: DID GOD TALK TO PAUL?

The ancient Greeks and Romans were both very superstitious and religious. One of their many ways of discovering the will of the Gods was to consult special intuitive persons at some twenty religious sanctuaries throughout the ancient Mediterranean world. These diviners of the will of the Gods were called "oracles." They were the mediums through whom a God transmitted revelations and oracles (as the sayings of a God were called). The most famous of these religious sanctuaries was Delphi, located on the slopes of Mount Parnassus overlooking the Gulf of Corinth. People, from kings to paupers, came from all over the ancient world to Delphi to consult the Pythian oracle; she was the prophetess of the God Apollo, one of the sons of Zeus. She received her revelations while being possessed by the God in a cave located under the temple of Apollo, whose ruins still exist, and she would speak for Apollo to those seeking answers to questions (compare Acts 16:16–18: where a young girl is described as possessed by a "Pythian spirit").

In the latter part of the first century and early second century CE, a philosopher and literary figure, Plutarch, who was a priest at Delphi, wrote an essay explaining why many oracular centers in Greece had ceased to function.[15] In other words a customary religious practice of ancient Greek religion was dying out.

In the first third of the first century after the death of Jesus (around 30 CE) certain followers of the Christ were also believed to be prophets (see Did. 11:3–13:7; 1 Cor 12:10, 29); they were moved by the Spirit to utter "the Word of the Lord" to their contemporaries, just as was done by the oracles in the religious sanctuaries of ancient Greece and Rome. One such early Christian prophet was the author of Matthew's Gospel, who channeled a saying of the resurrected Christ in Matt 28:18–20.

But perhaps more interesting is the claim of the apostle Paul that he himself, like the Pythia at Delphi, possessed the Spirit of God (1 Cor 7:40), and said that Christ spoke through him (2 Cor 13:3). Hence he was able to channel sayings (or oracles) of the deity, as the Pythia and the early Christian prophet Matthew had done. Here is an instance of Paul claiming to be privy to "an abundance of revelations," channeling a saying of the Lord:

> And to keep me from being too elated by the abundance of revelations, a thorn was given me in the flesh, a messenger of Satan, to harass me, to keep me from being too elated. Three times I besought the Lord about this that it should leave me; but he said to me "My grace is sufficient for you, for my power is made perfect in weakness" (2 Cor 12:7–9 RSV).

Paul claims further that the gospel he preached was not something he learned from others or something he came up with on his own, but rather that it came to him directly "through a revelation of Jesus Christ" (Gal 1:11–12). He even claimed that he was directed "by revelation" to do certain things (Gal 2:2), and on occasion he "would speak a revelation" to the assembly of saints (1 Cor 14:6). He was not that unusual in this regard, however, for others in the gatherings of saints also were believed to utter divine revelations to those assembled (1 Cor 14:26; for the divine gifts in the Pauline assemblies see also 1 Cor 12:4–11). These spiritual abilities were not given to everyone but only to certain individuals (1 Cor 12:28–30). Paul used the word "revelation" to describe what he claimed to receive from God and applied it also to the prophetic writings of the Jewish Scriptures (Rom 16:25–27). In other words, it would appear that he considered his revelations as authoritative as the Scriptures.

15. Plutarch, "Obsolescence of Oracles."

To judge by the experience of John, oracular utterances are received while the oracle is possessed by the spirit in a state of spiritual ecstasy (Rev 1:9–20); that is to say, while the oracle is in a state of rapturous delight and beyond reason and self control. Even today in certain charismatic churches glossolalia (speaking in tongues) is believed to be a revelation from God.[16] Like the ancient oracle, the individual is thought possessed by the deity when bringing a revelation to the assembly (see Paul's description of such an occasion: 1 Cor 14:1–25). But for most of those churches, which historically descend from the Reformation of the sixteenth century, glossolalia is a thing of the past. (2-9-16)

§77 COULD GOD HAVE A CHARACTER FLAW?

From my very earliest memory in Sunday school I learned that the Bible teaches that "God is Love." For example, in 1 John 4:8, 16 the writer describes the essence of God's character as love. Imagine my surprise one Sunday morning in Baptist Bible study we stumbled across another facet of God's character: God also hates, and even bears grudges. The prophet Malachi "quotes" God as saying, "I loved Jacob but I hated Esau; I laid waste his hill country and left his inheritance to jackals of the desert" (Mal 1:2–3, RSV; cf. Rom 9:13). And apparently God continues to bear a grudge against them, for Malachi adds: they are a "people with whom the LORD is angry forever" (Mal 1:4).

Why would God hate Esau and treat his inheritance so cruelly? Recall that Esau had sold his right of primogeniture (rights of the firstborn, Deut 21:15–17) to his brother Jacob (Gen 25:29–34); Esau's poor judgment in selling his birthright (Gen 25:29–34) for a little bread and a bowl of lentils may have been the cause of God's hatred of Esau and might explain why his descendants (the Edomites, Gen 36:9, 43) were later conquered by the Israelites (2 Chr 25:11–25; 2 Sam 8:12–14). At any rate, the descendants of Jacob, the Israelites (Gen 32:28), were ascendant over the Edomites because it was what God wanted (2 Chr 25:20) because God favored Jacob's descendants (Gen 32:28) and apparently bore a grudge against Esau's descendants. I can understand God being irritated with Esau for his poor judgment, but that seems an insufficient reason to *hate* him and to continue bearing a grudge against his descendants.

---

16 Wikipedia, "Glossolalia."

Hate seems to have been another character trait of God as understood in the Hebrew Bible, for Esau is not all that God hates. Job thought God hated him as well (Job 16:9), and even the Israelites at one point thought God hated them (Deut 1:27). And John did portray God claiming to hate the Nicolaitans (Rev 2:6), as God also did the Ephraimites (Hos 9:15).

God also hates human character flaws: robbery (Isa 61:8), evil in the heart and false oaths (Zech 8:17). A list of other human character flaws that God hates appears in Prov 6:16–19 (haughty eyes, a lying tongue, hands that shed innocent blood, a heart that devises wicked plans, feet that run to evil, bearing false witness, and the one who sows discord). God also hates certain Judean feasts and celebrations (Isa 1:14; Amos 5:21) along with evildoers (Ps 5:5) and idol worship (Ps 31:6; Jer 44:4).

In the Baptist tradition I have always been told that "God loves the sinner but hates the sin." But that really does not appear to be the case in the Bible. God also seems to hate those who do the "sin" (that is, whatever God may disapprove of). It is true that the Deuteronomist claimed that God hated every abominable thing (again, what God disapproves of, Deut 12:31), but it also seems to be the case that God hates those that perpetuate abominations, including those, for example, described in Prov 6:16–19.

Unless a person holds the view that the Bible is literally the words of God or words in some way inspired by God, one might recognize that describing God as "hating" is a quite primitive, anthropomorphic description of God—that is to say, it attributes human characteristics to God. In other words the biblical writers were describing God in their own image, as if God were only a bigger and more powerful human being—something the Greeks and Romans suggested by the physical size of their statuary in representing the Gods, and their descriptions of the sometimes reprehensible behavior of the Olympians.[17] The biblical writers simply transferred human characteristics to God, including gender. However, God as spirit (John 4:24) does not have gender (i.e., God is neither he nor she), and God therefore does not experience human emotions, either those we consider positive or negative. God (if God there be) is not of the human tribe, but rather wholly other. And if God does not hate, then neither does God love. In truth, however, each of us invents God in a way that satisfies us. (6–13–15)

17. Plato, *Republic*, II.377D–383; Shorey, trans., *Republic*, 1:177–99.

§78 DOES GOD PROVIDE SIGNS THAT PORTEND FUTURE EVENTS?

Does the God of modern Christian faith deal in portents? I suppose in the final analysis, it will depend on who you ask. Portents are well-known phenomena in the ancient Greek and Roman worlds. Occurrences that otherwise might seem to be simply natural happenings in the world are regarded as omens or signs of future events, sent by the gods; for example, a flight of birds, the movements of the stars, the falling of trees in the woods, and so forth. Some in the ancient world were thought to be endowed with the ability to recognize and interpret the signs that portended future events, and thus to avoid disasters. The practice of foretelling the future through such signs was called divination, for the portents were thought to be sent by the gods.[18]

Although the practice of divination was forbidden in Israelite law (Deut 18:9–12), nevertheless portents do show up in the Old Testament. For example, Isaiah's nudity was thought to be a portent (Isa 20:2–3; 8:18), and the "handwriting on the wall" was a portent of doom for Belshazzar (Dan 5:5–31). Some prophets thought that the Day of the Lord would be preceded by fearful portents in the heavens (Isa 13:9–11; Joel 2:30–31). Some New Testament writers thought that the end-time would be preceded by similar portents in the heavens (Mark 13:24–27; Luke 21:8–28). The Apocalypse describes some specific portents (Rev 12:1; 15:1). The birth of the messiah in Matthew was preceded by the portent of a star in the heavens leading the three magi to Bethlehem (Matt 2:1–23). The ripping of the curtain of the Judean temple at the death of Jesus Mark 15:37–38) is likely a portent, which Mark declines, or neglects, to clarify.

A case on point may be the crowing of the rooster that portends Peter's denial of Jesus. Before they went out to Gethsemane where Jesus was arrested, Jesus told Peter that "before the cock crows twice you will deny me three times." (Mark 14:30). Matthew (26:34), Luke (22:34), and John (13:38), however, have Jesus predict only one crowing of the cock followed by the three denials. I have often wondered why it is that the other canonical gospels have Jesus predict only one crowing of the cock, while Jesus in Mark predicts two. It may well be because in the narration of the events Mark narrates only one crowing of the cock (Mark 14:66–72). The first crowing of the cock is *apparently* not stated in the passage, although some reliable manuscripts add a first crowing at the end of Mark 14:68:

---

18. Cicero, "On Divination."

"and the cock crowed." New Testament textual critics add a first crowing appearing in some manuscripts to the end of 14:68 [in square brackets].[19] With the square brackets textual critics are indicating that they are not completely convinced of the authenticity of the words enclosed in the square brackets. In any case, a first crowing of the cock, whether or not Mark narrated it, must have served as the portent of Peter's great denial and initiated the sad drama, which concluded immediately upon Peter's third denial (Mark 14:72).

The motif of crowing cocks as portents also appears in the Greco-Roman tradition. Such a sign was thought to portend victory in battle for the Thebans over the Spartans,[20] but the portent is ridiculed by the first-century-BCE Roman writer, Cicero.[21]

Does God actually warn human beings of events, whether good or bad, through seemingly inconsequential natural occurrences such as the flight of birds, the crowing of roosters, the cawing of crows, or other natural events? Portents are attributed to God in the Bible, but how about today? Should modern users of the Bible regard portents as superstition, or "gospel truth"? And if they consider such events as reliable signs, do they consult modern diviners or augurs for a reading of the signs before undertaking significant activities in their lives? If, on the other hand, one determines that portents and divining the future are simply the stuff of ancient superstition, which have no basis in fact, how then should one regard their appearance in the Bible? (8–7–14)

§79 WHO DECIDES WHAT OFFENDS GOD?

I can almost hear someone saying, this is a trick question! Obviously, it is the injured party who decides what offends him or her. But the problem is more complicated. The Jewish/Christian God hasn't really spoken for himself (audibly) since Old Testament time or New Testament time. At least certain ancient texts claim that God at one time spoke audibly for himself. In the Bible, however, others also spoke for God by putting words in God's mouth (so to speak). In modern times some are more skeptical that God speaks (or ever spoke) audibly. People hearing voices

---

19. Metzger, *Textual Commentary*, 97.
20. Cicero, "On Divination," I.xxxiv.74
21. Cicero, "Divination," II.xxvi.56–57.

(divine or otherwise) are thought mentally unstable, and generally are locked away if they are thought to be dangerous to themselves or others.

The absence of God's audible voice is likely one (subconscious) reason that fundamentalist and evangelical Christians tout the Bible as "the Word of God." Without the words coming directly from God in some fashion, however, the message attributed to God is suspect, and we can never be certain what offends God. We only know what we have been told.

However impermeable we may think the Bible is as a stable platform for specifying God's likes and dislikes, the fact is that the Bible is permeable and porous, composed of several layers, and includes voices other than the Divine.

The English translator of the ancient Greek or Hebrew text one reads as being "from God" is another voice added to the mix. Each ancient word has a range of possible translations in each literary context, and the translator chooses what seems to the translator to be the best fit for a given word in a particular context. Hence what one reads in English is the product of the translator's mind, experience, and personal theological views.

For example, the NIV translation of the Bible, a favorite of evangelical Christians, for Matt 19:12 reads in part: "for some are eunuchs because they were born that way; others were made that way by men; and *others have renounced marriage* because of the kingdom of heaven." The RSV translation of this same verse reads, "for there are eunuchs who have been so from birth, and there are eunuchs who have been made eunuchs by men, and *there are eunuchs who have made themselves eunuchs* for the sake of the kingdom of heaven" (a eunuch is a castrated male). The translators render the text so differently that the general reader is left wondering what the text actually says.

Textual critics who prepare critical editions of the ancient texts that are read in modern translations also contribute to the permeability of the text. To establish the critical edition, they compare all copies of ancient manuscripts—no two of which are exactly alike in all particulars. They evaluate all of the variations in the manuscripts, debate them, and then vote to decide what they think the text originally read. Their decisions are made on the basis of the scholars' reading of the evidence, their experience, expertise, personal theological views, and debating skills.

The composers of the ancient texts themselves, however, contribute the greatest permeability to their texts. The texts of the Bible, according to fundamentalist and evangelical belief, are "inspired" by God. The expression "inspired" is explained as meaning "God-breathed" (2 Tim 3:16–17), suggesting that even though God no longer speaks audibly, the words of the Bible are imbued with the authority of God, meaning that they tell readers what God expects of them as human beings. Of course any putative "inspiration" from God would compete in the mind of the original writer with the writer's experience, background, prejudices, inherited theological beliefs, and so forth. For example, the writer of Leviticus did not create that text in a moment of time, but its author composed the text out of the earlier experiences of ancient Israel as a people. The original composition has drawn on Israelite traditions that evolved out of the life of the community.[22]

So who decides what is offensive to God? Likely the modern religious community decides which ancient offenses should be avoided and which ancient prohibitions can be ignored. Here is a case on point: The ancient writer in Leviticus represents God as audibly saying that it is forbidden for a male "to lie with a male as with a woman," for "it is an abomination" (Lev 18:22). And God is likewise cited as finding it an abomination to eat anything that comes out of the water, if it does not have fins and scales (Lev 11:9–12). It leads to the odd conclusion that eating shrimp or catfish is as offensive to God as homosexuality. Modern religious leaders have a lot to say about the sinfulness of homosexuality, but, so far as I am aware, most of them say little about the sinfulness of eating shrimp or catfish. Is God still offended by the eating of shrimp and catfish do you suppose?

Religious leaders are fond of reminding their congregations that the biblical view of marriage is one man married to one woman, but God wasn't always offended by a man having multiple wives. Laws regulating the treatment of multiple wives are found in the Israelite law code (Deut 21:15–17). King Joash of Judah, who had two wives, was commended by the biblical writer for "doing what was right in the eyes of the Lord" (2 Chr 24:1–3). And other heroes in biblical history having more than one wife (viz., Jacob, Elkanah, and David) were never condemned as sinners for that reason.

While there is not, so far as I know, a contemporary comprehensive list of sins that are agreed to by all, nevertheless someone is always willing

---

22. Davies, "Leviticus."

to tell us what sin is. It would seem that in today's society sin is whatever we allow ourselves to be convinced is sinful. (5–7–15)

§80 DOES GOD COMMUNICATE IN DREAMS?

Like most everything else in religion, it depends on who you ask. People have remarkably different ideas about what God does and does not do. In contemporary Christian belief, to judge by the popular religious media on the internet, God does communicate with human beings through their dreams.[23] No matter the God under discussion, this view was common in early and late antiquity. For example, Homer (Greek, early eighth century BCE) describes the various Gods appearing in disguise in dreams, offering their guidance.[24] The God Asclepius encouraged the practice of "incubating" in his temples; that is, seeking cures from the God during dreams.[25] Plutarch (Greek, first-century CE) said, "In popular belief . . . it is only in sleep that men receive inspiration from on high."[26] Cicero (Roman, first century BCE) thought that it was "an ancient belief handed down from mythical times" that the Gods gave people the "foresight and knowledge of future events" through dreams and other means.[27] Artemidorus (Greek, second century CE), who wrote an extensive study on dreams, thought that the soul alone produced dreams, although the Gods may play a role in configuring them.[28] Aristotle (Greek, fourth-century BCE) in contrast to the common view of antiquity argued that dreams are latent remnants of sense perceptions[29] and not prophetic messages from the Gods.[30] In sleep our sense perceptions emerge in the mind as dreams. In the Israelite tradition God appeared in dreams either in person or through messengers ("angels") to give guidance (Gen 20:3–7; 31:11–13, 24; Num 12:4–8; 1 Sam 28:6; 1 Kgs 19:5–15). In the New Testament dreams play a role in only the Gospel of Matthew, specifically in Matthew's birth narrative (Matt 1:18—2:23). In Matthew's narrative Joseph

---

23. Goodwyn, "Dreams and Visions."
24. Homer, *Od.* IV.795–847. Athena sends a message in a dream to Penelope.
25. Ferguson, *Backgrounds*, 222–26.
26. Plutarch, "On the Sign of Socrates," VII.589D.
27. Cicero, *Div.*" I.i—ii.3. The person speaking in book 1 is Cicero's dialogue partner Quintus, who appears as a straw man for Cicero's own views in book 2.
28. Harris-McCoy, *Artemidorus' "Oneirocritica,"* 543–44.
29. Aristotle, *Somn.* 462a.30.
30. Aristotle, *Div. somn.*

is the main protagonist, and all the significant elements of plot turn on God's guidance in dreams (1:20–24; 2:12–13, 19–20, 22). Luke's story (Luke 1:5—2:22) and Matthew's story are dramatically different. Joseph is not the protagonist in Luke; he appears in the narrative only incidentally and then only three times by name (Luke 1:27; 2:4, 16, 33, 43), and no elements of plot in Luke turn on dreams, which are not even mentioned. Matthew also describes a troubling dream of Pilate's wife, who warns him to "have nothing to do with Jesus, a righteous man" (Matt 27:19). There is no other indication that God communicates through dreams in the New Testament. There is only one other reference to dreams in the New Testament: in Acts 2:17 the author quotes Joel 2:28 ("your old men shall dream dreams" while "young men see visions"), but no indication that God invades anyone's dreams. Traditional Christianity after the New Testament period distrusted the popular idea that the Gods communicated through dreams, and early Christians were inclined to regard supernatural communication through dreams among the pagans as the work of demons.[31]

Dreams occur during the REM (rapid eye movement) stage of sleep, between unconsciousness and beginning consciousness.[32] The modern understanding of dreams originates with the work of Sigmund Freud. According to Freud, dreams are wish fulfillment deriving from our deepest desires or anxieties.[33] In short, we are the source of what we dream; dreams do not come from a foreign initiative outside an individual but arise from within, from things we have repressed and what is latent within us. Modern theories begin with Freud and agree that dream works derive from within the dreamer.[34]

So it appears that ancient and modern thought clash. Are dreamworks only the product of an individual's id and repressed ego, or are dreams due to outside influence; that is to ask, do the Gods invade dreams for the purposes of divine communication? The problem is more complex for someone who wants to champion what might be called the "Bible view" (that is, to champion the view that God communicates through dreams), because Matthew's description of Joseph's dreams appears to be only Matthew's idea (or that of the author of the birth narrative), since Luke does not corroborate Joseph's dream works in his different story

31. Tertullian, "Treatise on the Soul," 224–26 (chapters 46–48). Dreams originated from three sources: demons, God, and the soul.

32. Van der Linden, "Science behind Dreaming."

33. Freud, *Interpretation of Dreams*, ix, 6–86.

34. Van der Linden, "Science behind Dreaming."

of the birth (Luke 2:1–39). Matthew's birth narrative, as far as dreams are concerned, appears to be based on the common view in antiquity that Gods communicate through dreams. The New Testament as a whole neither confirms nor denies that God communicates through dreams.

The only evidence that God has communicated something in a dream is the dreamer's claim to be able to sort out the divine presence from the repressed desires and anxieties issuing from the id and ego. I wouldn't bet my lifestyle on the prophetic guidance and oracular utterances a dreamer claims come from God. (5–16-13)

§81 YAHWEH—THE GOD WHO CHANGED HIS WAYS[35]

You wouldn't think it possible that a God could change his or her ways; Gods are, after all, supposed to be consistent and reliable. But it did happen, and here is the story. Yahweh, the God of Israelite faith, is known as a covenant-making God; that means he liked to make agreements. Yahweh chose a particular people in the ancient world, and made an agreement with them to be their God (Gen 12:1–3; 17:1–14; 1 Chr 16:14–18). He told Abraham that this agreement was to be *everlasting* (Gen 17:7–8); in other words, he would always be the God of Abraham's progeny. To Abraham's descendants he gave the land of Canaan for an *everlasting* possession (Gen 48:4). He established a sanctuary in Canaan in the midst of his people where he would dwell *forever* (Ezek 37:26–37). In his sanctuary incense would burn *perpetually* (Exod 30:8). He established the seventh day (the Sabbath) as a *perpetual* day of worship for the people (Exod 31:16). And he appointed a special priesthood (Num 25:12–13) to attend the sacrifices *perpetually* in his sanctuary.

Yahweh established a kingship to rule his people, and promised that the line of David, his ideal king, would rule over Israel *forever* (2 Sam 7:12–16; Ps 89:34–37). He promised as an *everlasting* statute that the high priest would annually enter the holy of holies of Yahweh's sanctuary to make atonement for the people's sins (Lev 16:34). Yahweh had a number of these *everlasting* statutes for his sanctuary (for example, Lev 23:14, 31, 41; 24:2, 3–4, 8, 9); some of them seem a little odd (for example, Lev 3:17, 10:9, 16:29, 17:7). Yahweh promised *never to alter* his agreements

---

[35]. This essay appeared under the same title in the *Fourth R* 27/3 (May–June 2014), 21; used by permission.

(Ps 89:34); even if the people broke the agreements, God would *always* keep them (Ezek 16:59–63).

But something happened; the literature of the Israelite people never clarifies exactly what occurred, but a change in God's attitude is unmistakable in Jer 31:31: Yahweh intends to establish a new covenant that would effectively undermine the old covenants (Jer 31:32). By the second century of the Common Era the God of Israelite faith had found a new people, the Christians, and with them Yahweh adopted new ways. God's new people regarded the old agreements as obsolete; that is, they were no longer in force (Heb 8:13). One second-century writer described the moment God's ways changed. In 2 Esdras Yahweh categorically rejects his former people, something he said that he would never do, and officially adopts a new people (2 Esd 1:24–25, 35–37).

The apostle Paul was uncomfortable with the idea that God's choice of a new people meant rejecting the Jewish people and tried to reconcile the God of the old ways with the God of the new ways, the old people of God with God's new people (Rom 9–11). Paul was seriously conflicted. On the one hand, he could not consider for a moment that God had rejected his people (Rom 11:1), since he considered the call of God irrevocable (Rom 11:28–29). But on the other hand, he was absolutely convinced that the gospel he preached was sanctioned by God (Rom 1:16; 10:8–9); in the end he resolved his dilemma by reassuring himself that all Israel would eventually be saved (Rom 11:25). In short, his solution was that the Jewish people would "see the light," as the God of the old ways had seen the light, and convert to faith in God's Anointed.

The new ways adopted by the God of the New Agreement is a complete abandonment of the *everlasting* agreements he had previously made with Abraham and his progeny. For the new people of God there is no longer an *everlasting* sanctuary with *perpetual* statutes, and hence no *perpetual* priesthood (Heb 9:11–14); the Sabbath has been turned over to humankind to do with as they will (Mark 2:27), and the new people of God worship on the first day of the week (Acts 20:7; 1 Cor 16:2) rather than on the seventh day (i.e., the Sabbath); there is no longer a Davidic throne; and in the minds of the new people of God the ancient *everlasting* agreements are things of the forgotten past.

Modern Jewish theologians reject out of hand the Christian claims that God has abandoned his agreements with Abraham's progeny. Christian theologians, on the other hand, are equally convinced that those "old agreements" are completely obsolete (Heb 8:8–13), and obviously, from their perspective, Yahweh has indeed adopted new ways. They explain their situation this way: it was always the intention of God to change his old ways and become Christian, although how they could possibly know God's intentions is far from clear.

And we are still left with the nagging problem of the supposedly *everlasting* agreements that Yahweh broke when he adopted his new ways. Perhaps one could think about his behavior like this: adopting Christian ways is an absolute requirement for divine converts just as it is for human converts; everything must change, or as Paul put it: "The past is finished and gone, everything has become fresh and new" (2 Cor 5:17, Phillips). Perhaps so, but such an answer does not address Yahweh's behavior in breaking his earlier agreements; and it certainly calls into question the future prospects of the new agreement; especially since the old agreements were so easily dismissed. Clearly, the ways of God are completely inscrutable (Rom 11:33)—go figure! (8-6-11)

§82 *ḤĒREM*: GOD'S HOLY WAR

As I walked into the Bible study classroom one Sunday, one of the class members had a question for me. He opened his Bible to Josh 6:15-21 and stabbed his finger at the text and said, "This bothers me greatly." I could see the pain in his face. "I was hoping you would have an answer," he added. The story that bothered him was the destruction of Jericho by the Israelites in which Joshua tells them, "The city and all that is within it shall be devoted to the LORD" (Josh 6:17 RSV), meaning that every person and thing in the city shall be destroyed. The only exceptions were that "all silver and gold and vessels of bronze and iron" were to go into the treasury of the Lord (Josh 6:19 RSV), and Rahab and her house were to be preserved (Josh 6:17). When the Israelites took the city, they followed Joshua's orders and "utterly destroyed all in the city, both men and women, young and old, oxen, sheep, and asses, with the edge of the sword" (Josh 6:21 RSV).

Such cruelty and utter disregard for life characterizes the nature of *ḥērem*, the ancient holy war. The bloody, inhuman rules of engagement are laid down in Deut 20:10-20. The conquest of the "promised land" by the Israelites was holy war. Another particularly egregious holy war engagement is the annihilation of the Amalekites (1 Sam 15), in which God (according to Samuel, his prophet, 1 Sam 15:1-3) took revenge on the

Amalekites for their opposition to Israel during the exodus from Egypt (Exod 17:8-13; Deut 25:17-19; Judg 6:3-5). God told the Israelites to destroy the Amalekites down to the last nursing baby (1 Sam 15:3).

My friend struggled with what these stories implied to him about the character of God; they implied something foreign to everything he had been taught about God, which was that God is a God of love. Two principal ideas that most conservative Christians affirm (that the Bible constitutes the revelation of God, and that the Bible is true—i.e., revealed truth) are largely responsible for his dilemma: If God is a God of love and compassion, then it could not be true that God is responsible for the unconscionable actions of Israel at Jericho and later against the Amalekites, but if the Bible is revealed truth, then what it says about God must be true: a kind of catch-22, as it were. This is a difficult position for one who believes the Bible, since both ideas are prime truths for many Christians, and my friend had inadvertently stumbled onto the clash, and what is more to the point, recognized the dilemma. It is a terrible thing to discover that God has a mean streak.

For a rational person the dilemma is an existential turning point; for both postulates cannot be correct. Hence, one must change one's view of God to match these biblical stories, or one must change how one views the Bible, although deeply held religious beliefs that support a religious view of reality generally find illogical ways to prevail over logic and reason. Changing one's understanding of God is not something like changing your socks, however, and is more difficult to do, in my opinion, than changing how one understands the Bible. In spite of what many claim, no one has ever had firsthand experience with God, since there is nothing substantive there to get your hands on (so to speak). God is invisible spirit (John 4:24; but cf. Exod 33:20-23) and does not speak audibly, as he was once believed to have done, making it rather difficult to "examine" God. Most of us don't hear God's audible voice, or see God's back as it was claimed Moses did (Exod 33:23), although we might claim experiences with burning bushes (Exod 3:1-6). What we believe about God is due to what we have learned from others, had taught to us from the Bible, and worked out in our heads—probably from our youngest years. Truth be told, one's "personal experience with God" is all in the mind (e.g., the quiet whisper, as it were, as it were, 1 Kgs 19:11-13), if anything.

It would seem far easier to change one's view of the Bible, since it is tangible, has a history, and can be examined directly more easily than one can examine God or putative experiences of God. A large body of helpful literature exists on evaluating the Bible as literature and history.[36] The way out of the dilemma is by examining the story *about* the Bible. The Bible is historical literature recording ancient quests for understanding God from the flawed human perspectives represented in its individual texts. If the Bible is revelation, it is revelation mediated through imperfections, flawed perspectives, and the social conditioning of its human authors. Its theologies and its ethical images of God are determined by the cultures and social environments in which they were written. The Bible has not one view of God, but many views of God are represented among its various authors. There is not one system of ethical values, but many conflicting systems of ethical values are reflected in its pages. In short, the various versions of the Bible (Jewish, Catholic, and Protestant) reflect what people thought and believed at various times over the some 750 years of its inscription (beginning around 600 BCE,[37] ending about 150 CE[38]).

Many Christians tend to demand too much from the Bible. Whatever more the Bible may be to true believers, it is first of all, an ancient record of humanity's search for God in the Judeo-Christian tradition. Let the Bible be what it is. Truth is not helped by denying the obvious. (4–27–13)

§83 WHAT DOES GOD DO?

Answering this question will depend on knowing which God is being considered and what is being said about that God, since not all Gods behave alike. With those two caveats stated, this is the rule: Gods do what they are believed to do—no more, no less! Basically God is an idea that "exists" in most human minds. Hence, God has no "objectified existence"; that is to say, God is not opposite me in an identifiable way that can be specifically quantified. God "is" (only in a sense) akin to an invisible, immaterial spirit, and even that description is too concrete. There is no spot in the entire universe where God can be located as an "existing thing" such as a person might be. Neither is God spread pervasively throughout

---

36. For example, a reliable beginning text at an accessible level is Hayes, *Introduction to the Bible*.

37. Around the time of the discovery of a "book of the law" in the "house of the Lord," 2 Kgs 22:3—23:25.

38. This is the date usually given for the composition of 2 Peter, the latest book of the New Testament.

the universe "in all things." To think in such a way is to objectify God by identifying God in some way with living creatures and plants (flora and fauna) and inanimate objects. A saying in the Gospel of Thomas attributed to Jesus, however, says precisely that: "Split a piece of wood; I am there. Take up a stone and you will find me there."[39] God, if God there be, does not inhabit a space-time continuum as the universe and human beings do.

Primitive societies, however, did make one-to-one identifications between their idols and the spirit of *mana* (the power of the elemental forces of nature), which they believed infused their idols. The Greeks and Romans also objectified their Gods, representing them in statuary, and even thinking that sometimes they had taken human form. They even believed their statuary possessed some of the essential power of the God. For example, in the council chamber of the city of Stratonicea (on the west coast of Asia Minor) stood the statues of Zeus and Hecate, which were said in a formal city decree to "perform good deeds of great power." The citizenry celebrated their miracles daily by offering sacrifices, burning incense, praying, and giving thanks.[40] Christians generally do not objectify God—with one noticeable exception. In the Nicene Creed Jesus the Jewish sage is elevated to "true God of true God" and "worshipped and glorified."[41] This is apparently a dual movement consisting of God becoming man and man becoming God: it may be thought of as either an instance of the divine spirit "infused" into flesh and blood, or an instance of the materializing of immaterial divine spirit into human matter (John 1:1–14).

A more easily answered historical question, however, is what is God *represented* as doing in the Bible? That question can at least be investigated. The Bible is divided into two divisions: Hebrew Bible and New Testament. Among other things these divisions are characterized by two completely different thought worlds: Semitic (Hebrew Bible) and Hellenistic (New Testament). The Hebrew Bible describes what God does from the perspective of Old Testament faiths according to Israelite tradition, and the New Testament, drawing on the Old Testament, describes what earlier followers of Jesus thought about God's behavior from the perspective of New Testament faiths.

---

39. Gos. Thom. 77b; Hedrick, *Unlocking the Secrets*, 141; compare Col 1:17.
40. La Bas and Waddington, *Inscriptions grecques et latines*, 142–43.
41. Bettenson and Maunder, eds., *Documents* (3rd ed.), 28.

"Christian" ideas about what God does come much later, as they are expressed in the early Christian creed, which is not part of the biblical tradition, although Christians argue that the biblical tradition informs Christian beliefs.

Between the two divisions of the Hebrew Bible/Old Testament and the New Testament lies Jesus of Nazareth. The thought world of Jesus is indebted to Israelite traditions. Christian theology is partly based on the thought of Jesus the Judean sage and partly on Greco-Roman ideas of divinity. The question becomes, according to Jesus the Judean sage, what does God do? The most critical sifting of all sayings attributed to Jesus in early Christian literature of the first and second centuries by the Jesus Seminar suggests that there is only modest God-language to be found in the residue of Jesus sayings that survived the lapses of memory and the piety of the church.[42] What little there is suggests that God is not sectarian but cares for good people and bad people alike (Matt 5:45b), even to the extent of providing for their daily needs, like feeding and clothing them (Matt 5:25–30; 7:11; 10:29–31). Jesus prayed for the daily provision of the basic necessities of life as if he were indigent (Matt 5:11), and he thought that God's watch-care over the world extended to "numbering the hair on people's heads" and micromanaging the deaths of sparrows (Matt 10:29–31). According to Jesus, God knows how to give good things to those who ask him (Matt 7:7–11). But Jesus also said that people of means will have difficulty entering God's imperial rule (Mark 10:28; Matt 6:24).

When it comes to Gods, the biggest mistake most people make is thinking that their *personal* beliefs control what God does. As Job said, in a sudden flash of understanding, "Shall we receive good at the hand of God and not evil?" (Job 2:10; cf. 30:26). In short, the ways of the Gods, if Gods there be, are inscrutable. (6–13-13)

§84 CONSIDER A UNIVERSE WITHOUT GOD

Is that possible—a universe without God? I suppose so, for there are many who do not believe in God, and who no longer try to explain the disjunction between our dangerous universe and a caring God. That is to say, such people have given up the idea of a compassionate God controlling

---

42. See Hedrick, *Wisdom of Jesus*, 91–144.

the universe, specifically because the universe is so evidentially hostile to those God is supposed to care about.

On the other hand, some continue to believe in God but have given up the idea that God manages the universe or is even active in the universe, for the same reason: the universe is so inhospitable that we are forced to live by our wits, luck, and experimentation without any evident help from God. Not even prayer helps such people because the only voice they hear in their heads when they pray is the echo of their own thoughts.

They continue to believe in God, however, for the simple reason that they cannot explain why there is a world abounding in abundant life, instead of nothing at all. Their inability to answer that purely technical question is why they believe in God; that is to say, they believe in some unknown x that gave us the universe and all we see about us, both good and evil. For such people God technically survives as an unknown x but not as an experienced reality in the physical world, and for that reason also God is not a spiritual reality, since they recognize that belief in a spiritual reality may only be a figment of their own imaginations or the result of undue influence by very persuasive people.

They no longer know anything about God's character. They recognize that what they know was only what they had been told, and what they were told contradicts what they experience in the world. For example, if God is active in the universe, how can we explain evil going unchecked? If God controls the world, how can we explain the incompetent management of the divine weather desk? Indiscriminately killing hundreds and thousands through floods, tornadoes, hurricanes, and other natural disasters is simply not competent or compassionate management of the weather. Other examples of Godly incompetence or malfeasance in the exercise of the divine prerogatives can be cited, but they all inevitably lead to the same conclusion: that God, as generally conceived in Christian faith (i.e., compassionate and caring), must be absent from the world.

The fact that people can live without relying on God's involvement in the universe raises the question: what is left to Christians who would be forced to surrender the idea that the physical world of matter can be spiritually manipulated through faith in the Christian God and prayer? The issue can be positively asked in this way: what does Christianity have left to offer if God is absent from the universe? Here, very briefly, is what may be left.

- A *caring church community*: where joys are jointly celebrated and sorrows commiserated.
- A *sharing church community*: where members share the same traditions, know the same hymns, speak in the same idiom, and share similar values—the bedrock of which is the welfare and worth of the individual.
- A *common goal*: which is to be "the light of the world" and "the salt of the earth" (Matt 5:13–14; Gos. Sav. 1:4[43]): that is to say, the goal is to transform society by the humanitarian values of Jesus of Nazareth.

But spiritual magic, i.e., manipulating the physical world by spiritual means, is no longer an option in the face of modern science's success in explaining much of what previously belonged to the domain of religion. Christians must face the vicissitudes of life alone, with only the palliative comfort and encouragement of the community.

Will that be enough, or will Christianity, an ancient blending of religions of East and West, meet the same fate as the Greco-Roman religions? (5–24–14)

---

43. Miller, ed., *Complete Gospels*, 401–10.

6

Jesus of Nazareth

§85 THE BASIC PROBLEM OF HISTORICAL JESUS STUDIES[1]

Criticism: to make judgments in the light of evidence.

Everyone interested in Jesus of Nazareth should be interested in this short essay. I am not certain who first stated the basic problem of historical Jesus studies in so many words, but any historian who works comparatively and critically with the gospels today immediately becomes aware of the problem. Here is how the German scholar Wilhelm Wrede formulated the problem in 1901: "How do we separate what belongs properly to Jesus from what is the material of the primitive community?"[2] Wrede may actually have been first to state the problem in this way. Albert Schweitzer, who critiqued all the scholarly lives of Jesus in German and French written from 1778 through 1901, was in the best position to have recognized the problem, but in fact Schweitzer did not. Schweitzer rejected Wrede's literary-critical analysis of Mark in 1906 and assumed that the earliest two Synoptic Gospels (Mark and Matthew) were historically reliable in what they reported.[3] He also was less than critical in what he generally

---

1. This essay appeared under the same title in the *Fourth R* 28/1 (2015), 21; used by permission.
2. Wrede, *Messianic Secret*, 4.
3. Schweitzer, *Quest*, 394, and xiv–xvi.

regarded as authentic Jesus tradition.[4] After Schweitzer's book, no critical studies of Jesus were written until 1956, in part because of the difficulty of separating Jesus from the church's beliefs about him.[5] An axiom of critical Jesus studies is this: the gospels contain some reliable historical information about Jesus, but that data must be separated out from the faith descriptions of Jesus that obscure them.

To judge from the spate of critical Jesus books published at the end of the twentieth century, it appears that the situation has changed.[6] In spite of scholarship's failure to solve the basic problem, scholars have once again begun writing "biographies" of Jesus. Some even confidently combine an extensive "course of life" with a psychological analysis of Jesus. Nevertheless, these studies fail to lay out for readers, first and foremost, exactly where they draw the line between the good-intentioned machinations of the early community and Jesus himself.

Actually in the two-hundred-fifty-year history of history-of-Jesus research only once has it happened that a large group of scholars has convened to address formally the basic problem of Jesus research.[7] The Jesus Seminar did its study in the public eye (not behind the ivy-covered walls of academia), reached a consensus (that did not please everyone), and published a report to the public, which included their findings and the reasons for their findings. One would have supposed that this report should have become the basic point of reference for all future Jesus studies. Scholars could cite the report by adding or subtracting sayings and giving the reasons for their judgments. But the report was generally treated at best with benign neglect by the guild of scholars, and Jesus studies continued apace without first carefully sorting out what properly belongs to Jesus from the material of the early community. In other words the basic problem of Jesus studies continues to be routinely ignored.

How should we regard books on Jesus of Nazareth (1) that do not recognize this axiom of critical Jesus studies: not everything attributed to Jesus in the gospels originated with Jesus, (2) that do not include a specific list of the historical raw data on which the author bases a description of Jesus; (3) that do not include a justification for regarding such raw data

---

4. Robinson, "Introduction," xix.
5. Bornkamm, *Jesus*, 13–14.
6. Hedrick, *Wisdom of Jesus*, 163–79.
7. Funk et al., *Five Gospels*.

as historical, and (4) that do not carefully distinguish between the data and their own interpretation of it?

It is easier for me to respond by describing the extremes. At their very worst such studies are romantic and devotional, and are intended, either consciously or subconsciously, to buttress the faith of the believing community. Hence they are not critical studies but fall into the category of propaganda or devotional literature.

On the other hand, at their very best they are still flawed studies because they confuse the raw data with their analyses and fail to justify what they do use. Hence at best they are unreliable and misleading. (6-6-14)

§86 A NEARLY UNKNOWN EARLY CHRISTIAN TITLE FOR JESUS

Two titles conferred on Jesus by his early followers are so well known that many think of them as part of his personal name: i.e., Lord Jesus Christ. *Jesus*, however, is the personal name that his mother gave him. Christ (*Christos*) is a title coming out of the Israelite tradition meaning "anointed." Another title, Lord (*kurios*), is a term addressed to a person who commands respect or exercises authority; it is used in Hebrew Bible/Septuagint of Yahweh, God of Israel, where he is referred to as the Lord, the Lord God, or both. The title carries the idea of high authority. Hence Jesus' two best-known titles are the Lord and the Anointed.

An odd, little-known title barely surviving in the New Testament is *archēgos*, but how should it be translated? In the Greek tradition it is used to refer to the founder of a city, among other things. In the Septuagint it refers to political and military leaders of various sorts, both tribal and national. In English translations the title has appeared variously as "beginner," "leader," "instigator," "author," "captain," "chief," "prince," and the like

There are only four instances of its use in the New Testament, and all appear in confessional statements:

- Acts 3:15 refers to Christ as "(*archēgos*) of life."
- Acts 5:31 refers to Jesus as "(*archēgos*) and Savior."
- Heb 2:10 refers to Jesus as "(*archēgos*) of salvation."
- Heb 12:2 refers to Jesus as "(*archēgos*) and perfecter of our faith."

The word also appears in 2 Clem. 20:5, where it refers to Jesus as "the Saviour and prince (*archēgos*) of immortality."[8] In Ep. Pet. Phil. 139:27 and 140:4 the word refers to Jesus as "the author (*archēgos*) of our life."[9] In the German translation of Peter to Philip, *archēgos* is translated as *Urheber*,[10] which carries the dictionary meanings of "author," "creator," "founder," or "originator." It was argued in 1981 that the term should be translated "prince," and explained as a christological understanding of Jesus as "the fulfillment of the Davidic hope" (Ezek 34:24; 37:25).[11]

From my perspective *archēgos*, as used in the New Testament, is a clearly secular word that takes on secondarily a religious sense only by the word with which it is paired and the confessional context in which it appears. A place in Hebrew Bible where an early follower of Jesus might have encountered it, while looking for messianic "prophecies," is Num 24:17: "A star shall rise out of Jacob, a man shall spring out of Israel, and shall crush the princes (*archēgos*) of Moab and shall spoil all the sons of Seth" (LXX). In the early second century Irenaeus[12] and Justin[13] cited this verse as a messianic prophecy, which Jesus fulfilled, but they gave no explanation as to how the prophecy applied to Jesus.

Simon bar Kosiba, the Judean rebel leader of the second Jewish revolt (early second century) appealed to Num 24:17 to support his messianic claims. His supporters and followers called him Bar Kohkba, "son of a star." During his occupation of Jerusalem Simon even minted coins featuring a star.[14] Eusebius (fourth century) said this of him:

> The Jews were at that time led by a certain Bar Kokhba, which means star, a man who was murderous and a bandit, but relied on his name, as if dealing with slaves, and claimed to be a luminary who had come down to them from heaven, and was magically enlightening those who were in misery.[15]

Although Bar Kokhba may have presented himself as a messianic figure, he is clearly a military/political leader and war chieftain. Those

---

8. Lake, trans., *Apostolic Fathers*, 1:163.
9. Wisse, "Letter of Peter to Philip," 397.
10. Bethge, *Brief des Petrus an Philippus*, 29.
11. Johnston, "Christ as Archegos," 384.
12. *Haer.* 9.2.
13. *Dial.* 106.
14. Isaac and Oppenheimer, "Bar Kokhba."
15. *Hist. eccl.* 4.6.1–3.

who view God as working in the world in a spiritual way, like Irenaeus and Justin, however, would see *archēgos* in a religiously spiritual sense. Hence Jesus is the "leader" who, as precursor, first led the way in faith. He was *archēgos* in the sense that his faith (that is, Jesus' own confidence in God, Gal 2:16) first established the spiritual path. He was the pioneer, trailblazer, or *archēgos* of that Way of faith (Acts 9:2; 19:9, 23; 22:4; 24:14, 22).[16] Such a secular title had little chance of succeeding, however, against early orthodoxy's idea of a crucified and resurrected Savior, and its use simply died out as too bland or as clearly inappropriate for a dying and rising Savior who was far more than simply a "leader" or "beginner" of a path of faith.

Titles given to Jesus tell us nothing substantive about the man, however; they only tell us what early Christians thought about him. (5-3-16)

§87 THE BEGINNING OF CHRISTOLOGY[17]

Where does the process begin that turns Jesus from a man into God? What was there about this first-century lower-class Judean[18] man that set him apart from others? We know very little about him and his situation in life in the early years of the first century. Jesus was born under the ideology of the Israelite religion and became a lower-class artisan by trade.[19] At one point he became a follower of John the Baptizer, who preached a message of Israelite renewal, repentance, and baptism in the face of the coming Judgment of God (Mark 1:4-8). About his early life nothing more is known, for the sources report virtually nothing historically reliable about the period from his birth to the beginning of his own public career, which followed the arrest of John.

The early Christian gospels are of little help, other than perhaps at providing us hints about the earlier period, since Jesus is already portrayed in the gospels as larger-than-life, the Messiah and Son of God; he was basically described as a divine figure who appears to be a man.[20] In

---

16. See §76, p. 180, above.

17. This brief essay appears as the second half of an essay titled "Early Christian Confessions. An Intertextual Dialogue," *Fourth R* (forthcoming). For the first half of the essay see §91, below.

18. Early gospel literature portrays Jesus as being from Galilee, but the entire region was known as Judea; Elliott, "Jesus the Israelite."

19. Hedrick, *Wisdom of Jesus*, 182-83; 186-88.

20. John 1:1-14; Phil 2:5-8.

their reports the process is well advanced on the way to the declaration of Chalcedon in 451, which was that Jesus is "fully God and fully man."[21] We must search, however, for hints that might take us backwards toward the beginning of the process.

It seems probable that the process of turning Jesus into God happened as a result of Greek influence during the early history of the church. With the influx of non-Judeans into the early community gatherings, Eastern religious traditions meet Western religious traditions. The right conditions for accelerating the process are provided by the Greek tendency to ascribe divinity to people of unusual abilities[22] and by the pervasive influence of the mystery religions in the Greco-Roman world, in whose secret ceremonies the initiate was brought into close relationship with the deity.[23] To judge from the Pauline letters, by the early 50s the process of elevating Jesus to divinity was well advanced, a situation likely due to the fact that Gentiles associated themselves with Jesus gatherings shortly after the crucifixion (Acts 6:1-6).

What unusual ability might Jesus have had that would prompt his elevation from artisan to divinity? Josephus (*Ant.* 18.3.3 [§§63-64]) provides one suggestion. In the well-known *Testimonium Flavianum* Josephus refers to him as a wise man (*sophos anēr*), although the entire statement about Jesus in Josephus (first century) suggests that he is more than simply a man. Because the description of Jesus as a "wise man" conflicts with the statement as a whole, the view that Jesus was a "wise man" may be an authentic early memory. Another hint appears in a remarkable statement made by Justin Martyr (second century), who attests a similar view of Jesus: "Now the son of God, called Jesus, even if only a man by ordinary generation, yet on account of his wisdom (*sophia*) is worthy to be called the Son of God."[24] Justin tells the reader nothing about what he regards as the content of Jesus' wisdom.

The association of Jesus with wisdom is more pointedly made in the New Testament by the author of the Gospel of Matthew (Matt 23:34-36) in revising an earlier Q tradition, represented by Luke (11:49-51). Q attributes the oracle of doom on the people of "this generation" to Jesus,

---

21. Bettenson and Maunder, eds., *Documents* (3rd ed.), 56.
22. Talbert, *What Is a Gospel*, 25-52.
23. Meyer, "Mystery Religions."
24. Justin *1 Apol.* 22. Coxe, "First Apology of Justin," 170.

who says, "I will send you prophets, wise men (*sophous*) and scribes."[25] In Matthew, on the other hand, the oracle of doom is attributed to "the Wisdom of God," who "will send prophets and apostles." In other words Matthew has identified Jesus as personified Wisdom, and attributed Wisdom's oracle to Jesus. Before the earth was formed, (personified) Wisdom worked alongside God in the creation of the heavens and the earth (Prov 8:27-30). But more to the point "in every generation she (Lady Wisdom) passes into holy souls and makes them friends of God and prophets" (Wis 7:27). Matthew again revises an earlier Q tradition; Q identifies John the Baptizer and Jesus as emissaries (i.e., children) of Lady Wisdom in spite of their different lifestyles (Luke 7:31-35) while Matthew by revising Q makes Jesus the embodiment of Lady Wisdom herself (Matt 11:16-19) by virtue of the deeds Jesus performs (Matt 11:19).

There is no trace of Jesus' reputation as savant or sage in any of the early Christian creeds, and only traces of it can be found in the early Christian gospels. His reputation as a Galilean sage virtually disappears from the tradition; the creeds also suppress his public career.

Only these few hints remain to suggest what may have been the case in Galilee and Judea only twenty years or so before Paul: Jesus was a man of unusual but native abilities with a quick mind who was remembered for his memorable sayings. Although he was an unlettered savant or a rustic sage, he became celebrated for his wisdom; eventually he came to be regarded by his associates as a "friend of God" and one of his generation's "holy souls" sent by Lady Wisdom (Wis 7:27). His unusual natural abilities gave him a position of special prominence and respect among his peers in Galilee.

Being regarded as an emissary of Lady Wisdom and a "wise man," however, would not inevitably lead to divinity, for "wise men" were ubiquitous in the ancient world. Nevertheless, the right conditions might spark the beginning of the process. Those "right" conditions are provided by the influence of non-Israelites in the early gatherings of his later followers; they likely began the process resulting in divine honors for him. Consider the early pre-Pauline Hellenistic confession that Jesus was a human being chosen by God to be his son by virtue of his resurrection from the dead (Rom 1:3-4). Such a conjecture about the status of Jesus among

---

25. The hypothetical early Christian Gospel Q is reconstructed by scholars from the agreements between Matthew and Luke against Mark. Luke's wording for the Q Gospel is preferred by scholars. They use Luke's chapter and verse to designate Q.

his peers plausibly tracks the beginnings of Christology to circumstances in the life of the Judean man Jesus in Roman Palestine. (11–5–14)

§88 WAS JESUS AN EXORCIST?

The synoptic evangelists agree that the public career of Jesus could best be summed up in the following way:

> His mission was primarily that of a prophet (Mark 1:15), teacher (Luke 4:15), and healer (Luke 4:40, 13:32), or exorcist (Luke 4:41, 6:17–19); his message was the announcement of the impending arrival of the reign (or kingdom) of God (Luke 4:43), and the requirements which were to be met before admission into this kingdom.[26]

I personally would have said healer *and* exorcist based on the Q saying (Matt 12:28=Luke11:20) attributed to Jesus. In other words, his exorcisms (casting demons out of people unfortunate enough to have been possessed by them) and his healings of diseases and infirmities are two sides of the same activity, for in the view of the synoptic evangelists illness is also caused by demons (Mark 9:14–29/Matt 17:14–21/Luke 9:37–43a). Hence exorcizing demons, healing the sick, and proclaiming the kingdom are all aspects of the emerging reign of God, which initiates the end of the age.[27] Therefore Jesus is generally described as an apocalyptic prophet who announces the blessings of the soon-to-arrive kingdom, of which his exorcisms and healings in the present are a foretaste. Such is the default understanding of Jesus on the part of the authors of the synoptic evangelistic tracts, a view shared by the confessing church and by many (if not most) in the contemporary academic community, although this is not the image of Jesus in the Gospel of John.[28]

"A belief in the existence and activity of demons is not limited to the [New Testament]. Some conception of evil spirits or demons was held almost universally by the religions of the ancient world."[29] But not all people in antiquity shared this view of possession by evil spirits and the therapeutic activity of exorcising them. For example, the satirist Lu-

---

26. Grant, "Jesus Christ," 882.

27. See Hedrick, *Wisdom of Jesus*, 164–79 for a summary of academic views about Jesus at the end of the twentieth century.

28. Hedrick, *When History and Faith Collide*, 42–44.

29. Reese, "Demons," 140.

cian of Samosata (second century CE) ridicules the gullibility of people who are willing to believe all sorts of things about a supernatural world, and takes exorcism of evil spirits as an example of their gullibility.[30] Hippocrates of Cos (fifth century BCE), the most famous physician of antiquity, regarded possession by God (what he calls the "sacred disease") as due to natural causes, and the idea that it was due to divine action was the result of superstition, gullibility, and quackery. Hippocrates avers that the real source of this serious disease is to be found in the brain, and it can be cured without recourse to purifications or magic.[31] Among the things that Marcus Aurelius (Roman emperor, second century CE) claimed that he learned was to be incredulous about sorcerers and imposters regarding the driving out of spirits.[32]

Doubt is cast on the historical value of the general picture of Jesus (quoted above) emerging from the Synoptic Gospels by a number of the Jesus sayings that the evangelists preserve, and, in particular, on the therapeutic value of exorcism. For example, the narrative parables, in the main, contain no evident trace of the apocalyptic features that the synoptic evangelists associate with the career of Jesus. Nevertheless one of the stories attributed to him in Matthew and Luke does describe demon possession, but it in fact casts doubt on the general efficacy of exorcism. The story is found in the earliest gospel, Q (Luke 11:24-26=Matt 12:43-45), and Matthew and Luke repeat it with minor differences; in short, the story in Matthew and Luke is repeated virtually verbatim. Oddly, however, the Jesus Seminar printed Matthew's version in grey (meaning the ideas in this version were thought to be close to Jesus' own), and Luke's version was printed in pink (meaning Jesus probably said something like this) even though the differences are only stylistic and few in number.[33] Here is the story in Luke's version:

> When the unclean spirit has gone out of a man, he passes through waterless places seeking rest; and finding none he says, "I will return to my house from which I came." And when he comes he finds it swept and put in order. Then he goes and brings seven other spirits more evil than himself, and they enter and dwell there.

30. Lucian, "Lover of Lies," 16, 31-32.
31. Hippocrates, "Sacred Disease," I.1-4; II.1-46; V.1-21; VI.1-2; XXI.22-26.
32. Marcus Aurelius, *Meditations*, I.6.
33. Funk et al., *Five Gospels*, 189, 330-31.

Luke's concluding statement (11:26, "and the last state of that man becomes worst than the first") is the Q interpretation of the story and is repeated by Matthew (12:45); Matthew (12:45) adds another interpretation: "So shall it be also with this evil generation." While the story reflects the widespread superstition in antiquity that demons and evil spirits possess people, it portrays the practice of exorcism as futile. In that sense it challenges the traditional image of Jesus as an exorcist. One will recall that there are no accounts of demon possession or exorcism in the Gospel of John. This short story seems to link Jesus to the attitudes expressed by Lucian, Hippocrates, and Marcus Aurelius.

For what reason would Jesus as a practicing exorcist cast doubt on the therapeutic value of his own exorcisms, or was this story perhaps not told by Jesus? Have the synoptic evangelists simply capitalized on a tendency in the Jesus tradition to see Jesus as an exorcist and developed it further? After all, they had no personal knowledge of Jesus. (8–24–16)

§89 "SCRUBBING" THE EARLY JESUS TRADITIONS

In my experience members of the U.S. military use the expression "scrubbing a list" when it is being checked for accuracy. To clean a list of errors, typos, inaccuracies, and the like, one "scrubs" the list. I am using the term to describe a Jesus-Seminar-like exercise, which aims to determine in so far as is possible what in the gospels is left of the essentially historical Judean man Jesus of Nazareth.[34] Everyone "scrubs" the Jesus traditions: the gospel writers, Paul, translators, ministers, true believers and liberals, even historians! When a critical historian "scrubs" the Jesus traditions, however, his/her Jesus comes out as a radical figure having little in common with the figure worshiped in either the modern or ancient Christian church. In the first place, Jesus was not Christian but a Judean Israelite by tradition. The rituals with which he would have been familiar would have been those at home in the Israelite faith rather than those reflected in the Christian calendar. Jesus knew nothing of Christian baptism, Eucharist (Lord's Supper), Christmas, Easter, confirmation, invitation hymns, ordained clergy, bishops, or praying in Jesus' name.

Jesus is portrayed as undergoing the Israelite rite of circumcision; as celebrating the Feast of Tabernacles, the Feast of Dedication, and Passover; as observing the Sabbath; as going to the synagogue and the

---

34. As was done in Funk et al., *Five Gospels*.

temple; and as arguing with Pharisees about Torah. (He knew nothing of the books of the New Testament.) So how did we get Christian rites, Christian theology, and celebrations out of this Israelite man? In part, it was due to the fact that traditions about Jesus were "scrubbed" by the evangelists in their narratives, and then by the later church. Their literary contexts and "Christian" spins of the oral Jesus traditions, out of which they composed their narratives, made Jesus more amenable to the Christian Greek mentality, and Greeks were the target audience of the evangelists.

Most scholars accept that Jesus was baptized by John the Baptizer, but John's baptism was a baptism of repentance for the forgiveness of sins (Mark 1:4-5; Acts 19:1-4). The Christian view (Paul's) sees baptism as immersion into the death and resurrection of Jesus, the Christ (Rom 6:3-4). Matthew, on the other hand, was bothered by the suggestion that Jesus might also be thought to have "confessed his sins" like everyone else when he was baptized by John, and completely eliminates this as a possibility by having Jesus explain to John why it was necessary that John baptize him (Matt 3:13-15). In Luke, apparently John does not baptize Jesus, for Luke writes that John was put in prison (Luke 3:19-20) immediately before the baptism of Jesus (Luke 3:21); this appears to be how Luke handled Jesus being baptized for the remission of his sins; he wasn't baptized by John but rather at a later time, and who baptized him is left unclear. In the Gospel of John, John's baptism was not a baptism of repentance for the forgiveness of sins; rather John was baptizing so that Jesus might be revealed to Israel (John 1:31). The baptism of Jesus in John's Gospel is a baptism of the spirit, which John only witnesses, rather than a water baptism (John 1:30-34). On the other hand, in an unusual passage John represents Jesus as baptizing others (John 4:1), but then in the very next verse (John 4:2) John actually denies that Jesus is doing the baptizing himself, a statement that contradicts John 4:1![35]

The sayings of Jesus that pass historical/critical muster (if I can put it that way) do not offer guidance for living, talk about God or salvation, predict the future, warn about the end of the world, anticipate the foundation of an ecclesiastical institution that would last for two thousand years, establish a cult of a dying and rising God, or authorize the change of theology from a radical form of Israelite religion to an entirely new

---

35. See the discussion of the feature of "asides" in John's Gospel in Hedrick, "Authorial Presence and Narrator."

Greek/Roman religion.[36] Here are three radical sayings that probably originated with Jesus of Nazareth; shorn of their literary contexts they appear to prescribe actions that are completely impractical and unworkable in practice in either the ancient or modern worlds:

> Luke 6:27: "Love your enemies." The seriously radical character of this saying is camouflaged by its literary context; that is, by including it among other plausible but challenging acts one can render to an "enemy": do good to those who hate you, bless those who curse you, pray for those abuse you. In this way readers are led to believe that "loving your enemy" means something a little less than how one "loves" family, wife, parents, friends.

> Luke 6:29: "When struck on the cheek, offer the other; when someone takes your outer garment, offer your undergarment" (which is worn next to the skin); putting this act into practice would leave one nude, without a stitch of clothing to cover one's nudity.

> Luke 6:30: "Give to everyone who begs from you." Follow this principle literally, and how long do you suppose it would be before you find your savings exhausted, the bills piling up, and the mortgage long overdue?

Another saying camouflaged by its literary context in all three Synoptic Gospels and the Gospel of Thomas is, "Pay both Caesar and God what is due them" (Mark 12:17). The oblique character of the saying is mitigated by the controversy story in which it appears. In that context it comes across as an evasive answer by which Jesus avoids a trap laid for him by his interlocutors; in its literary context the saying is a shrewd quip allowing Jesus to best his interlocutors in the exchange. In itself as an oral survival from Jesus' public career, however, it is simply ambiguous, offering no clear guidance, since it does not specify the content of what is due to Caesar and what is due to God. One has to work that out for oneself with no help from Jesus. These types of sayings are characteristic of what most probably originated with Jesus. The literary contexts of the pronouncements in the gospels are not the actual living social contexts of Jesus' public career but the inventions of the evangelists. As a result,

---

36. See my summary of sayings that originate with Jesus in Hedrick, *Wisdom of Jesus*, 91–131.

when the literary context is "scrubbed," we are left in general with sayings characterized by perplexing ambiguity or unrealistic idealism. (2–24-13)

§90 PARSING[37] THE RESURRECTION OF THE CHRIST

Christian communities in the Western world celebrated Easter in 2016 on Sunday, March 27, but the Easter celebration in Orthodox Christianity did not happen until May 1, 2016. Easter, as virtually everyone in this country knows, celebrates the revivifying of a dead Christ. At some point between 26 and 36 CE Jesus was crucified near Jerusalem (Mark 15:22; John 19:17–20) under the administration of the Roman prefect Pontius Pilate.[38] There are no eyewitness accounts describing either crucifixion or resurrection that are contemporary with the event. The earliest mention of the resurrection is little more than a formulaic confession, which is thought to derive from the early Palestinian Christians, some twenty years or so before Paul; he quoted the brief confession in a letter (ca 50):

> I have delivered to you [the Corinthian Christians] as of first importance what I also received,
> *That Christ died for our sins*
> *according to the scriptures,*
> *and that he was buried,*
> *and that he was raised on the third day*
> *according to the scriptures,*
> *and that he appeared to Cephas, then to the twelve.* (1 Cor 15:3–5)

The confession is frustrating in its lack of detail. It doesn't describe specifically what the disciples saw: did Christ appear bodily (compare Matt 27:51–53), or was it a vision (Acts 9:10, 17), or a dream (Matt 1:20–21)? Did they see a spirit (Luke 24:37) or a phantom (Mark 6:49)? Perhaps they only saw his "angel" (Acts 12:15)? The nature of the experience is conditioned by what they saw, or thought they saw.

Paul himself had no personal knowledge of what had occurred earlier except for what he learned through the confessional report delivered to him by others. He himself claimed, however, to have had an experience similar to what is suggested by the Palestinian confession (1 Cor 15:8; Gal

---

37. "Parsing" is to sort into its component parts.
38. Rajak, "Pontius Pilatus."

1:15–16), but he does not describe this experience further (but compare another claim, 2 Cor 12:7–9).

Paul's early analysis of the postcrucifixion "sighting" by the Palestinian followers of Christ finds it to be a spiritual experience, which specifically denies that the Christ was seen in some sort of bodily state (1 Cor 15:44, 50). In short, the physical remains of the Christ had been transformed (1 Cor 15:20, 51–53), and he came forth a "life-giving spirit" (1 Cor 15:21–22, 45).

Some twenty years or so after Paul, the gospel writer we call Mark, in describing the origins of the gospel that his church preached (Mark 1:1), reports only that Jesus was raised (16:6); there are no reports of sightings. Only an empty tomb and the promise that he could be seen in Galilee (16:7) greeted the mourners coming to the tomb that first Easter morning; it was a terrifying experience (16:8).[39] Towards the end of the first century the resurrection state of the Christ became something more substantial than a vision, dream, or bodiless spirit. In the romantic accounts of the later gospels he was described as being seen in a bodily state (Matt 28:9; Luke 24:36–43; John 20:24–29). In the early second century such statements suggesting a bodily state were seized upon to argue that "he was in the flesh even after the resurrection" (Ign. *Smyrn.* 3:1–3).

Is the resurrection of the Christ a historical event? A reported sighting of a dead person following his burial is not what we usually think of as a historical event; that is, it is not an event open to verification by a neutral third party. The putative witnesses to the resurrection mentioned in the report (Peter and the disciples, Paul, and the others he described as also having seen the resurrected Christ [1 Cor 15:6–8]) all shared faith in Jesus as the Christ, and, hence, were scarcely neutral third parties. The historical event of Easter is that they *claimed* to have seen him. That they *claimed* to have seen him is open to historical verification. *What* they claimed to have seen is a part of a salvation or theological history (a history that traces out the claims of the perceived acts of God in the movement of human events). It is not a common human experience that people are raised from the dead by the activity of God. People that die remain dead. Hence it is only the *claim* that God has intervened in human history and performed a miracle by raising Jesus from the dead that is verifiable as historical event. The resurrection itself is a part of

---

39. Mark 16:8 admittedly is an abrupt ending. Later scribes added other endings; see Metzger, *Textual Commentary*, 102–6.

a theological history.⁴⁰ What can be observed by anyone should not be confused with what can be seen only by a few. In this case what the few saw they saw with the eye of faith, like John (20:3–9); the many, however, see with the natural eye.⁴¹ (3–25–16)

§91 EARLY CHRISTIAN CONFESSIONS: AN INTER-TEXTUAL DIALOGUE⁴²

One of the earliest Christian confessions is "Jesus Christ has come in flesh" (1 John 4:2; 2 John 7; dated around the end of the first century; and Pol. *Phil.* 7:1, dated middle second century). These references all describe the statement as a "confession"; that is, it is a formal statement of religious belief. The words of the confession do not describe, however, how the confessor understands the expression but merely states that Jesus Christ "has come" to a location described as "in flesh," which begs the question, where was he prior to having come to the "in flesh" location?

The Gospel of John 1:1–18 may perhaps clarify somewhat his previous location. John describes the Word as Jesus Christ (1:17), who existed before creation (1:1–5), and who later "became flesh" (1:14); that is to say the divine Word was "en-fleshed." Oddly John 1:14 does not claim that Jesus Christ became human (*anthrōpinos*), or even that he became a man (*anēr*), but rather that he became "flesh" (*sarx*). Does the confession in the Johannine letters and Polycarp communicate the idea that his being "in flesh" was a state foreign to his prior state, as is suggested by the second half of John 1:14: "and he took up (temporary) residence (*eskēnōsen*) among us"? Not being equipped to read minds, all that I can say is that such an explanation is at least a possible understanding of the confession.

The confession basically only claims that Jesus Christ is not a "phantom," a condition suggested by the disciples' experience in Mark 6:49, where it is suggested that to the disciples Jesus briefly appeared to be only a ghostly apparition. On the contrary, the confession affirms that he is actual substantive flesh (and blood), such as the rest of us are (1 John 1:1).

40. Hedrick, *When History and Faith Collide*, 1–13.
41. Hoover, "Was Jesus' Resurrection an Historical Event?"
42. §91 (combined with §87, p. 203, above) will appear as the first half of a longer essay titled "Early Christian Confessions and the Language of Faith," in the *Fourth R* (forthcoming).

The confession does not speculate on the nature of his fleshly condition, but such a speculation does exist in Paul, where he states that the "flesh" of Jesus Christ was of a different kind than that characterizing the normal human condition. Paul asserts that God sent "his own son in the *likeness* of sinful flesh" (Rom 8:3)—meaning that his flesh only *appears* to be like that of the rest of us sinful fleshly human beings; his "flesh," however, is distinctly different. These are very strange words indeed, suggesting that the flesh of Jesus was of a different sort, and that it was only "similar" to the sinful flesh human beings share.[43]

Paul's statement and the idea that Jesus is different corresponds to an early Christian "hymn," which Paul quotes: that Christ was "born in the *likeness* of men" (Phil 2:7); that is to say, he was not really a man or a human being, but he only appeared to be so.

A confession in 1 Timothy echoes language similar to Phil 2:7, the Pastor (a name given by scholars to the author of the Pastoral Epistles[44]) begins a confession as follows: "he was *made visible* in flesh" (1 Tim 3:16). This statement takes up a middling position affirming that Jesus was "visible in flesh" but does not necessarily agree with either John 1:14 (where he *became* flesh) or Rom 8:3 (where his flesh was of a *different sort*). Prior to his having become visible in flesh, the suggestion in 1 Tim 3:16 seems to be that he was invisible, a state that is characteristic of deity (Col 1:15; 1 Tim 1:17; Heb 11:27).

Paul describes on one occasion that Jesus came into the world in the manner of a human birth: "when the time had fully come God *sent forth* his son, born of a woman" (Gal 4:4), but the "sending forth" language suggests that it was something different from a normal, natural birth: the force of the statement evokes something akin to what is expressed in John 1:14. The birth narrative in Luke likewise has the façade of a natural birth (Luke 1:31; 2:7), but clearly something else is going on (Luke 1:35). Matthew's story also shares the façade of a natural birth, but clearly it is not (Matt 1:18, 24–25).

Summarizing the view that seems to be reflected in these early texts, it appears that Jesus was not conceived as a human being. Rather he was a "divine other" who did not share the human condition but only took up temporary residence in our midst, appearing among us "in flesh."

---

43. The statement is not that unusual for Paul; in 1 Cor 15:39 he describes different kinds of flesh.

44. First and 2 Timothy and Titus in critical scholarship are not regarded as Pauline letters. See Feine et al., *Introduction*, 258–72.

Imagine my surprise then to read the decision of the Council of Chalcedon (in 451 AD); in seeking to resolve the christological disagreements in the church, the council decreed that Jesus Christ was "truly God and truly man"; that is, he had two natures, human and divine, both of which resided indivisibly in the same persona.[45] This orthodox creed, which has existed in the Western church since the middle of the fifth century, is that Jesus Christ was "fully God and fully human." It is somewhat ironic, however, that the earliest followers of Jesus do not seem to have shared that confession.

The ancient Greek Gods, Zeus and company, were known to have encounters with men and women. The Gods assumed human disguises for these encounters and in some cases even appeared as animals. Zeus is particularly famous for his liaisons with human females. In the form of a swan he consorted with Leda and had two sons with her (Castor and Pollux/Polydeuces, the Dioscuri).[46] Here is another example: Zeus came to Alcmena, and "becoming like" her husband Amphitryon, Zeus "lay down" with her, and she bore two sons, Hercules and Iphicles.[47] Such intimate situations clearly suggest that there was "fleshly" contact. This description is similar to that in the Valentinian Gospel of Truth (possibly second century), where Jesus "came by fleshly form."[48] The writer of Hebrews notes that as children "shared blood and flesh, he [Jesus] himself similarly shared these" (Heb 2:14); some manuscripts add the word "misfortunes" to clarify the indefinite "these" of Heb 2:14. "Sharing" flesh and blood is imprecise. It is scarcely a claim that Jesus was human but only a claim that he was "human-like," as the Greek Gods were also described.

Twice more the author of Hebrews uses "flesh" to describe Jesus. In Heb 5:7 the writer refers to "the days of his flesh." The expression suggests that the "days of his flesh" constituted only a temporary passage of time in an otherwise longer existence, and that he himself was not to be identified by "flesh" in the same way the rest of us are; his fleshly state was something he only "shared" temporarily with us. Flesh and blood were only the means by which he opened up for us "a new and living way" into the presence of God (Heb 10:20).

---

45. Bettenson and Maunder, eds., *Documents* (3rd ed.), 56.
46. Graves, *Greek Myths*, 206–7 (62c).
47. Ibid., 85–86 (118c–d).
48. Gos. Truth, 31:4–6.

A somewhat rambling creedal-like statement appears in the Epistles of Ignatius (early second century):

> There is one physician
> Both fleshly and spiritual
> Born and unborn
> In humankind, God
> In death, true life
> Both from Mary and from God
> First capable of suffering and then incapable.
> Jesus Christ, our Lord.[49]

The statement shows the difficulty Ignatius had in describing Jesus precisely, and reveals the inherent potential for misunderstanding statements that attempt to be comprehensive and yet brief. This statement is clearly dualistic even as it gropes toward a unified description for the nature of Jesus, the Christ.

The strange passage in John 6:51–58, where Jesus promises eternal life to the one who "eats his flesh and drinks his blood," is frequently taken as an anachronistic allusion to the church's celebration of Eucharist.[50] Ignatius seems to echo this John passage when he describes Eucharist as the "medicine of immortality."[51] These latter passages suggest that there was something special about the flesh of Jesus. It was not simply common human flesh, for *his* flesh possessed a spiritual power and was the means by which he brought eternal life. Hence his flesh was hardly ordinary.

Judging from this evidence, it appears that in the early days of the church (later first and early second centuries) no uniform way existed to describe Jesus as Christ. There were attempts to form some kind of plausible explanation that would do full justice to what everyone knew (i.e., he was a man) and to what everyone believed (i.e., he came from God). So one might say about this early period that wide speculation existed, but that no definitive explanation emerged claiming general acceptance. In truth, there never has been a description satisfactory to everyone. While the "definitive" Chalcedon statement ("truly God and truly man") ended speculation in 451 for the orthodox churches, on the fringes

---

49. Ign. *Eph.* 7.2.
50. For example, Brown, *John*, 1:284–85.
51. Ign. *Eph.* 20.2.

of orthodoxy speculation continued, and still does continue. (10-11-14 and 10-24-14)

§92 WILL CHRIST COME AGAIN?

Modern Christian fundamentalism touts belief in a future return of Christ as one of the fundamental truths essential to Christian faith.[52] The belief is part of the Nicene Creed (fourth century), which confesses that "Jesus Christ . . . is coming again with glory to judge living and dead."[53] The earliest use of the expression "second coming of Christ" occurs in Justin Martyr (second century),[54] but the earlier writer of Hebrews (9:28) also expected that "Christ . . . will appear a second time . . ."

The hope of a future coming of Christ is part of the earliest extant Christian text (1 Thess 1:10; 3:13; 4:13—5:11), where the event is referred to as "his [God's] son from heaven," "the coming of the Lord Jesus," and "the day of the Lord." There is also evidence that the earliest Christians prayed for his coming. Paul concludes a letter with what is thought to be a prayer of early Aramaic Christians: *marana tha*, "our Lord come" (1 Cor 16:22). The latest writing in the New Testament (ca. 150) also warns that "the day of the Lord will come like a thief," and describes the event as "the coming of the day of God" (2 Pet 3:9-13). Hence a future return of (the Lord Jesus) Christ is a belief shared by virtually all the early Christians.

It is questionable, however, whether the earliest gospel (Mark) shares the belief in a second coming of Christ. In Mark Jesus is not quoted as saying, "I am coming again," or I will come a second time." Instead in the Gospel of Mark it appears that Jesus anticipated a future coming of a "son of man" (Mark 8:38—9:1; 13:24-27; 14:60-64).[55] He speaks in these passages of the coming son of man in the third person, as though he were someone other than himself. Other statements in Mark refer to the son of man as a contemporary figure who suffers, is betrayed, is killed, and rises from the dead (Mark 9:9, 12, 31; 10:33, 45; 14:21, 41). The events that identify Jesus as the son of man clearly reflect the faith of the early church (e.g., 1 Cor 15:1-5; Acts 2:22-24). The question is, however, did these sayings originate with Jesus, or are they faith statements of the

---

52. Dillenberger and Welch, *Protestant Christianity*, 226-31.
53. Bettenson and Maunder, eds., *Documents* (3rd ed.), 28-29.
54. *Dial.* 14.
55. Soards, "Parousia/Second Coming," 646-47.

church retrofitted into the career of Jesus to justify the church's belief that the coming son of man was Jesus? No saying of Jesus exists in which he unambiguously promises to return sometime in the future.

Nevertheless, virtually all scholars accept that Jesus referred to himself as "son of man" (e.g., Mark 2:10, 27–28 and Q [Luke 9:58=Matt 8:20][56]), but in what sense did Jesus use the expression of himself? Its meaning (loosely construed) was something like "man of the people"; that is to say, "a common human being"; the expression is used in Mark 3:28: "sons of men," meaning "human beings."

The term "son of man" is used in three different senses within the Hebrew Bible: Job 25:4–6 describes an insignificant human creature, Ps 8:3–6 describes a human being a little lower than God, and Dan 7:13–14 describes an apocalyptic figure of the end time.[57] The early church understood the term "son of man" (an Aramaic expression for "I") as a claim to be the apocalyptic figure of Dan 7:13–14.

Mark 2:10 was rejected by the Jesus Seminar as a Christian formulation giving Jesus the present authority of the coming apocalyptic figure, the son of Adam.[58] They accepted Mark 2:27–28 as a genuine saying of Jesus; it is then the only surviving son of man saying in the Gospel of Mark that likely originated with Jesus. If the Sabbath was made for human beings (Mark 3:27), then a human being (i.e., the "son of man" in the sense of Job 25:4–6) rules over the Sabbath as he was ordained to rule over the earth (Gen 1:26–30; spoken to Adam). It is not a messianic claim but rather a logical argument that dissolves Sabbath rules.[59]

It seems probable to me that Jesus anticipated the imminent appearing of an apocalyptic figure other than himself (Mark 8:38—9:1; 13:24–27), and the early church identified this figure (i.e., the son of man from Dan 7:13–14) as Jesus. How could such a thing happen? It likely occurred among his early followers under the influence of Judean messianic expectations and their reading of the Jewish Bible as a book of prophecy. Such a situation is actually depicted in John 2:13–22, where an incident in the Judean temple during the public career of Jesus (2:13–20)

---

56. Q (*Quelle*; i.e., source) is the hypothetical source scholars construe that Matthew and Luke used in addition to Mark; Q is reconstructed on the basis of close verbal agreements between Matthew and Luke in material not found in Mark; see Hedrick, *When History and Faith Collide*, 95–109.

57. Funk et al., *Five Gospels*, 76–77.

58. Ibid., 44–45.

59. Hedrick, *Wisdom of Jesus*, 104–5.

is understood differently after the death of Jesus by his followers; they came to the new understanding by reading the Jewish Bible like a book of prophecy (John 2:21-22).

In the synoptic tradition there is no future coming of the Lord Jesus Christ—at least, not in so many words. The Synoptic Gospels describe a future coming of a "son of man." The early church in the main abandoned "son of man" language and identified the resurrected Christ as the figure of a future apocalypse.

Will there be a second coming of Christ as the early Christians expected and modern Christians believe? It depends. I regard the belief that Jesus is coming again as a "faith fact." That is to say, it is a fact if you believe it to be so; nevertheless one should always remember that believing a thing to be so does not make it so. (10-29-15)

§93 READING JESUS' MIND

Today's average Christian if asked whether Jesus thought of himself as the Son of God and the Messiah would likely answer in the affirmative. Most critical scholars in general would likely avoid the question for obvious reasons, for who can possibly know anyone's thoughts? Confessional scholars would likely side with the average Christian. Nevertheless, even some scholars who approach the Jesus tradition from a critical perspective are not at all uncomfortable talking about what was going on in Jesus' mind. Marcus Borg, for example, affirms some things that "Jesus was *aware of*": "The power or authority which others sensed in him"; "the power of the Spirit flowing through him"; "his teaching also shows an *awareness* of a numinous authority not derived from tradition." And if you allow Borg to define carefully the terms he uses, he is willing to affirm, "in this Jewish sense, Jesus may have thought of himself as 'son of God.'"[60]

At the turn of the previous century Albert Schweitzer (holding three doctorates—in music, theology, and medicine) wrote a short work titled *The Psychiatric Study of Jesus*. The book was his medical dissertation. In it he countered the views of those in the medical profession who at that time were arguing that Jesus, "who considered himself the 'Son of Man' and the 'Messiah,' is to be adjudged in some fashion as psychopathic."[61]

---

60. Borg, *Jesus*, 47-49. He specifically rules out "*the* Son of God" in a Christian sense (p. 49), however.

61. Schweitzer, *Psychiatric Study*, 27.

Even Schweitzer himself felt comfortable telling readers what Jesus thought: Jesus "did not permit the conviction that he was destined to be the coming Messiah to play a part in his message."[62] The idea that Jesus believed himself to be the Messiah was something Schweitzer reiterated again: "That Jesus of Nazareth knew Himself to be the Son of Man who was to be revealed is for us the great fact of His self-consciousness, which is not to be further explained."[63]

Even the gospel writers knew what went on in the mind of Jesus, or claimed they did. Here are a few of their comments: "Jesus knowing their thoughts said . . ." (Matt: 9:4); "knowing their thoughts, he said . . ." (Matt 12:25); "he knew their thoughts and said . . ." (Luke 6:8); "But when Jesus perceived the thought of their hearts, he took . . ." (Luke 9:47).

Providing readers with interior views of characters in a narrative is a function of the narrator (i.e., the voice telling the story). Such a narrative technique is a standard feature of narrative fiction and qualifies the narrator as omniscient, i.e., a narrator who knows everything.[64] Matthew and Luke also engaged in reading Jesus' mind; hence they are omniscient narrators, because they know everything, even what goes on in the minds of their characters. John, on the other hand, features an unreliable narrator, for the principal narrator's story is frequently corrected by a second, more knowledgeable narrative voice at points in the narrative.[65]

An author's use of the literary technique of reading minds calls into question the realism of the narrative. The use of such a technique results in a less realistic narrative because it provides readers with something they could not possibly know in real life. Hence the realism of the early Christian gospels is more akin to romantic fiction than history.[66] For historians to use this technique in historical narrative is irresponsible, because it misleads readers in that the historian presents as a datum of history something that is obviously a fantasy of fiction.

The truth is that we never know what people are thinking even when they tell us what they claim to be thinking. (9-2-14)

---

62. Ibid., 51.
63. Schweitzer, *Quest of the Historical Jesus*, 367.
64. Arp and Johnson, *Perrine's Literature*, 238–45.
65. Hedrick, "Unreliable Narration."
66. Hedrick, "Realism in Western Narrative," 355–59.

§94 IS BELIEF IN THE DIVINITY OF JESUS ESSENTIAL TO BEING CHRISTIAN?[67]

Someone recently asked me, can you be a Christian without believing in the divinity of Jesus? The short answer is, it depends on whom you ask. Everyone believes their own answers to questions about personal religious faith are the right answers; would anyone admit their own religious beliefs are wrong? Not likely! If they really thought they were wrong, they would change their views.

Let's change the question a bit to inquire about data rather than opinion: did *every* early follower of Jesus believe in his divinity? With this question we hit another brick wall. Of course we can never know what *every* follower believed; we have no idea even how many followers there were, so we must ask the question another way: what do the extant early sources reveal about belief in the divinity of Jesus? That is a question that can be answered. From the beginning, beliefs about Jesus varied widely; the followers of Jesus believed different and contradictory things about him, and the canonical literature in particular reveals the range of these very surprising differences!

No primary sources relating to Christian origins exist before Paul (around 45 CE). Beginning with Paul the extant sources reveal a striking diversity in belief, particularly with respect to belief in the "divinity" of Jesus. This diversity was gradually driven underground following the events of the fourth and fifth centuries (the political patronage of the Roman emperors and the development of canon and creeds) when one wing of the different groups that existed as competitors in the first through third centuries consolidated its political and ecclesiastical influence. In the fifth century and later the view of the one group that described itself as "orthodox" became the standard for what constituted Christianity. Other views were dismissed as "heretical."

The Religious Situation in the First Century

Describing Jesus as the son of God in the first century would not have seemed unusual to the average citizen on the streets of Rome and particularly throughout the eastern provinces of the early Roman Empire.[68]

---

67. This essay subsequently appeared in the *Fourth R* 24/5 (September–October 2011) 3–4; used by permission.

68. Ferguson, *Backgrounds*, 199–207.

Long before the time Jesus was born, the Greeks had bestowed divine honors on kings and great men who were thought to have been unusually outstanding, referring to them variously as "heroes," "demigods," "immortals," or "divine men." The ancient Greeks believed these human beings had a divine origin; they were born as a result of a union between a God and a human being, and this explained their unusual abilities. They were honored, or worshiped, at various centers throughout the Greek world. They were not gods in the narrow sense of the pantheon of the twelve traditional gods of the Greco-Roman world, but they were nevertheless divine, or half divine, because of their deeds and parentage.[69] That is how the birth narratives in Matthew (1:18) and Luke (1:35) would likely have been understood outside Christian circles in the climate of the ancient world of their time.

Here is the description of the beginning of a hero cult reported by the second-century-CE Roman tourist Pausanias:

> Theagenes of Thasos, the Thasians say, was not the son of Timosthenes, who was a priest of the Heracles of Thasos, but that Heracles disguised as Timosthenes had an intrigue with the mother of Theagenes ... The most notable of his successes at Olympia have already been recorded and how he beat Euthymus in boxing [in 480 BCE] and how he was fined by the people of Elis. At that time Dromeus of Mantinea won the victory in the pancratium,[70] for the first time without a contest. But he was beaten by Theagenes the following Olympiad [in 476 BCE] in the pancratium. Theagenes also won three victories in the Pythian games for boxing, and nine at Nemea and ten at the Isthmus for the combined pancratium and boxing ... he beat all comers in the long race ... The total number of crowns he won was fourteen hundred ... [When his statue fell on someone and killed him], the Thasians threw the statue into the sea ... [Later some fishermen recovered the statue.] The Thasians set it up again where it used to be, and offer sacrifice to it as to a god. I know that there are many statues of Theagenes in many different parts of Greece, and also among the barbarians; and that he cures diseases and receives honors from the natives.[71]

---

69. Burkert, *Greek Religion*, 203–15.

70. —Ed. The *pancratium* is a Greek athletic contest combining boxing and wrestling.

71. Pausanius, *Descr.* 6 (Eleia 2) 11:1–9 (Pausanius, *Guide* [Levi, trans.], 315–17).

In the Roman period the Greek custom of offering divine honors to kings and great men influenced the rise of the Imperial cult (emperor worship) after the Roman Republic.[72] Here is how the second-century biographer Plutarch described Alexander the Great's visit to the temple of the God Ammon in the eastern desert of Egypt:

> When he came to the place of the oracle, the prophet of Ammon gave him salutation from the god as from a father; whereupon Alexander asked him if any of the murderers of his father [Philip of Macedon] had escaped him. To this the prophet answered by bidding him be guarded in his speech, since his was not a mortal father... And a story became current that the god had addressed him with... O son of Zeus... His own opinion on the idea [of how he was related to god] was that God was indeed a common father of all humankind, still, he made peculiarly his own the noblest and best of them. In general, [Alexander] bore himself haughtily towards the Barbarians, like one fully persuaded of his divine birth and parentage, but with the Greeks it was within limits and somewhat rarely that he assumed his own divinity.[73]

In the chaos of civil war after the failure of the Roman Republic, Octavian assumed absolute control of Rome, which he then transferred to the Roman Senate, which bestowed on him the name of Augustus (meaning "worthy of veneration"). Thus began the period of Empire in Rome's history. At death Augustus and the emperors that succeeded him were accorded divine honors. The Senate of Rome recognized (by a vote) that the *genius*, the higher spiritual essence, of the emperor deserved to be honored. Temples were built to the emperors, sacred rites appointed, and a college of priests set over their rites. The cult of the emperors (like the Greek hero cult) perpetrated their memory through sacrifice and prayer. In the eastern provinces of the Roman Empire especially, honors paid to the emperor easily became worship. The Senate, however, did not declare the emperors "gods" (*deus*), rather they were "divine" (*divus*) by virtue of their superior spiritual essence and accomplishments.[74]

Here is the declaration of the deification of Emperor Augustus by the Roman Senate:

> [The senate] declared Augustus immortal, assigned to him a college of priests and sacred rites and made Livia, who was already

---

72. Jones, "Roman Imperial Cult."
73. Plutarch, *Life of Alexander*, 27–28 (Perrin, trans., *Plutarch's Lives*, 7:305–307)
74. Ferguson, *Backgrounds*, 207–11.

> called Julia and Augusta, his priestess. They also permitted her to employ a lector [reader] when she exercised her sacred office ... A shrine voted by the senate and built by Livia and Tiberius was erected to him in Rome, and others in many different places ... While his shrine in Rome was being erected, they placed a golden image of him on a couch in the temple of Mars and to this they paid all the honors that they were afterwards to give to his statue.[75]

And here is the dedication of an altar to Augustus in Southern France:

> The populace of Narbo [Narbonne] has dedicated the altar of the divine spirit of Augustus ... "O divine spirit of Caesar Augustus, father of his country! When this day I give and dedicate this altar to you, I shall give and dedicate it under such regulations and such rules as I shall here this day publicly declare to be the groundwork both of this altar and its inscriptions ... Under these regulations and these rules, just as I have stated, on behalf of the Emperor Caesar Augustus, father of his country, *pontifex maximus* [high priest], holding the tribunician power for the thirty-fifth year; of his wife, children, and house; of the Roman Senate and people; and of the colonists and residents of the Colonia Julia Paterna of Narbo Martius, who have bound themselves to worship his divine spirit in perpetuity, I give and dedicate this altar to you."[76]

It is against this ancient practice of recognizing a divine essence in certain human beings, erecting temples and altars in their honor, and conducting cultic rites in their name that the divinity and worship of Jesus must be considered.

Transition into the Greco-Roman World

The "nature" of Jesus would not have been a problem during Jesus' public career in Galilee. What we associate with his career from the canonical gospels: proclamation of the sovereign rule of God (Isa 24:23; Mic 4:6–7; Ps 146:10), healing (2 Kgs 5:1–14), the early title Messiah (that is, the Anointed, Isa 45:1), and manipulation of nature (1 Kgs 17:8–16; 2 Kgs 4:4–37) are all part of the fabric of ancient Israelite tradition. These

---

75. "Deification of Augustus," in Lewis and Reinhold, eds., *Roman Civilization*, 1:640

76. "Emperor Worship," in Lewis and Reinhold, eds., *Roman Civilization* 1:621–22.

particular aspects reflected in the public career of Jesus, rare though they may be in Israelite tradition, were performed by human beings—by men of God; it was God's power working through a human being that accomplished them. In ancient Israel Yahweh was the source of suffering, misfortune, and disease, and even of torment by evil spirits (1 Kgs 22:19-23) that troubled human beings. Sometimes it was possible to expel them with music (1 Sam 16:14-17, 23), but it did not always work (1 Sam 19:10-11; 19:9-10). Exorcism does not fit within the framework of ancient Israelite traditions. It is not found until the later Hellenistic period (roughly 323 BCE to 410 CE), when it became widespread throughout the ancient world.[77] In the Hellenistic period a widespread ancient belief in demonology eventually influenced the Israelite traditions, and as early as the second century BCE demons were exorcised by a kind of "magic" (Tobit 6:6-8, 15-17; 8:1-3), a means that would have been prohibited in ancient Israel (Deut 18:9-14). One did not need to be a god or be divine to exorcise demons; human beings exorcized demons and evil spirits. Josephus reports:

> And God granted [Solomon] knowledge of the art used against demons for the benefit and healing of men. He also composed incantations by which illnesses are relieved, and left behind forms of exorcisms with which those possessed by demons drive them out, never to return. And this kind of cure is of very great power among us to this day, for I have seen a certain Eleazar, a countryman of mine, in the presence of Vespasian, his sons, tribunes and a number of other soldiers, free men possessed by demons, and this was the manner of the cure: he put to the nose of the possessed man a ring which had under its seal one of the roots prescribed by Solomon, and then, as the man smelled it, drew out the demon through his nostrils, and, when the man at once fell down, adjured the demon never to come back into him, speaking Solomon's name, and reciting the incantations which he had composed.[78]

The point of all this background information is that from the Israelite perspective there is nothing that Jesus said or did that automatically made his "nature" different from that of other human beings. Until the followers of Jesus moved out into the broader Greco-Roman world and encountered the competition of healing gods and hero cults, questions

77. Mendelsohn, "Exorcism"; Gaster, "Demon, Demonology."
78. Josephus, *Ant.* 8.2.5 (§§45-47); Thackeray and Marcus, trans., *Jewish Antiquities*, 5:594-97.

about his "nature" did not emerge. To be competitive in a world of hero cults, healing gods, and divine emperors Jesus needed to acquire credentials that were equally as good. To meet that challenge, Hellenistic Christians had only their human reason, the Septuagint (the Greek translation of the Hebrew Bible), and whatever traditions they brought with them into the new faith community. Some turned to Scripture and read it allegorically as prophecies about Jesus (Isa 7:14; Matt 1:18–25). Others turned to philosophical traditions, mystery religions, and religious-philosophical speculation for help. How they went about resolving the problem can be deduced only by noting the result of their speculation and then looking back, adducing parallels between their stated conclusions and what are presumed to have been their sources. Attempts to puzzle out the "nature" of Jesus in the Hellenistic world began quite early and likely mark the beginning of Christian theologizing. Most of the inferences about Jesus noted below are clearly indebted to Hellenistic thought. Whereas the ancient Israelite view of the constitution of a human being is that s/he was a unified entity, an animated body (Gen 2:7), the views about Jesus draw on the Greek notion that human beings are a duality composed of a body inhabited by a soul.[79] Beginning from such a perspective made it easier to think of Jesus having a complex constitution, human and divine. Judging from the texts in which they are reflected, these views did not originate on Palestinian soil but elsewhere in the Greco-Roman world. Hence one might theorize that this type of christological speculation arose sometime after 70 CE, when nascent "Christianity" was forced out into the Greek world after the destruction of Jerusalem. There may, of course, be other ways of understanding Jesus in the early period that remain unknown due to the paucity of sources. All views about the "nature" of Jesus sketched out below are inferences drawn by the early followers of Jesus, and none of them is necessarily to be preferred over the others.

Diverse Theories about the Nature of Jesus in Early Christian Literature

1. Jesus was not divine but was by nature essentially a human being whom God "adopted" or "appointed" for a special purpose.

This position is clearly affirmed in what appears to be a creedal statement used by Paul; it likely originates in one of the Hellenistic communities where Paul learned the basics of Christian faith. In the statement it

---

79. Annas, "Plato," 1192.

appears that Jesus was not appointed the son of God from the beginning of his life but was promoted to that status at the moment God raised him from the dead:

> The gospel concerning his [i.e., God's] son who was descended from David according to the flesh and appointed son of God in power by his resurrection from the dead according to the Spirit of holiness, Jesus Christ our Lord. (Rom 1:3-4)

Another profession of faith also associates Jesus' status as son of God with his resurrection:

> What God promised to the fathers this he has fulfilled to us their children by raising Jesus; as also it is written in the second psalm "You are my son; today I have begotten you." (Acts 13:32-33, quoting Ps 2:7)

In another passage Jesus is clearly not preexistent or of the same nature as the Father, but rather a human being whom God "made" both Lord and the Anointed:

> Let all the house of Israel know for certain that God has made him both Lord and Christ. (Acts 2:36)

The baptism of Jesus played a role in an understanding of the nature of Jesus as an adoptive son of God. Unlike Matthew and Luke, Mark gives no birth narrative, and there is no insistence on either the divinity or preexistence of Jesus in Mark. Jesus steps on the stage of history a fully grown human male, and it is at his baptism that a heavenly voice proclaims him to be "my beloved son" (Mark 1:11). Since the second century, Eastern churches have celebrated the baptism of Jesus as Epiphany, the moment Jesus was manifested to the world as son of God. Whether or not Mark intended that Jesus' baptism be understood as the moment he *became* son of God is not clear, but it is clear that it was understood that way, and the allusion to Ps 2:7 in Mark 1:11 is hard to miss. In some early manuscripts the passage in Luke 3:22, the parallel to Mark 1:11, reads like Ps 2:7: "You are my son; today have I begotten you." This reading in Luke signals an understanding of how the baptism of Jesus was understood in the first few centuries of the Christian era: Jesus became the son of God at his baptism, when the Holy Spirit descended on him (Luke 3:22).

2. Jesus was by nature a human being who came to be inhabited at his baptism by a divine spirit, the "Christ," or "the living Jesus."

This inner divine presence was the source of all the wondrous activities that characterized the public career of Jesus in the gospels. At the end of his public career the divine force departed from Jesus prior to his crucifixion. Such were the teachings of Cerinthus, a Christian teacher from Asia Minor who is thought to have lived near the end of the first century and been a contemporary of the apostle John.[80] The idea of this kind of "spirit possession" is usually most closely associated with radical Christian groups generally labeled Gnostic. The distinct dual natures are explained in the Apocalypse of Peter by the savior himself to Peter:

> He whom you see above the cross, glad and laughing, is the living Jesus. But he into whose hands and feet they are driving the nails is his physical part, which is the substitute. (Apoc. Pet. 81:15–21)[81]

And later in the same text the living Jesus further explains that he who was crucified (that is, Jesus) was a substitute that remains behind, but he himself (the living Jesus) was "the intellectual spirit filled with radiant light," who unites with the perfect light (Apoc. Pet. 82:18–83:15) before the crucifixion.[82] So the man Jesus was not divine but merely a temporary host for a spiritual power that came from the Perfect Light.

A similar idea is reflected in the early Christian Christ-hymn in Paul's letter to the Philippians. Like the situation in the prologue to the Gospel of John, the hymn in Philippians stresses an originally preexistent divine figure whom Paul identifies as Jesus (Phil 2:5). The statements about this preexistent figure do not clarify exactly how it happened that the divine figure came to take on a "servant form" and came to be in "human likeness" (Phil 2:7), but his closeness and equality (though not identity) with God are clear (Phil 2:6). The language used to describe his presence in the world emphasizes a distinction between an earlier divine God-like status and a later human-like slave existence (Phil 2:6–7). Eventually the divine figure leaves his temporary residence in human form and resumes his originally exalted status (Phil 2:9–11):

---

80. Cockerill, "Cerinthus."
81. Brashler, trans., "Apocalypse of Peter," 241.
82. Ibid., 241–45.

> Christ Jesus, who being in the form of God, did not count equality with God a thing to be grasped, but emptied himself, taking a slave's form, coming to be in human likeness. And being found in human form he humbled himself, becoming obedient unto death, even death on a cross. Therefore God has highly exalted him and bestowed on him the name that is above every name, that at the name of Jesus every knee should bow, in heaven and on earth and under the earth, and every tongue confess that Jesus Christ is Lord, to the glory of God the Father. (Phil 2:5–8)

Compare a similar idea in John's Gospel:

> In the beginning was the Word and the Word was with God and the Word was God. He was in the beginning with God . . . The Word came to be flesh and dwelt among us. (John 1:1–2, 14)

3. Jesus was partly divine and partly human.

The centurion's comment on the death of Jesus in Mark suggests another way that Jesus was understood. The statement, "Truly this man was *a* son of God" (Mark 15:39), includes Jesus among the many demigods (half god, half human) of the Greco-Roman period rather than making him the *only* son of God, as the Gospel of John has it: "For God so loved the world that he gave his only begotten son" (John 3:16). In some ways the nature of Jesus reflected in the centurion's comment is similar to the understanding presupposed in the infancy narratives of Matthew and Luke: Jesus like the Greco-Roman demigods had a heavenly Father and an earthly mother. Some Christians, however, vigorously opposed thinking of Jesus in the context of the pagan immortals. For example, the second-century Christian philosopher Justin Martyr theorized that the Greco-Roman "myths" about the immortals were influenced by wicked demons who initiated such tales in order to lead people astray. The demons, having read in the Prophets that the Christ was to come, put forward many as sons of Jupiter hoping that such fabricated stories would discredit the Christ when he finally came.[83]

---

83. Justin Martyr, *1 Apol.* 21–22; Coxe, "*First Apology*," 170–71.

4. *Jesus was not a human being at all. He was completely divine and only seemed to be human.*

The understanding of Jesus reflected in #2 above is slightly different, although similar. In #2 Jesus was clearly characterized by physicality, but in the view of the Docetists (from the Greek word *dokei*, "it seems"), a designation given to the groups holding this position, Jesus only *seemed* to be real.[84] Docetists viewed Jesus as something like a phantom (cf. Mark 6:49 for "phantom"). Such an understanding of Jesus is rigorously denied in the First Letter of John, where the essential physicality of Jesus is insisted on, and the idea that Jesus was characterized by becoming flesh (that is, an insistence on his physicality) is also emphasized by the Johannine tradition:

> What was from the beginning, what we have heard, what we have seen with our eyes, what we have looked at and our hands have touched (1 John 1:1)

> Every spirit that confesses that Jesus Christ has come in flesh is of God. (1 John 4:2)

> And the word became flesh and dwelt among us. (John 1:14)

5. *Jesus (the Christ) was both divine and human, but he did not have two natures; rather his nature was at once both completely human and divine.*

Readers will recognize this belief as the one that became dominant among the "orthodox" Christians in the fifth century, and survives today. This view, which has continued to be the orthodox definition of the nature of Jesus Christ was stated in 451 by the Council of Chalcedon:

> We will teach and acknowledge the same Son, our Lord Jesus Christ, at once complete in Godhead and complete in manhood, truly God and truly man, consisting of a reasonable soul and body; of one substance with the Father as regards his Godhead, and at the same time of one substance with us as regards his manhood... one and the same Christ, Son, Lord, Only-begotten, recognized IN TWO NATURES, WITHOUTCONFUSION,

---

84. Van Voorst, "Docetism."

WITHOUT CHANGE, WITHOUT DIVISION, WITHOUT SEPARATION.[85]

6. *The humanity of Jesus is incidental to his nature.*

This view is also expressed in the early creeds of the church. In those creeds the humanity of Jesus almost disappears and is virtually assimilated into his divinity. For example, the Apostles' Creed completely skips over his public career; indeed his entire life is treated as of no significance. Birth and death are all that remain of his life in the creedal statement. The pointed brackets indicate where his public career should have been:

> I believe in God Almighty and in Christ Jesus, his only son, our Lord, who was born of the Holy Spirit and the Virgin Mary < . . . > who was crucified under Pontius Pilate and was buried. And the third day rose from the dead, who ascended into heaven and sits on the right hand of the father, whence he comes to judge the living and the dead—and [I believe] in the Holy Ghost, the holy church, the remission of sins, the resurrection of the flesh, the life everlasting.[86]

The Nicene Creed, coming near the end of the fourth century, still ignores his public career but has the barest indicators of his human life, while the language associating him with God becomes more elaborate:

> We believe in one God the Father All-sovereign, maker of heaven and earth and of all things visible and invisible; and in one Lord Jesus Christ, the only-begotten Son of God, begotten of the Father before all the ages, Light of Light, true God of true God, begotten not made, of one substance with the Father, through whom all things were made; who for us men and for our salvation came down from the heavens and was made flesh of the Holy Spirit and the Virgin Mary, and became man and was crucified for us under Pontius Pilate.[87]

Both these creeds essentially reflect the later judgment of the Council of Chalcedon as to the nature of "the Lord Jesus Christ." But it seems clear where the emphasis has come to rest: on the divinity of Jesus, and

---

85. Bettenson and Maunder, eds., *Documents* (3rd ed.), 56. The statement as reproduced here is a slight abridgment of the source.

86. Ibid., 26.

87. Ibid., 28–29.

his equality or identity with the Father is emphasized. These creeds barely evade the "heresy" of Monophysitism (literally "one nature-ism), which maintained that Jesus had one nature that was partly divine, partly human. Monophysites acknowledged that there was a human element in Jesus' nature, but because that finite and frail human element coexisted with infinite and all-powerful divinity, Jesus' humanity was virtually overwhelmed by his divinity.[88]

Here is a fragment of a Coptic Revelation discourse of Jesus, which is likely Monophysite. Its inscription dates from the seventh century to the tenth century:

> I am Jesus the son of the Almighty. I have come to this world to save from [death]. My corporeal divinity was not parted from my humanity by a blink of an eye. I am the first word that came from the Father. I exist(ed) with my Father before all time. My divinity is within me concealed within my inner part. It was not divided from my humanity by a blink of an eye. It was constant in me until the Jews lifted me up on the cross. When my [humanity] tastes death [within] me, my divinity [remains] within my [inner] part.[89]

In other words, one nature exists, part divine and part human, indistinguishable, but the dominant part is divine: When Jesus' humanity dies, his divinity remains.

CONCLUSION

Persons holding any one of the views sketched out above believed it was what everyone should believe, and would have rejected other views as mistaken. One might well ask which view is correct. My answer would still be, it depends on whom you ask. But it seems clear that some people in the early period of the church thought of themselves as Christians but but did not think that belief in the divinity of Jesus was an essential part of being "Christian." How should one adjudicate these different views of the "nature" of Jesus of Nazareth? It seems to me that there are two options and two options only! One can simply accept the fifth-century orthodox creed of the Western church (or one of the other views), and raise no more questions. The orthodox view has length of years on its

---

88. Walker, *History*, 153–60.
89. Hedrick, "Revelation Discourse," 15.

side, even if it does lack in logic: how is a human being at once both completely human and completely divine at one and the same time? Some in the early faith communities clearly recognized the inherent illogic in trying to combine divinity into humanity and actually appealed to "divine mystery" to resolve the lack of logic:

> Avowedly great is the mystery of our religion:
> He was manifested in flesh,
> vindicated in spirit,
> seen by angels,
> proclaimed among the nations,
> believed on in the world,
> taken up in glory. (1 Tim 3:16)

The second option is to go back and face the same issue confronting the earliest followers of Jesus when they found themselves in a culture that divinized human beings: how to explain the "nature" of the Judean man, Jesus of Nazareth? Today one must begin with the bits of tradition that most probably originated with Jesus of Nazareth and proceed to make up one's own mind without favoring ahead of time one of the above solutions over another. This strategy increasingly recommends itself to modern human beings who are coming to recognize that they are rational beings in a secular world no longer influenced by unseen spirit powers.

Some churches today have taken this approach: they consider themselves "Christian," but they no longer think faith in the divinity of Jesus is an essential part of what it means to "be Christian." They organize their faith around the teachings of Jesus of Nazareth, and many have come together in the Center for Progressive Christianity to encourage mutual support in order to work out a new program for the church.[90] (6-2-10)

§95 JESUS WAS A GALILEAN STORYTELLER

Whatever else he may have been, Jesus was clearly a teller of tales. His stories are similar to the world's first photographic process, the daguerreotype. His tales, like those old photos, were black and white, grainy, and often blurry, but nevertheless provided realistic images of life in first-century rural Galilee. For the most part the stories replicated common

---

90. *Progressive Christianity.*

life in small peasant villages.⁹¹ Chances are that all his characters in peasant village life were accurate to type, but those few modeled on characters from the upper classes may very well be lacking in verisimilitude because their exclusive social circles were inaccessible to the oral "folk poet." Few of the stories reflect religious motifs, however general, and none of the stories are eschatological in character or concern the activities of Gods. Theology and eschatology, however, are regularly attributed to them by contemporary pious readers, and before them by the early "Christians," who preserved them purely for theological and religious reasons.

With the exception of two stories, the narratives treat human beings in Palestinian antiquity momentarily caught in the act of being human.⁹² One of these (Luke 16:19–31) contrasts the states of the rich and the poor after death. The other, a Q story (Matt 12:43–45a = Luke 11:24–26a), describes "unclean" spirits who take possession of an individual. This last narrative provides the only confirmation in story form that the artistic creator of the parables shared in the mythology of evil spirits, and demons endemic to the ancient world. According to the Jesus Seminar, the Lucan version of demon possession probably originated with Jesus.⁹³ Brandon Scott, Craig Blomberg, and Arland Hultgren, however, do not include the story in their surveys of the parables of Jesus.⁹⁴ Graham Twelftree does not include the story in his book on spirit possession and exorcism in Palestine.⁹⁵

The story of the twice-possessed person, however, is narrative in form, as is the classic form of "parable." In form the story is not unlike other better-known stories Jesus told. The story of the twice-possessed person narrates a case of possession by an "unclean spirit," later described as "evil." Contrary to what the highly respected German scholar Joachim Jeremias asserts, the spirit is not "cast out" but merely goes out of the person of its own volition. It passes through the desert (i.e., "waterless places") seeking rest, but finding none (why the Spirit needed rest is not stated), the spirit returns to its "house," that is to say to the person in whom it formerly resided. It found the "house" cleaned up and put in

91. See the summary of their subjects and themes in Hedrick, *Wisdom of Jesus*, 138–44.

92. Perrin, *Language of the Kingdom*, 104.

93. Funk et al., *Five Gospels*, 329.

94. Scott, *Hear Then the Parable*, 457–60; Blomberg, *Interpreting the Parables*, 334; Hultgren, *Parables*, 492, 496.

95. Twelftree, *Jesus*, 13–14.

order (Matthew adds that it was "empty"). Apparently during its residency this possessing spirit had not only disarranged and cluttered the house but also left a dirty floor. The spirit went out again, and found seven other spirits "more evil" than itself. And all eight entered and dwelled there. Q added an interpretive conclusion (Matt 12:45a = Luke 11:26a), "and the last state of that person becomes worse than the first." Matthew adds a second interpretation (12:45c): "So shall it also be with this generation."

The story describes the helpless and the hopeless condition of a person possessed by a spirit: if for some reason the possessing spirit decides to vacate its "house," nothing prevents it from returning and causing even more serious harm to its host, who had in the interim regained an ordered life. Jeremias argues that the relapse is not "predetermined and inevitable" but merely possible, and makes the individual responsible for keeping free of future possession by not letting the "house" become empty, and hence subject to repossession.[96]

In short the story describes the absolute control that evil spirits exert in the ancient world. Apparently anyone could be possessed or repossessed at the whim of any spirit. Matthew regards the story as a curse upon "this evil generation" (Matt 12:45c; 12:38-39). In Luke it becomes a warning about the dangers of demon possession (Luke 11:14-26). Jeremias turns it into Christian theology. He thinks the life of the healed individual must be filled with a spiritual element—"the word of Jesus."[97]

The canonical gospels, with the exception of John, relate several stories about the exorcism of demons. Oddly there is only one story about possession by an evil spirit in the Jewish Scriptures[98] (1 Sam 16:14-16; 18:10; 19:9), but the amelioration of Saul's depression by David's harp playing is scarcely an exorcism in the later Hellenistic style (cf. Tobit 3:7-8; 6:7-8, 16-17). None of the other seven exorcism stories in the gospels concern repeat possessions by evil Spirits. (7-23-14)

§96 WHY DID JESUS TELL PARABLES?

He actually told stories, or if I must use the technical literary term for story, his characteristic way of speaking was in *narrative*. Narratives (stories)

---

96. Jeremias, *Parables*, 198.
97. Ibid.
98. There is a story about the LORD putting a lying spirit in the mouths of prophets (1 Kgs 22:19-23; 2 Chr 18:18-22).

have as a minimum a beginning, middle, and end, and consist of a series of related events that develop and continue through the narrative to the end. In other words a story is not a simple statement. Calling a story a "parable," implying that it is figurative, is a reading strategy applied to the narrative, describing how one intends to read the story. In other words, the designation "parable" does not describe a distinct literary form; a parable is simply a brief narrative read in a particular way.[99]

In the early Christian gospels parables are generally viewed as brief stories intended to make a comparison, draw an analogy, or illustrate a moral or religious principle. Some of the parables are regarded as example stories that provide an example of proper human conduct. Some scholars theorize that parables are stories making a single comparison between an unstated reality and the situation in the story. The single point where the unstated reality and the situation in the story come together is best rendered as a broad single moral point. The stories of Jesus have also been described as metaphors: a narrative description of one thing under the guise of another, unlike thing. On this reading strategy parables are described as stories intended to bring the kingdom of God into expression in vivid, memorable language. All the theories take their place among other reading strategies for the parables of the early Christian gospels.

Basic to all these strategies, however, is the story: i.e., the narrative. In my view the stories Jesus told are freely invented secular fictions, that are subjected to various reading strategies by the writers of the gospels and subsequently by modern critics. A parable works when readers put themselves into the story and identify with one of the characters; they are then positioned to make discoveries about themselves.

Why would Jesus tell what are principally secular stories that have been so confusing to understand? The earliest recorded answer to that question is found in the Gospel of Mark around 70 CE. We have no idea what Jesus thought of his stories; all we have to go on are the stories themselves in order to investigate the earliest period of Christian origins. Some forty to fifty years after the death of Jesus Mark thought the stories were allegories, which is another reading strategy for the stories. A narrative read as an allegory assumes that the story is composed of a series of figures or metaphors: see Mark 4:3-8: a story about farming in the first century and Mark's reading of it (Mark 4:14-20) as a series of individual

---

99. See the discussion in Hedrick, *Many Things in Parables*, 1-9.

figures; Mark's reading understands the story to be an allegory about reactions to early Christian preaching.[100]

Why did Mark think Jesus told figurative stories? Mark said that parables are intended for those outside the inner circle of Jesus' associates. Parables were designed to keep "those outside" in the dark so that they would not learn the "secret" of the kingdom of God and turn and be forgiven (Mark 4:11–12). Matthew, on the other hand, blames the crowds to whom Jesus addresses his parables for deliberately hardening their hearts (Matt 13:10–15) but omits Mark's strange phrase, "lest they turn again and be forgiven" (Mark 4:12). Luke says that the parables conceal the secrets of the kingdom, which are only meant for disciples. Luke leaves it open that the crowds might still understand other things Jesus speaks about in parables (Luke 8:9–10), and like Matthew he also omits Mark's offensive phrase, "lest they (the crowds) turn again and be forgiven" (Mark 4:12).

When I was teaching classes in the parables of Jesus at Missouri State University, students delighted in telling me that Jesus used parables because it was a good teaching technique and made things clearer to the audience, as good examples should do. The difficulty with this explanation is that not even the evangelists agree among themselves on what a parable is and what it was about. For example, Matthew and Luke come to opposite interpretations of the parable of the Lost Sheep and even disagree on what the parable says (Matt 18:10–14/Luke 15:3–7).

I have never found anyone to agree with Mark that Jesus used parables in order to keep people from understanding "lest they turn again and be forgiven." (12-26-16)

§97 THE INCARNATION: IS JESUS GOD INCARNATE?

At Christmastime Christians celebrate the incarnation; the word means "en-fleshment" or "embodiment in flesh." Today what the average church member understands by "incarnation" is reflected in Matt 1:23 (date: 80–100[101]): Jesus, a child born to Mary, is Emmanu-el, which means God is with us, although Matthew never explains how God is with us in Jesus. A similar idea appears in Luke 1:35 (date 70–90[102]). Mark (date: around

---

100. See the discussion of Mark's theory of parables in Hedrick, *Many Things in Parables*, 27–35.

101. Feine et al., *Introduction*, 119–20.

102. Ibid., 151.

70[103]), however, does not use incarnation language about Jesus and does not know the birth traditions of Matthew and Luke. The idea that God is *incarnate* in Jesus, however, takes several centuries to become rooted in Christianity, in spite of statements suggesting that "God was in Christ" (2 Cor 5:19).

Matthew's idea was not a new concept. Antecedents existed in the Greco-Roman world. For example, the twelve traditional Greek Gods appear in the form or guise of human beings; or the legendary heroes of Greek tradition, such as Herakles, and real human beings like Alexander the Great, were thought to be sons of Zeus by human mothers.[104] Even the Jewish writer Philo portrayed certain human beings as the embodiment of divine Wisdom.[105]

In Matthew, Mark, and Luke Jesus is portrayed as claiming "to speak with divine inspiration and authorization as in some sense the representative of God. But there is nothing of consequence to support the thesis that Jesus saw himself in some sense as God, as the incarnation of deity."[106] In Paul's writings the classic statement of Jesus as a divine figure "incarnated" in bodily form is found in an early Christian hymn quoted in Phil 2:5–11. The hymn uses incarnation language but is also dualistic; that is, the divine figure does not *become human* but merely assumes the form or guise of a human being. The theology of the hymn scarcely meets the standards of later Christian orthodoxy:

> Christ Jesus, who though he was in the *form of God*, did not count *equality with God [not God, but equal to God]* a thing to be held onto, but emptied himself, taking the *form of a slave [not really human, but only a divine figure in the form of a slave]*, being born in *the likeness of human beings [a divine figure in a human likeness]*. And being found in human form [*human in form only*] he humbled himself . . . (Phil 2:5–8)

Paul thought of Jesus as "God's Son," but how Jesus came by that relationship to God is different from what is portrayed in the synoptic birth narratives. Paul uses language suggesting that he thought of Jesus as a human being (Gal 4:4) whom God *appointed* to sonship when he was raised from the dead (Rom 1:3–4); that is, he was not born son of God. I

---

103. Ibid., 98.
104. See §94, p. 221 above.
105. Dunn, "Incarnation," 399.
106. Ibid., 401.

find no incarnation language in Paul's writings rivaling the synoptic birth narratives.

At the end of the first century the prologue of John (1:1-18), in language reminiscent of that describing Lady Wisdom's role in the creation (Prov 8:22-31), describes the divine Word as preexistent with God, adding a divine character to the Word with this statement, "and the Word was God" (John 1:1-3). The Word (which was also the true Light, John 1:9), "became flesh" and temporarily resided among us (John 1:14). Other passages in John support the idea that John 1:14 is incarnation language (10:33; 20:28; 14:9).

"Became Flesh" (John 1:14) is very odd and obscure incarnation language at best. Clearly John thought of Jesus as a human being, for he describes him as "the son of Joseph" (1:45, 6:42), and John knows how human beings are born (John 16:21). So why use such an odd expression ("becoming flesh") for describing the advent of the Word into the world? The language is hardly a personal description for the birth of a child. John uses *sarx* ("flesh"), meaning a living being (in this case, of the human variety, John 17:2) rather than *anthrōpos* or *anthrōpinos*, meaning "human being." Such language suggests that the Word, while a living physical being like the rest of us, nevertheless is not one of us, which makes the expression at best a dualistic motif.

The statement likely is formulated to oppose Docetism, an early ideology opposed by Christian orthodoxy.[107] The Docetists argued that the body of Jesus was a phantasm (an unreal apparition, Mark 6:49). Hence, they argued that Jesus suffered and died in appearance only. From the perspective of that early Christian debate, John 1:14 is insisting that the Word was not intangible or immaterial luminance, but rather something actual, substantial, and physical—fleshly even. Opposition to Docetism is a feature of the Johannine letters (1 John 1:1-2; 4:2-3; 2 John 7), which were written about the same time as the Gospel of John, and which echo the same sensory language of John 1:14.

The issue addressed by the strange language in John 1:14 concerns the substantiality of the Word. The situation is similar to Lady Wisdom becoming substantially incarnate in Torah (Bar 3:37—4:1), although there, as in John, there is not a one-to-one relationship between Lady Wisdom and the book of the Torah. The prologue of John sets readers up to understand that Word and Light are "en-fleshed" in Jesus Christ. The

---

107. Van Voorst, "Docetism."

term "Light" is specifically applied to Jesus in the narrative (John 8:12, 9:5, 12:35-36, 12:46), but oddly the principal term used in the prologue, "Word," is not. John's language created huge problems for later theologians, since it never explained how the divine, incarnate Word and the human being Jesus are related.

Is Jesus God incarnate? The earliest followers of Jesus did not think so, and it was not until the fourth century, particularly in the Nicene Creed, that such an idea became the official belief of Christian orthodoxy, where Jesus is thought of as "true God of true God."[108] (12-21-12).

---

108. Bettenson and Maunder, eds., *Documents* (3rd ed.), 27.

7

Traditional Christian Beliefs

§98 PONDERING THE ORIGINS OF THE CHURCH

The word *church* is several centuries and cultures removed from the word it is used to translate in the earliest Christian texts. *Church* and its various cognates through the centuries is descended from a Late Greek word *kuriakon*, derived from ecclesiastical Greek and meaning "belonging to the Lord" or the "Lord's house"; from this word has come the Teutonic word *kirche* or *Kirk* (still used in Scotland), which is the equivalent of the English word *church*. It appears that translators of the New Testament have pressed into service what is today a "brick and mortar" Christian word in order to render into English the pre-Christian *ekklēsia*, used in the earliest extant Christian texts. Paul uses *ekklēsia* to describe a local gathering of Jesus people, and the basic idea of *ekklēsia* is an assembly of people called out for some purpose. The original idea of the word, its secular use, survives in Acts 19:32, 39, 41, where it is translated correctly as assembly. Another word Paul uses to describe the people in the gathering is *agioi*, or "holy ones," usually translated "saints" (1 Cor 1:2).

It is an egregious chronological error, an anachronism, to translate *ekklēsia* as "church," because in the middle first century there was no developed organization in the sense that the word "church" is used today. Technically speaking what we know as the "church" arose several centuries later, although certain earlier theological developments led up to what we recognize as the church in the fourth and fifth centuries. In the earliest period for which there are extant texts, only local gatherings of Jesus people existed.

Paul's gatherings were made up of Judeans and non-Judeans; in Paul's mythological thinking people in the gathering were made "holy" in Jesus, whom he believed to be God's Anointed (i.e., Christ, 1 Cor 1:2). These gatherings met in private homes (Rom 16:3–5; Gal 1:1) and were somewhat freewheeling assemblies not bound by formal rules, procedures, or guidelines. Paul described these gatherings in the following ways: "the gatherings of the Anointed in Judea" (Gal 1:22), "the gatherings of God in Jesus the Anointed in Judea" (1 Thess 2:14), "the gatherings of the holy ones" (1 Cor 14:33), or he referred to the gatherings by the name of the location or region in which they assembled: for example: "to the gatherings of Galatia" (Gal 1:2). Paul's later disciples came to think in terms of a united phenomenon, such as "the household of God, which is the church (*ekklēsia*) of the living God, the pillar and bulwark of the truth" (1 Tim 3:15). Using the word "church" as a translation for *ekklēsia* in this latter designation does not seem inappropriate. It is one of those evolutionary developments that led up to the church as it emerged in the fourth and fifth centuries.

Paul did not invent the idea of a "gathering," for there was already a gathering in Jerusalem led by people he did not meet until some seventeen years after his conversion. Peter, James, and John (Gal 1:17–24), who earlier had been part of Jesus' inner circle (Mark 14:32–33), composed the leadership of the Jerusalem gathering.

It is improbable that Jesus invented the concept for these gatherings. The gospels do not portray Jesus forming small gatherings in the communities he visited. *Ekklēsia* is used only three times in the gospels, and all three appear in Matthew. The first of these is a passage whose historicity is questionable (Matt 16:16–19), in which Jesus says to Peter, "You are Peter (*petros*) and upon this rock (*petra*) "I *will* build my *ekklēsia*." That is to say, the *ekklēsia*, however conceived and translated, was something for the indefinite future. *Ekklēsia* also appears in Matt 18:15–18, where it appears to relate to a formal religious organization with developed rules for disciplining "brothers"; hence it is not like the gathering reflected in the Corinthian correspondence. The passage Matt 16:17–19 is a Matthean insertion into a text borrowed from Mark 8:29–30.[1] The developed concept of the primacy of Peter does not appear until the third century and

---

1. Funk et al., *Five Gospels*, 206–7.

later.² Hence these two segments in Matthew are best thought of as bolts out of the later ecclesiastical blue. In short, they are chronologically out of place in time.

A more cogent occasion for the origins of the Pauline gatherings is most likely to be the widespread private clubs and associations in the Greco-Roman world.³ In the early Roman Empire many belonged to private associations of one sort or another, based on common interests and needs. The broad purposes for people associating themselves with such clubs were economic, religious, and social. There were, for example, associations of the trades and professions (merchants, scribes, woodworkers and metalworkers), burial societies, dining societies, sports groups, groups of ex-servicemen, and some that were specifically religious.⁴ As the fledgling cults of the risen Christ emerged in the Roman world, naturally like-minded persons in a given location would assemble together on the basis of their shared interests, following the model of private clubs and associations. Outsiders aware of such gatherings would have seen them as just one more private association.

In short, what eventually became the church in Greco-Roman culture likely began as small independent gatherings around certain ideas about Jesus, the Anointed. The origins of these gatherings, which led in the fourth and fifth centuries to what became the Christian church, had no one single point of beginning.

§99 IS THE TRINITY FOUND IN JOHN'S GOSPEL?⁵

Toward the end of the first century the situation is remarkably different from what one finds in the letters of Paul at the middle of the century. Around the end of the century, the Gospel of John makes a definite advance in defining the relationship between Jesus and God, but there is no stated concept of a Triune God; that is to say, of Father, Son, and Holy Spirit as three persons conceptualized as One God. Conceptualizing and describing a divine Trinity requires abstract logical thinking and systematic description, which are not found in John.

---

2. McKenzie, "Peter," 666.
3. Ferguson, *Backgrounds*, 142–47.
4. Ascough et al., *Associations*.
5. See also above §74, p. 177: Is the Holy Spirit Part of a Trinity?

In John God is understood as spirit (John 4:24), which seems to describe God's nature or character (spirit; not *the* spirit, which indicates identity). Jesus is presented as God's "son" (John 1:49; 5:18; 10:36; 11:27; 19:7; 20:31). The son (John 1:14), was "with God" and "was God" (John 1:1–2, 18), and came forth from God, having been sent here by God (John 8:42). He became flesh (John 1:14; not quite the same as being born a human being). The essential identity of God and Jesus is made certain by the confession of Thomas: "My Lord and my God" (John 20:28). Other, less certain clues appear in John reflecting an identity between Jesus and God (John 10:30; 17:11, 21–22). The unity is apparently primordial (John 17:24). No attempt is made by the writer, however, to explain how that unity/identity could be so. In John there seems to be a duality of two distinct personae conceived as one God.

How the Holy Spirit should be conceived in relation to the divine Duality, however, is complicated, and unclear. At the beginning of Jesus' public life, John the baptizer testifies that he saw *the* spirit descend and remain (John 1:32) on Jesus, who as a result baptizes with (in?) the Holy Spirit (John 1:33). The descending spirit must also be holy, for the "Father" is holy (John 17:11) and is apparently the source of the Holy Spirit with which Jesus baptizes. The spirit is thus involved in the activities of Jesus (John 3:3–8; 4:23–24; 6:63), and God is not stingy in giving the spirit (John 3:34).

On one occasion, however, surprisingly an intrusive explanatory voice interrupts the narrative, asserting that there was no spirit yet, for Jesus had not yet been "glorified" (John 7:39; "glorification" in John is a cryptic allusion to the crucifixion/resurrection: John 12:23–24, 27–33; 17:1–5). Hence John 7:39 clearly contradicts John 1:32–33, for spirit remains with Jesus through his public career, enabling his words (John 6:63), making true worship possible (John 4:23–24), and generating new birth (John 3:3–8). Opposed to this idea that the spirit is active in the public life of Jesus is the surprising statement at the end of the Gospel of John that the Holy Spirit is finally given (John 20:22–23).

Before the crucifixion, Jesus tells his followers that he is going to the one who sent him (John 16:7) and at his departure the *paraklētos* (John 16:4b–11) will come to them. The meaning of this word is unclear, and translations vary. Immediately following this statement his followers learn that another figure is also coming to them: the spirit of truth (John 16:13). The temptation is to harmonize and read the *paraklētos* and the spirit of truth as one and the same, but the figures have different functions: *paraklētos* (in John 16:8–11); spirit of truth (in John 16:13–14). Nevertheless the two figures are awkwardly identified as one and the same (John 14:16–17). How seriously should one regard the reference to "another *paraklētos*" (John 14:16)? Should one consider the spirit of truth as an additional (second) *paraklētos*?

The Holy Spirit is awkwardly identified as the *paraklētos* in John 14:25–26, almost as an afterthought. Its appearance in John 14:26 seems like an intrusion into the sentence, similar to the explanatory observation at John 7:39 (among many others). All three figures—*paraklētos*, spirit of truth (i.e., *paraklētos* number 2?), and Holy Spirit—have different functions, but they all come to replace Jesus, the son (John 14:25–26, 16:7–8, 16:12–13). This figure or these figures are not clearly identified as one with Jesus in the same sense that Jesus was identified with God; rather they are cast as performing Jesus' role in the community after he is gone. The language that the writer of John employs to describe Jesus in relation to them puts a certain distance between Jesus, the *paraklētos*, and the spirit of truth. John 14:25–26: "*paraklētos*, whom the father will send in my [Jesus'] name; he will remind you of all I have said"; John 16:14: "He [spirit of truth] will glorify me"; John 16:7: "I will send him [*paraklētos*] to you . . ." This language, carefully distinguishing Jesus and the figure(s) who replace him, does not encourage readers to sense a close unity or union between the son and his replacement(s).

There are no Trinitarian formulae in John; the closest statement to such an idea is John 1:32–34, and John does not seem to be aware of the later theological concept of Father, Son, and Holy Spirit—three figures in one Godhead. (12-9-15)

§100 DOES HELL EXIST?

In the contemporary popular imagination hell is a fiery abyss into which the ungodly are cast at the end of the ages, where they will suffer throughout eternity. Oddly enough, the word *hell* as such does not appear in the Bible. In ancient Israelite and Greek thought there are two principal words that describe the abode of the dead. In Israelite thought *Sheol*, generally translated by the English words "grave," "hell," and "pit," is the underworld where a person's shade went at death; they continued there in a shadowy semiexistence. *Sheol* included both the good and the wicked (for example, Gen 44:29, 31; Ps 31:17). It was only later that the distinction between the wicked and the righteous occurred.[6]

In the ancient Greek tradition Hades is the God of the underworld and the area he rules is the "house" of Hades. Hades (frequently translated "hell" in the New Testament) is the universal destination of humankind upon death, although even in the fifth century BCE some special dead ascended to the "upper air,"[7] and a privileged few enter the "Isles of the Blessed."[8]

In the early Christian tradition the designations Hades and *Gehenna* are exclusively places of torment in fire for the unrighteous (Matt 5:22; Luke 16:23–24; Rev 20:11–14). Gehenna is the valley of Hinnom, where it has been suggested that the killing by cremation of children as an offering to Baal and Molech possibly gave rise to the notion of a hell of fire (Matt 5:22; 2 Kgs 16:3; 23:10; 2 Chr 28:2–3).[9] The Israelite tradition was also likely influenced by ideas of the underworld as a fiery place of punishment during Judah's captivity in Babylon (587 BCE; 2 Kgs 25).[10] The concept of a fiery punishment appears in later Israelite writings (2 Esd 7:36; Sir 7:17; Jdt 16:17; 2nd Isa 66:24; 1 En 90:25–27 and 54:1–5).

Other words for the abode of the dead or the place of punishment also occur in the New Testament. *Tartarus* (2 Pet 2:4) is the lowest part of the underworld, even deeper than Hades.[11] The underworld is also described as the Abyss, the Bottomless Pit (Luke 8:31; Rom 10:7; Rev 9:1–2), and the Outer Darkness (Matt 8:11–12; 22:13; 25:30).

In the Middle Ages Dante Alighieri (1265–1321) wrote a poetic imaginary vision of a guided trip through hell, purgatory, and paradise, the three spiritual realms of departed spirits, reflecting the views of the medieval Christian church.[12] His vivid descriptions of the suffering of the dead rival in many ways the later (1743–1758) preaching of Jonathan Edwards, who terrified his congregation with warnings of the damnation awaiting them unless they repented:

6. Jacob, *Theology*, 299–305.
7. Henrichs, "Hades."
8. Warmington, et al., "Islands of the Blest."
9. Watson, "Hinnom Valley," 202.
10. Carroll, "Israel History of," 573; Gaster, "Gehenna."
11. Lewis, "Dead, Abode of," 105.
12. Alighieri, "Divine Comedy," 2.160–201.

The God that holds you over the pit of hell, much as one holds a spider, or some loathsome insect over the fire, abhors you, and is dreadfully provoked: his wrath towards you burns like fire; he looks upon you as worthy of nothing else, but to be cast into the fire . . . Therefore, let everyone that is out of Christ, now awake and fly from the wrath to come.[13]

This view of hell as a place of terrifying punishment is still alive and well in modern Christian churches and even in the popular imagination of the unchurched. Does such a place exist? Of course it did in the imagination and faith of Dante; and Jonathan Edwards clearly believed that it did, and it was likewise very real to his audiences, who responded to his preaching with hysteria, distress, and weeping.

But does it actually *exist* in the material universe as well as "exist" in imagination and belief? The short of the matter is this: if you believe hell exists then surely it does, as might other specific locations of faith, such as the pearly gates and streets of gold (Rev 21:21), the New Jerusalem (Rev 21:2), and purgatory (not in Protestant and Jewish Bibles, but in Catholic Bibles: 2 Macc 12:40–45). These latter "places" are part of the imagination and belief of the writer of Revelation.

We don't know hell by means of our primary senses (seeing, touching, smelling, tasting, hearing), but rather through our minds (i.e., as an idea, or item of faith and/or superstition). Hell does not in fact exist in the normal ways we think of things existing. That is to say, it does not exist as a locatable and visitable "somewhere" in the universe, or as something that occupies space and time at a certain longitude and latitude or parsecs location. Could it "exist" as part of a spiritual universe that perhaps overlays our material universe, or is "over there spiritually" in parallel to our material universe, although not a part of it? If so, it does not exist, except in our minds.[14] (8-29-15)

§101 WHAT IS SIN?

For no particular reason I began wondering what acts or attitudes are specifically named as sin in the Bible (*hamartia* in the New Testament). The writers, of course, use an assortment of words to describe acts or attitudes on which they frown. For example the deception of Eve was called a

---

13. Edwards, "Sinners," 547.
14. See §12, p. 38 above, Are Religion and Science Incompatible?

transgression (*parabasis*, 1 Tim 2:14) but not a sin. I was only interested, however, in acts or attitudes specifically designated as "sin" (*hamartia*).

I was surprised to discover that very few acts or attitudes are specifically designated "sin." While the Bible uses the generic word "sin" quite frequently, very few specific acts or attitudes are ever specifically named as sin. That is to say, few authors write: "X is sin." This lack of specificity raises the question, exactly to what are biblical writers referring when they use the general word "sin" or describe someone as a sinner with no specific acts or attitudes being described? For example, when people came to John the Baptizer for baptism (Mark 1:5) "confessing their sins," exactly what did they confess? Or when the "woman of the city" who washed Jesus' feet with her hair (Luke 7:37) was described as a "sinner" (Luke 7:39), what exactly had she done to earn such a harsh condemnation? And when Jesus later in the narrative "forgave her sins" (Luke 7:48), exactly what was he forgiving? The New Testament writers seldom give specific reasons for why certain people are described as sinners.

In order to make the survey manageable I limited myself to Hebrew and Greek words that English translators of the Bible decided to render by the English word *sin*. Note that there are a number of different Hebrew terms with subtle differences, all of which translators choose to render by the generic word "sin."

The following acts and attitudes are specifically designated as sin:

Old Testament/Jewish Scriptures/Hebrew Bible

- Unfulfilled vows to God (Deut 23:21)
- Rebellion and witchcraft/divination; stubbornness and idolatry (1 Sam 15:23)
- Idol worship (1 Kgs 12:30; 16:26)
- Rebellion and speaking without knowledge (Job 34:35–37)
- Haughty eye and proud heart (Prov 21:4)
- Speaking against the LORD and Moses (Num 21:7)
- Killing David without a cause (1 Sam 19:5)
- David's numbering of Israel (1 Chr 21:8)

The Apocrypha

- The beginning of pride (Sir 10:13)
- Always swearing and uttering the Name [of God] (Sir 23:10)
- Proud speech (Sir 32:12)

New Testament

- Blaspheming the Holy Spirit (Mark 3:28–29)
- Immorality (unlawful sexual acts) (1 Cor 6:18)
- Acts that cause a person to stumble and whatever does not proceed from faith (Rom 14:21–23)
- All wrongdoing (1 John 5:17)
- Lawlessness (1 John 3:4)
- Betraying innocent blood (Matt 27:4)
- Knowing to do right and not doing it (Jas 4:17)

Looking over this strange list, one can only wonder at the arrogance of contemporary religious leaders who seem to know a much longer list of acts or attitudes they regard as sin.

The use of the word *sin* with no specifics seems to be similar in content and style to a general slander charge in Greco-Roman antiquity. For example, the first charge against Socrates, aside from corrupting the youth, was that he did not pay customary respect to the Gods of the city of Athens (*nomizonta*, *Apology* 24b, which is equivalent to a general charge of impiety or atheism).[15] Actually Socrates was very pious and diligently sacrificed to the Gods. Dutiful respect for the Gods of one's family and community is one way of describing a respectable citizen of the community and carries the general idea of being devout, pious, or upright (Dan 11:37–38).

The charge against Socrates is the same sort of calumny leveled against the early Christians. Among other general accusations against them, they were called atheists in that they did not participate in the worship of the traditional Gods or make sacrifices in behalf of the emperor.[16]

15. Plato, *Apology* (Fowler, pp. 90–91).
16. "Propaganda against Christians," in Lewis and Reinhold, eds., *Roman*

Calling someone a "sinner" works in a similar, slanderous way. Jesus, for example, was accused of being a sinner (John 6:19, 24); it was a malicious misrepresentation and was tantamount to a slur designed to ruin his reputation. The reason given was that he didn't keep the Sabbath; in other words, he was called a sinner, not because of something he did, but because of something he did not do, and the charge lacked in specificity. Even Paul was apparently accused of being a sinner (Rom 3:7).

Jas 4:8, like the other two examples above, has the earmarks of a general slur made by someone on one side of an argument against those on the other side, and the obscure accusations accompanying the slur lack specifics (you need to "cleanse your hands, and purify your hearts"; you are "double-minded").

It appears that calling someone a sinner or accusing someone of committing sin, both in the abstract, may be the equivalent of a Christian slur. The charge "sinner" without specificity has no more significance than affirming that people so designated do not agree with the accuser's way of thinking.

What is sin, anyway? Is it possible that it is simply a figment of the pious imagination? At least one ancient text claimed that there was no such thing as sin (Gospel of Mary, 3:3–5).[17] Paul, on the other hand, seemed to think that sin is built into our DNA (Rom 7:11–23). (4-26-15)

§102 PROPHECY, DIVINATION, AND FATE

My description of the situation in the ancient world must necessarily be a tight compression of a great amount of data, which will inevitably result in some distortion of the ancient situation. The ancient world was religiously very diverse, and the following brief description of divination in all its forms merely scratches the surface.

I use the term *pagan* to describe the religions and culture of the ancient world. The term was used in the later Christian period to describe the last vestiges of the formally rich culture of the ancient world preceding the Christian period (roughly before Constantine, fourth century CE). In the early Christian period pagan culture and religions did not survive in cities where Christian influence was concentrated, but in the byways of the countryside. The term "pagan" is adapted from a Latin word *paganus*

Civilization, 2:553–56.

17. King, *Gospel of Mary*, 13.

meaning "someone who lives in the villages of the countryside."[18] Hence it was in the countryside that the ancient culture and Gods of the old world survived for a time.

Human beings as a species have always had an insatiable desire to know what their personal future holds, as well as the future prospects of the state and the earth. It has always been the case. In the ancient past there appear to have been three broad avenues to knowing the future. Cicero, a Roman politician and philosopher of the first century BCE, disagrees and describes only two ways of knowing the future (*Div.* II.xi.26), which he designated as the natural (prophecies made by inspired persons) and the artificial (divination based on observation and deduction from signs people believed were sent by the Gods). Hence, according to Cicero, in order to learn about the future using a natural source, one would consult an individual who was believed to have the gift of prophetic utterance, through whom the Gods revealed the future.

These men and women were believed to be inspired by the Gods. They were called by various names: seers, oracles, and prophets (1 Sam 9:9; 2 Sam 16:23) and were consulted for a wide range of reasons: on matters of state, personal issues, medical questions, battle outcomes, and so forth. The divine utterances they spoke were called "words of God," or oracles and prophecies.

The ancient Hebrew prophets belonged to this category, as did the famous Greek oracle at Delphi in ancient Greece, among many other oracular shrines devoted to various Gods. There were even prophetic or oracular centers in ancient Israel at Bethel (2 Kgs 2:2–3), Jericho (2 Kgs 2:4–5), and Gilgal (2 Kgs 4:38), where one finds guilds or schools of prophets. They were called "the sons of the prophets."

Cicero's second avenue for determining the future, called the artificial, was by divination; that is, by reading signs believed to be sent by the Gods that appear as chance events in the natural world. A widespread belief in the Hellenistic period[19] asserted that all Gods reveal the future to certain persons of their choosing, but to the vast majority of us they only give indirect signs, omens, and portents, which if carefully interpreted enlighten us about the future.

Cicero mentions a number of these signs in the natural world: for example, dreams, the direction lightning takes in the sky, the direction

---

18. Rousseau, "Pagan, Paganism," 1091; Purcell, "Pagus," 1092.

19. A period of time calculated from the death of Alexander the Great in 336 BCE to the beginning of the Roman period in 30 BCE.

of flights of birds, the entrails of animals during times of sacrifice, prodigies (something extraordinary, inexplicable, or marvelous), omens (an occurrence believed to portend a future event), and wandering stars. In other words both the common and extraordinary in life may be a sign that portends the future. The general attitude in antiquity was that if one disregarded these signs sent by the Gods, it was tantamount to disbelieving in the Gods.[20]

The Romans institutionalized the observation of signs by means of a college of augurs, a group of fifteen who regularly "took the auspices" (i.e., read the signs) on matters of importance for the state. They also kept a roost of "sacred chickens" that were regularly consulted by eminent Romans on matters of importance. The eating behavior of the chickens was observed for predictions of future events.[21] When the sacred chickens ate so greedily that the food dropped from their beaks to the ground, a favorable omen was predicted (called the *tripudium*).[22] They also kept a set of ancient Sibylline books; these were collections of prophetic utterances of the Sibyls, who were female visionary figures from the classical tradition. They consulted these books at times of crisis and national emergency.[23]

What I regard as a third distinct way of determining the future, which Cicero included with his artificial category, is astrology. In the Hellenistic period it was believed that one's destiny was fated and determined by the movement of the heavenly bodies. Fate may be defined as the principle, power, or agency by which events are unalterably predetermined from eternity.[24]

By the third century BCE ancient Greeks had developed from Babylonian astral observations the idea that "the movements of the heavenly bodies control earthly events up to the smallest detail."[25] Hence, our future destiny is unalterably written in the movements of the stars, which also hold the secrets of our eventual fate. Not even prayer and sacrifice could help one escape one's inevitable fate. The best one could do was to understand and affirm it. Even the Gods themselves were subject to the

---

20. Cicero, *Div.* I.xlvi.104.
21. Lewis and Reinhold, eds., *Roman Civilization*, 1:139.
22. Cicero, *Div.* I.xxxv. 77; I.xv.28; I.xxxiv.72–I.xxxv.73.
23. Lewis and Reinhold, eds., *Roman Civilization* 1:147–48.
24. *OED*, s.v. "Fate."
25. Ferguson, *Backgrounds*, 41–42.

inevitable force of fate, as the priestess at Delphi told the envoys of King Croesus of Lydia.[26]

To discover one's destiny one would consult an astrologer, who was learned in the arcane knowledge of the heavenly spheres. Knowing that all things were predetermined gave one a sense of freedom from anxiety. Fate was not a God but an impersonal force described by one philosopher as "an orderly succession of causes wherein cause is linked to cause and each cause of itself produces an effect."[27] Some philosophers suggested that while bodily existence was subject to fate, the soul, however, was free.

Astrology, the idea that life is determined by the movement of the heavenly bodies, is still today believed by many to be a viable way of discovering the future through consulting horoscopes, tarot, astrological almanacs, and psychic readings.

It is surprising to note that the authors of the Bible in the main shared these ancient pagan ideas about divination and prophecy. The fact that they have so much in common with pagan thinking should not be surprising, however, since the biblical authors themselves in aspects of their thinking and faith were products of ancient pagan culture.

The Israelites clearly believed that their God (Yahweh), like the other pagan gods of antiquity, chose certain people to be channels for his revelations (Deut 18:17–18). But, on the other hand, diviners, soothsayers, augurs, sorcerers, wizards, charmers, mediums, and necromancers were forbidden in Israel (Deut 18:10–12); nevertheless such things still occurred, as, for example, when Saul consulted the medium of Endor to resuscitate the prophet Samuel from death (1 Sam 28:3–25).

The literary prophets of Israel's history were believed to write "words of God." While there is an element of futurity in their prophecies, the prophecies concerned the near future in general detail on matters relating to the Israelites and their welfare. Some of their prophecies did not come true, as, for example, the prophecy that there would always be a descendant of David ruling Israel (2 Sam 7:1–7; Jer 33:17–18). Today, however, Israel is no longer a monarchy, and its leaders do not claim descent from David!

Here is a second failed prophecy: Ezekiel prophesied that the ancient city of Tyre would be utterly destroyed and no longer inhabited (Ezek 26:17–21), but today Tyre is a thriving city in Lebanon. Cicero's dialogue

---

26. Dillon, "Fate," 2:777. Herodotus, *Histories*, 1.53, 91.
27. Martin, *Hellenistic Religions*, 41–42.

partner argued that occasional failed prophecies must inevitably occur, but that did not disprove the effectiveness of divination,[28] for every art reflects some fault.

Early Christians co-opted some of the "Old Testament" prophecies to prove that the founding events of their faith had been foreseen by the prophets. For example, they took over a prophecy that Isaiah made to King Ahaz of Judah during a political crisis of the eighth century BCE. The birth of a child in Judah, Isaiah said, prophesied the survival of the kingdom of Judah (Isa 7:1–17). The prophecy came true; Judah did survive.

Matthew, however, took over one verse of this prophecy out of the context in which Isaiah used it (Isa 7:14), claiming that the prophecy related to the birth of Jesus, the Anointed of God (Matt 1:18–23). Early Christians treated the Bible as a book of prophecy that related specifically to them in a way similar to the way Romans treated the Sibylline books.

Divination also occurs in the biblical texts by means of all the usual pagan signifiers and language, as Cicero described them: dreams (Matt 1:20; 2:12–13, 19, 22); signs and wonders (Acts 4:30; 2:43; Heb 2:4; 2 Cor 12:12; Rom 15:19); portents (Dan 5:5–31; Joel 2:30–31; Isa 13:9–11; 20:2–3; 8:18; Mark 13:24–27; Luke 21:8–28; Rev 12:1; 15:1); marvels (Exod 34:10; John 7:21); signs (John 2:1–11; Judg 6:37–40; Matt 24:29–30) omens (Sir 34:5; 2 Macc 5:4); apparitions (2 Macc 5:1–4); wandering stars (Matt 2:2, 9–10); prodigies (Rev 13:1–9, 11–18). Those who think the Bible establishes the true contours of what is real when it describes divination and prophecy should think again. The Bible simply provides more examples of what occurred in paganism.

One definite difference between the Bible and the views of paganism, however, is the Bible's understanding of fate.[29] In the Bible fate is not an impersonal force that determines human destiny. Rather Yahweh himself predetermines both chance and outcomes: thus human destiny lies in God's hands (Pss 16:5; 31:15; Prov 16:33; Eccl 3:11, 15; 7:13; 8:17; 1 Sam 16:14; 1 Kgs 22:22; Rom 9:18; 2 Thess 2:11). Nevertheless some of the biblical writers are aware of Fate as an impersonal force determining human destiny (Isa 47:13; Jer 10:2; Ezek 21:21; Matt 2:2), and astrologers still read the heavens to determine fate on earth (Dan 2:27; 4:7; 5:7. 11).

---

28. Cicero, *Div.* I.xiv.24
29. Cook, "Fate," 2:434–35.

Cicero's essay (*On Divination*) is in the form of a dialogue between Cicero and his brother Quintus. The paper character Quintus (invented by Cicero for the purposes of the essay) makes the case for divination in the first section of the essay (I), and in the second section (II) Cicero makes the case against divination.

Personally, I am more convinced by Cicero's argument against divination. It is simply implausible that anyone possesses sufficient clairvoyance to see into the distant future, although it is certainly possible to read a particular immediate situation through human logic and reason and have a pretty good idea what the possible outcomes of that situation might be. But I hasten to add that this insight is based on human logic and experience rather than a divine endowment of insight.

Cicero summarized the issue of divination at one point in this way: "Divination is compounded of a little error, a little superstition, and a good deal of fraud."[30] And he lamented at one point that he spent "so much time in refuting such stuff" that he was "more absurd than the very people who believe it."[31] And later he wondered, "Why do immortal Gods see fit to give us warnings which we can't understand without the aid of interpreters?"[32] Even his (invented) dialogue partner Quintus, who made the case for divinations and prophecy, concludes his comments as follows: "I will assert, however, in conclusion that I do not recognize fortune-tellers, or those who prophesy for money, or necromancers, or mediums"[33]; yet Quintus still claimed "that the gods advise and often forewarn him" (through the chance events of nature). In short, Quintus approved of "divination," which he regarded as "not trivial and free from falsehood and trickery."[34]

Cicero, on the other hand, regarded divination as superstition, "which is widespread among the nations." It "has taken advantage of human weakness to cast its spell over the mind of almost every other person," and he quickly added "I want it distinctly understood that the destruction of superstition does not mean the destruction of religion."[35] I am inclined to agree with him. Religion will survive in some form with-

30. Cicero, *Div.* II.xxxix.83.
31. Ibid., II.xxiii.51.
32. Ibid., II.xxv.54.
33. Ibid., I.lviii.132.
34. Ibid.
35. Ibid., II.lxxii.148.

out those features that tax the credulity of a twenty-first-century human being.

Cicero concludes his essay in this way: "It is a duty to weed out every root of superstition. For superstition is ever at your heels to urge you on; it follows you at every turn. It is with you when you listen to a prophet, or an omen; when you offer sacrifices or watch the flight of birds; when you consult an astrologer or a soothsayer; when it thunders or lightens or there is a bolt from on high; or when some so-called prodigy is born or made. And since necessarily some of these signs are nearly always being given, no one who believes in them can ever remain in a tranquil state of mind."[36]

The truth is, there is no fixed inevitable future that preexists in the foreknowledge of God. The only future we will ever know ahead of time is what rushes into the present in the next second. The future is always in a state of becoming; beyond that it exists only as an uncertain contingency of plans, fears, and hopes in the human mind. (3–28–17; 4–10–17)

§103 LIFE IS WHAT YOU MAKE IT—OR IS IT?

I have come to think that life is what you make it! There are no built-in assurances that one's life will be happy or successful, nor is one's life fated to be filled with unhappiness or end in disaster. When one is born, life is as full of possibilities, as one's historical circumstances allow and one's capabilities permit. I did not always think of life as my own creation, however. The fresh air of philosophical secularism rarely penetrated into the heavy religious atmosphere of the Mississippi Delta, where I spent my youth.

> I was taught that God had a plan for every life, which (if one could find it) would lead to success, but only as God counts success. That is to say, one's life may not appear successful as the secular world counts success, but God would regard it so. And one could count on God helping one achieve success in life (as, I was taught, God valued success), provided one resisted the wiles of Satan, God's archenemy.

What is surprising is that this narrative, which I learned in the church, is not part of the views of some writers in the Bible. For example, consider the case of Judas Iscariot, who appears to have been destined for

36. Ibid., II.lxxii.149.

infamy from the beginning. Luke even describes Judas's traitorous act as being prophesied in Scripture (Acts 1:16; Ps 41:9), meaning that Judas's life became not what he made it but what God had forced upon him. The evidence is mixed for Judas, however. John describes Judas's betrayal of Jesus as caused by demon possession (John 6:70-71; 13:2), while Matthew describes the betrayal as inspired by Judas's greed (Matt 26:14-16; Mark 14:10-11). A classic Old Testament example of God's interfering in our lives to work his inscrutable ways is the account of King Saul's clinical melancholia. It was caused by an evil spirit sent from God (1 Sam 16:14-23) after the departure of God's (holy) spirit (1 Sam 16:14). If the Bible is correct, neither Judas nor Saul had much of a chance for success in life; their lives failed because of invisible powers over which they had no control.

Is it true that invisible supernatural powers are at work on all of us (as Eph 6:12 has it) to our detriment or benefit, and that we have no control over them, and we become what we are as a result of what they impose on our lives? It calls to mind comedian Flip Wilson's immortal line: "the devil made me do it!" It is true, however, that certain historical circumstances beyond our control do influence the outcomes of our lives (for example, economic, political, social, or other circumstances). But these are neither invisible nor supernatural. Thinking that supernatural powers are at work in the world is a matter of personal belief; it is not objective reality. Naturally if one believes such things, one thereby creates an objective reality for oneself, and it is that *belief* that influences one's life, rather than the putative supernatural power. This idea works as well for those who do not think that life is influenced by supernatural powers, for their *nonbelief* becomes the objective reality that sets them free to make what they will of life.

Some biblical writers seem to think that God interferes in our lives in the sense that some are predestined to greatness and others to failure by God electing or choosing them for the fate that they come to realize in their lives (e.g., Isa 42:1; 45:4; 65:9; Mark 13:20, 27; 1 Pet 1:2; Rom 11:5; Deut 7:6; 1 Kgs 11:34; Ps 78:70-71). The clearest passage of which I am aware (perhaps the only one) where God swears "hands off" interfering in peoples' lives are the surprising statements attributed to Paul in Rom 1:18-32, where God "gave up" certain people to what Paul calls their impurity, dishonorable passions, and base minds. With this exception the biblical view seems to be that God interferes in all our lives. But secular belief can trump biblical faith in the sense that we can create our own realities. (3-15-17)

§104 CAN THE CHURCH GRANT ABSOLUTION FOR SINS?

To be absolved means to be "set free from the consequences of guilt." And yes, some churches do claim to be able to absolve people of their sins. In the Episcopal Church, for example, a penitent may confess their sins to God in the presence of a priest or bishop and receive from them the assurance of pardon and the grace of absolution. Upon their confession the priest then pronounces this absolution:

> Our Lord Jesus Christ, who has left power to his Church
> to absolve all sinners who truly repent and believe in him,
> of his great mercy forgive you all your offenses; and by his
> authority committed to me, I absolve you from all your sins:
> In the Name of the Father, and of the Son, and of the Holy
> Spirit. Amen.[37]

The rationale behind this Episcopal Church tradition (also found in the Roman Catholic, Anglican, Orthodox, and Lutheran traditions) is that Jesus is portrayed as forgiving sins (Matt 9:1–8; Mark 2:1–12; Luke 5:17–26; 7:36–50), and he passed on to Peter the authority to "bind and loose" (Matt 16:18–19); and in the Gospel of John Jesus passes on to all his disciples the ability to forgive sins (John 20:19–23). The custom of the church granting absolution for sins, however, does not appear to be known in the rest of the New Testament. Ignatius does not seem to be aware of the practice of ecclesial absolution for sin in the early second century, but he does advise that the repentant should turn in repentance to the bishop's council.[38] The Shepherd of Hermas (100–150 CE), however, disagreed with those who believed that if anyone sinned after baptism, there was no opportunity for repentance (compare Heb 6:1–6, where forgiveness is not possible after apostasy). The Shepherd asserted that there was opportunity for the church to repent.[39] In the third century those about to undergo martyrdom or who underwent torture or imprisonment were deemed to be able to absolve those who had commit-

---

37. Episcopal Church, *Book of Common Prayer*, 447–48.
38. *Phld.* 8.1
39. *Herm. Vis.* 2.2–3; *Herm. Mand.* 4.1–4; 12.3–6; *Herm. Sim.* 8.11,1–5.

ted the sins of adultery and fornication. A shocked Tertullian reported that a certain bishop issued an edict saying that "I remit to such as have discharged repentance the sins of both adultery and fornication."[40] Such is the evidence for absolution in the earliest period. After the late second century the custom became institutionalized in the later church for sins in general.

It seems to me that the church practice of absolving people of their sins is a usurpation of what should be God's prerogative on the assumption that the authority Jesus is believed to have had and extended to his disciples falls by default to the institutional Christian church. That is to say: *someone* has to pronounce absolution for sins, and who is in a better position to do it than the church? Hence, those who take upon themselves the pronouncement of absolution for the sins others commit may believe they have the authority to do so by virtue of church custom and their ordination, but in my view they are deceiving themselves about the limits of their ability. The scribes asked the correct question: "who can forgive sins but God alone?" (Mark 2:7).

In the context of religious faith it would seem that only God has the authority to pronounce absolution for sins. Even though God doesn't speak audibly anymore, those who have sinned must still by themselves seek absolution from God, according to their own understanding of God. In the context of human life, however, absolution for sins (i.e., injuries, ills, harms, etc. done to others) must ultimately be sought from those they have injured.

If the statements in the previous paragraph are correct, it would appear that the priestly pronouncement of absolution is like the counsel of Eliphaz, the Temnite, to Job—just so many "windy words" (Job 16:2, RSV); what they advised were vaporous words, full of well-meaning intent perhaps, but signifying little. Absolution for sins must be sought in two venues: 1. a person must stand, nakedly remorseful, before the injured party and humbly petition for absolution; and 2. during a personal dark night of the soul penitents must make their own peace with God, if God there be. The church may assist the penitent seeking absolution, but it seems an arrogance of the first order to assume it can grant absolution, or even assure the penitent that absolution has been granted. A third party has no standing in this matter. God cannot be "bound or loosed" by church tradition (compare Exod 33:19; Rom 9:15). Believing oneself

---

40. Tertullian, "On Modesty," 74, 100 (chapters 1 and 22).

capable of committing the God of the universe to anything on one's own personal authority, however they may think it is delegated to them, seems very much like thinking one can bridle a giant fire-eating dragon: it is the stuff of romantic fiction and mythology. (7-20-15)

§105 GOD'S VIEW OF MARRIAGE?[41]

I am always astonished when anyone claims to know what God thinks! It is a rash claim, at best. A case in point is an editorial by James D. Hernando of Springfield, Missouri. Hernando claimed that "Marriage is God's idea. He created us as sexual beings and His loving plan for the fulfillment of our sexuality is a monogamous heterosexual union in marriage."[42] Actually Hernando is reciting his own ideal of marriage based on the Bible (Genesis). The Bible, however, is inconsistent on the subject of marriage. For example, polygamy was practiced among the ancient Israelites (Gen 4:19; 16:1-4; 25:6; 26:34; Deut 21:15; Judg 8:30; 1 Sam 1:1-2; 1 Kgs 11:1-10; 1 Chr 4:5; 2 Chr 11:21; 24:3). Particularly relevant is Deut 21:15, which shows God condoning polygamy. First Kings 11:1-10 portrays God as opposed to Solomon's marriage to foreign women because it would lead to the worship of foreign Gods, not because God had placed a high view on monogamous marriage—that is, on marriages of one man and one woman. In 2 Chr 24:1-3 Joash is extolled as "doing what was right in the eyes of the LORD all the days of Jehoiada," while at the time he was married to two wives. So God apparently did not always, if ever, hold to the ideal of monogamous marriage that Hernando attributes to him.

Even in the New Testament the ideas about marriage do not measure up to Hernando's ideal view of marriage that he attributes to God. Paul, for example, preferred that men and women should remain single (1 Cor 7:6-9), but he granted marriage as a concession to human weakness ("better to marry than burn with [sexual] passion," 1 Cor 7:9). Paul's rationale for his view lies in his mistaken idea that the end of the world was imminent (1 Cor 7:25-31). He sets out his reasons for singularity (not monogamy) in 1 Cor 7:32-35, where he claims that marriage distracts from undivided devotion to God. His view of a kind of sexless or spiritual "marriage" is odd, to say the least. Apparently at Corinth unmarried men

---

41. A shorter version of this essay appeared in the *Springfield News-Leader*: Hedrick, "Bible Varies."

42. Hernando, "Marriage."

and women were living together without being married, or engaging in sexual intercourse. Paul reassured them that if a couple decided to marry "it was not a sin" (1 Cor 7:36: a reference to marriage as "not a sin" reflects a rather low view of marriage). Paul concludes that the man who marries his virgin does well, but the man who refrains from marriage does better (1 Cor 7:38). With this statement Paul seems to put his stamp of approval on a kind of continent spiritual living together. And Paul argued, this kind of "union" (being accompanied by a sister as wife) was his "right," a right he shared with "the other apostles and the brothers of the Lord and Cephas" (i.e., Peter: 1 Cor 9:5). Later writings in the New Testament after Paul do reflect Hernando's idea of "one man and one woman" (viz., 1 Tim 3:2, 12; Titus 1:6). In Paul's earliest letter a passage, usually considered to be about marriage is unclear even for a reader of the Greek text (1 Thess 4:4–8). Tertullian (second/third century), a presbyter of the Latin church, in trying to deal with the large number of virgins in the church (that is, those having taken a vow of chastity) recommended that widowers take a virgin as a kind of spiritual wife into their homes. Indeed, "a plurality of such wives is pleasing to God."[43]

Cyprian (bishop of Carthage, middle third century) dealt with a similar situation differently than did Paul and Tertullian. He stopped the practice of a man and a virgin living together, excommunicating the men who had been involved but permitting the virgins who remained virgins and were resolved to continue as virgins to remain in the church.[44] What today we see as radical actions, in antiquity were attempts to deal with the large number of women who had taken vows of chastity. Celibacy was a religious ideal that was honored by the Christian church and thought to be approved by God—as Paul said, however, we don't all have the same gift. And a similar statement is attributed to Jesus about male castration: "whoever is able to receive it, let him receive it" (Matt 19:12).

Human beings are not privy to knowing the mind of God. No less a prophet than Isaiah said: "Who has known the mind of the LORD and been his counselor so as to instruct him?" (Isa 40:13 LXX; quoted by Paul in 1 Cor 2:16). Paul wanted all his saints to have the "mind of Christ" (Phil 2:5), but not even Paul claimed to know the mind of God (1 Cor 2:11), even though he claimed to have the mind of Christ (1 Cor 2:16), which likely refers to Christ's self-giving attitude in life (Phil 2:2–10). The

---

43. Tertullian, "Exhortation to Chastity," 56 (chapter 12).
44. Cyprian, "Epistles," 356–58 (Epistle 61).

Bible, neither as a collection nor in its individual essays, embodies the mind of God, but represents one record of the human quest for God in the Judeo-Christian tradition. The best practice is steer clear of anyone who claims to have God's ear or know God's mind. (4-16-13)

§106 WHO DECIDES WHAT IS "TRUE CHRISTIANITY"?

In a "Voice of the Day" editorial in a local newspaper Rev. Michael Haynes, director of the Greene County Baptist Association in Springfield, Missouri, criticized Rev. Dr. Roger Ray, pastor of Community Christian Church.[45] Community Christian Church is a nontraditional, progressive Christian community.[46] Mr. Haynes said of Mr. Ray, "Ray is not a Christian"; Ray should "stop the charade and not call himself a Christian"; and Ray should "stop making Jesus into whomever he wants him to be." What follows is a slightly longer version of my response, which was not accepted for publication in the newspaper.

Dear Brother Haynes, it seems unfair of you to evaluate Brother Ray's Christianity, or lack thereof, by the Baptist Faith and Message Statement,[47] a statement, that likely represents only your view of "true Christianity." Such a view is only definitive if one shares your belief. Christianity has always been a "Big Tent" religion, encompassing very divergent views. There has never been one true view of Christian faith, not even from the beginning. What much later became the so-called orthodox view in the fourth century came about with the political support of the first Christian emperor, Constantine, aided by a self-appointed orthodoxy's aggressiveness, in stamping out the competition.[48]

There was no standardized view of Christianity until the creeds of orthodoxy in the fourth century,[49] and also no Christian Bible (Hebrew Scriptures plus New Testament) until the fourth century.[50] In short, there were no generally agreed-upon standards that could be used to judge another's beliefs. In the second century there were charismatic teachers with divergent views. Paul, for example, had to argue his positions against

---

45. Haynes, "Ray's Work for Poor," 9A.
46. Ray, "Emerging Church."
47. Southern Baptist Convention, "2000 Baptist Faith & Message."
48. Eusebius, "Life of Constantine."
49. Bettenson and Maunder, eds., *Documents* (3rd ed.), 25–29.
50. Athanasius, "Letter XXXIX," 552.

those with whom he disagreed. The early postresurrection-belief followers of Jesus used only the Greek translation of the Hebrew Bible as their Scriptures. The writing of the New Testament texts was yet years in the future; one text (2 Peter) was not written until the second century. Not until the fourth century did it become possible to cite New Testament texts and church creeds as authoritative proofs of what some regarded as true faith. Before that, each group promoted its own version of faith as the true faith, as is still the case.

In this early period before the Constantine-led suppression of the diversity of beliefs about Jesus, there were numbers of ways of interpreting Jesus. In the end-of-the-first-century canonical gospels clearly Jesus was regarded as the divine Son of God. But oddly the title "Son of God" is never found as an admission on Jesus' own lips; the title is bestowed on him by others.[51] And only once does Jesus accept the title messiah ("anointed" Mark 14:61–62). In the passages parallel to Mark (Matt 26:63–64; Luke 22:67–68) he is presented as avoiding a claim of messiahship. In Rom 1:3–4, a pre-Pauline confession or hymn, Jesus was not presented as divine, but it is asserted that he was by nature essentially a human being, appointed or adopted for a special purpose. Others believed that Jesus was not human after all, but rather that he was completely divine and only seemed to be human (cf. Phil 2:9–11 and John 1:1–2, 14). Jesus' humanity, including what he said and did, essentially disappears in the later ecclesiastical creeds.[52] Still other groups regarded Jesus as a human being who came to be inhabited at his baptism by a divine spirit—"the Christ,"[53] or believed that he was the natural-born son of Mary and Joseph, a human being like the rest of us except that he was better.[54] Throughout the first and second centuries the Judean man Jesus became an originating principle for a variety of ways of understanding him and his role in faith.

With such diversity in the early days, how does anyone have the authority to rule that any of Jesus' followers is misguided when it appears that the faith once delivered to the saints (Jude 3) turns out to be only a statement of one's personal belief? On one occasion, Jesus' disciples censured a stranger for exorcizing demons in Jesus' name. Jesus said they

---

51. Brown, *Introduction to New Testament Christology*, 89.
52. Bettenson and Maunder, eds., *Documents* (3rd ed.), 25–29.
53. Irenaeus, *Haer.*, 1.24.3–4; in Foerster, comp., *Gnosis*, 1:59–61.
54. Hedrick, "Cerinthus," 580.

should let him alone . . . "For he that is not against us is for us" (Mark 9:38–41; compare John 10:16). (4-1-14)

§107 HOLINESS IS A STATE OF MIND

In primitive societies persons, places, and things were thought to be imbued with a general supernatural force or power, generally referred to as *mana* by anthropologists. This force was considered sacred or holy, and consequently that in which mana resided must never be dealt with casually or carelessly. It required a shaman, tribal chief, or holy person of the community who understood such things to deal with them.[55] Treat them casually and there could be catastrophic results. In the Hebrew Bible, for example, when the ark of the covenant was being moved on a cart drawn by oxen, the oxen stumbled, and one of the cart drivers, Uzzah, reached forth his hand to steady the ark so that it would not fall, and died for his efforts (2 Sam 6:1–7). In other instances the force could be beneficial. For example, objects taken away from the body of Paul to the sick, infirm, and demon possessed cured the ailments and drove out the evil spirits (Acts 19:11–12). Holy objects must be given due deference!

Today, Christians, on their best days, tend to think of the supernatural force associated with holy objects and places as a spiritual force from God: that is, the power does not reside in the object itself but ultimately comes from God through the sacred object. Such a view has some intellectual respectability to it; at least it shields Christians who trade in sacred objects from a charge of shamanism. But who knows what a person in the pew, or the pulpit for that matter, really thinks? Likely there are a range of views in religious communities that trade in religious objects and locations, ranging from superstition to a sophisticated theological rationale. Official statements of a religious group only represent the views of the majority drafting the statements.

A case on point is the way the elements of the Eucharist are viewed in the Catholic and the Lutheran traditions. In Catholicism it is asserted that the bread and wine at a sacred moment in the Mass are actually transformed into Christ's body and blood.[56] Hence one would assume that the elements are not holy by virtue of a spiritual force coming from outside, but the bread and wine are now holy in themselves; that is to

---

55. Albright, *From the Stone Age to Christianity*, 168–69.
56. Bettenson and Maunder, eds., *Documents* (3rd ed.), 162–66.

say, the power resides in them. Lutherans, on the other hand, say that the presence of Christ substantially invests the elements; hence the bread and wine remain bread and wine but now have an added spiritual force.[57] The Catholic view resonates with the ancient primitive idea of a spiritual force innate to a sacred object, while the Lutheran view *seems* more in line with an outside spiritual force permeating the elements of the Eucharist. I say *seems* because the "substantial presence" in the Eucharist appears to be a special instance that does not apply to other objects. Some theologians describe the spirit of God actually permeating the entire universe—rocks, trees, animals, comets, suns, and so forth.[58] But the Lutheran view of the Eucharist seems to hold the Eucharist to be a special instance.

In Eastern and Western Christianity holy shrines are still believed to bring healing to the masses even today. The miraculous icon of the Virgin, our Lady of the Greek Island of Tinos, and the icon of our Lady of Lourdes, France, bring sight to the blind, hearing to the deaf, and cures of all sorts, just as Asclepius did at his ancient Greek sanctuaries of Epidauros and Kos. Protestant Christianity, on the other hand, has traveling shrines where healings occur wherever faith healers like Benny Hinn happen to pitch a tent or hire an auditorium.

The word *holy* as applied to certain things often means little more than worthy of deference or respect. For example, in describing the church auditorium as a "sanctuary" (that is, a holy space) many would agree that the word simply means the space is to be respected, like one respects the Senate chambers of the federal government, for example. Not everyone thinks that way, however, and would affirm the auditorium as God's house, meaning that God is in that place in a special way; the space is therefore holy or sacred. This latter way of thinking about a church auditorium is more like the primitive idea of a supernatural force or power residing in rocks and trees, as it does not reside in neutral places, like, for example, a football stadium.

The line between faith and superstition is exceedingly fine. Since the eighteenth century, the rise of critical thinking and a reliance on human reason for explaining what we regard as extraordinary have challenged the idea of the holy as a sacred presence permeating things we regard as special or unusual. A view of objects and places as supernaturally endowed, and even a sacral view of the cosmos itself, has been steadily

---

57. Dillenberger and Welch, *Protestant Christianity*, 51–52.
58. Robinson, *Exploration into God*, 88–96.

falling before scientific questions and answers. The primitive view of world as sacred space, alive with spirits and mysterious powers surrounding human beings who must be protected by magic and religious ritual, survives in Western thinking, but for many of us it likely only survives in the dark recesses of our minds. Nevertheless, in many parts of the world primitive ideas of the holy still, quite literally, hold human minds hostage. In the West, however, rational thinking and human reason are gradually overcoming superstition. The line between faith and superstition is drawn with great difficulty, and perhaps with the loss of many of the assured tenets of one's chosen faith. (2–10–11)

§108 HOW DID MOSES COME BY THE TORAH?

Most everyone knows the biblical tradition portraying Moses as the great "lawgiver" of the Israelite people. In Exodus and Deuteronomy he is described as receiving the Torah directly from God. He tells the Israelite people, "I went up to the mountain to receive the tables of stone ... And the LORD gave me two tablets of stone written by the finger of God" (Deut 9:9–10; and for the second giving of the tablets to Moses see Deut 10:1–5; Moses had broken the first set). It is surprising to learn, however, that the apostle Paul did not agree that God had given the law *directly* to Moses. According to Paul (Gal 3:19) and other New Testament writers (Acts 7:38, 53; Heb 2:2), the law was "ordered through angels." This tradition was also shared by Josephus, a first-century Jewish writer, in a statement attributed to Herod: "We have learned the noblest of our doctrines and the holiest of our laws from the messengers [angels] sent by God."[59]

This tradition of an indirect passing of the law to Moses is unknown in the Hebrew Bible, although angels are part of the coterie of God in the Septuagint version of Deut 33:2, where God comes with his "holy ones," and "on his right hand were his angels with him." In one of the apostolic fathers (the Shepherd of Hermas), the archangel Michael was said to have "put the law into the hearts of those who believe."[60] Angels were long thought to act as mediators between God and human beings (see, for example, Testaments of the Twelve Patriarchs: T.Levi 5:5–6; T.Dan 6:1–2; Philo, On Dreams, 1.141–42; Jub. 1.27—2.1; 32:21–22). Cerinthus, according to Epiphanius, claimed that the Law and Prophets were given by

---

59. Josephus, *Ant.* 15.5.3 (§136).
60. Herm. Sim. 8.3.3.

angels, and that the lawgiver was one of the angels who made the world.[61] Barnabas (9.4), another of the apostolic fathers, reports that an evil angel misled the Israelite people into thinking that circumcision was an actual fleshly act.

Obviously we have here an interesting contradiction between the Old Testament and the New Testament: did Moses actually receive the law directly from God, or was it "ordered through angels"? Both assertions cannot be correct at the same time! The situation is much more complicated, however. These claims about the law are traditions validating the authority of the Torah. A tradition is a "handing down" orally of a belief from generation to generation. Traditions are living "things," and as such they change, evolve, and mutate. Because they exist in memory and surface in oral communication, no sequential history of the evolution of an ancient tradition survives. Each generation inevitably modifies what they receive, because it is not written in stone (so to speak). If there ever had been a point of origin and an original form of the tradition, it would have long since vanished into the dense fog of the past. With time, written stories do emerge explaining the origin of this or that particular belief. These various written forms of the tradition often represent diverse, contradictory versions of the tradition. Such versions represent what individuals or groups believed about them at a given moment in time. Oral tradition, however, goes on evolving into still later multiple forms as interpreted by those who receive it and pass the tradition on to other auditors.

Neither of these two attempts to explain how the Torah came to Moses (i.e., directly from God or ordered through angels) is a historically verifiable datum about the origin of the Torah; they are rather ancient traditional beliefs and as such do not provide a historical description of origins. Rather each is a then current religious belief representing what people thought at the time.

Many if not most statements about origins in the Bible work the same way. For example, early Christians validated the divinity of Jesus by various narratives: of a physical birth (Matt 1:18–25; Luke 1:26–55; 2:1–20), of the infusion or mutation of the preexistent heavenly Christ into flesh (John 1:1–14), and of a baptismal theophany (Mark 1:9–11). The diversity of explanations presents critical readers with an interesting contradiction between biblical writers.

61. Epiphanius, *Pan.*, 28.1, 2.

Which of these contradictory traditions about the Torah, if either, makes more sense? Or to put the question another way, with whom should one agree: "Moses" (i.e., directly from God), Paul (i.e., ordered through angels), or Hedrick (i.e., traditions, not history)? (9–30–14)

§109 HOW RELEVANT IS THE CHRISTIAN WORLDVIEW TODAY?[62]

Nascent Christianity emerged in the early first century CE as a tiny Judean religious sect. Its religious heritage was shaped by the Holy Scriptures of the ancient Israelites and the temple at Jerusalem. What little we know about this small Judean sect derives from the writings of their later descendants: the gospels and the Pauline letters.

When nascent Christianity emerged, the city of Rome controlled the Mediterranean basin and had divided its territories into a number of provinces. Judea was an imperial province, governed by the emperor of Rome rather than by the Roman senate.[63] The religion of Rome in general was characterized by the worship of the traditional Greek Gods in Roman garb, plus new religions that the Romans had allowed into the city.

In the Greco-Roman world the Judean sect of Jesus followers was rapidly transformed into a religion of salvation. With the patronage of Constantine, the first Christian emperor of the Roman Empire (325 CE), the transformed faith rapidly replaced the old religious traditions, which survived outside the cities in the countryside (cf. *paganus*: Latin for "countryside" and the source of our word "pagan"). After 440 CE no pagan names are listed among the elite of the city of Rome.[64]

Since the fourth century CE, Christianity has been a formidable force in the Western world. Only recently, however, with the rise of modern science and a growing reliance on reason rather than faith has Christianity begun to show signs of irrelevance. There had been warnings about the demise of the "pagan" worldview before the Christian hegemony. For example, in the first century CE, about the time nascent Christianity was emerging and some three hundred years before the ancient pagan worldview was replaced by the Christian, Plutarch, a priest of

---

62. This essay was later published in the *Fourth R* 28/3 (May–June 2015) 17–18; used by permission.

63. Ferguson, *Backgrounds*, 43.

64. Hedrick, *History and Silence*, 57.

Apollo, recounted a strange story; he had heard reports of an anonymous voice announcing the death of the Great God Pan.[65] Even if the story is fictional, it attests a discomfort with the pagan hegemony.

Similar warnings have been sounded about the Christian worldview, which has now survived some 1700 years. Toward the end of the nineteenth century German philosopher Friedrich Nietzsche in *The Joyous Science* described a madman who ran into a marketplace seeking God. "Where is God?" he cried. "I will tell you," he says. "We have killed him." The man delivered a short speech about the loss of moorings in a world in which God is dead. He looked around at his audience, and throwing his lantern to the ground, he lamented, "I come too early; my time is not come yet. This tremendous event is still its way, still wandering; it has not yet reached the ears of man." On the same day he entered numerous churches and sang an eternal requiem to God saying, "What are these churches now if they are not the tombs and sepulchers of God?"[66]

In the 1960s a group of scholars briefly emerged who wrote about the "death of God" as an event in our time. One of these scholars, Thomas Altizer, took the incarnation quite seriously:

> God has negated and transcended himself in the Incarnation, and thereby he has fully and finally ceased to exist in his original or primordial form. To know that God *is* Jesus, is to know that God himself has become flesh: no longer does God exist as transcendent Spirit or sovereign Lord, now God is love . . .[67]

> Once God has ceased to exist in human experience as the omnipotent and numinous Lord, there perishes with him every moral imperative addressed to man from a beyond, and humanity ceases to be imprisoned by an obedience to an external will or authority.[68]

Altizer's view clearly suggests that there are more than a few cracks in the Christian "conglomerate" (the heterogeneous mixture we call Christianity). It is now evident that fissures, spearheaded by reason and science, have begun to appear in the seemingly impregnable Christian worldview. The Christian conglomerate holds that God controls the natural world,

---

65. Plutarch, *Mor.* 5.419A–E ("Obsolescence of Oracles").
66. Kaufman, ed. and trans., *Portable Nietzsche*, 95–96.
67. Altizer, *Gospel of Christian Atheism*, 67.
68. Ibid., 127.

but Mr. Darwin's scientific views on the origin of our species make a more convincing case than do theological ones, and the weather is frequently a destructive force in the natural order, causing unconscionable loss of life and property damage. By the early nineteenth century, in the face of compelling science, all opposition to the view that the sun was the center of our solar system had ceased. The notion that earth rather than the sun was the center of our solar system had been a near item of faith for around 1700 years, and for his dissent Gordiano Bruno was convicted of heresy and burned at the stake at the end of the sixteenth century.[69]

The Christian conglomerate holds that the Bible is a special religious text that puts human beings in touch with the divine will, but over three hundred years of historical-critical study has shown it to be a human collection, and God has been reduced, at best, to a peripheral role, as perhaps inspiring some of its ideas. The idea that God was in Christ reconciling the world to himself (2 Cor 5:19) is an item of faith that is not demonstrable except to those who already believe it. The church is not, as Paul believed, a divinely gathered community of saints of the end-time, but through the years has become a seriously flawed, thoroughly human institution.

Could the church in the Western world, like ancient paganism and its temples, simply fade into oblivion for lack of relevance? Put differently, exactly how is Christianity relevant to life in the twenty-first century? (3-6-15)

§110 THE CHURCH AND SKELETONS, GHOSTS, SPIRITS, AND DEMONS

Many from childhood have learned from the Bible and the church that surreal encounters can happen: for example, witches can raise the dead by spirit power (1 Sam 28:7-15); strange visions can occur about disassociated bones reconnecting and being revivified (Ezek 37:1-10); evil spirits can inhabit our bodies (Mark 5:6-13), or ghosts (phantasms) perhaps walk among us (Mark 6:49-50). Of course, a modern scientific worldview excludes such possibilities. Nevertheless revivified skeletons, ghosts, spirits, and demons are still a part of the modern landscape, although not as the Bible or the church would always have them.

---

69. Stimson, *Gradual Acceptance*, 52; see also §15 (pp. 44-46) above.

If we have lived for any length of time, most all of us have a skeleton or two in our respective closets. I define a skeleton as something from our past that we have buried but that still lurks in an out-of-the way corner of our conscious mind being involuntarily recalled at odd moments. That skeleton, if it were rattled about in public, might cause us embarrassment perhaps, but no real harm, except for a slight tarnishing to our egos and reputations.

Then there are our personal ghosts, the demons we have suppressed deep within our subconscious; they cast shadows over our conscious mind and at times debilitate our emotional and physical health. These ghosts are psychological; that is to say, they exist only in our minds, but they are nevertheless very real in the sense that they are mental remainders of experiences so powerfully frightening or painful that we deny them, and consequently bury them so deep in our subconscious they are soon forgotten by our conscious minds. But they remain with us. From deep within our subconscious they continually chaff against our consciousness, bringing to the surface feelings of inferiority and depression, excessive negative behaviors, and even more serious personality disorders. We would do well to pay attention to the warning signs that suggest some may well be inhabited by "ghosts and demons of the past." If so, one should seek the help of an "exorcist"; that is, someone specifically trained in the medical art of therapy. To exorcize these shadows of our past we need the help of skilled therapists. A general counselor, spiritual advisor, or religious life coach is ill-equipped for this task.

Then there are the metaphysical spirits, ghosts, and demons. By definition metaphysical ghosts and demons are not part of the physical world; that is, they do not exist in the sense that they occupy common space and time like you and I do, and in that sense they are not actually real, like you and I are. They belong to an imagined spirit world totally apart from the physical cosmos in which we exist. Nevertheless they are very real as ideations of the mind. They and many other such ideations are remainders left over from humanity's superstitious, primitive childhood. In our naïve past the natural world was not an "it" but a "thou."[70] Rocks, trees, bushes, mountains, and the like were endowed with *mana* (a general supernatural force concentrated in objects or persons), and the physical world was populated by spirit beings both helpful and harmful to humans. One learned to placate them by spells, charms, and sacrific-

70. Frankfort, et al., *Before Philosophy*, 11–36.

es.[71] All religions to some degree have perpetuated belief in such spirits, but in the modern Western world Christianity with its use of the Bible must accept a larger share of the blame for perpetuating such primitive superstitions.

If they are imaginary, what possible harm would it do to believe in metaphysical spirits, ghosts, and demons? I suppose none, unless one attributes physical illness, disease, or accidents to these metaphysical ideations of the mind, and ignores medical science by resorting to prayer or charms, or both, as a first-line of defense against them. Tragically even in the modern world people have died as the result of misguided attempts to exorcise possessing demons and spirits.

The use of the Bible as an authoritative religious text without proper disclaimers is not only irresponsible: it borders on the criminal by endangering the mental health and welfare of the public. (3-9-14)

§111 PROPHECY FULFILLED, OR SIMPLY CREATIVE READING?

In Baptist Bible study one Sunday morning the lesson for the day was a part of John's account of the crucifixion. In the student quarterly the lesson writer pointed out several "fulfilled prophecies" in John's crucifixion story. A fulfilled prophecy is something that a New Testament writer believed happened in order to fulfill a prediction by a Hebrew Bible/Old Testament writer. In this case the writer of John believed that certain Old Testament writers had "foretold" (predicted) that certain events would take place during the crucifixion of Jesus. The "prophecies" being fulfilled are Ps 22:18 (John 19:24), Ps 69:21 (John 19:28), Exod 12:46/Num 9:12 (John 19:36), and Zech 12:10 (John 19:37).

I checked the purported prophecies John identified in the Old Testament, and surprisingly discovered there was no indication in the context that the Old Testament writers were even aware of a future event, and what they had written had nothing to do with the crucifixion of Jesus. Nevertheless John relates his statements about Jesus' crucifixion to passages in the Old Testament with the formula "in order that the scriptures might be fulfilled..." or the like. The specific "prophecies," that John cites

---

71. The control of this spirit world continued in the Christian period; see Meyer et al., eds., *Ancient Christian Magic*.

are not marked out in the Old Testament as prophecies and a crucifixion is not mentioned in connection with the Old Testament statements.

The Old Testament texts give no hint that they should also apply to some distant future situation, and they clearly fit the context in the time of the ancient authors. John seems to have arbitrarily lifted statements out of their contexts in the Old Testament and applied them to the crucifixion story because they are similar in language to John's story. How can the similarity in language be explained? 1. Under the belief that the entire Old Testament was a book of prophecy, John adapted his crucifixion narrative to fit the statements in the Old Testament; or 2. John searched out statements in Old Testament having similar language to support his narrative; or 3. John was using a traditional list of early Christian prophecies concerning the Christ, from which he selected appropriate "prophecies."

If any of these alternate explanations seems plausible, how then is it possible to claim that the Old Testament statements are deliberately intended prophecies on the part of the writers? The writer of the students' quarterly had an answer for this question and explained Ps 22:18 (John 19:24) as a prophecy this way: The soldiers who divided up the garments of Christ were not aware that they were fulfilling prophecy when they decided to cast lots for the inner garment of Jesus. As John was writing his gospel, however, John knew they were prophecies. "The Spirit led John to include a reference to Ps 22:18, where the psalmist foretold these very events," says the lesson writer. Thus, although the psalmist was apparently unaware that he was foretelling a future event, what he wrote becomes prophecy at a later time due to the "inspired" reading of the Old Testament by John. The lesson writer described the prophecy as a revelation to John, rather than as a revelation to the Old Testament writer. Hence the "prophetic" statements only become prophecy after the crucifixion, when John wrote about it.

Fulfilled prophecy is frequently used in contemporary religiously conservative circles to demonstrate the inspiration of the Bible and the divinity of Jesus. The modern writer of this Bible study lesson on the crucifixion, for example, argued that because of the fulfilled prophecies "we can be assured that He [Jesus] is the Savior and worthy of our devotion." As early as the second century, Justin Martyr had argued that the fulfillment of prophecy proves that Jesus is "the firstborn of the unbegotten God."[72]

---

72. Coxe, "First Apology of Justin," 180 (chap. LIII).

Apart from John's assertion that his quotations from the Old Testament are prophecies, the Old Testament statements quoted in the crucifixion story cannot be objectively demonstrated to have first occurred in the mind of an Old Testament writer, for the Old Testament writers do not identify their statements as prophetic utterances! In order to see these passages as prophecy fulfilled, one must have faith that the prophecy first occurs in John's mind by revelation, and that John through the inspiration of the Holy Spirit is thereby enabled to see what is generally unavailable to others; perhaps not even the Old Testament writer was aware that he had uttered a prophetic statement. These quotations seem to be simply cases of John's "creative reading"; that is to say, John reads prophecy back into a text where it never existed, except in John's mind.

An assertion whose proof is ultimately based on faith is not proven true by the belief of the one who makes the assertion; the faith statement only proves that one believes the assertion. If other purported prophecies in the Old Testament fail to reflect the specific character of a deliberate prophecy, then the arguments that prophecy proves both the inspiration of the Bible and the divinity of Jesus are seriously undermined. Similarity of language is not enough. (2-14-14)

§112 FAITH, REASON, AND MYSTERY

The term *mystery* as used positively in the New Testament relates to a cognitive dissonance; that is to say, to a disconnect between faith and reason. Positively used, it describes the incomprehensible working of divine power, which the early followers of Jesus struggled to understand rationally. At least six issues perplexed them; some of these same issues still remain rational problems to the modern Christian mind.

1. The mystery of the failure of the Judean mission

Paul was perplexed about the failure of the Jewish mission. Why hadn't the Judean people as a group embraced the "good news" about Jesus that Paul preached? In Paul's view it had always been God's plan (Rom 9:1-5) to save the world through the sacrifice of Jesus. Why had the Judean people not understood the Scripture, their own holy books, which early followers of Jesus believed "testified of Jesus" (John 5:39)? That "a hardening had come upon Israel" until the proper number of Gentiles had "come in" was a "mystery" according to Paul (Rom 11:25-29). Paul appealed to the holy books of the Judean people, showing that this "hardening" had always been part of God's plan (Rom 11:8; Deut 29:3-4; Isa 6:9-10).

2. The mystery that Gentiles are heirs of the promise of Christ

After Paul's day the historical situation changed, and a new problem was created by the failure of the Judean mission. At this later point Judean religion and the church were recognized essentially as two different religions. From the later perspective the question then became, how is it that Gentiles (of which the church was then mostly composed) are also heirs of the promise of Christ (Eph 3:3-6)? They had come to recognize that the inclusion of the Gentiles was a promise made to Israel in the new covenant spoken of by Jeremiah (Jer 31:31-34; Heb 8:8-13).

Today the church no longer considers either of these a mystery. From the perspective of history it is clear that by the middle first century the movement represented by Paul had already turned the corner. Judean religion and the early followers of Jesus actually represented two distinct social and religious groups, and Paul was too close to the situation to recognize it.

3. The mystery of the spirit body

Paul also considered the resurrection of the believer a mystery; it involved the transformation of the physical body into a "spirit body" (1 Cor 15:51-52). How could such a thing as the transformation of a physical body into a spirit body occur? How could the perishable become imperishable in "the twinkling of an eye"? Paul never answers the question how but simply calls it a mystery, signaling by this term that it was something he did not understand. His arguments for understanding the resurrection as a spiritual experience (1 Cor 15:35-50) are analogies rather than substantive logical arguments. What he clearly does understand, however, is that the fleshly, physical, and perishable "cannot inherit the kingdom of God," which is innately imperishable and spiritual (1 Cor 15:44, 50). A later Pauline disciple reinterpreted his idea of the spirit body by arguing for the ascent of the spirit or the soul apart from the body rather than for a "spirit" body.[73] Why should a spirit need "embodiment" anyway?

73. Treat. Res. 45:14—46:2; 47:30—48:6; 49:9-16.

The resurrection still remains a mystery to the Christian mind. In an age of reason and scientific thinking a resurrection in whatever form is a problem for many. But many modern believers persist in believing in the resurrection of the physical body and simply ignore Paul's view, arguing instead that the resurrection will be physical (i.e., the resuscitation of the natural body), a view that is encouraged in the gospels (Matt 28:9; John 20:17; 21:12–13; Luke 24:30) and 2 Clem. 9:5.[74]

4. The mystery of all things united in Christ

Some Pauline disciples believed that "in the fullness of time" God intended to gather into Christ the sum total of everything in heaven and on earth (Eph 1:9–10); it included all things and all beings. Christ becomes a "receptacle," as it were, for everything in the universe in the fullness of time so as to establish a kind of cosmic harmony and unity, just as all things had begun in Christ (Col 1:16–17; cf. Rom 11:36; 1 Cor 8:6).

The very concept is breathtaking, albeit a bit strange: all things are united in Christ and nothing exists outside him. Christ in a sense becomes "the all in all" of the universe, i.e., its plenitude. With the universe gathered "in Christ," it would be sanctified, i. e., made holy. The distance between the sacred and profane would be overcome, and the profane transformed into the sacred. At the same time, it was clearly an odd idea even for those who lived in the first century, hence their description of it as mystery. But it is even odder for those of us who live in the twenty-first century. How exactly can such a concept be understood in the modern scientific age? The universe is clearly expanding rather than contracting—and what exactly is "sanctified matter" anyway?

5. The mystery of lawlessness already at work

In 2 Thess 2:1–12 the author corrects a misapprehension that the day of the Lord had already come. The assertion is that it cannot have come, since it must first be preceded by "the rebellion" and by the appearance of the "man of lawlessness." The mystery lies in the fact that already "lawlessness" is at work, although the lawless one has not yet been revealed. In other words, there is in this writer's view apparently an established timetable for the coming of the day of the Lord, and the mystery is that

74. This first part of the essay was posted online July 27, 2013.

the scheme has been partially breached or compromised. How can that be? How to explain that lawlessness is already at work even though "what restrains" (2 Thess 2:7) is still in place and the man of lawlessness has not yet appeared? This kind of thinking is called apocalyptic eschatology, a kind of thinking in which imagined schemes are devised to account for what will transpire at the end-time (cf. 2 Esd 6:1–34). Such thinking imposes a fictive plot on history and time that never comes to pass. On the other hand, Christianity was clearly more successful with its fictive plot on time, separating a pagan time frame from a Christian time frame by using BC and AD.

6. The mystery of Christ

The "Christ event" is by far the most perplexing of these mysteries. This mystery, more than anything, revealed the difficulty that later followers of Jesus had with the most basic concept of their faith (1 Tim 3:16). They preached the mystery of Christ (Col 4:2–4); that is to say, how could it be that God was in Christ reconciling the world to himself (2 Cor 5:19)? How could it be that all the treasures of wisdom had come to be in Christ (Col 2:1–3)? How could the gospel of a crucified wisdom teacher be the wisdom of God destined from the ages to bring about human glorification (1 Cor 2:7)?

The early followers of Jesus did not settle the questions evoked by these mysteries; in fact, they never even really grappled with them. They contented themselves with the idea that the solutions to these mysteries reside in the mind of God and naturally remain incomprehensible to the human mind (Rom 11:33). A surprising lack of curiosity or inquisitiveness on their part apparently resulted in a reluctance to pursue the mysteries. Certainly part of this mind-set arose from the idea that they regarded their teaching as absolutely true, but in part it evolved because they considered inquisitiveness (*ekzētēsis*) a negative attribute (1 Tim 1:4). The word appears in the New Testament where it is translated "speculations" (RSV). Inquisitiveness also carries with it the idea of getting to the bottom of things, or making an investigation. Hence a kind of anti-intellectualism characterized the early Christians. They simply ignored these issues, until much later when diversity in the church forced later leaders to address them. The mystery of Christ was eventually directly addressed in the Council of Nicaea in 325, but not really resolved. It was simply glossed over by the eventual adoption of an arbitrary scheme (the Trinity).[75]

7. Mystery is a puzzle to be deciphered.

The word *mystery* is used only three times in the canonical gospels, and all in the same parallel context (Mark 4:11–12 = Matt 13:11, 13 = Luke 8:10). The word does not indicate a divine mystery, as it does elsewhere. In the gospels a mystery is a deliberate strategy used by Jesus to present information about the kingdom of God in oblique language in order to obfuscate the understanding of the masses. Yet in the Apocalypse it is generally used almost as the equivalent of *puzzle*, a puzzle to be solved (Rev 1:20; 17:5, 7). On the other hand, in Rev 10:7, a divine mystery will be accomplished at the trumpet call of the seventh angel. This obscure reference to the "mystery of God" is not made clear to readers, but here the mystery clearly refers to a divine secret about to be unveiled.[76]

My contention is that early followers of Jesus applied the term mystery to aspects of their belief system that they could not understand rationally; that is to say, a mystery was something they believed even though it seemed contrary to reason. Instead of revising their beliefs to accord with reason, they admitted cognitive dissonance and branded what was not understandable as a mystery, which allowed them reasonably to continue affirming a belief they could not understand rationally. They trusted that these acknowledged disconnects between reason and faith would be worked out in the divine economy. In the modern Christian church the term *mystery*, as far as I know, is not extensively used. One notable exception is the mystery of the Mass—the sacred moment at which the bread and wine become the *actual* body and blood of Christ.[77]

These several uses of the term *mystery* surveyed above raise the question whether or not nascent Christianity of the Pauline type might be regarded as a mystery religions cult, not in the sense of dependence on one of the ancient cults of the Greco-Roman world, but as a parallel development. In other words, the spirit of the age evoked these religions of personal salvation and also led to the transformation of the early Jesus people into a nascent Christianity of the Pauline type. At least one highly

75. Teselle, "Trinity."
76. This second part of the essay was posted online on August 8, 2013.
77. Bettenson and Mauder, eds., *Documents* (3rd ed.), 162–66.

respected New Testament scholar of a previous generation thought of the "religious history of the Mediterranean world in the early imperial period as 'the age of mysteries.'"[78]

The mystery religions cults were rather diverse in their public celebrations, sacred objects, and theological content. So they had a public face as well as a hidden, secret side. Although different, they did have several things in common. They were all voluntary associations in which people must choose to present themselves as initiates. At the heart of the cult was a private mystery rite, a secret not to be divulged to anyone. In the mystery rite the individual was brought into a close personal relationship with the deity. The myth behind the rite and the rite itself consisted of things said to the individual, performed in the presence of the individual, or done to the individual. Since these rites were secret and not divulged, scholars are left to guess from clues here and there as to the content and meaning of the different secret rites. Participation in the mystery granted individuals redemption from the evils of the earthly life and assurance of a blessed immortality, i.e., the expectation of eternal life. Usually a sacred meal was celebrated by those initiated into the mystery cults. The goal of the initiation rite was not to impart a particular body of knowledge, but rather to produce a certain experience in the individual that would result in a particular state of mind about God, life, and the hereafter. Some scholars describe the rite of initiation as "an extraordinary experience that could be described as death and rebirth."[79]

Meyer finds several close similarities between the nascent Christianity of the first century and the mystery religions. Like adherents of the mystery religions, followers of the Christ voluntarily associated themselves together in the early Pauline communities, which also were communities of redemption and salvation. In the community they experienced baptism, a ceremonial ritual (Rom 6:1–11) in which initiates were baptized "into Christ's death" and with Christ experienced death and rebirth. Another rite was the Eucharist (1 Cor 11:17–31), which commemorated the death of Christ. "By eating of the bread and drinking of the wine [i. e., Christ's body and his blood] in the Eucharist Christians participated in the passion of Christ, and assimilated the saving power of the Cross into their lives"[80] (Meyer gives a number of other parallels).

78. Case, *Social Origins of Christianity*, 113.
79. Meyer, "Mystery Religions," 941–45.
80. Ibid., 944.

The "myth" behind both these rituals is the mystery of Christ (1 Tim 3:16): that God was in Christ reconciling the world to himself (2 Cor 5:17–19; Gal 6:14). Christ is described by Paul as the wisdom of God (1 Cor 1:24), and Paul writes: "We proclaim *in a mystery* a hidden wisdom of God, which God decreed before the ages for our glorification" (1 Cor 2:7, italics added; cf. Rom 16:25). It is difficult to make detailed comparisons between nascent Christianity and the Greco-Roman mysteries, however, because little extant firsthand information can be found on the mysteries.[81]

These parallels are well known, but generally scholars exclude Christianity from consideration as a Greco-Roman mystery religion with the argument that the mystery in Christianity is an open secret; in spite of the fact that nascent Christianity uses similar language, concepts, and rites, and shares similar objectives with the mystery religions. Nascent Christianity of the Pauline type evolved out of the early Jesus people into a religion of personal salvation, which is clearly a type of mystery religion. It managed to survive into modernity by evolving again into an institutional, creedal religion, which enjoyed the political patronage of the Roman emperor Constantine, in the fourth century.[82] The institutionalized religion seems a far cry from the earlier Pauline mysteries. Paul regarded himself and the initiates in his gatherings as "servants of Christ and stewards of the mysteries of God" (1 Cor 4:1).[83] (8-21-13)

---

81. See Meyer, ed., *Ancient Mysteries*.

82. Eusebius, "Life of Constantine."

83. This third part of the essay was posted online on August 21, 2013. The combination of the three parts will appear in the *Fourth R* as "Myth and Mystery. Profiling the Early Christian Mind."

8

On Being Christian in the Contemporary World

§113 LEARNING TO LIVE WITHOUT GODS

Believing in greater-than-human spirit entities and being superstitious are two sides of the same coin: one does not exist without the other! Superstition and religious faith appear to be opposite ends of a spectrum that meet somewhere around the middle. What some define as faith, others describe as superstition:

> 1a: a belief or practice resulting from ignorance, fear of the unknown, trust in magic or chance, or a false conception of causation; 1b: an irrational abject attitude of mind toward the supernatural, nature, or God resulting from superstition; 2: a notion maintained despite evidence to the contrary.[1]

Until the Renaissance (the fourteenth through seventeenth centuries) and the Enlightenment (the eighteenth century), average persons would not have been prepared to live without recourse to God and other spiritual or mythical entities to explain themselves and the world. The Western world was dominated by the thinking of the medieval Catholic Church, and until the Enlightenment no rationale existed that would have permitted an average human being even to conceive of such a possibility.

---

1. *Webster's Ninth New Collegiate Dictionary*, s.v. "superstition."

With the dawning of the "Age of Reason" in the eighteenth century, the church's hegemony over human thinking was finally broken, and human reason became a serious competitor to religious faith as a way of organizing one's life and understanding of the world. Human reason and religious faith/superstition have since been competitors for primacy in the human mind.

Theoretically, people today can learn to live without practical recourse to God; since everything we think we know about God we either learned from someone else or made up in our own minds. Therefore we can simply continue learning, for since the time of the Enlightenment people have come up with answers to questions that were once the exclusive prerogative of the church to answer. For example, science has developed a theory for the origin of the universe; it is described as the big bang; think of the explosion of a dense cosmic egg the size of a tiny mathematical decimal point containing all matter and energy in the universe. Such an event is at least as plausible as the poetic explanation found in the biblical creation myth (Gen 1).

Science, through the diligence of Mr. Darwin, has given to posterity a plausible theory for the origin and development of the human species, which is, again, at least as plausible as the mythical story of Adam and Eve (Gen 2:4–24). In his theory human beings are classified as evolving mammals (at our present stage we are *Homo sapiens*, intelligent man), rather than creations in one instant in the image of God (Gen 1:26).

The natural world has in the main already been dedivinized (or better, naturalized) to some extent. In the Western world we are more conditioned to seek answers from biologists and meteorologists (who use satellite imagery) to explain anomalies in nature than to consider that matters out of the ordinary are caused by spirit entities of various sorts. For example, we follow television weather reports and consult our weather apps. Having such scientific resources available makes praying about the weather a last resort rather than our first inclination.

The most difficult adjustment in the shift from faith to reason, however, has been the persistent idea that an invisible spirit world "exists" parallel to the world of matter. All of the spirit entities in current fashion (they have changed over time and from religion to religion) reside in the spirit world, but because the borders between the material and spirit world are thought to be permeable to these entities, it is believed they can suddenly emerge into the material world at any time to do either good or evil in accordance with their nature, and then they return to the spirit world until their next trip into the material world.

I personally have never experienced the "visit" of a spirit entity, whether of the night demon Lilith (Isa 34:14) or of a satyr (Isa 34:14) or of a spirit that causes muteness or deafness (Mark 9:25) or of a spirit causing jealousy (Num 5:14) or of an evil spirit from the LORD (1 Sam 16:14) or of an angel (Matt 4:11) or of a spirit causing infirmity (Luke 13:11)—or of any of those other spirits that all religions seem to number among their pantheons of good and evil spirits in order to explain things adherents don't understand. I have always been told about demon possession but have never actually known for certain that a demon caused the reaction (Mark 5:1–5). How could one possibly know for certain? Is it a demon that causes obscene language suddenly to erupt from an individual, or is it an aspect of Tourette Syndrome, specifically *coprolalia*?[2]

I look to natural causation in order to explain such things. If you don't "believe" in invisible spirits, how could they possibly affect you? They are after all invisible and are not even "there" in the way we usually think of things being "there." Physical scientists also deal with unseen things (quarks for example), but a quark even though invisible to the naked eye is still material, whereas demons and Gods are really not part of the physical cosmos, unless you happen to believe they are. (6-25-16)

§114 THE NULL HYPOTHESIS, EPILEPSY, AND EVIL SPIRITS

"A null hypothesis is a type of hypothesis used in statistics that proposes that no statistical difference exists in a set of given observations. The null hypothesis attempts to show that no variation exists between variables, or that a single variable is no different than zero. It is presumed to be true until statistical evidence nullifies it for an alternative."[3]

A discussion about belief in spirits can easily bog down into a null hypothesis—my worldview against yours, so to speak. In other words it is just as plausible to believe in spirits as not to believe in them. If that is true, the question becomes, is there a scientific study showing that not believing in spirits is a more reasonable position than accepting such entities as spirits. In this brief essay I will try to avoid the null hypothesis

2. Mayo Clinic Staff, "Tourette Syndrome."
3. *Investopedia*, "Null Hypothesis."

by attempting to show that it is more plausible to attribute the effects of illness, disease, and mental abnormalities to natural causes than to possession by unseen spirits.

In the common tradition shared by Matthew, Mark, and Luke the three evangelists report the same stories in their common material, each in different ways. The current, generally accepted theory of the synoptic relationship is that Mark wrote first, and then Mark's narrative was used as a source independently by Matthew and Luke.[4] Mark (9:14–29) recounts that a boy possessed by a "mute" spirit (Mark 9:17, i.e., a spirit causing muteness) was brought to the disciples, who could not "cast it out" (Mark 9:18). The description of the spirit's effect on the boy is frightening (Mark 9:20–22). Jesus casts the spirit out, adding that it was also a spirit causing deafness (Mark 9:25–26). Luke's narrative (Luke 9:37–43a) is shorter and attributes the boy's ailment simply to "a spirit" (Luke 9:38), which later turns out to be "an unclean spirit" (Luke 9:42), which Jesus "rebukes" as he "heals the boy" (Luke 9:42).

Matthew's narrative (17:14–21) is also shorter than Mark's version and adds that the boy is an epileptic (17:15) and, more to the point, describes his epilepsy as caused by a demon (17:18), which Jesus rebukes as he cures the boy. The word "epilepsy" was chosen by translators for a word that literally translates as "moonstruck," for "in the ancient world epileptic seizure was associated with the transcendent powers of the moon."[5] Matthew gives the disease its "proper" medical term for antiquity but regards epilepsy as a disease caused by demon possession.

Today the medical profession (and most of the Western world) does not regard epilepsy as being caused by demon possession. In the twenty-first century epilepsy is thought to be "caused by abnormal activity in brain cells."[6] Medical practitioners have shown that it is more effective to treat epilepsy with medication than it is to subject a patient to an exorcism[7]

The history of the diagnosis and treatment of epilepsy, which brings the rational world to a medical explanation for epilepsy, is anything but reassuring. The stigma attached to epilepsy lasted well into the 1990s, and the disease has not always been treated competently.

4. On the synoptic problem see Hedrick, *When History and Faith Collide*, 76–94.
5. Bauer and Danker, eds., *Greek-English Lexicon*, 919.
6. Mayo Clinic Staff, "Epilepsy: Symptoms & Causes."
7. Mayo Clinic Staff, "Epilepsy, Diagnosis & Treatment."

Hence I offer this single statistic, a single variable: it is that epilepsy responds to medical treatment.[8] This datum shows, conclusively in my judgment, that believing epilepsy is caused by evil spirits is a flawed perception of reality and may very well be dangerous to the welfare of those afflicted with epilepsy if their immediate caregivers persist in believing that epilepsy is caused by evil spirits. While it is only a single variable, I suggest that the number of variables will greatly multiply if one makes a study of other illnesses and diseases previously thought to have been caused by evil spirits, which with the advent of modernity have been shown to be the result of natural causes.

Nevertheless, not all who live in the twenty-first century are really completely a part of the twenty-first century, and they persist in believing that evil spirits can cause disease. A case in point is Dr. Richard Gallagher, a board-certified psychiatrist who is described as a professor of clinical psychiatry at New York Medical College. Mr. Gallagher seems clearly to believe in demon possession.[9] Has Mr. Gallagher matched my single variable with multiple variables of his own? If so, we are still mired in the null hypothesis; that is to say, because of Mr. Gallagher's medical training and testimony about exorcising evil spirits, one might conclude that it is as reasonable for someone to seek help from exorcists for illness, disease, and mental abnormalities as it is to seek help from medical professionals. (7–8–16)

§115 FATHER GEORGE AND THE SACRED MYSTERIES OF FAITH

Father George is a priest of the Greek Orthodox Church, but only his cassock reveals his professional standing in society. Everything else about him seems out of character. He sports a long ponytail and a neatly trimmed beard; he wears cowboy boots even during the liturgy. As a priest he is a cigarette-smoking, ouzo-drinking, girl-watching enigma! But when he sings the liturgy, his deep mellow bass voice obscures his man-of-the-world trappings in favor of his priestly image, and one only sees the dispenser-of-the-bread-of-life. When not performing the most sacred mystery of the faith, he manages his own small farm, tends to the needs of his own family, and regularly visits the *kafeneion* (coffee shop)

---

8. Magiorkinis, et al., "Highlights in the History of Epilepsy."
9. Gallagher, "As a Psychiatrist."

to socialize. Except for his priestly garb he is like other men very much at home in the world.

What makes someone choose such a high-profile role of standing in the gap ostensibly between the profane and the sacred? I cannot actually say, and I doubt anyone can, for the reasons may be as numerous as the men and women who choose such professions, and even they in their more reflective moments may not be able to say. But the question prompts me to wonder about what motivates these high-profile practitioners of the religious arts. Positive motivation must lie in the distinctive religious practices of each group in which each must be most at home; surely there is negative motivation as well: think of the fiction narrative, *Elmer Gantry*.[10] Speaking broadly, there appear to be three primary appeals for entering into the religious arts as practiced in certain religious groups; these appeals lie at a level deeper than the usual cultic practices of Christian religious groups such as marrying, burying, indoctrinating neophytes, and other such activities.

In the liturgical traditions (Roman Catholic, Orthodox) lies the obvious appeal of dispensing the primary sacred mystery of the faith; that is to say, dispensing the actual body and blood of Christ (compare John 6:52–59). This heady responsibility sets the priest apart as the most holy point where the sacred and the profane coalesce in the modern world. Essentially, the appeal is to practice the religious art as a priest, who mediates between human beings and God.

Protestant groups feature as an appeal that an individual might become God's authoritative spokesperson, one who proclaims God's Word, which proclamation is believed to lead to an improvement of the human condition. The religious professional conceives of him- or herself, and is conceived by the religious community, as God's messenger through whom one hears the voice of God, and comes to know the will of God. Essentially, the appeal is to the prophetic function, in which the prophet speaks in God's behalf.

A new form of Christianity is rapidly becoming a serious competitor to these two models of the Christian faith, namely, the ancient priestly model and the prophetic Reformation model. Churches practicing this recent form of Christianity describe themselves as progressively Christian in faith. There is no central authority, but progressive churches do seek a loose and unofficial association for collegial purposes. Such

---

10. Lewis, *Elmer Gantry*.

churches represent a reform movement among the traditional Protestant churches left over after the sixteenth-century Reformation. Progressive churches aim at reinterpreting the mythical and mystical categories in which the older forms of Christianity expressed themselves. Whereas the earlier forms focused on bringing the divine to expression in a secular world, progressive churches view themselves primarily as helpers of human beings, which means feeding the hungry, helping the poor, and such like. They practice an aggressive social activism aimed at justice in the social order, seeking to improve the world for all God's creatures.[11] Essentially, the appeal is to become a helper of human beings. There was such a role recognized in the Pauline churches of the first century. A helper was a person set aside by God for a higher purpose than self (1 Cor 12:28). The function of the helper is not described, but one must suppose that a helper was one who gave rather than received.

Do these essentially different views of the role of the religious professional in the contemporary world of Christianity have anything in common, except the designation "religious," however broadly construed? That is a tough question, having many possible answers, but the more I think about it, George's cowboy boots may turn out to be symbolic for the religious professional in the Christian tradition. The cowboy is an iconic figure of the Old West as portrayed in American western films of the 1940s; the cowboy was a resourceful, solitary figure who rode into a tragic human situation with the "right stuff" for righting wrongs and repairing the breach in the common good. Every kid in my generation wanted to be the cowboy who wore the white hat and sported pearl-handled revolvers.

The iconic cowboy, as I have described him above, is also not too far-fetched as a description of Jesus of Nazareth as portrayed in the canonical gospels. He was a solitary figure with the right stuff, who entered into the tragic human situation to heal the breach in the common good. Such a description in general is not a bad fit, not even for the religious professionals of the modern Christian period. (9–27–11)

§116 ON WEARING A CHRISTIAN LABEL

All of us wear unofficial labels of one sort or another. For example, Jesus had a status label, which is something about oneself that cannot be

---

11. Ray, *Progressive Faith and Practice*.

denied. He surely was an Israelite from Judean Galilee (John 1:47; Mark 1:9, 14:70). Other labels we give to ourselves. Jesus, for example, by all accounts called himself "son of man" (meaning something like "man of the people," Luke 9:58).[12] Others sometimes give us labels that are not complimentary. For example, Jesus was called a "glutton and a drunkard" (Matt 11:19; Luke 7:34), likely because of the dinner parties he attended (Mark 2:15-16; Luke 15:1-2).

This third kind of label is apparently what became affixed to the followers of Jesus: "They were first called 'Christians' at Antioch" (Acts 11:26). *Christian* was a term used by the Greco-Roman citizens of Antioch to designate them as followers of the god Christos; this was a general way of designating the adherents of a particular leader: for example, followers of Herod were called "Herodians" (Mark 3:6). The only other uses of the term *Christian* in the first century (Acts 26:28; 1 Pet 4:16) are not inconsistent with this understanding. Luke apparently thought that followers of Jesus originally regarded themselves "disciples" (Acts 11:26; 9:10; 6:1-2, 7; 16:1; 19:1; 21:16).

By the second century, however, the name *Christian* was clearly embraced as a self-designation by Jesus followers (e.g., Did. 12:4; Mart. Pol. 10:1; 12:1; Ig. *Mag.* 4:1). In 1 Pet 4:16 the name "Christian" was associated with suffering and persecution: "If anyone suffers as a Christian, let him not be ashamed, but under that name let him glorify God" (1 Pet 4:16). In the early second century (ca. 112) Pliny the Younger, a Roman administrator in Asia Minor, reported to the Emperor Trajan that he tried those accused of being Christian and executed the ones who refused to deny the name. An act of denial would have taken the form of sacrificing to the Roman Gods and cursing Christ.[13]

The Letter to Diognetus (from the second or third century CE) has an interesting sociological description of Christians; it suggests that Christians appeared to be little different from the rest of the Greco-Roman population except that they did not expose infants, practiced free hospitality, and guarded their purity (Diogn. 5.1-17).

Who were these people who embraced the label *Christian* in the second century in spite of its negative associations? One may not simply assume that the label *Christian* means today what it did in the past. For one reason, the term means different things to different people today, and this was no less true in antiquity. Those who acknowledged the name

12. Funk et al., *Five Gospels*, 76-77.
13. Kee, comp., *Origins of Christianity*, 51-53.

Christian to Pliny confessed (according to Pliny) "the whole of their guilt or error" to be that they met on a certain fixed day before light, sang a hymn to Christ as a God and took a solemn oath not to commit fraud, theft, or adultery, and not to falsify their word, or to deny a trust, and later they ate together.[14] On the other hand, Cerinthus, an early second-century Christian gnostic teacher in Asia Minor taught that the world was not created by God but by a lesser power. In his view Jesus was not virgin-born but the natural son of Mary and Joseph, although he was better than other men. The (heavenly) Christ descended on Jesus before his baptism and departed before his death.[15]

In the third century the author of the Gospel of Philip, a Christian gnostic text from the Nag Hammadi library, claimed to be Christian (Gos. Phil. 53:21–24; 64:22–27; 74:12–14), but the kind of Christianity reflected in the text is very different from that reflected in Paul, John, and the Synoptic Gospels. For example, the author writes:

> The chrism [i.e. the anointing] is superior to baptism, for it is from the word "chrism" that we have been called Christians, certainly not because of the word "baptism" (Gos. Phil. 74:12–15) . . . He who has been anointed [i.e., by chrism] possesses everything. He possesses the resurrection, the light, the cross, the Holy Spirit. The Father gave him this in the bridal chamber . . . (Gos. Phil. 74:17–22).

Philip's community would have been declared heretical (i.e., not genuine) by those defining themselves as orthodox. The orthodox group later adopted the Nicene Creed (fourth century), which assumes in part a three-tiered universe (heaven, earth, and hell) and spirit entities, and affirms that Jesus was not a human being but a divine figure from heaven who was "made flesh" of the holy spirit and the virgin Mary. It affirms "one holy Catholic and Apostolic Church" and "one baptism unto the remission of sins."[16]

The label *Christian* has had a wide variety of meanings in the past, and the situation is no different today. A large number of different religious groups are categorized as Protestant Christians. They exist alongside Christians of a different sort: Catholic, Orthodox, and Mormon. They all claim the term *Christian*, and yet all believe and practice different

14. Ibid., 52.
15. Hedrick, "Cerinthus."
16. Bettenson and Maunder, eds., *Documents* (3rd ed.), 28–29.

religious customs. It appears that the label has no specific content to which all would agree; or put another way, the term *Christian* means just about anything one wants it to mean. So what does one imply by identifying oneself by the term? Has it outlived its usefulness? (10–14–15)

§117 IS IT POSSIBLE TO BE SPIRITUAL WITHOUT BEING RELIGIOUS?

Clearly the answer to the question depends on what one means by *spiritual* and *religious*. In contemporary Christianity the question has become important as the numbers of those associated with the "church alumni association" continue to rise. In a 1999 Gallup poll "30% [three in ten] say they would define themselves as 'spiritual but not religious.'"[17] In a CNN/*USAToday*/Gallup poll January 2002 50 percent of Americans described themselves as religious, while 33% claimed to be spiritual but not religious.[18] A poll conducted by *Newsweek* and *Beliefnet* in 2005 reported a lower percentage (24%) claiming to be spiritual but not religious, while 9% claimed to be religious but not spiritual.[19] A 2007 Baylor Religion Survey found that only 10% of those polled claimed to be spiritual but not religious.[20]

The words *religious* and *spiritual* are used in the New Testament and suggest something other than simply "organized religion" (*religious*) and "personal and individual attitudes" (*spiritual*). The words *religion* and *religious* are rare in the New Testament, but in Greek antiquity their cognates are fairly common. In general, being religious is showing devotion to a transcendent power through cultic practice, which corresponds somewhat to the idea of "organized religion," although modern Christian "cultic" practice is quite different from what occurred in ancient Greek and Roman temples.

In the New Testament the term "religious" appears only once (*thrēskos*); it is used of persons who are able to control their tongues (in Greek antiquity it carries the idea of "god-fearing" or "pious"). Those who cannot control their tongues have a worthless religion (Jas 1:26; compare 3:1–2). That is to say, what they do in their formal worship by showing

---

17. Newport, "Americans Remain Very Religious."
18. Winseman, "I Am a Person Who Is Spiritually Committed."
19. Beliefnet, "*Newsweek/Beliefnet* Poll Results."
20. Stark, *What Americans Really Believe*, 88.

devotion to a transcendent power is worthless unless they look after orphans and widows in affliction and keep themselves from the negative influences of the world (Jas 1:27). Hence, a religious person is someone whose worship is defined in terms of what we might call service to others; in James it is regarded as the only kind of cultic practice that is "pure and undefiled."

The specific term "spiritual" with reference to certain people is used primarily in the letters of Paul. The term "spiritual" is used to describe the nature of the abilities with which God endows certain persons (1 Cor 12:4–11, 28–31). These abilities are given mystically through a divine spirit and are considered mystically endowed gifts. They are not natural abilities with which a person is endowed at birth that can be developed through one's own human powers. Paul described himself as a source of certain spiritual gifts that he could impart to others (Rom 1:11). Hence he apparently regarded himself as a spiritual person and apparently not the only one with this ability (1 Cor 2:12–3:3). Others also regarded themselves as "spiritual" (1 Cor 14:37). A spiritual person was endowed with a spiritual gift for the common good (1 Cor 12:7) and hence was a helper of others through their spiritual gifts (Rom 1:11; 1 Cor 9:11; Gal 6:1).

In Paul's view, however, being spiritual was not a static state; there were degrees to spirituality (1 Cor 3:1–4). The degree of spirituality at its lowest end was characterized by "ordinary fleshly people" (or "babes in Christ"), and at its highest end were the "spiritual people." One presumes that the designations fleshly/spiritual come together at the midpoint halfway through the scale. Paul distinguishes these two extremes only in terms of human behaviors, and he gives his readers an example. Ordinary people act jealously and create strife (1 Cor 3:3). Presumably the spiritual people at the upper end of the scale would act just the opposite; that is to say, they would be characterized by trust and would create harmony. Elsewhere Paul describes a series of spiritual behaviors (Gal 5:22–23) and behaviors of the flesh (Gal 5:19–21, what he regards as human lower nature).

People in the twenty-first century who describe themselves as spiritual but not religious would not have been understood by a follower of Jesus in the first century, since in the ancient idiom both terms are closely related. It may also be true that many today who describe themselves as religious would not be understood by followers of Jesus in the first century for the same reason. The term *spiritual*, in the sense of the answers given to the pollsters in 1999 and later, seems to suggest the idea that such persons have no active involvement with either organized religion or any practice of being a source of aid to others. In today's vernacular to be spiritual apparently means being wrapped up in oneself. It does not even suggest such things as meditation, mystical trance, contemplation, or thinking about matters beyond one's own self, something Paul would clearly not have understood (Rom 8:6–7).

Can one be spiritual without being religious? Like so many other things in life, it depends on how one defines the terms and who is answering the question. (6-1-15)

§118 DOING RIGHT AND WRONG

Sin and *sinner* are words that belong to the vocabulary of religion and are primarily oriented toward God. In the final analysis even when one "sins against" someone else (Matt 18:21; Luke 17:4), it has the effect of an offense against God (Luke 15:18, 21). In a secular society (with the exception of life within religious communities) the concept of sin is an oxymoron. Secular societies in representative democracies function on the basis of laws, and actions are judged, from the perspective of the law, either legal or illegal. Something illegal is "against the law" or "against the body politic"; that is, it is against the people who compose the community with whose approval the laws are made. Something legal is "permissible," not necessarily "right."

Doing right and wrong are moral and ethical concepts; they are not legal or illegal concepts. For example, I personally would judge it wrong to obey immoral laws; or put another way, breaking immoral laws is ethically the right thing to do. Of course, whoever breaks even an immoral law will nevertheless suffer the consequences, even if their actions are seen as a moral act (i.e., the right thing to do). That is, "If you do the crime, you must do the time."

An example of immoral laws, now recognized by all civilized nations, are laws regulating the purchase, sale, and ownership of slaves; that is to say the buying and selling of human beings as chattel (property). It may be a shocking thought today, but two hundred years ago such laws were not only legal but regarded as natural and "right."

This way of stating the situation raises the question, on what basis does one judge the morality of one's actions? Or put another way, how does one know what is right (moral) and what is wrong (immoral)? In my view an action is only right if it benefits one's fellow human beings in some way, and it is wrong if it does harm to a fellow human being. Or put another way, actions done for the greater "good" of others are right and any action that brings harm to another is wrong. Hence the standard of right and wrong is how one treats a fellow human being.

What is the theory that might lead one to this principle of behavior? Oddly I have come to a humanist ethic through traditional Christianity and the Bible. It began with this concept:

> If anyone says "I love God," yet hates his brother; he is a liar. For he who does not love his brother, whom he has seen, cannot love God whom he has not seen. (1 John 4:20)

Of course, as it is stated, this statement reflects a narrow community ethic (i.e., love for one's fellow congregant), but the principle is much broader: love for a fellow human being is made the standard for judging one's love for God. Paul's idea that "the whole law is fulfilled in one saying: you shall love your neighbor as yourself" (Rom 13:8-10; Gal 5:14) may actually go beyond the narrow limits of the saying in Hebrew Bible (Lev 19:18), where it refers to fellow Israelites. In Paul's letter it borders on achieving the ethically broader concept of love of humanity (cf. Gal 5:13). That is to say, love for humanity meets the requirements of the Israelite law.

Clearly a saying attributed to Jesus in Q, "love your enemy" (Matt 5:43-45; Luke 6:27-35), does exceed the narrow limits of a community ethic; the saying includes one's fellow human beings, even up to and including a hated enemy whose goal it is to destroy the one aiming to love even the enemy. The sayings attributed to Jesus in Matt 25:34-45 are clearly not a community ethic, and evoke a broad humanitarian concern: one serves God by extending compassion and aid to "the least of these" in human society (Matt 25:40, 45). In other words regular service in a soup kitchen is higher up on the scale of service to humanity than teaching Sunday school; or put another way, love is greater than faith and hope (1 Cor 13:13).

In many ways this ethical standard is an impossible ethic to keep when viewed on a broad scale in terms of whole companies, communities, and nations; for in acting in the best interests of some, one will inevitably injure others. For example, a major employer in a small town is faced with the problem of radically reducing the company's number of employees and drastically cutting the wages and benefits of the remaining workers in order to keep the company from failing altogether. In this example what faces the employer is a mixed decision that will injure all employees: some it will ruin economically, while the economic viability of others will be compromised. In other words in a complex world often all one can do is aim for the greater good of the largest number of people, while keeping the injuries incurred by the rest as small as possible, a decision that is neither black nor white but rather a dirty shade of gray.

To judge by the blind impact of natural disasters not even God can do any better. (5-19-15)

§119 WHY GO TO CHURCH?

My title assumes that you do go to church, but that may not be the case. The rates of regular church attendance have declined dramatically over the last fifty years.[21] That is particularly true in the United Kingdom and Europe. This question crossed my mind one Sunday morning as I was preparing to attend a church service. I should admit, however, that I do not attend formal worship services, for I have joined what has been referred to as "the church alumni association" (former church members who previously were actively involved in church activities). On the other hand, I regularly participate in a men's Bible study group every Sunday morning at a local Southern Baptist church in Springfield, Missouri.[22] While tying my tie, I began to wonder why I even do that.

Readers of things I have published in the past will attest that my personal faith, whatever it may have been, is no longer traditional. I affirm very few of the religious concepts I was taught in my youth, and yet I continue to be involved in Baptist Bible study. The Bible study group as a whole, however, continues to hold traditional Baptist views for the most part. On one occasion Bishop John Shelby Spong asked me in front of a small dinner party, "Why do you continue with that church; are you doing mission work?" (I suppose he meant, are you spreading the "gospel of critical thinking"?) I have no memory of what I replied that evening, but what follows are several things that should have come to mind.

I go to Baptist Bible study because of a sense of community. Church is not really about theology for most people. The major reasons most people "find a church home" are family, friends, a shared common experience, and familiarity with traditions. Creeds and theology may attract those considering themselves "true believers," but comfortable sociability

---

21. Stark, *What Americans Really Believe*, 8–10.
22. First Baptist Church, 525 South Avenue, Springfield, Missouri, 65806-3193.

is a greater attraction for most. In short, these are my people, pebbles off the rock from which I too was hewn. I know them, their songs, and their unwritten traditions. I know whence they came and how they got here. In short, I am one of them—granted, a bit odd perhaps, and as one former pastor admitted to a news reporter, "sometimes it is an uncomfortable fit"! I am not sure that Bishop Spong, a creedal Episcopalian, can appreciate the free-church Baptist mentality, but Baptists have no creeds or common theology, at least not formally! In practice, "The Baptist Faith and Mission Statement" is as close as it comes to a formal "creed" for Southern Baptists.[23] This document, however, has changed over time and does not mandate what Baptists *must* believe, but rather it claims to document what a *majority* of them *do* believe. Dissenting ideas and beliefs have always existed between Baptists; my voice is one of those dissenting voices on many items of faith.

I go to the Sunday Bible study for myself, not for the church. The reason for my regularity is not to enrich myself spiritually or to "hear a word from the Lord," or any such pious religious sentiment. In spite of the authoritative claims that all churches make, their confessions and creeds, like the Bible itself, are only human opinions. In my past experience Baptist Christianity has always been a big-tent religion, and the church as a collective with its various gospels through the centuries has yet to speak the final word on God and things religious. There is still something to be said for the individual conscience and finding one's own way. The issue is too important to be left to the professionals.

I have deliberately set aside one hour each week to reflect on biblical texts that I seldom read (the Song of Solomon, for example) in order to ponder the human condition, to consider my own practical religious behavior, and to ponder the eternal unknowns. Such ideas seldom ever emerge in the course of my professional work, in which I am always a critical scholar of religion. In this one hour of the week, however, I try to think about my professional subject a little more personally.

I go to Bible study as opposed to church because I can ask questions and speak my mind freely; worship services do not give me that prerogative. In discussing the texts I can serve as a resource on historical issues, comment on, "what are they saying about that in biblical scholarship today," raise questions, disagree or agree with a class consensus, and always receive polite consideration for what I have to say; not that I sway many minds, but I am not trying to do that. Like I said, I do this for what

---

23. Southern Baptist Convention, "2000 Baptist Faith & Message."

I get out of it rather than for what the class gets out of it. Of course one does need a thick skin from time to time, but I must admit on the whole they are a tolerant bunch.

Whatever the faults of religious institutions in general and traditional Christianity in particular, as institutions they have at least maintained through the centuries a formal space in society where people may individually or collectively ponder the human condition and the eternal verities, if such there be. (2-26-14)

§120 END-OF-LIFE ISSUES: HOSPICE, A LINGERING DEATH, AND PALLIATIVE CARE

When physicians recognize that their patients who are near the end of life are suffering severe pain, they prescribe palliative care; that is to say, the patients are made as comfortable as possible with medication, while they linger, awaiting an inevitable death. Comatose patients, for example, may have feeding tubes inserted into their stomachs, and, unless fortunate, are housed in "nursing" homes while awaiting their end. It is not a pretty sight.

Prolonging a life that is clearly at its end is based on the idea that life of any quality is precious and that being alive is better than not being alive. In the Judeo-Christian tradition it is believed that all life is given by God (Gen 2:7, 21–22), and that the taking of human life is prohibited by Exod 20:13: "You shall not kill" (usually understood as "not kill unjustifiably"[24]). Hence all life is cherished and must be continued, including even the lives of those who are not able to reverse a painful terminal illness caused by disease. Such persons are sedated by narcotics that hopefully render them impervious to their worst suffering, while their lives continue slowly to dribble away. Persons who are fully cognizant of their situation and who desire help from a physician in ending their lives before the terrible suffering of their anticipated inevitable end may or may not be able to find the help they need. I am assuming here that the decision to end life by choice is to save one's self and loved ones the indignity of the unnecessary suffering. There are likely other reasons as well; for example, one possibility is that a person may fear the suffering.

---

24. Compare Gen 9:5–6, and see the brief comment on the sixth commandment in Collins, "Ten Commandments," 385–86.

Public opinion is decidedly opposed to what many consider suicide, euthanasia, "mercy killing," or even murder. Southern Baptists, for example, devote one Sunday each year to study what they call "sanctity of life" issues. (*Sanctity* means "holiness" or "sacredness."). For Catholics suicide, euthanasia, and murder (1 John 3:15) are "mortal" sins (the term is taken from 1 John 5:16–17[25]), meaning that it is a serious sin for which one is condemned to hell if the sin is not forgiven.[26]

Christian tradition uniformly condemns suicide, although neither the Hebrew Bible nor the New Testament prohibits it, and throughout antiquity suicide was "accepted, admired, and even sought after."[27] The Hebrew Bible does narrate several accounts of suicide, and those committing suicide are neither criticized nor commended by the biblical writers (Judg 9:54; 16:29–30; 1 Sam 31:4–5; 2 Sam 17:23; 1 Kgs 16:18).

At the time this essay was composed, physician-assisted suicide was legal in four states (California, Oregon, Vermont, and Washington); one state had legalized physician-assisted suicide by a court ruling (Montana); forty-one states prohibited it, and in four states the situation was unclear.[28]

My personal view of this situation is that being conscious even with pain is better than being insentient; or put another way, life lived with physical difficulties and pain is better than a death that instantly banishes all pain, for as long as there is life there is hope! But I must also admit that I have been at the bedside of those who were suffering a lingering, untimely death (specifically my sister and my mother, as well as others). It seems to me that being at the extremity of life and being fully conscious of the inevitable fact that my own life is dribbling away in suffering is a very different thing than living with difficulty and pain. Hence I cannot fault those who might choose a quick death over an inevitable and painful lingering death.

What is the state's interest in prohibiting rather, than regulating, physician-assisted suicide? Should the state even be involved in enacting laws that prohibit people from ending life with dignity (as they might see it), and forcing them to choose between either enduring unconscionable suffering or spending their last days in a drug-induced virtual coma? Opinions vary and are hotly debated. (3–15–16)

25. Wikipedia, "Mortal Sin."
26. Wikipedia, "On Suicide."
27. Droge, "Suicide," 225.
28. *ProCon.org/*, "State-by-State Guide to Physician-Assisted Suicide."

§121 AN IMPOSSIBLE SITUATION: THE BISHOP VERSUS THE NUN

Here is the situation: in late 2009 at Saint Joseph's Hospital and Medical Center in Phoenix, Arizona a nun, Sister Margaret Mary McBride, was part of a committee consultation to decide a course of treatment for a woman eleven weeks pregnant. The medical team treating the woman had determined that the woman's medical situation was life-threatening. She suffered from "a rare and often fatal condition in which pregnancy can cause the death of the mother ... The condition [pulmonary hypertension] limits the ability of the heart and lungs to function and is made worse, possibly fatal, by pregnancy."[29] The consultation was composed of the patient, her doctors, and McBride, who is a nurse and a representative of the hospital's ethics committee. The decision was made to terminate the pregnancy.[30]

Bishop Thomas J. Olmsted of the Roman Catholic Diocese of Phoenix learned of the abortion after the fact, and in a subsequent news release is quoted as saying, "While medical professionals should certainly try to save a pregnant mother's life, the means by which they do it can never be by directly killing her unborn child. The end does not justify the means ... If a catholic formally cooperates in the procurement of an abortion, they are automatically excommunicated."[31]

The situation was impossible. It pitted the mother's life against that of the eleven-week fetus. It was a true dilemma, a choice between two equally unpleasant alternatives! If the pregnant woman tried to carry the fetus to term, the medical prognosis was that she could die trying to do so. The fetus was only eleven weeks at the point the decision was made to abort. Generally a fetus becomes viable at the beginning of the third trimester (sometime between the beginning of the twenty-fourth and twenty-eighth weeks. No baby has ever been successfully delivered before the middle of the twenty-second week).[32] Had the mother died in the next eleven or twelve weeks (three months), the baby would have died as well. And if the mother placed her life in jeopardy by trying to carry the fetus to term, the medical prognosis was that she *might* die, although the baby *might* survive if the mother died after the beginning of the twenty-

---

29. Associated Press, "Hospital Nun Rebuked."
30. Clancy, "Abortion Leads to Reassignment," 8A.
31. Ibid.
32. Foer, "Fetal Viability."

third week. On the other hand, an abortion removed the serious threat to the life of the mother. There was no good alternative. The choice was a dirty shade of gray—a choice between two bad alternatives. And no matter what the decision was, the result would be devastating for the family.

Sister McBride apparently recognized the nature of the medical dilemma and supported the decision to abort. The bishop, on the other hand, put church doctrine over a sensitive weighing of the situation. The perspectives of each were no doubt influenced by their own situations in life: the bishop, an administrator and enforcer of church dogma; the sister, a healer and caregiver.

It would be nice if all our choices were as crystal clear as the bishop seemed to think this one was. But, alas, there are few absolute rights and absolute wrongs.[33] What I mean is this: in our complex world when we choose a particular course of action we think is "right," more often than not that "right" choice will result in harm to someone else somewhere along the line, as in this situation. Sister McBride seemed to recognize that. Many think that abortion in itself could never be judged "right," but in this case it was the least worst of two "wrong" choices. Apparently the bishop in his zeal to protect the fetus did not recognize that his choice could lead directly to the death of the mother—using the bishop's word, his choice could "kill" the mother, and the fetus still might not survive, a true no-win situation!

Contrary to the bishop's view, this particular situation at bottom was not theological or ecclesiastical. It was not even a societal moral issue. Rather it was a life-and-death dilemma facing a particular woman eleven weeks pregnant. Such a decision is best left to the mother in consultation with her physicians and others *she* chooses to consult. Pondering whether you will suffer and live or die is a very personal decision, and it is best left to you. Everyone else is merely a spectator, and spectators have no skin in the game. (5-21-10)

§122 ON DYING ALONE AND BEING KEEPERS OF SISTERS

We all die alone, no matter how many family and friends crowd into the room at the end. Before the final moment, however, family and close friends can be a great comfort. Being connected to others who care for

---

33. See Fletcher, *Situation Ethics*.

you and for whom you care helps us ease the hurts that life inevitably brings to all of us. We may want to be alone during certain times of crisis to process a situation or to try and make sense of things, but eventually we need the comfort and counsel of trusted friends and family. I suspect we all know this. It is the rare person who deliberately and consistently shuts out everyone. Everyone needs somebody. Human beings are social creatures and do not make successful islands!

That is why the striking complaint of the psalm writer, "no one cares for me" (Ps 142:4), evokes such pathos in even the casual reader. Apparently, the psalmist had reached a point in life where s/he felt completely isolated and utterly alone. A recent personal experience brought home to me the psalm writer's sense of abandonment with a force. My wife and I had noticed an unusual number of newspapers in a neighbor's drive, and took it upon ourselves to place them out of sight. Upon finding the back door standing open, and receiving no response from our knocking and calls, we called 9-1-1. The police found her dead on the floor of her home with only her dogs for company. I have since pondered at what point in the preceding days she may have died, and wrestled with the idea that had I been more observant, she might have gone to the hospital rather than the morgue. But she was a private person, and we didn't want to intrude.

We did our civic duty, I suppose; seeing something irregular, we checked, and called the police. Nevertheless, I can't help but feel that a higher human obligation may have gone unmet. We are all members of the human family and have obligations for each other's welfare, even for those we do not know. Meeting that higher obligation requires a personal involvement of more than just a casual "Good morning" in the human community. Clearly, however, there are limits to how involved one can be with those around us every day, but being sensitive to what is going on even with casual acquaintances is something toward which we should all aspire.

What I am suggesting, however, raises questions. For example, when does unsolicited care become unwanted meddling? Are care and meddling two qualitatively different sorts of intrusion in someone's life, or are they both simply intrusion, and the only difference is a matter of perspective? In other words, what one person may consider a welcome expression of concern, in the mind of another person can turn out to be an unwanted intrusion.

It puts me in mind of Cain's answer to Yahweh's question: "how goes it with your brother Abel?" (Gen 4:9). Cain's dismissive and curt response has become proverbial in our day: "am I my brother's keeper?" Cain says (Gen 4:9). In Cain's case, however, he was his brother's executioner! But it is the wont of proverbs to apply in a variety of situations; in my case Cain's question became, should I have been my sister's keeper?—meaning, should I long ago as a concerned neighbor have interrupted her privacy? A saying attributed to Jesus suggests I likely should have done precisely that: "Treat others like you want to be treated" (Luke 6:31), he said. The saying, however, assumes that the other party wants what you would have wanted under the same circumstances, and that may not be the case.

Cain's answer raises another question. By intruding myself into her life unsolicited, would I have been looking to meet her needs or mine? Or does that really matter if one is reaching out to meet what one perceives as a need of a fellow human being? The answer likely turns on what one perceives. Yet, what I perceive about another may not be what the other perceives about herself.

After assessing a few of the vagaries of such unclear social situations, we are still left with the disturbing image of a woman dying alone with only dogs for company, and the plaintive complaint of the unknown psalm writer: "no one cares for me." (8-23-11)

§123 SKY IS NOT BLUE

The truth is, we live by individual perceptions of reality rather than by reality itself. The perception is that on cloudless days the sky is blue and that the earth does not move. But the reality is that the sky is not blue, and the earth does move. The blue color, caused by the sun's light, is made up of all colors of the spectrum, refracted through the oxygen and nitrogen of the atmosphere under which we live. Without the atmosphere the light would appear white.[34] In any case the sky becomes red in the evening on a clear night. With regard to the mobility of the earth, every junior high school student knows that the earth spirals on its axis in an ellipsis around the sun, even though it appears to be stable. We *perceive* sky as blue and earth as immobile, but that is not the reality.

---

34 Woodwose, "Evidence."

What we see, or think we see, must be processed by the brain for interpretation. Hence our knowledge is at least thrice removed from reality: reality is out there, and something registers on the retina, the eardrum, or the skin, which the brain interprets. The same is true for everything we know, or think we know. The truth is, all human beings perceive their own "truth." Such is the unwavering principle of all human life, as the following examples show:

With respect to the history of religion, Yahweh, the Israelite God of the Hebrew Bible, since the fourth century has seen the light, converted to Christianity, and adopted new ways, as the attachment of New Testament texts to the Hebrew Scriptures shows. But for modern Judaism the Israelite God still maintains his old ways.

With respect to church practice, Catholics and the Orthodox, for whom Scripture is subordinate to church tradition, will baptize babies by sprinkling them with water. But Baptists, for whom Scripture is generally the final authority, will only baptize adults by immersing them.

With respect to morality, for many Americans homosexuality is regarded as an "abomination before God"; yet many states have recently legalized same- sex marriage.

With regard to ethical behavior, in the Gospel of Matthew Jesus is described as contrasting his own ideas with what the Hebrew Bible regards as behavior acceptable to God (Matt 5:21–48). For example, the Hebrew Scripture demanded "an eye for an eye and a tooth for a tooth" (Exod 21:22–25; Lev 24:19–20; Deut 19:16–21). But Jesus proposed a new way: when you are injured, take the hit and move on—"do not resist one who is evil. But if anyone strikes you on the right cheek, turn to him the other also" (Matt 5:38–42).

With regard to aesthetics, Kurt Vonnegut's *Slaughterhouse-Five* is listed as number 51 of the greatest fiction books since 1900 (distilled from numerous such best books listings).[35] Nevertheless in 2011 the Republic School District in southwest Missouri banned the book again.[36] And so it goes! Banning any competing perspective sets a dangerous precedent for a community and the country. It is a grave warning that your views might be next on the banned list. (7–28-11)

---

35. *The Greatest Books*, "Greatest Books since 1900."
36. Morais, "Neverending Campaign."

Postscript

The Authority and Religious Value of the Bible: A Dialogue

The early twentieth-century New Testament scholar, C. H. Dodd, argued that "the measure of any authority which the Bible may possess must lie in its direct religious value, open to discovery in experience; and this value in turn will be related to the experience out of which the Scripture came."[1] One reviewer (J. Y. Campbell) objected, arguing that "I cannot see that anything is gained by talking of authority if what we really mean is religious value."[2] Dodd defined *authority* "in its primary form" as "the authority of the truth itself, compelling and subduing," and added to that a "secondary sense of the term 'authority,'" which he sees as the following: "the authority of persons who being presumed to know the truth communicate it to others."[3] Hence for Dodd the authority we meet in the Bible is in this secondary sense, which is "the authority of experts in the knowledge of God, masters in the art of living; the authority of religious genius."[4] We cannot, however, engage these "experts in the knowledge of God" in person. They can only be met, however, in written texts passed down to us.

Campbell counters, however, that "any such authority is certainly quickly destroyed when we discover our 'authorities' [i.e., the written texts] making erroneous statements,"[5] which modern critical studies of

1. Dodd, *Authority*, xiii.
2. Campbell, "Interpretation of Biblical Authority," 423.
3. Dodd, *Authority*, 21.
4. Ibid., 25.
5. Campbell, "Interpretation of Biblical Authority," 424.

the Bible have clearly demonstrated to be the case with the Bible, as Dodd himself acknowledges.[6]

The preeminent "religious genius" in the Bible in Dodd's view is Jesus. According to Dodd, "His inner life possessed a unique moral perfection, which would account for the unique authority His words have actually carried in spite of all local and temporal limitations."[7] Sayings of Jesus as reported by the evangelists, however, do not possess the same authority as the man, for in the gospels one finds sayings, as Dodd admits, that "either are simply not true, in their plain meaning, or are unacceptable to the conscience or reason of Christian people."[8] This acknowledgement by Dodd of the clearly flawed condition of the gospels leads Campbell to conclude: "This crucial instance suffices to show that no authority of this secondary sort can be claimed for the Bible."[9] In other words, the religious authority of those living "experts in the knowledge of God" is not passed on to the texts that contain writings about and by them. On the other hand, Campbell agrees that modern biblical scholarship "has revealed more clearly than ever" the "abiding spiritual value" of the Bible "as Mr. Dodd has shown so excellently."[10]

This brief exchange contrasting the ideas of Dodd and Campbell uses two words in assessing the relevance of the Bible: *authority* and *value*. Dodd had considered and rejected the word *infallible*, in the sense that "the biblical writers infallibly set forth the truth."[11] And Campbell rejects Dodd's claim that the Bible has authority. Both agree, however, that the Bible has religious value.

Both scholars, however, were speaking as men of faith and evaluating the Bible from within the house of Christian faith rather than from a disinterested, broader historical perspective in a universal and timeless sense. Objectively speaking, the Bible has no inherent or intrinsic religious value or authority in itself; the Bible has only that religious authority or value (or both) that one chooses to give it. According to Dodd, "the Bible itself does not make any claim to infallible authority

---

6. Dodd, *Authority*, 233.
7. Ibid., 240–41.
8. Ibid., 233.
9. Campbell, "Interpretation of Biblical Authority," 424.
10. Ibid.
11. Dodd, *Authority*, 8–18; the quote is from page 8.

for all its parts."[12] How could it? Later people of faith collected its various parts to make it a whole long after the individuals who lived and wrote it had passed from the historical scene. It is the product of modern critical scholarship and represents only two episodes (Israelite and Christian) in a longer and broader human quest for God.

Calling the Bible "the Word of God" is a learned personal opinion about the Bible and is not a description of the Bible. The Bible consists of human words about how God was understood in two religious communities long before the modern era commenced. Hence its words and ideas need to be vetted for contemporary religious relevance. Quite clearly the Bible has historical significance as part of the religious history of Western civilization, but whether or not it has a claim to exclusive authority and value for shaping religion in contemporary life is a personal choice on the part of its readers.

---

12. Ibid., 15.

Bibliography

Abell, George. *Exploration of the Universe*. 2nd ed. New York: Holt, Rinehart & Winston, 1969.
Adamantinus, Origen. *De principiis*. In *ANF*, translated by Frederick Crombie, 4:239–382.
Aelian (Claudius Aelianus). *On the Characteristics of Animals*. Translated by Alwyn Faber Scholfield. 3 vols. LCL 446, 448, 449. Cambridge: Harvard University Press, 1958–59.
Aftermath. "What Are the Four Stages of Human Decomposition?" http://www.aftermath.com/content/human-decomposition/.
Albright, William Foxwell. *From the Stone Age to Christianity: Monotheism and the Historical Process*. 2nd ed. with a new introduction. Doubleday Anchor Books. Garden City, NY: Doubleday, 1957.
Alighieri, Dante. *The Divine Comedy*. In *WIL* 2.160–201.
Allison, Dale C. "Jesus Christ." In *ABD* 1:583–94.
Altizer, Thomas J. J. *The Gospel of Christian Atheism*. Philadelphia: Westminster, 1966.
Annas, Julia. "Plato." In *OCD*, 1190–93.
Arp, Thomas R., and Greg Johnson. *Perrine's Literature: Structure, Sound, and Sense*. 8th ed. Boston: Heinle and Heinle, 2002.
Ascough, Richard S., et al. *Associations in the Greco-Roman World: A Sourcebook*. Waco: Baylor University Press, 2012.
Associated Press. "Hospital Nun Rebuked for Allowing Abortion. She Agreed That Seriously Ill Woman Needed Procedure to Survive." *Healthcare on NBC News* (website). Updated May 15, 2010. http://www.nbcnews.com/id/37171656/ns/health-health_care/t/hospital-nun-rebuked-allowing-abortion/.
Athanasius, Alexandrinus. "Easter Letter XXXIX." In *NPNF*[2], edited by Archibald Robertson, translated by Henry Burgess and revised by [Jessie] Payne-Smith, 4:551–52.
Attridge, Harold W. *The Epistle to the Hebrews: A Commentary on the Epistle to the Hebrews*. Hermeneia. Philadelphia: Fortress, 1989.
Auerbach, Erich. *Mimesis: The Representation of Reality in Western Literature*. Translated by Willard R. Trask. Princeton: Princeton University Press, 1953.
Aungerville, Richard. "The Love of Books: The Philobiblion of Richard de Bury. http://www.aolib.com/reader_626_0.htm/.
Aurelius, Marcus. "Meditations." In *Marcus Aurelius Meditations; Epictetus Enchiridion*. Translated by George Long, 1–165. Gateway Edition. Chicago: Regency, 1956.

Azar, Beth. "The Faces of Pride." *American Psychological Association.* http://www.apa.org/monitor/mar06/pride.aspx/.
Babbitt, Frank Cole, trans. *Plutarch's Moralia with an English Translation.* 15 vols. LCL. Cambridge: Harvard University Press, 1962.
Babcock, Maltbie D. "This Is My Father's World." In the *Baptist Hymnal,* edited by Walter Hines Sims, hymn no. 59. Nashville: Convention, 1956.
Barrett, C. K., ed. *The New Testament Background: Selected Documents.* London: SPCK, 1956.
Bauckham, Richard. "Descent to the Underworld." In *ABD* 2:156–59.
Beliefnet. "*Newsweek/Beliefnet* Poll Results." (August 2005). http://www.beliefnet.com/news/2005/08/newsweekbeliefnet-poll-results.aspx/.
Bauer, Walter. *A Greek–English Lexicon of the New Testament and Other Early Christian Literature.* Revised and edited by Frederick William Danker. 3rd ed. Chicago: University of Chicago Press, 2000.
Bent, James Theodore. *Aegean Islands: The Cyclades, Or Life among the Insular Greeks.* New and enl. ed. Argonaut Library of Antiquities. Chicago: Argonaut, 1966.
Bethge, Hans-Gebhard, ed. and trans. *Der Brief des Petrus an Philippus: Ein neutestamentaliches Apokryphon aus dem Fund von Nag Hammadi (NHC VIII.2).* TUGAL 141. Berlin: Akademie, 1997.
Bettenson, Henry, ed. *Documents of the Christian Church.* Edited by Chris Maunder. 3rd ed. Oxford: Oxford University Press, 1999.
Betz, Hans Dieter, ed. *The Greek Magical Papyri in Translation, including the Demotic Spells.* 2nd ed. Chicago: University of Chicago Press, 1992.
Blomberg, Craig L. *Interpreting the Parables.* Downers Grove, IL: InterVarsity, 1990.
Booth, Wayne C. *The Rhetoric of Fiction.* 2nd ed. Chicago: University of Chicago Press, 1983.
Borg, Marcus J. *Jesus: A New Vision; Spirit, Culture, and the Life of Discipleship.* San Francisco: Harper & Row, 1987.
Bornkamm, Günter. *Jesus of Nazareth.* Translated by Irene and Fraser McLusky with James M. Robinson. London: Hodder & Stoughton, 1960.
Bragg, William. "The Universe of Light." In *Exploring the Universe,* edited by Louise B. Young, 283–92. 2nd ed. New York: Oxford University Press, 1971.
Brashler, James A., trans. "Apocalypse of Peter: Text, Translation, and Notes." In *Nag Hammadi Codex VII,* edited by Birger A. Pearson, 218–47. NHMS 30. Leiden: Brill, 1996.
Bronowski, Jacob. *The Ascent of Man.* Boston: Little, Brown, 1973.
Brown, Francis, S. R. Driver, and Charles A. Briggs. *A Hebrew and English Lexicon of the Old Testament with an Appendix Containing the Biblical Aramaic. Based on the Lexicon of William Gesenius as translated by Edward Robinson.* Oxford: Clarendon, 1968.
Brown, Raymond E. *The Gospel according to John.* 2 vols. AB 29–29A. Garden City, NY: Doubleday, 1966–1970.
———. *An Introduction to New Testament Christology.* New York: Paulist, 1994.
Bultmann, Rudolf. *The History of the Synoptic Tradition.* Translated by John Marsh. Oxford: Blackwell, 1963.
———. *Theology of the New Testament.* Translated by Kendrick Grobel. 2 vols. New York: Scribner, 1951–1955.

Burkert, Walter. *Greek Religion*. Translated by John Raffan. Cambridge: Harvard University Press, 1985.
Campbell, J. Y. "An Interpretation of Biblical Authority." *JR* 10 (1930) 422–24.
Carroll, Robert P. "Israel, History of (Post-Monarchic Period)." In *ABD* 3:567–76.
Cartlidge, David R., and David L. Dungan, eds. *Documents for the Study of the Gospels*. Rev. and enl. Minneapolis: Fortress, 1994.
Case, Shirley Jackson. *The Social Origins of Christianity*. New York: Cooper Square, 1975.
Chadwick, Henry. "Some Ancient Anthologies and Florilegia, Pagan and Christian" in *Studies on Ancient Christianity*. Variorum Collected Studies Series. Burlington, VT: Ashgate, 2006.
Charlesworth, James H. "Apocrypha." In *ABD* 1:292–94.
Chaucer, Geoffrey. "The Parson's Tale: A Translation into Modern English." The Middle English text is from Larry D. Benson, gen. ed. The Riverside Chaucer. https://sites.fas.harvard.edu/~chaucer/teachslf/parst-tran.htm/.
Cicero, Marcus Tullius. "On Divination." In *Cicero De Senectute, De Amicita, De Divinatione*. Translated by William Armistead Falconer, 214–539. LCL. Cambridge: Harvard University Press, 1959.
———. "On the Nature of the Gods." In *Cicero De Natura Deorum, Academica*. Translated by H. Rackham, 1–396. LCL 268. London: Heinemann, 1933.
Clabeaux, John J. "Marcion." In *ABD* 4:514–16.
Clancy, Michael. "Abortion Leads to Reassignment." *Springfield News-Leader* (Missouri), 16 May 2010, 8A.
Cline, Austin. "Religion vs. Superstition." ThoughtCo, March 17, 2017. https://www.thoughtco.com/religion-vs-superstition-250714.
Cockerill, Gareth Lee. "Cerinthus." In *ABD* 1:885.
Cohen, Nick. "What Are the Various Methods Used to Identify Planets in Other Solar Systems as Well as the Distances of Those Planets from Their Suns?" https://www.quora.com/What-are-the-various-methods-used-to-identify-planets-in-other-solar-systems-as-well-as-the-distance-of-those-planets-from-their-suns/.
Collins, John J. "Sibylline Oracles." In *ABD* 6:2–6.
Collins, Raymond. "Ten Commandments." In *ABD* 6:383–87.
Condon, Edward Uhler. "The Two Theories of Light." In *Exploring the Universe*, edited by Louise B. Young, 278–83. 2nd ed. New York: Oxford University Press, 1971.
Conner, Robert P. "The Shadow as a Magical Assistant." https://www.scribd.com/document/70353722/The-Shadow-as-a-Magical-Assistant/.
Conybeare, Frederick Cornwallis, trans. *Philostratus; The Life of Apollonius of Tyana; The Epistles of Apollonius; and the Treatise of Eusebius*. 2 vols. LCL. Cambridge: Harvard University Press, 1966.
Conzelmann, Hans. *1 Corinthians: A Commentary on the First Epistle to the Corinthians*. Translated by James W. Leitch. Bibliography and References by James W. Dunkly, edited by George W. MacRae. Hermeneia. Philadelphia: Fortress, 1975.
Cook Stephen L. "Fate." In *NIDB* 2:434–35.
Copernicus, Nicolas. "The Revolutions of the Heavenly Bodies." Translated by William S. Knickerbocker. In *WIL* 2:499–503.
Costandi, Mo. "Life after Death: The Science of Human Decomposition." *Guardian*, May 5, 2015. https://www.theguardian.com/science/neurophilosophy/2015/may/05/life-after-death/.

Cross, Frank Moore. *The Ancient Library of Qumran and Modern Biblical Studies*. The Haskil Lectures 1956–57. Rev. ed. Anchor Books. Garden City, NY: Doubleday, 1961.
Cuddon, J. A., and C. E. Preston. *The Penguin Dictionary of Literary Terms and Literary Theory*. 4th rev. ed. London: Penguin, 1999.
Coxe, A. Cleveland, ed. "First Apology of Justin Martyr." In *The Apostolic Fathers with Justin Martyr and Irenaeus*, translated by Philip Schaff, ANF 1:158–87.
Cyprian, Thascius. "The Epistles of Cyprian." Translated by Ernest Wallis. In *ANF* 5:275–409.
Darwin, Charles Robert. *The Origin of Species: With Introduction, Notes, and Illustrations*. Harvard Classics. New York: Collier, 1909.
Dave. "Weather Dudes. Weather Facts. What Causes Wind?" (last modified November 27, 2008) http://www.weatherdudes.com/facts_display.php?fact_id=35/.
Davies, G. Hinton. "Leviticus." In *IDB* 3:117–22.
Dewey, Arthur J., et al., trans. *The Authentic Letters of Paul: A New Reading of Paul's Rhetoric and Meaning; The Scholars Version*. Salem, OR: Polebridge, 2010.
Dibelius, Martin. *From Tradition to Gospel*. Translated by Bertram Lee Woolf. New York: Scribner, 1965 (1st German ed. 1919).
Dillenberger, John, and Claude Welch. *Protestant Christianity Interpreted through Its Development*. New York: Scribner, 1954.
Dillon, John M. "Fate." In *ABD* 2:776–78.
Dodd, C. H. *The Authority of the Bible*. 2nd ed. London: Nisbet, 1938.
Droge, Arthur J. "Suicide." In *ABD* 6:225–31.
Dunn, James D. G. "Incarnation." In *ABD* 3:397–404.
Edwards, Jonathan. "Sinners in the Hands of an Angry God." In *WIL* 2:543–47.
Ehrman, Bart D. *Jesus, Apocalyptic Prophet of the New Millennium*. Oxford: Oxford University Press, 1999.
Eissfeldt, Otto. *The Old Testament: An Introduction. The History of the Formation of the Old Testament*. Translated by Peter R. Ackroyd. New York: Harper & Row, 1965.
Eliot, T. S. "The Waste Land." Wikipedia: https://en.wikipedia.org/wiki/The_Waste_Land/.
Elliott, John H. "Jesus the Israelite was neither a 'Jew' nor a 'Christian': On Correcting Misleading Nomenclature." *JSHJ* 5 (2007) 119–54.
———. "Peter, Second Epistle of." In *ABD* 5:282–87.
Encyclopedia Britannica. "Archimedes Principle." https://www.britannica.com/science/archimedes-principle/.
Episcopal Church.*The Book of Common Prayer and Administration of the Sacraments and other Rites and Ceremonies of the Church together with the Psalter or Psalms of David according to the Use of the Episcopal Church*. New York: Church Hymnal, 1979.
Estrada, Andrea. "Pride—Sin or Incentive?" UC Santa Barbara *Current*. http://www.news.ucsb.edu/2017/017673/pride-sin-or-incentive.
Eusebius (of Caesarea). *The Life of the Blessed Emperor Constantine*. Revised translation by Ernest Cushing Richardson. In $NPNF^2$ 1:481–559.
Evans, Craig C. "John." *NIDB* 3:344–51.
Fee, Gordon D. *The First Epistle to the Corinthians*. NICNT. Grand Rapids: Eerdmans, 1987.

Feine, Paul, et al. *Introduction to the New Testament.* Translated by A. J. Mattill, Jr. 14th ed. Nashville: Abingdon, 1966.

———. *Introduction to the New Testament.* Translated by Howard Clark Kee. 17th rev. ed. Nashville: Abingdon, 1975.

Ferguson, Everett. *Backgrounds of Early Christianity.* 3rd ed. Grand Rapids: Eerdmans, 2003.

Fitzmyer, Joseph A. *The Gospel according to Luke.* 2 vols. AB 28-28A. New York: Doubleday, 1970-1985.

Fletcher, Joseph. *Situation Ethics: The New Morality.* Philadelphia: Westminster, 1966.

Foer, Franklin. "Fetal Viability." The Slate Gist: A Cheat Sheet for the News. *Slate*, May 25, 1997. http://www.slate.com/id/1060/.

Foerster, Werner, comp. *Gnosis: A Selection of Gnostic Texts.* Translated by R. Mcl. Wilson et al. English translation edited by R. McL. Wilson. 2 vols. Oxford: Clarendon, 1972.

Frankfort, Henri, et al. *Before Philosophy: The Intellectual Adventure of Ancient Man; An Essay on Speculative Thought in the Ancient Near East.* A Pelican Book. Baltimore: Penguin, 1946.

Frazer, James George. *The Golden Bough: A Study in Magic and Religion.* 1 vol. abridged ed. New York: Macmillan, 1951.

The Free Dictionary by Farlex. "Spirit." https://www.thefreedictionary.com/spirit.

Freud, Sigmund. *The Interpretation of Dreams.* Translated by A. A. Brill. New York: Gramercy, 1996.

Fuller, Russell E. "Text Criticism, OT." In *NIDB* 5:531-34.

Funk, Robert W., et al. *The Five Gospels: The Search for the Authentic Words of Jesus; A New Translation and Commentary.* San Francisco: HarperSanFrancisco, 1993.

Funk, Robert W., and the Jesus Seminar. *The Acts of Jesus: The Search for the Authentic Deeds of Jesus.* San Francisco: HarperSanFrancisco, 1998.

Gallager, Richard. "As a Psychiatrist, I Diagnose Mental Illness. Also I Help Spot Demonic Possession." *Washington Post*, July 1, 2016. https://www.washingtonpost.com/posteverything/wp/2016/07/01/as-a-psychiatrist-i-diagnose-mental-illness-and-sometimes-demonic-possession/?utm_term=.b353a1da1e81/.

Gamow, George. "Toward the Limits of the Unknown." In *Exploring the Universe*, edited by Louise B. Young, 382-98. 2nd ed. New York: Oxford University Press, 1971.

Gaster, Theodor H. "Demon, Demonology." In *IDB* 1:817-24.

———. "Cosmogony." In *IDB* 1:702-709.

———. "Gehenna." In *IDB* 2:361-62.

Gay, Peter. "Introduction." In *The Enlightenment. A Comprehensive Anthology*, edited by Peter Gay, 13-26. New York: Simon & Schuster, 1973.

Goodspeed, Edgar J. *How Came the Bible?* New York: Abingdon, 1940.

Goodwyn, Hannah. "Dreams and Visions: God Uncensored." *Christian Broadcasting Network.* http://www1.cbn.com/biblestudy/dreams-and-visions%3A-god-uncensored/.

Graves, Robert. *The Greek Myths.* 2 vols. in 1. New York: Braziller, 1959.

Gesenius, Wilhelm. *Hebräisch-Deutsches Handwörterbuch über die Schriften des Alten Testaments mit Einschluss der Geographischen Nahmen und der Chaldäischen Wörter beym Daniel und Esra.* Leipzig: Vogel, 1810.

Gesenius, William, and Edward Robinson, trans. *A Hebrew and English Lexicon of the Old Testament including the Biblical Chaldee.* 8th ed. rev. Boston: Crocker & Brewster, 1857.

Gesenius, William. *A Hebrew and English Lexicon on the Old Testament from the Latin of William Gesenius with Corrections and Large Additions Partly Furnished by the Author in Manuscript and Partly Condensed from his Larger Thesaurus as Completed by Roediger.* Edited and translated by Edward Robinson. 20th, rev. ed. Boston: Crocker & Brewster, 1868.

Gesenius, Wilhelm. *Wilhelm Gesenius' Handwörterbuch über das Alte Testament.* Edited by Frants Buehl, et al. 17th ed. Leipzig: Vogel, 1921.

Gesenii, Gvlielmi. *Thesarvrvs Philologicvs Criticvs Lingvae Hebraeae et Chaldaeae Veteris Testamenti.* Based on the 2nd ed. Leipzig: Vogel, 1829.

Grant, Frederick C. "Jesus Christ." In *IDB* 2:869–96.

The Greatest Books. "The Greatest Books since 1900." http://thegreatestbooks.org/the-greatest-fiction-since/1900?page=2/.

Griffiths, Alan H. "Centaurs." In *OCD*, 308–9.

Harkness, Georgia. *Mysticism: It's Meaning and Message.* Nashville: Abingdon, 1973.

Harris-McCoy, Daniel E. *Artemidorus' "Oneirocritica": Text, Translation, and Commentary.* Oxford: Oxford University Press, 2012.

Hartmann, Lars. "Baptism." In *ABD* 1:583–94.

Hayes, John H. *Introduction to the Bible.* Philadelphia: Westminster, 1971.

Haynes, Michael P. "Ray's Work for the Poor Isn't Christian." *Springfield News-Leader* (Missouri). 3 February 2014, 9A.

Heber, Reginald. "Holy, Holy, Holy." In *Baptist Hymnal*, compiled by William J. Reynolds, hymn no. 1. Nashville: Convention, 1975.

Hedrick, Charles W. "Authorial Presence and Narrator in John: Commentary and Story." In *Gospel Origins and Christian Beginnings: In Honor of James M. Robinson*, edited by James E. Goehring, et al., 74–93. ForFasc 1. Sonoma, CA: Polebridge, 1990

———. "The Basic Problem of Jesus Studies." *The Fourth R* 28/1 (January–February 2015) 21.

———. "Bible Varies on the Topic of Marriage." *Springfield News-Leader* (Missouri). 11 July 2013, 3B.

———. "Cerinthus." In *NIDB* 1:580.

———. "Conceiving the Narrative: Colors in Achilles Tatius and the Gospel of Mark." In *Ancient Fiction and Early Christian and Jewish Narrative*, edited by Ronald F. Hock et al., 177–97. SBLSymSer 6. Atlanta: Scholars, 1998.

———. "Early Christian Confessions and the Language of Faith." *Fourth R* (forthcoming).

———. "Halloween: Do the Dead Walk?" *Fourth R* 25/1 (2012) 25–26.

———. *House of Faith or Enchanted Forest? American Popular Belief in an Age of Reason.* Eugene, OR: Cascade Books, 2009.

———. "How Relevant is the Christian Worldview Today?" *Fourth R* 28/3 (May–June 2015) 17–18.

———. "Introduction: Making Personal Sense of Ancient Religion in the Modern World." In *When Faith Meets Reason: Religion Scholars Reflect on Their Personal Journeys*, edited by Charles W. Hedrick, xiii–xxi. Santa Rosa, CA: Polebridge, 2008.

———. "Introduction: The Tyranny of the Synoptic Jesus." In *The Historical Jesus and the Rejected Gospels*, edited by Charles W. Hedrick, 1–8. *Semeia*. Atlanta: Scholars, 1988.

———. "Is Belief in the Divinity of Jesus Essential to Being Christian?" *Fourth R* 24.5 (September-October, 2011) 15–20, 26.

———. "Is the Baptism of Jesus by John Historically Certain?" *PRSt* 44/3 (2017) 311–22.

———. *Many Things in Parables: Jesus and His Modern Critics*. Louisville: Westminster John Knox, 2004.

———. "Out of the Enchanted Forest." In *When Faith Meets Reason: Religion Scholars Reflect on Their Spiritual Journeys*, edited by Charles W. Hedrick, 13–24. Santa Rosa, CA: Polebridge, 2008.

———. *Parables as Poetic Fictions: The Creative Voice of Jesus*. 1994. Reprinted, Eugene, OR: Wipf & Stock, 2005.

———. *Parabolic Figures or Narrative Fictions? Seminal Essays on the Stories of Jesus*. Eugene, OR: Cascade Books, 2016.

———. "Putting Paul in His Place." *Fourth R* 31/1 (2018) 5–8.

———. "Realism in Western Narrative and the Gospel of Mark: A Prolegomenon." *JBL* 126 (2007) 345–59.

———. "A Revelation Discourse of Jesus." *JCoptS* (2005) 13–15.

———. "Satyrs or Wild Goats? The Politics of Translating the Bible." *Fourth R* 24/5 (2012) 21–22, 24.

———. "The 34 Gospels." *BRev* 18/3 (2002) 20–31, 46–47.

———. *Unlocking the Secrets of the Gospel according to Thomas: A Radical Faith for a New Age*. Eugene, OR: Cascade Books, 2010.

———. "Unreliable Narration: John on the Story of Jesus; The Chronicler on the History of Israel." In *Perspectives on John: Methods and Interpretation in the Fourth Gospel*, edited by Robert B. Sloan and Mikeal C. Parsons, 121–43. NABPR Special Studies Series 11. Lewiston, NY: Mellen, 1993.

———, ed. *When Faith Meets Reason: Religion Scholars Reflect on Their Spiritual Journeys*. Santa Rosa, CA: Polebridge, 2008.

———. *When History and Faith Collide: Studying Jesus*. 1999. Reprinted, Eugene, OR: Wipf & Stock, 2013.

———. "Where Does Evil Come From?" *Fourth R* 26/4 (2013) 15–16.

———. *The Wisdom of Jesus: Between the Sages of Israel and the Apostles of the Church*. Eugene, OR: Cascade Books, 2014.

———. *Wry Thoughts about Religion*. A Blog First Appearing in 2007. http://blog.charleshedrick.com/

———. "Yahweh—The God Who Changed His Ways." *Fourth R* 27.3 (2014) 21.

Hedrick, Charles W., and Lee M. McDonald. "Is the Bible the Word of God?" *Fourth R* 29/3 (2016) 3–10; Part 2: 29/4 (2016) 13–16, 19–20; Part 3: 29/5 (2016) 9–14.

Hedrick, Charles W., Jr. *History and Silence: Purge and Rehabilitation of Memory in Late Antiquity*. Austin: University of Texas Press, 2000.

Heidegger, Martin. *Introduction to Metaphysics*. Translated by Gregory Fried and Richard Polt. New Haven: Yale University Press, 2000.

Henley, William Ernest. "Invictus." In *Poems: Wadsworth Handbook and Anthology*, edited by C. F. Main and Peter J. Seng, 74. 2nd ed. Belmont, CA: Wadsworth, 1965.

Henrichs, Albert. "Hades." In *OCD*, 661–62.

Hernando, James D. "Reject God's Intent for Marriage at Our Peril." *Springfield News-Leader* (Missouri), 4 April 2013, 3B.

Herodotus. *The History*. Translated by David Grene. Chicago: University of Chicago Press, 1987.

Hippocrates (of Kos). "The Sacred Disease." In *Hippocrates with an English Translation*. Translated by W. H. S. Jones, 2:127–83. LCL. 8 vols. Cambridge: Harvard University Press, 1967.

Hock, Ronald. "Cynics." In *ABD* 1:1221–26.

Hollister, C. Warren, and Judith M. Bennett. *Medieval Europe: A Short History*. 9th ed. Boston: McGraw-Hill, 2002.

Holmon, C. Hugh, and William Harmon. *A Handbook to Literature*. 6th ed. New York: Macmillan, 1992.

Holmes, Michael W. "Text Criticism, NT." In *NIDB* 5:529–31.

Holmyard, Eric John. *Alchemy*. Baltimore: Penguin, 1957.

Homer. *The Odyssey*. Translated by E. V. Rieu. Penguin Classics 51. Harmondsworth, UK: Penguin, 1946.

Hoover, Roy W. "Was Jesus' Resurrection an Historical Event? A Debate Statement with Commentary." *Fourth R* 23/5 (2010) 5–12, 24.

Hultgren, Arland J. *The Parables of Jesus: A Commentary*. The Bible in Its World. Grand Rapids: Eerdmans, 2000.

International Union of Pure and Applied Chemistry. "Periodic Table of Elements." https://iupac.org/what-we-do/periodic-table-of-elements/.

Investopedia. "Null Hypothesis." https://www.investopedia.com/terms/n/null_hypothesis.asp.

Isaac, Benjamin, and Aharon Oppenheimer. "Bar Kokhba." In *ABD* 1:598–601.

Jeremias, Joachim. *Jerusalem in the Time of Jesus: An Investigation into Economic and Social Conditions during the New Testament Period*. Translated by F. H. and C. H. Cave. Philadelphia: Fortress, 1969.

———. *The Parables of Jesus*. Translated by S. H. Hooke. 2nd rev. ed. New York: Scribner, 1972.

Jacob, Edmond. *Theology of the Old Testament*. Translated by Arthur W. Heathcote and Philip J. Allcock. New York: Harper & Row, 1958.

Jerome (Eusebius Sophronius Hieronymus). "Commentary on Isaiah." In *St. Jerome: Commentary on Isaiah Including St. Jerome's Translation of Origen's Homilies 1–9 on Isaiah*, translated by Thomas P. Scheck, 67–880. ACW 68. New York: Newman, 2015.

———. "Letter LVII, 9." In *NPNF*[2], translated by W. H. Fremantle et al., 6:116–17.

Johnson, James Turner, ed. *The Bible in American Law, Politics, and Political Rhetoric*. SBLBAC 4. Philadelphia: Fortress, 1985.

Johnston, George. "Christ as Archegos." *NTS* 27 (1981) 381–85.

Johnston, Harold Whetstone. *The Private Life of the Romans*. Lake Classical Series. New York: Scott, Foresman, 1903.

Jones, Donald L. "Roman Imperial Cult." In *ABD* 5:806–809.

Josephus, Flavius. *Jewish Antiquities*. Translated by H. St. J. Thackery and Ralph Marcus. LCL. 9 vols. Cambridge: Harvard University Press, 1934.

———. *The Jewish War*. Translated by H. St. J. Thackeray. LCL. 9 vols. Cambridge: Harvard University Press, 1989.

Jost, Madeleine. "Arcadian Cults and Myths." In *OCD*, 139.

———. "Pan." In *OCD*, 1103.
Keener, Craig S. *The Gospel of John: A Commentary*. 2 vols. Peabody, MA: Hendrickson, 2003.
Kim, Chan-Hie. *Form and Structure of the Familiar Greek Letter of Recommendation*. SBLDS 4. Missoula: SBL for the Seminar on Paul, 1972.
Kitchen, K. A. "Exodus, The." *ABD* 2:700–708.
Koester, Helmut. *Ancient Christian Gospels: Their History and Development*. Philadelphia: Trinity, 1990.
Kohlenberger, John R., III, and James A. Swanson. *The Hebrew-English Concordance to the Old Testament: With the New International Version*. Grand Rapids: Zondervan, 1998.
Krause, Tom. "Interpreting God's Word." *Springfield News-Leader* (Missouri). 30 November 2014, 7E.
Kuemmerlin-McLean, Joanne K. "Demons (Old Testament)." In *ABD* 2:138–40.
Kuntz, J. Kenneth. *The People of Ancient Israel: An Introduction to Old Testament Literature, History and Thought*. New York: Harper & Row, 1974.
———, trans. *Eusebius: The Ecclesiastical History with an English Translation*. LCL. 2 vols. Cambridge: Harvard University Press, 1926. Reprinted, 1965.
Kaufman, Walter, ed. and trans. *The Portable Nietzsche: Selected and Translated with an Introduction, Preface and Notes*. Viking Portable Library 62. New York: Viking, 1954.
Kearns, Emily. "Elysium." In *OCD*, 521.
Kee, Howard Clark, comp. *The Origins of Christianity: Sources and Documents*. Englewood Cliffs, NJ: Prentice-Hall, 1973.
King, Karen L. *The Gospel of Mary of Magdala: Jesus and the First Woman Apostle*. Santa Rosa, CA: Polebridge, 2003.
La Bas, Philippe, et al. *Voyage archéologique en Grèce et en Asie Mineure fait par ordre du Gouvernement Français pendant les années 1843 et 1844 et publié sous les auspices du Ministère L'Instruction Publique*. Vol. 3.2: Philippe La Bas and W. H. Waddington. *Explication des Inscriptions grecques et Latines recueillies en Grèce et en Asie Mineure*. 3 vols. in 6. Paris: Didot, 1870.
Lake, Kirsopp, trans. *The Apostolic Fathers, with an English Translation*. LCL. 2 vols. Cambridge: Harvard University Press, 1965.
Lewis, Naphtali, and Meyer Reinhold, eds. *Roman Civilization: Selected Readings*. 2 vols. 3rd ed. New York: Columbia University Press, 1990.
Lewis, Sinclair. *Elmer Gantry*. New York: Harcourt Brace, 1927.
Lewis, Theodore J. "Dead, Abode of." In *ABD* 2:101–5.
Liddell, Henry George, and Robert Scott, comps. *A Greek-English Lexicon*. Revised and augmented by Henry Stuart Jones with Roderick McKenzie and the cooperation of many scholars. 9th ed. Oxford: Clarendon, 1940 (with a supplement 1996).
Lindars, Barnabas. *The Gospel of John*. NCBC. Grand Rapids: Eerdmans, 1972. Reprinted, 1986.
Lovell, A. C. B. "Theories of the Origin of the Universe." In *Exploring the Universe*, edited by Louise B. Young, 404–25. 2nd ed. New York: Oxford University Press, 1971.
Lucian (of Samosata). "The Lover of Lies or the Doubter." In *Lucian with an English Translation*, 2:127–83. Translated by W. H. S. Jones. LCL. 8 vols. Cambridge: Harvard University Press, 1967.

Mack, Burton L. *A Myth of Innocence: Mark and Christian Origins*. Philadelphia: Fortress, 1988.
Magiorkinis, Emmanouil, et al. "Highlights in the History of Epilepsy: The Last 200 Years." *Epilepsy Research and Treatment*. Vol. 2014 (2014). Article ID 582039. https://www.hindawi.com/archive/2014/582039/.
Martin, Luther H. *Hellenistic Religions: An Introduction*. Oxford: Oxford University Press, 1987.
Mayo Clinic Staff. "Epilepsy: Diagnosis & Treatment." http://www.mayoclinic.org/diseases-conditions/epilepsy/diagnosis-treatment/treatment/txc-20117241/
———. "Epilepsy, Symptoms & Causes." https://www.mayoclinic.org/diseases-conditions/epilepsy/symptoms-causes/syc-20350093
———. "Tourette Syndrome." https://www.mayoclinic.org/diseases-conditions/tourette-syndrome/symptoms-causes/syc-20350465.
McDonald, Lee Martin. "Canon of the New Testament." In *NIDB* 1:536–46.
McKenzie, John L. "Peter." In *DBib*, 663–66.
Mendelsohn, Isaac. "Exorcism." In *IDB* 2:199–200.
Metzger, Bruce M. *A Textual Commentary on the Greek New Testament. A Companion Volume to the United Bible Societies' Greek New Testament (Fourth Revised Edition)*. 2nd ed. New York: United Bible Societies, 2000.
Meyer, Marvin W. "Affirming Reverence for Life." In *Finding Lambaréné*, by Donald Desfor et al., 3–13. Orange, CA: Chapman University Albert Schweitzer Institute, 2007.
———. *The Ancient Mysteries: A Sourcebook; Sacred Texts of the Mystery Religions of the Ancient Mediterranean World*. San Francisco: Harper & Row, 1987.
———. "Mystery Religions." In *ABD* 4:941–45.
Meyer, Marvin W., et al., eds. *Ancient Christian Magic: Coptic Texts of Ritual Power*. San Francisco: Harper, 1994.
Michaels, J. Ramsey. "The Redemption of Our Body: The Riddle of Romans 8:19–22." In *Romans and the People of God: Essays in Honor of Gordon D. Fee on the Occasion of His 65th Birthday*, edited by Sven K. Sondurlund and N. T. Wright, 92–114. Grand Rapids: Eerdmans, 1999.
Migne, J.-P., ed. *Sancti Eusebii Hieronymi stridonensis presbyteri. Opera Omnia* (1985). In *Patrologia Latina* 24. *Commentaria in Isiam prophetam*. Columns 17–687B, pages 174–75: https://books.google.com/books?id=mHTciI6-7dcC&printsec=frontcover&source=gbs_ge_summary_r&cad=0#v=onepage&q&f=false/.
Miller, Frank Justus, and G. P. Goold, trans. *Metamorphoses*, by Ovid. 6 vols. 2nd ed. Cambridge: Harvard University Press, 1984.
Miller, Robert J., ed. *The Complete Gospels: The Scholars Version*. Salem, OR: Polebridge, 2010.
Milton, John. "Paradise Lost. Book 1: The Argument." *John Milton Reading Room*. https://www.dartmouth.edu/~milton/reading_room/pl/book_1/text.shtml.
Morais, Betsy. "The Neverending Campaign to Ban 'Slaughterhouse Five.'" *The Atlantic* (August 12, 2011). https://www.theatlantic.com/entertainment/archive/2011/08/the-neverending-campaign-to-ban-slaughterhouse-five/243525/.
Morris, Simon Conway. "Evolution and the Inevitability of Intelligent Life." In *The Cambridge Companion to Science and Religion*, edited by Peter Harrison, 148–72. Cambridge Companions to Religion. Cambridge: Cambridge University Press, 2010.

Mother Jones. "Here is the Supreme Court's Decision in the Hobby Lobby Contraception Case." *Mother Jones,* June 30, 2014. http://www.motherjones.com/mojo/2014/06/supreme-court-hobby-lobby-ruling-document/.
Moulton, James Hope, and George Milligan. *The Vocabulary of the Greek Testament: Illustrated from the Papyri and Other Non-Literary Sources.* London: Hodder & Stoughton, 1930.
Newport, Frank. "Americans Remain Very Religious, but not Necessarily in Conventional Ways." *Gallup News,* December 24, 1999. http://news.gallup.com/poll/3385/americans-remain-very-religious-but-not-necessarily-in-conventional-ways.aspx/.
Nickle, Keith F. *The Synoptic Gospels: An Introduction.* Rev. and exp. 2nd ed. Louisville: Westminster John Knox, 2001.
Nickelsburg, George W. E. "Resurrection: Early Judaism and Christianity." In *ABD* 5:684–91.
Nicoll, W. Robertson, et al., eds. *The Expositor's Greek Testament.* 5 vols. Grand Rapids: Eerdmans, 1956.
Noll, Mark A. "The Bible and American Culture." https://www.hbu.edu/museums/dunham-bible-museum/influence-in-history-and-culture/the-bible-and-american-culture-by-mark-noll/.
Noss, John B. *Man's Religions.* 3rd ed. New York: Macmillan, 1963.
Oskin, Becky. "Japan Earthquake & Tsunami of 2011: Facts and Information." LiveScience. May 7, 2011. https://www.livescience.com/39110-japan-2011-earthquake-tsunami-facts.html/.
Palmer, Jason. "Amondawa Tribe Lacks Abstract Idea of Time, Study Says." *BBC News.* http://www.bbc.com/news/science-environment-13452711.
Pausanias. *Guide to Greece.* Translated by Peter Levi. Rev. ed. 2 vols. Penguin Classics. London (vol. 1) and Harmondsworth (vol. 2) UK: Penguin, 1979.
Perrin, Norman. *Jesus and the Language of the Kingdom: Symbol and Metaphor in New Testament Interpretation.* Philadelphia: Fortress, 1976.
Persinger, Michael A. "Religious and Mystical Experiences as Artifacts of Temporal Lobe Function: A General Hypothesis." *Perceptual and Motor Skills* 57 (1983) 1255–62.
Petronius (Titus Petronius Arbiter). *The Satyricon.* Edited and annotated by Evan T. Sage and revised and expanded by Brady B. Gilleland. New York: Irvington, 1982.
Phy, Allene Stuart, ed. *The Bible and Popular Culture in America.* SBLBAC. Philadelphia: Fortress, 1985.
Planer Felix E. *Superstition.* Rev. ed. Buffalo: Prometheus, 1988.
Plato. *The Apology.* In *Plato in Twelve Volumes: Euthyphro; Apology; Crito; Phaedo; Phaedrus,* translated by Harold North Fowler, 1:68–145. LCL 36. 12 vols. Cambridge: Harvard University Press, 1977.
———. *The Republic.* Translated by Paul Shorey. LCL. 2 vols. London: Heinemann, 1930.
Plutarch (Plutarchus Chaeronensis). "On the Sign of Socrates." In *Plutarch's Moralia in Fifteen Volumes,* translated by Phillip H. De Lacy and Benedict Einarson, 7:362–509. LCL. Cambridge: Harvard University Press, 1959.
———. *Plutarch's Lives with an English Translation.* Translated by Bernadotte Perrin. 11 vols. LCL. London: Heinemann, 1919.

———. "The Obsolescence of Oracles." In *Plutarch's Moralia in Fifteen Volumes*, translated by Frank Cole Babbit, 5:348–501. LCL. Cambridge: Harvard University Press, 1962.

———. "Superstition." In *Plutarch's Moralia in Fourteen Volumes*, translated by Frank Cole Babbit, 2:452–95.

Potter, David S. "Oracles." In *OCD*, 1071–72.

Potts, Richard, and Christopher Sloan. *What Does It Mean to Be Human?* Washington DC: National Geographic, 2010.

ProCon.org/. "State-by-State Guide to Physician-Assisted Suicide." https://euthanasia.procon.org/view.resource.php?resourceID=000132/.

Progressive Christianity. https://progressivechristianity.org/.

Purcell, Nicholas. "Pagus." In *OCD*, 1092.

Rajak, Tessa. "Pontius Pilatus." In *OCD*, 1220.

Randall, John Herman. *The Making of the Modern Mind: A Survey of the Intellectual Background of the Present Age.* Boston: Houghton Mifflin, 1926.

Rawley, Cliff. "Scripture Can Teach Us Life Truths." *Springfield News-Leader* (Missouri), 7 July 2014, 2C.

Ray, Roger L. "The Emerging Church." http://spfccc.org/.

———. *Progressive Faith and Practice: Thou Shalt not Stand Idly By.* Eugene, OR: Wipf & Stock, 2014.

Reese, David G. "Demons." In *ABD* 2:140–42.

Rios, Jaime Martin del Campo. "Religion and Superstition through a Cognitive Perspective: Examining the Relationship of Religious and Superstitious Beliefs to Cognitive Processes." PhD diss., University of Leicester, 2014. https://lra.le.ac.uk/bitstream/2381/32224/1/2015MARTINDELCAMPOJPhD.pdf.

Robertson, Noel, and B. C. Dietrich. "Fate." In *OCD*, 589–90.

Robinson, James M. "Introduction." In Albert Schweitzer, *Quest of the Historical Jesus: A Critical Study of Its Progress from Reimarus to Wrede*, xi–xxxiii. Translated by W. Montgomery. New York: Macmillan, 1968.

Robinson, James M., et al., eds. *The Critical Edition of Q.* Hermeneia Supplements. Minneapolis: Fortress, 2000.

Robinson, John A. T. *Exploration into God.* Stanford: Stanford University Press, 1967.

Rogers, Eric M. "The Triumph of a Theory." In *Exploring the Universe*, edited by Louise B. Young, 121–29. 2nd ed. New York: Oxford University Press, 1971.

Rotman, Youval. "The Imperial Eunuch: Traces of Hellenistic Institution in Roman Epigraphy." *Dike Rivista di Storia del Dritto Greco ed Ellenistico* 18 (2015) 143–57. https://riviste.unimi.it/index.php/Dike/article/view/8031/.

Rousseau, Philip. "Pagan, Paganism." In *OCD*, 1091.

Rowe, Christopher R. "Soul." In *OCD*, 1428.

Rudolph, Kurt. *Gnosis: The Nature and History of Gnosticism.* Translated and edited by Robert McLachlan Wilson et al. San Francisco: Harper & Row, 1983.

Sagan, Carl. *Cosmos.* New York: Wings, 1980.

Sanders, E. P. *The Historical Figure of Jesus.* Penguin Books. London: Penguin, 1993.

Schweitzer, Albert. *Out of My Life & Thought: An Autobiography.* Translated by C. T. Campion. Harvard Medicine Preservation microfilm project., Part 4 New York: Holt, 1933.

———. *The Psychiatric Study of Jesus: Exposition and Criticism.* Translated by Charles R. Joy. Boston: Beacon, 1948.

———. *The Quest of the Historical Jesus: A Critical Study of Its Progress from Reimarus to Wrede*. Translated by W. Montgomery. New York: Macmillan, 1968.
Scott, Charles Archibald Anderson. "Jesus and Paul." In *Essays on Some Biblical Questions of the Day by Members of the University of Cambridge*, edited by Henry Barclay Swete, 329–76. London: Macmillan, 1909.
Scott, Bernard Brandon. *Hear Then the Parable: A Commentary on the Parables of Jesus*. Minneapolis: Fortress, 1989.
Scheid, John. "Superstitio." In *OCD*, 1456.
Shriver, George H., ed. *Dictionary of Heresy Trials in American Christianity*. Westport, CT: Greenwood, 1997.
Simundson, Daniel J. "Suffering." In *ABD* 6:219–25.
Slick, Matt. "Permissive Will." *Christian Apologetics and Research Ministry (CARM)*. https://carm.org/dictionary-permissive-will/.
Sloan Digital Sky Survey / SkyServer. "The Expanding Universe." http://skyserver.sdss.org/dr1/en/astro/universe/universe.asp.
Soards, Marion L. "Parousia/Second Coming." In *MDB*, 646–47.
Southern Baptist Convention. "The 2000 Baptist Faith & Message." http://www.sbc.net/bfm2000/bfm2000.asp/.
Stanglin, Doug. "Demand for Exorcisms Is Up Threefold in Italy, So Vatican Is Holding a Conference." *USA Today* February 23, 2018. https://www.usatoday.com/story/news/world/2018/02/23/vatican-host-international-exorcism-conference-meet-growing-demand/367735002/.
Stark, Rodney. *What Americans Really Believe: New Findings from the Baylor Surveys of Religion*. Waco: Baylor University Press, 2008.
Stevens, Wallace. *Letters of Wallace Stevens*. Selected and edited by Holly Stevens. New York: Knopf, 1966.
Stimson, Dorothy. *The Gradual Acceptance of the Copernican Theory of the Universe*. Glouster. MA: Smith, 1972.
Sumney, Jerry L. "Anthropology, NT Theological." In *NIDB* 1:168–70.
Tabor, James D. "Heaven, Ascent to." In *ABD* 3:91–94.
Talbert, Charles H. *What Is a Gospel? The Genre of the Canonical Gospels*. Philadelphia: Fortress, 1977.
Tanglao, Leezel, and Ben Forer. "Tornadoes and Storms Tear through South; at Least 292 Dead." April 28, 2011. *ABC News*. http://abcnews.go.com/us/tornadoes-storms-tear-south-292-dead/story?id=13474955/.
Taussig, Hal. "Disparate Presence." In *When Faith Meets Reason: Religion Scholars Reflect on Their Spriitual Journeys*, edited by Charles W. Hedrick, 149–60. Santa Rosa, CA: Polebridge, 2008.
Tennyson, Alfred Lord. *In Memoriam*, canto 56." *The Literature Network*. http://www.online-literature.com/tennyson/718.
Tertullian (Quintus Septimius Florens Tertullianus). "A Treatise on the Soul." Translated by S. Thelwall. In *ANF* 3:180–235.
———. *De praescriptione haereticorum*. Translated by Peter Holmes. In *ANF* 3:243–65.
———. "On Exhortation to Chastity." Translated by S. Thelwall. In *ANF* 4:50–58.
———. "On Modesty." Translated by S. Thelwall. In *ANF* 4:74–101.
Teselle, Eugene. "Trinity." In *NIDB* 5:678.
Theissen, Gerd, and Annette Merz. *The Historical Jesus: A Comprehensive Guide*. Translated by John Bowden. Minneapolis: Fortress, 1998.

Theophrastus. *The Characters of Theophrastus: Newly Edited and Translated; Herodes, Cercidas and The Greek Choliambic Poets (except Callimachus and Babrius)*. Edited and translated by J. M. Edmonds. LCL. Cambridge: Harvard University Press, 1967.

———. *Theophrastus Characters, Herodas Mimes, Cercidas and the Choliambic Poets*. Edited and translated by Jeffrey Rusten et al. LCL 225. Cambridge: Harvard University Press, 1993.

Thomas, Dylan. *The Collected Poems of Dylan Thomas*. 1st New Directions paperback ed. New York: New Directions, 1971.

Tillich, Paul. *Systematic Theology*. 3 vols. Chicago: University of Chicago Press, 1951–1963.

Traub, Helmut. "οὐρανός." In *TDNT* 5:497–502.

Twelftree, Graham H. *Jesus the Exorcist: A Contribution to the Study of the Historical Jesus*. Peabody, MA: Hendrickson, 1993.

VanderKam, James C. "Jubilees, Book of." In *ABD* 3:1031–32.

Van der Linden, Sander. "The Science behind Dreaming." Mind. *Scientific American*. https://www.scientificamerican.com/article/the-science-behind-dreaming/.

Van Voorst, Robert E. "Docetism." In *NIDB* 2:154.

Versnel, H. S. "Deisidaimonia." In *OCD*, 441.

Vonnegut, Kurt, Jr. *Slaughterhouse-Five or The Children's Crusade. A Dance with Death*. New York: Delacorte, 1969.

Walker, Williston. *A History of the Christian Church*. Student's ed. New York: Scribner, 1946.

Ware, Timothy. *The Orthodox Church*. Harmondsworth: Penguin, 1964.

Warmington, Eric Herbert, et al. "Islands of the Blest (*Fortunatae insulae*)." In *OCD*, 769.

Watson, Duane F. "Hinnom Valley." In *ABD* 3:202–203.

Webster's Third New International Dictionary. 1961.

Webster's Ninth New Collegiate Dictionary. 1990.

Westcott, Brooke Foss. *The Bible in the Church: A Popular Account of the Collection and Reception of the Holy Scriptures in the Christian Churches*. New York: Macmillan, 1887.

Wikipedia. "Conservation of Energy." https://en.wikipedia.org/wiki/Conservation_of_energy/.

———. "Dragon." https://en.wikipedia.org/wiki/Dragon/.

———. "Exorcism in the Catholic Church." https://en.wikipedia.org/wiki/Exorcism_in_the_Catholic_Church/.

———. "Glossolalia." https://en.wikipedia.org/wiki/Glossolalia.

———. "List of Superstitions." https://en.wikipedia.org/wiki/List_of_superstitions.

———. "*Man of La Mancha*." https://en.wikipedia.org/wiki/Man_of_La_Mancha.

———. "Mortal Sin." https://en.wikipedia.org/wiki/Mortal_sin.

———. "Near-death Experience." https://en.wikipedia.org/wiki/Near-death_experience/.

———. "On Suicide." https://en.wikipedia.org/wiki/Christian_views_on_suicide.

———. "Philosopher's Stone." https://en.wikipedia.org/wiki/Philosopher%27s_stone.

———. "2011 Joplin Tornado." http://en.wikipedia.org/wiki/2011_Joplin_tornado/.

———. "*Waiting for God* (TV Series)." https://en.wikipedia.org/wiki/Waiting_for_God_(TV_series)/.

———. "*Waiting for Godot.*" https://en.wikipedia.org/wiki/Waiting_for_Godot/.
Wilson, John Francis. *Caesarea Philippi: Banias, the Lost City of Pan.* London: Tauris, 2004.
Wimsatt, W. K., Jr. *The Verbal Icon: Studies in the Meaning of Poetry.* Kentucky Paperbacks. Lexington: University of Kentucky Press, 1967.
Winseman, Albert L. "I Am a Person Who Is Spiritually Committed." May 28, 2002. *Gallup News.* http://www.gallup.com/poll/6097/person-who-spiritually-committed.aspx?version=print/.
Wisse, Frederik, trans. "Letter of Peter to Philip." In *The Nag Hammadi Library in English*, edited by James M. Robinson, 394–98. San Francisco: Harper & Row, 1977.
Woodwose, T. E. "Evidence That the Sky Is not Blue?" http://wiki.answers.com/Q/Evidence_that_the_sky_is_not_blue.
Woolley, Kate Wilkins. "Free to Be Me." In *Baptist Hymnal*, edited by William J. Reynolds, hymn no. 331. Nashville: Convention, 1975.
Wordsworth, William. "Ode: Intimations of Immortality from Recollections of Early Childhood." In *Poems of William Wordsworth*, edited by Howard Judson Hall, 192–98. Lake City Edition. Chicago: Scott, Foresman, 1924.
Wrede, William. *The Messianic Secret.* Translated by J. C. Greig. Library of Theological Translations. Cambridge: Clarke, 1971.
Young, Louise B. "Editor's Note on Scientific Reasoning and Terms." In *Exploring the Universe*, edited by Louise B. Young, 22–24. 2nd ed. New York: Oxford University Press, 1971.
———, ed. *Exploring the Universe.* 2nd ed. New York: Oxford University Press, 1971.
Zoll, Rachel. "Catholics: More Exorcists Needed." *Springfield News-Leader* (Missouri). 13 November 2010, 8A.
Zoroya, Gregg. "Young Veterans Tally 'Alarming' Suicide Numbers." *USA Today.* In *Springfield News-Leader* (Missouri), 11 January 2014, 2A.

Index of Ancient Sources

OLD TESTAMENT/ HEBREW BIBLE/ SEPTUAGINT

Genesis

1	282
1:1	13
1:6–8	13
1:26–30	218
1:26	55, 282
1:27–28	102
1:28	59
1:31	13, 35, 120
2–3	130
2:4–24	282
2:7	120, 125, 226, 296
2:17	13, 80, 130
2:18–23	131
2:21–22	296
2:23–24	130
2:23	130
2:24	131
3:1–13	130
3:1–5	15
3:16–19	13
3:17	120
3:19	130
4:9	301
4:19	260
6:5	18
7:4	35
7:21–23	35
8:1	49
8:20–22	35, 64
8:21	18
9:5–6	296n24
9:11–17	35
12:1–3	190
15:12	6n27
16:1–4	260
17:1–14	190
17:7–8	190
19:1–3	57
19:24–25	26
20:3–7	188
22:1–18	108
25:6	260
25:29–34	182
26:34	260
31:11–13	188
32:28	182
36:9	182
36:43	182
44:29	246
44:31	246
48:4	190
50:20	18

Exodus

3:1–6	193
4:24–26	146
7:9	97
7:10	97
7:12	97
12:46	272
14:21	49

Exodus (continued)

15:10	49
17:6	34
17:8–13	193
17:12	6n27
19–23	169
20:2–17	102
20:4	13
20:5	130
20:11	13
20:13	296
20:20	103
21:22–25	302
21:32	132
24:1–7	90
30:8	190
31:16	190
32:14	18
33:19	259
33:20–23	193
33:23	193
34:10	254
34:25–35	177
34:29–30	178
34:35	178

Leviticus

3:17	190
4:1–6:7	64
7–10	101
10:9	190
11:9–12	187
15	127
16:29	190
16:34	190
17:7	14, 109, 110, 111, 190
18:8	125
18:22	187
19:18	293
19:33–34	57
20:10	102
23:14	190
23:31	190
23:41	190
24:2	190
24:3–4	190
24:8	190
24:9	190
24:19–20	302
26	169
26:3–5	169
26:6–13	169
26:14–33	169

Numbers

5:14	283
9:12	272
11:31	49
12:4–8	188
19	127
20:8–11	34
21:7	248
21:15–35	146
22:21–30	14
24:17 LXX	202
25:12–13	190

Deuteronomy

1:27	183
5:7–21	102
6:2	103
6:4–5	177
6:5	103
7:6	257
8:15	34
9:9–10	95, 266
10:1–5	95, 266
10:12	103
12:31	183
15:1–3	57
17:2–5	95
18:9–14	225
18:9–12	184
18:10–12	253
18:17–18	253
19:16–21	302
20:10–20	192
21:15–17	182, 187
21:15	260
21:18–21	95, 102
21:22–23	113
22:6–7	29

22:6	32	16:14–15	179
22:13–21	102	16:14	254, 257, 283
23:21	248	16:23	18, 225
25:17–19	193	17:40–50	99
29:3–4	275	17:47	99
32:13	34	18:10	18, 235
32:33	97	19:5	248
33:2	266	19:9–10	225
34:4	80	19:9	18, 235
34:5–6	80	19:10–11	225
34:7	80	19:24 LXX	166, 167
		21:1–6	147
Joshua		22:20–23	147
6:15–21	192	28:3–25	253
6:17	192	28:6	188
6:19	192	31:4–5	297
6:21	192		
10:6–14	6	**2 Samuel**	
10:12–14	6, 14, 146	1:1–10	29
23:15	18	1:6	29, 32
		6:1–7	264
Judges		7:1–7	253
6:3–5	193	7:12–16	190
6:21	33	8:12–14	182
6:37–40	254	16:23	251
8:30	260	17:14	18
9:23	18, 21	17:23	297
9:54	297	24:1	19
14:18	6n27	24:16	18
16:29–30	297	28:7–15	270
19:21	57		
		1 Kings	
1 Samuel		9:9	18
1:1–2	260	11:1–10	260
6:1–9	29	11:34	257
6:9	29, 32	12:22	90
9:9	251	12:30	248
9:27	90	14:10	18
15	15, 102, 192	16:18	297
15:1–35	146	16:26	248
15:1–3	26, 192	17:8–16	6n27, 224
15:3	193	18:12	126
15:23	248	19:1–18	53
16:14–23	257	19:1–5	188
16:14–17	225	19:9–13	171
16:14–16	18, 235	19:11–13	193

1 Kings (continued)

19:11–12	193
19:12	170, 171
19:13	171
22:13–23	14, 18
22:19–23	179, 225, 235n98
22:22	254
19:12	170, 171

2 Kings

2:2–3	251
2:4–5	251
4:1–7	6n27
4:4–37	224
4:38	251
5:1–14	224
6:1–7	5
6:4–7	14
6:33	18
13:20–21	3
16:3	246
21:12	18
22:3–23:25	194
22–23	90
23:10	246
24:1–14	26
25	246

1 Chronicles

4:5	260
16:14–18	190
17:3	90
21:1	19
21:8	248
25:5	90

2 Chronicles

7:13–14	31
7:14	10
11:15	109, 110, 111
11:21	260
12:7	10
18:18–22	235n98
18:34	6n27
24:1–3	187, 260
24:3	260

25:11–25	182
25:20	182
28:2–3	246
32:26	10
33–34	90

Ezra

1:1–11	18
9:4	90

Nehemiah

2:13	97
9:15	34
13:18	18

Esther

4:14	60

Job

1–2	180
1:1–2:13	76, 169
1:1	169
1:6–13	18
1:8–12	170
1:8	76
1:9–11	76
1:18–19	51
2:1–6	18, 76
2:3–6	170
2:4–6	218
2:10	18, 196
3:1—42:6	47, 169
4:7	76
6:24–30	76
6:24–25	76
8:1–6	76
9:20–21	76
10:5–7	76
11:4–6	76
12:4	76
13:2–5	76
16:9	183
16:2	259
16:2–3	32, 76
19:4	76

INDEX OF ANCIENT SOURCES 327

22:29	10
23:3–7	32, 76
25:4–6	218
27:1–6	32
27:2–6	76
27:3–6	32
28:28	103
29:6	34
30:17–21	32
30:26	196
32:6—37:24	76
34:35–37	248
36:8–12	76
38–41	76
38:1—43:6	76
38–39	47
40:1–5	76
42:1–6	32, 47, 76
42:7–17	47, 169
42:7–9	77
42:7	77
42:11	18

Psalms

1	64
2:7	226
5:5	183
8:4–8	55
8:3–6	218
16:5	254
22:18	272, 273
24:3–4	127
31:6	183
31:15	254
31:17	246
35:1 LXX	103
41:9	257
41:10	132
69:9	157
69:21	272
69:26	132
74:13	98
78:15–16	34
78:20	34
78:70–71	257
81:16	34
89:34	191
89:34–37	190
90:10	80
91:6	14
91:13	97
105:41	34
109:8	132
114:8	34
118:24	81
119	64
135:6	13
135:7	50
142:4	300
146:10	224
148:7–8	50

Proverbs

1:7	103
3:7	103
3:34	10
6:16–19	183
8:13	10
8:22–31	239
8:27–30	205
8:27–29	13
16:33	254
21:4	248
22:4	10
29:23	10
30:5	90

Ecclesiastes

1:1	81
1:14	81
2:17	81
2:24	81
3:11	80, 254
3:15	254
3:16	81
3:17–18	170
3:22	81
4:1	81
4:7	81
5:13	81
5:18–19	71
6:1	81
7:13	254

Ecclesiastes (continued)

7:15	81
7:18	170
8:9	81
8:12–13	170
8:17	81, 254
9:2–12	29
9:4	81
9:7	71
9:9	71
9:11	29, 32, 81
9:13	81
10:5	81
10:19	81
12:1–14	81
12:13–14	170
12:13	81

Isaiah

1:14	183
6:9–10	275
7:1–17	254
7:1–10	127
7:14	226, 254
8:18	184, 254
9:9	10
11:15	50
13:9–11	184, 254
13:11	10
13:21–22	112
13:21	109, 110, 111
14:12–15	20
16:6	10
20:2–3	184, 254
20:2 LXX	166
24–27	35
24:23	224
27:1	98
34:14	14, 109, 110, 111, 112, 283
40:3–5	117
40:3	147
40:8	49, 90
40:13 LXX	66, 261
42:1	257
45:1	224
45:4	257
47:13	254
48:21	34
51:9	98
61:8	183
65:9	257
65:17–20	35
65:17	35, 120
66:24	246

Jeremiah

10:2	254
10:13	50
26:13	18
26:19	18
29:1–4	90
31:31–34	88, 275
31:31	191
31:32	191
33:17–18	253
36:1–4	90
44:4	183
45:1–5	90
48:2	10
48:29	10
49:36	50
51:34	97

Ezekiel

2:12–15	126
5:13–17	18
8:3	126
11:24–25	126
16:59–63	191
21:21	254
26:17–21	253
34:24	202
37:1–10	270
37:1	126
37:12–14	25
37:25	202
37:26–37	190
40:2	126

Daniel

2:27	254
4:7	254

5:5–31	184, 254
5:7	254
5:11	254
7:13–14	218
9:2	87
11:37–38	249

Hosea

1:1–2	169
1:4–8	169
2:4–5	169
3:1–5	169
4:1–19	169
9:15	183
11:1–12	169

Joel

2:28	189
2:30–31	184, 254

Amos

5:21–23	64
5:21	183
5:24	64

Jonah

1:4	50
3:10	18

Micah

4:6–7	224
6:6–8	64
6:8	64, 71

Habakkuk

2:11	33

Zephaniah

1:14–18	35
3:1–8	35
3:11	10

Zechariah

3:1–2	14
8:17	183
9:9	157
11	132
11:12	132
11:13	132
12:10	272
14:5 LXX	114

Malachi

1:2–3	182
1:4	182
3:1	147

APOCRYPHA

2 Esdras

1:20	34
1:24–25	191
1:35–37	191
6:1–34	277
7:36	246
14:44–48	90

Tobit

3:7–8	235
6:6–8	225
6:7–8	235
6:15–17	225
6:16–17	235
8:1–3	225

Judith

15:9	10
16:17	246

Wisdom of Solomon

7:27	205
11:4	34

Sirach

Prologue	90
2:15–16	103
7:17	246
10:13	249
23:10	249
24:23	90
32:12	249
34:5	254
39:28–31	19
47:17	164n121
50:1	10

Baruch

3:37–4:1	239

Bel and the Dragon

33–36	126

2 Maccabees

5:1–4	254
5:4	254
12:40–45	247

PSEUDEPIGRAPHA

1 Enoch

54:1–5	246
90:25–27	246

2 Baruch (Syriac)

8:14	66

Jubilees

1:27–2:1	266
10:8	19
32:21–22	266

Testament of the Twelve Patriarchs

Testament of Dan 6:1–2	266
Testament of Levi 5:5–6	266

NEW TESTAMENT

Matthew

1:18—2:23	188
1:18–25	267
1:18–23	254
1:18	214, 222
1:20–24	189
1:20–21	211
1:20	254
1:23	237
1:24–25	214
2:2	254
2:1–23	184
2:9–10	254
2:12–13	189, 254
2:19–20	189
2:19	254
2:22	189, 254
3:3	147
3:5	142
3:9	33, 34
3:13–17	117, 137
3:13–15	209
3:13–14	198
3:17	136
4:1–11	100
4:1	19
4:3	33
4:11	283
5:11	196
5:21–48	302
5:22	246
5:25–30	196
5:38–42	302
5:39	150
5:43–45	293
5:43–44	58

5:44–45	26
5:44	58, 102, 150
5:45	6n27, 196
6:1–8	79
6:1	79
6:10	119
6:16–18	79
6:24	196
6:25–33	69
7:7–11	196
7:11	196
8:11–12	246
8:20	218
8:23	144
8:26–27	50
9:1–8	258
9:4	220
9:20–21	8
10:1	14
10:8	14
10:29–31	196
10:30	29, 77
11:12–15	162
11:16–19	205
11:19	205, 288
12:4	147
12:24	19
12:25	220
12:28	119, 152, 206
12:45	208
12:38–42	151
12:38–39	235
12:43–45	207, 234
12:45	235
13:10–15	237
13:11	278
13:13	278
13:33	173
13:58	143
14:13–21	6
14:20	6
14:26	86
16:1–4	149
16:16–19	242
16:17–19	242
16:18–19	258
17:2–5	117
17:14–21	21, 206, 284
17:15–18	14
17:15	284
17:18	284
18:10–14	237
18:10	14
18:15–18	242
18:21	292
19:9	102
19:12	186, 261
22:3–6	132
22:13	246
23:34–36	204
24:29–30	254
25:21	63
25:23	63
25:30	246
25:34–35	293
25:40	293
25:41	21
25:45	293
26:3–4	132
26:14–16	257
26:14–15	132
26:34	184
26:47–50	132
26:63–64	263
27:3–5	132
27:4	249
27:19	189
27:7–10	132
27:25	114
27:46	25
27:50	7n30, 25
27:51–54	14, 24
27:51–53	211
27:51	7n30, 25
27:53	7n30, 24, 25
27:54	25
27:55–56	7n30
28	25
28:1–2	25
28:4	103
28:9	25, 212, 276
28:18–20	117, 181

Mark

1:1–3	147

Mark (continued)

1:1	139, 212	5:1–20	21
1:4–8	203	5:1–10	14
1:4–5	137, 209	5:1–5	283
1:5	142, 143, 147, 248	5:6–13	270
1:9–11	136, 137, 267	5:22–24	106
1:9	135, 288	5:23	106
1:10–11	118	5:24–30	15
1:11	227	5:24	106
1:12–13	100	5:25–34	106
1:13	19	5:29	141
1:14–15	150, 152	5:30	141
1:14	114	5:34	47
1:15–19	152	5:35	106
1:15	206	5:35–43	106
1:27	140	5:36	106
1:28	142	5:38	106
1:33	142, 147	5:39	106
1:41	141	5:40	106
2:1–12	152, 158, 258	5:41–42	106
2:5	140	5:42	140
2:6	141	6:1	148
2:7	259	6:5	143
2:8	140	6:6	141
2:10	218	6:14–29	148
2:12	140	6:14	148
2:15–16	288	6:20	141
2:17	151n100	6:21	148
2:25–26	147	6:25–27	148
2:27–28	218	6:24–25	148
2:27	191	6:26	141
3:1–5	47	6:32–44	6, 152
3:6	288	6:34	141
3:21–27	152	6:41	118
3:27	218	6:42	6
3:28–29	249	6:43	43
3:28	218	6:45–52	14, 152, 158
4:1–12	149	6:45–50	86
4:2	143	6:45	148
4:3–8	236	6:49–50	86, 270
4:11–12	237, 278	6:49	211, 213, 230, 239
4:12	237	6:51–52	141
4:14–20	236	6:51	140
4:32	118	7:13	88
4:36	143	7:14–23	127
4:39	50	7:22	10
4:41	50, 104, 141	7:27	150
		7:34	118
		7:37	140

INDEX OF ANCIENT SOURCES 333

8:1–9	34	12:17	140, 210
8:11–13	149, 153	12:25	118
8:11–12	151	12:36	141
8:11	118	13:24–27	184, 217, 218, 254
8:12	141	13:20	257
8:29–30	242	13:25	118
8:38–9:1	217, 218	13:27	118, 257
9:2–8	145	13:31	118
9:6	141	13:32	118
9:9	217	14–16	131
9:12	217	14	152
9:14–29	206, 284	14:1–2	131
9:15	140	14:3–9	152
9:17	284	14:4	141
9:18	284	14:10–12	131
9:20–22	284	14:10–11	257
9:25–26	284	14:12	152
9:25	14, 283	14:21	217
9:31	217	14:22–25	152
9:38–41	264	14:30	184
10:1	152	14:32–50	131
10:10	102	14:32–42	100
10:14	119, 141	14:32–33	242
10:17–22	69	14:33	141
10:17	152	14:34–41	141
10:21	118, 141	14:34–36	141
10:23	119	14:41	217
10:25	119	14:49	131
10:26	140	14:53–72	148
10:28	196	14:54	148
10:32	140, 152	14:55–65	142
10:33	217	14:56	118
10:41	141	14:60–64	217
10:45	153, 217	14:61–62	263
10:52	47	14:66–72	184
11:1	152	14:66	148
11:12	141	14:68	184, 185
11:15—13:1	131	14:70	288
11:15–19	162	14:72	141, 185
11:15	152	15	114
11:18–19	131	15:5	141
11:18	140, 141	15:10	140
11:21	141	15:22	211
11:25	118	15:37–38	184
11:30–31	118	15:39	229
11:32	141	15:43	141
12:12	141	15:44	141
12:15	140, 141	16:2	6n27

334 INDEX OF ANCIENT SOURCES

Mark (continued)

16:5	149
16:6	212
16:7	212
16:8	103, 140, 141, 212n39
16:43	141

Luke

1:1	142
1:5–2:22	189
1:26–55	267
1:27	189
1:31	214
1:35	9n37, 214, 222, 237
1:51	10
2:1–39	190
2:1–20	267
2:4	189
2:7	214
2:16	189
2:33	189
2:43	189
3:4–6	147
3:8	34
3:18–22	137
3:19–20	209
3:21–22	117
3:21	209
3:22	227
4:1–13	100
4:3	19
4:15	206
4:23	151, 151n100
4:40	206
4:41	206
4:43	206
5:17–26	258
6:3	147
6:8	220
6:17–19	206
6:23	118 (Q)
6:27–35	293
6:27–31	58
6:27	58, 102, 150, 210
6:29	210
6:30	210
6:31	301
7:11–17	34
7:31–35	205
7:34	288
7:36–50	258
7:37	248
7:39	248
7:48	248
8:9–10	237
8:10	278
8:22	144
8:24–25	50
8:31	246
9:10–17	6
9:17	6
9:37–43	206, 284
9:38	284
9:42	284
9:47	220
9:58	218 (Q), 288
10:15	118 (Q)
10:18	19
10:30–35	30
10:29–35	29
10:31	29, 30
11:2	119 (Q)
11:11–12	42
11:13	118 (Q)
11:14–26	235
11:14–20	21
11:14	21
11:20	119 (Q), 152, 206 (Q)
11:24–26	207 (Q), 234 (Q)
11:26	208, 235 (Q)
11:29–32	151
11:29	149
11:49–51	204
12:2	vi (Q)
12:7	29
12:33	118 (Q)
13:11	14, 283
13:32	206
15:1–2	288
15:3–7	237
15:7	118 (Q)
15:18	292

15:21	292
16:16	163
16:17	118 (Q)
16:19–31	234
16:23–24	246
17:4	292
17:29	118 (Q)
18:2–5	103
18:2	103
18:4	103
19:40	33
21:8–28	184, 254
22:3	132
22:4–6	132
22:34	184
22:36	180
22:39	132
22:47–54	132
22:67–68	263
24:30	276
24:36–43	212
24:36–42	146
24:37	211

John

1:1–11:54	160
1:1–51	160
1:1–18	153, 158, 162, 213, 239
1:1–14	195, 203n20, 267
1:1–5	213
1:1–3	239
1:1–2	229, 244, 263
1:5	158
1:6–8	162
1:9–13	163
1:9–11	145
1:9	239
1:14	213, 214, 229, 230, 239, 244, 263
1:15	162, 163
1:17	213
1:18	244
1:19	163
1:20	163
1:29–34	137, 152
1:29	161, 163

1:30–34	209
1:31	209
1:32–34	245
1:32–33	244
1:32	163, 244
1:33	244
1:34	163
1:35	161
1:39	161
1:43	161
1:45	239
1:47	288
1:49	244
2:1–12:50	153
2:1–22	153
2:1–11	34, 47, 254
2:1	161
2:4	161
2:11	149
2:12	161
2:13–22	157, 162, 218
2:13–20	218
2:13	152
2:14–22	161
2:16	157
2:17	157
2:18	157
2:19	157
2:20	157
2:21–22	219
2:21	157
2:22	157
2:23	152, 161
2:25–30	152
3:1–21	160
3:1–10	163
3:1	161
3:3–8	244
3:6	159
3:7	51
3:8	50
3:11	163
3:12	163
3:13–21	163
3:16	229
3:22–30	152
3:22	161
3:25–30	163

John (continued)

3:25	161
3:31–36	163
3:34	244
4:1–3	105
4:1	104, 105, 161, 209
4:2	104, 105, 106, 209
4:3	104, 105
4:6	161
4:21	163
4:24	168, 170, 172, 183, 193, 244
4:25	163
4:22–24	163
4:23–24	244
4:35	155
4:42	162
4:43	161
4:44	161
4:46–54	153
4:53	84
4:54	149
5:1–9	152
5:1	152, 161
5:2–18	158
5:2	161
5:9	161
5:18	244
5:25	161
5:28	161
5:30	161
5:35	155
5:37	161
5:38	161
5:39	274
6:1–15	6, 152
6:1	161
6:2	105
6:4	161
6:5–14	105
6:10	105
6:12	6, 105
6:13	6, 105
6:14	105
6:16–21	86, 152, 158
6:16	161
6:19	250
6:22	161
6:24	250
6:26	105
6:29	161
6:38	161
6:42	239
6:44	161
6:51–58	216
6:52–59	286
6:52	161
6:53	79
6:63	244
6:66	161
6:70–71	132, 257
7:1	161
7:2	161
7:5	161
7:8	161
7:10	152
7:14	161
7:15	162
7:16	161
7:21	254
7:22	105, 163
7:28	161
7:37	161
7:39	244, 245
8:2	161
8:12	153, 161, 240
8:16	161
8:20	161
8:21	161
8:23	159, 161
8:31–37	60
8:32	73
8:42	161, 244
8:44–45	158
9:5	240
9:39	161
10:1–5	164
10:6	164, 165
10:7–18	164
10:7	161
10:16	264
10:19	161, 165
10:22	161
10:30	244
10:33	239

INDEX OF ANCIENT SOURCES 337

10:36	244	14:25–26	245
11:1	161	14:26	245
11:5	161	14:30	14, 19
11:6	161	14:31	160
11:7	152, 161	15:1–18:1	160
11:17	161	16:4–11	244
11:18	152	16:7–8	245
11:25–26	153	16:7	244, 245
11:27	244	16:8–11	245
11:47–53	133	16:11	14, 19
11:55–20:29	160, 161	16:12–13	245
11:55	152, 160	16:13–14	245
12:1–8	152	16:13	21, 244
12:1	160	16:14	245
12:3	155, 161	16:16–29	164, 165
12:4–8	132	16:20–28	164
12:6	132	16:21	239
12:12–19	157	16:25	161, 164
12:12–16	161	16:29–30	164
12:12	152, 160	16:29	164
12:14	157	16:32	161
12:15	157	17:1–5	244
12:16	167	17:1	161
12:20	161	17:2	239
12:23–24	244	17:11	244
12:27–36	153	17:14	161
12:27–33	100, 244	17:16	161
12:31–33	161	17:21–22	244
12:31	19	17:24	244
12:35–36	153, 240	18:1–12	133
12:46	240	18:2–3	133
13:1–20	152	18:12–13	162
13:1	160, 161	18:25	161
13:2	133, 160, 257	18:28	152, 161, 162
13:11	132	18:31–33	151
13:12	160	18:37–38	151
13:23	160	19:1	161, 162
13:25	160	19:6	162
13:27	133	19:7	244
13:29	132	19:14	152, 160
13:30	161	19:17–20	211
13:31–14:31	160	19:18	162
13:31–32	153	19:21	160
13:31	160, 161	19:28	161, 272
13:38	184	19:24	272, 273
14:9	239	19:31	152
14:16–17	245	19:36	272
14:16	245	19:37	272

John (continued)

19:38	161
19:42	152
20:1	160
20:3–9	161, 213
20:5–7	155
20:17	276
20:19–23	258
20:19	160
20:22–23	244
20:24–29	212
20:26	160
20:28	239, 244
20:31	244
21:1	161
21:7	155, 165, 166
21:12–13	276
21:15–19	156
21:20–23	156
21:20–22	156
21:20–21	156
21:22	157
21:23	156

Acts

1:6–11	146
1:8	83
1:14	82
1:16–20	132
1:16	257
1:24	82
2:1–21	83
2:4	83
2:7–8	83
2:16–18	83
2:17	189
2:23–24	217
2:33	82
2:36	227
2:37–38	83
2:38	83
2:42	82
2:43	83, 254
3:1	82
3:10	82
3:15	201
4:30	83, 254
4:31	83, 88
5:12	83
5:30–32	83
5:15	8
5:31	201
5:32	83
6:1–6	204
6:1–2	288
6:7	288
6:8	83
7:32–34	82
7:38	95, 266
7:49	82
7:53	266
7:55–56	82
8:6–8	83
8:14–18	83
8:17–18	79
8:39–40	126
9:2	203
9:10	211, 288
9:17	83, 211
9:36–41	83
10:2	103
10:4	82
10:9–35	125
10:9–19	83
10:10	82
10:22	103
10:34–35	103
10:44–48	83
10:43	83
11:1	88
11:4–5	83
11:5	82
11:13–18	84
11:26	288
12:5	82
12:6–11	83
12:9	86
12:11	21
12:12	82
12:15	86, 211
12:23	21
13:5	88
13:9	83
13:16	103
13:29–39	83

3:32–33	226	28:25	83
13:46	88		
14:8–10	83	Romans	
16	84		
16:1	288	1:3–4	178, 205, 227, 238, 263
16:12	84	1:4	178
16:14–15	84	1:11	291
16:16–18	83, 180	1:18–32	257
16:16	14	1:18	119
16:28–31	83	1:16	191
16:31	84	1:30	10
16:33	84	3:7	250
16:34	84	3:18	103
17:2–4	83	3:30	177
17:17–28	82	4:1–5:2	64
17:22	4	5:1	178
17:24	82	5:2	178
17:31	178	5:5	178
18	84	5:8–11	153
18:8	84	5:11	178
19	8, 9	5:12–21	130
19:1–6	83	5:12–14	13
19:1–4	209	5:12	80, 130
19:1	288	5:17	13, 80
19:6	79, 83	5:21	178
19:9	203	6:1–11	279
19:11–12	7, 8, 83, 264	6:3–5	241
19:12	8, 15	6:3–4	116, 209
19:21–28:30	83	6:3	79
19:21	83	6:6	113, 114
19:23	203	6:17–28	60
19:32	241	7:7–12	64
19:39	241	7:11–23	250
19:41	241	7:24–25	178
20:7	191	8:2	60
20:22	83	8:3	214
20:23	83	8:6–7	292
20:27	83	8:9–11	178
21:4	83	8:9	178
21:11	83	8:11	178
21:16	288	8:18–23	41
22:4	203	8:18–21	13
22:17	82	8:19–23	36, 120
24:14	203	8:19–21	173
22:22	203	8:20–23	80
25:19	4	8:20	120
26:18	83	8:21	120
26:28	288		

Romans (continued)

8:22-23	120
8:24-25	67
8:28	27, 31
8:38	171
9-11	191
9:1-5	274
9:13	182
9:15	259
9:18	254
10:5-11	94
10:6	119
10:7	246
10:8-9	191
10:9	64
11-13	114
11:1	191
11:5	257
11:8	275
11:16	127
11:20	104
11:25-29	191, 275
11:25-26	114
11:25	191
11:28-29	191
11:33-34	66
11:33	31, 192, 277
11:36	276
13:1	73
13:8-10	57, 293
14:17	120
14:21-23	249
15:1-2	57
15:16	114
15:19	254
15:25-29	69
15:27	69
16:25-27	114, 181
16:25	280

1 Corinthians

1:2	114, 123, 127, 178, 241, 242
1:4	178
1:13-17	116
1:17-22	113
1:17	113
1:18	114
1:24	280
2:2	113, 115
2:7	277, 280
2:11	261
2:12-3:3	291
2:16	66, 261
3:1-4	291
3:3	291
4:1	280
4:20	120
5:1-5	124
5:3-4	125, 126
5:3	125
5:4-5	125
5:6-7	128
6:1-8	122
6:3	123
6:9	120
6:11	114, 127
6:12-20	130
6:15-20	128
6:15-16	8
6:15	128
6:18	249
7:1-9	102
7:6-9	260
7:8	102
7:9	260
7:10-11	115
7:13-14	9
7:14	127, 128
7:25-31	260
7:25	115
7:29-31	123
7:31	36, 80
7:32-35	260
7:36	261
7:38	261
7:40	181
8:4-6	177
8:4	177
8:5	119
8:6	177, 178, 276
9:5	261
9:11	291
9:14	115
9:9-12	94

10:1–4	94
10:2	116
10:31	59
11:17–31	279
11:20–34	117
11:23–32	79
11:23–26	115
11:23–25	131
12:3	178
12:4–13	178
12:4–11	181, 290
12:7	291
12:10	181
12:13	116
12:28–31	291
12:28–30	181
12:28	287
12:29	181
13:1–13	58
13:1–2	58
13:3	58
13:4–7	58
13:4	104
13:5	104
13:7	104
13:11–12	58
13:12	36
13:13	58, 104, 293
14:1–25	182
14:6	181
14:26–33	83
14:26	181
14:33	114, 242
14:37	115, 291
15:1–5	217
15:3–5	211
15:3–4	157
15:6–8	212
15:8	211
15:20	178, 212
15:21–22	212
15:21	80
15:24	120
15:27–28	177
15:35–50	120, 275
15:37	29, 32
15:39	214n43
15:42–57	25

15:44	212, 275
15:45	212
15:47	119
15:50	120, 212, 275
15:51–53	212
15:51–52	275
15:57	178
16:1–4	69
16:2	69, 191
16:22	217

2 Corinthians

1:1	114
1:20	178
3:3	178
3:4–18	178
3:13–16	94
3:16–18	178
3:17	60, 178
3:18	178
4:3–6	94
5:1–4	119
5:1–5	120
5:6–8	120
5:8	121
5:10	121
5:17–19	280
5:17	192
5:19	178, 238, 270, 277
6:14–7:1	127
6:15	19
6:18	178
8–9	69
8:3–4	69
8:13	69
9:7	69
11:13–15	172
11:14	14, 21
12–13	69
12:1–4	61, 26
12:2–4	119
12:4	61
12:7–9	181, 212
12:12	254
13:3	181
13:13	114
13:14	177

Galatians

1:1	242
1:2	242
1:4	114
1:7	114
1:8	119
1:11–12	115, 181
1:15–16	212
1:17–24	242
1:22	242
2:1	114
2:2	181
2:10	69, 114
2:13	114
2:15–16	102
2:16	64, 108, 178, 203
2:20	114
3:1	114, 115
3:6–14	108
3:7	114
3:8–11	108
3:16	94
3:19–29	64
3:19–20	177
3:19	95, 266
3:27	116
4:4–7	178
4:4	115, 214, 238
4:6–7	178
4:22–31	94
5:1	73
5:13	293
5:14	57, 293
5:19–21	291
5:21	120
5:22–23	291
5:24	114
6:1	291
6:4	11
6:14	113, 114, 280

Ephesians

1:9–10	276
2:2	14, 19, 21, 171
3:3–6	275
3:10	171
4:8–9	25
4:26	6n27
6:5	104
6:10–12	21
6:12	14, 171

Philippians

1:1	114
1:11	178
1:21–22	71
2:2–10	261
2:5–11	238
2:5	115, 228, 261
2:5–8	203n20, 229, 238
2:6–7	228
2:6	228
2:7	214, 228
2:9–11	228, 263
2:12	65
3:3	177
3:20–21	119
3:21	120
4:21–22	114

Colossians

1:15	172, 214
1:16–17	17, 276
1:17	195
2:1–3	277
2:5	125
3:18–4:1	74
4:2–4	277

1 Thessalonians

1:10	114, 119, 217
2:9	114
2:12	120
2:13	88
2:14–16	114
2:14	242
2:15	113
2:16	114
3:2	114
3:13	217
4:3	114
4:4–8	261
4:8	178

4:10–12	74	5:7	100, 215
4:13–5:11	217	6:1–6	258
4:13–18	114	6:20	178
4:13–17	120	8–10	102
4:16–17	120	8:8–13	96, 191, 275
4:15–17	115	8:8–12	88
4:16	119	8:13	191
4:18	114	9:11–14	191
4:23	178	9:28	217
5:9–10	114	10:20	215
5:9	178	11:27	214
		12:2	201
		12:18–21	103
		13:7	88

2 Thessalonians

2:1–12	276
2:7	277
2:11	254

1 Timothy

1:4	277
1:17	214
2:8–15	95, 115
2:14	248
3:1–13	102
3:2	261
3:12	261
3:15	242
3:16	214, 233, 277, 280
4:14	79

2 Timothy

1:6–7	79
3:2	10
3:15–16	88, 91, 95, 96
3:16–17	187

Titus

1:6	261
3:1–2	74

Hebrews

1:1–4	88
2:2	95, 266
2:4	254
2:10	201
2:14	215

James

1:26	290
1:27	64, 291
2:1–13	57
2:2	166
2:14–26	64
2:15	166
2:18–26	108
2:21–26	102
2:24	64, 108
3:1–2	290
4:6	10
4:8	250
4:17	30, 249

1 Peter

1:2	257
1:23–25	88
2:13–15	74
2:17	103
3:18–19	25
4:11	59
4:16	288
5:5	10

2 Peter

1:16–18	117
1:19	19
2:4	246
2:22	164
3:5–7	88

2 Peters (continued)

3:9–13	217
3:10	36
3:13	120
3:14–17	179

1 John

1:1–2	239
1:1	213, 230
1:8	170
2:16	10
3:4	249
3:15	297
4:2–3	239
4:2	213, 230
4:8	171, 182
4:13–17	103
4:16	182
4:18	103
4:20	293
5:16–17	297
5:17	249

2 John

7	213, 239

Jude

3	44, 263

Revelation

1:8	174
1:9–20	182
1:10	126
1:20	278
2:6	183
4:1–2	126
9:1–2	246
10:7	278
12:1	184, 254
12:7–12	19
12:3	98
12:4	98
12:7	98
12:9	19, 98
12:13	98
12:17	98
12:18	98
13:1–9	254
13:2	98
13:4	98
13:11–18	254
13:11	98
14:7	103
15:1	184, 254
16:13–14	14
16:13	98
17:3	126
17:5	73, 278
17:7	278
18:2	73
19:11–18	88
20:2	98
20:11–14	246
21:1–4	36
21:1	120
21:2	247
21:10	126
21:21	247

GREEK AND LATIN AUTHORS

Aelian 307
On the Characteristics of Animals

16:15	110n39
16:18	110n39
19:9	110n39

Aristotle
Dreams

462a.30	188n29

Prophesying by Dreams

	188n30

Artemidorus
Oneirocritica

543–44	188n28

INDEX OF ANCIENT SOURCES 345

Athanasius 307
Letter XXXIX 91n9, 261n50

Cicero 309
On the Nature of the Gods
I.xlii.117 4n21
III.xv.39 4n20
On Divination 184n18, 255
I.i–ii.3 188n27
I.xiv.24 254n28
I.xv.28 252n22
I.xxxiv.72–I.xxxv.73 252n22
I.xxxv.77 252n22
I.xlvi.104 252
I.lviii.132 255n32
II.xi.26 251
II.xxiii.51 255n31
II.xxv.54 255n32
II.xxvi.56–57 185n21
II.xxxiv.74 185n20
II.xxxix.83 255n30
II.lxxii.148 255n35
II.lxxii.149 256n36

Cyprian 310
Epistles
61 261n44

Epiphanius
Panarion
28.1.2 267
51.3.6 151n103

Eusebius 310
Ecclesiastical History
4.6.1–3 202n15
Life of Constantine
 154, 154n104, 262n48, 280n82

Herodotus 314
Histories
1.53.91 253n26

Hippocrates 207, 208, 314
Sacred Disease
I.1–4 207n31
II.1–46 207n31
V.1–21 207n31
VI.1–2 207n31
XXI.22–26 207n31

Homer 314
Odyssey
10.495 61n12
11 61
4.795–847 188n24
Illiad
2.1–35 179
2.205 179

Irenaeus
Against Heresies
1.24.3–4 263
9:2 202n12

Jerome 314
Letters
57.9 146, 147
Commentary on Isaiah
232–33 110n40

Josephus 314
Jewish Antiquities
8.2.5 225n78
13.14.2 113n44
15.5.3 95, 266n59
18.2.5 225n78
18.3.3 204
18.5.2 148n97
Jewish War
1.4.6 113n44

Justin 229
1 Apology
21–22 229n83
22 204n24
53 273n72

346 INDEX OF ANCIENT SOURCES

Dialogue with Trypho
14 — 217n54
106 — 202n13

Lucian — 207, 208, 315
Lover of Lies
16.31–32 — 207n30

Marcus Arelius — 207, 208, 307
Meditations
I.6 — 207n32

Origen — 307
First Principles — 20n13

Ovid
Metamorphoses
XIV.130–53 — 145n92

Pausanias — 317
Description of Greece
6.11.1–9 — 44n8, 222n71

Petronius — 317
Satiricon
48:8 — 144n91

Philo
On Dreams
1.141–42 — 266

Philostratus
Life of Apollonius
6–8 — 98n21

Plato — 317
Apology of Socrates
24b — 249
90–91 — 249n15
Republic
II.376E–377A — 146n93
II.377A–383E — 146n95
II.377D–383 — 183n17

Plutarch — 317, 318
Life of Alexander
27–28 — 223n73
The Oracles at Delphi — 94n14
The Obsolescence of Oracles — 181n15
V.419 A–E — 269n65
On the Sign of Socrates
VII.589D — 188n26
Superstition
II.165 B–C — 4n19

Sibylline Oracles
5.512–30 — 19

Tertullian — 319
Exhortation to Chastity
12 — 261n43
On Modesty
1 — 259n40
22 — 259n40
Prescription against Heretics
7 — 38n1
The Soul
46–48 — 189

Theophrastus
Characters — 3

∽

APOSTOLIC FATHERS

Barnabas
9.4 — 267

2 Clement
9.5 — 276
20.5 — 202

INDEX OF ANCIENT SOURCES 347

Didache

| 11.3–13.7 | 181 |
| 12.4 | 288 |

Diognetus

| 5.1–17 | 288 |

Ignatius 216

To the Ephesians

| 7.2 | 216n49 |
| 20.2 | 79, 216n51 |

To the Magnesians

| 4.1 | 288 |

To the Philadelphians

| 8.1 | 258n38 |

To the Smyrnaeans

| 3.1–3 | 212 |

Martyrdom of Polycarp

| 10.1 | 288 |
| 12.1 | 288 |

Polycarp

To the Philippians

| 7.1 | 213 |

Shepherd of Hermas

Mandates

| 4.1–4 | 258n39 |
| 12.3–6 | 258n39 |

Similitudes

| 8.3.3 | 266n60 |
| 8.11.1–5 | 258n39 |

Visions

| 2.2–3 | 258n39 |

NEW TESTAMENT APOCRYPHA

Apocalypse of Peter

| 81:15–21 | 228 |
| 82:18–83:15 | 228 |

Gospel of Mary

| 3:3–5 | 250 |

Gospel of the Savior

| 1:4 | 198 |

NAG HAMMADI CODICES

Letter of Peter to Philip VIII 2

| 139:27 | 202 |
| 140:4 | 202 |

Gospel of Philip II 3

53:21–24	289
64:22–27	289
74:12–15	289
74:12–14	289
74:17–22	289

Gospel of Thomas

13	33
19	33
69	69, 150
77	195

Gospel of Truth
31:4–6   215n48

Treatise on the Resurrection I 4
45:14—46:2   27n73
47:30—48:6   275n73
49:9–16   275n73

Index of Modern Authors

Abell, George, 6n28, 307
Ackroyd, Peter R., 310
Albright, William Foxwell, 264n55, 307
Alighieri, Dante, 15, 16n3, 246, 246n12, 247, 307
Allcock, Philip J., 315
Allison, Dale C., 135, 135n74, 307
Altizer, Thomas J. J., 269, 269n67, 307
Anderson, George K., xxi
Annas, Julia, 125n61, 226n79, 307
Arp, Thomas R., 140n85, 220n64, 307
Ascough, Richard S., 243n4, 307
Attridge, Harold W., 100n25, 307
Auerbach, Eric, 160, 160n114, 307
Aungerville, Richard, 89, 89n5, 307
Azar, Beth, 12n48, 308

Babbit, Frank Cole, 94n14, 308, 318
Babcock, Maltbie D., 31, 31n21, 308
Barrett, C. K., 91n8, 308
Bauckham, Richard, 25n16, 308
Bauer, Walter, 5n23, 10n43, 308
Beckett, Samuel, 24
Bennett, Judith M., 3n13, 314
Benson, Larry D., 309
Bent, James Theodore, 109n37, 308
Bethge, Hans-Gebhard, 202n10, 308
Bettenson, Henry, 177n12, 195n41, 204n21, 215n45, 217n53, 231n85, 262n49, 263n52, 264n56, 278n77, 289n16, 308

Betz, Hans Dieter, 9n40, 308
Blomberg, Craig L., 234, 234n94, 308
Booth, Wayne C., 140n84, 308
Borg, Marcus J., 219, 219n60, 308
Bornkamm, Günter, 200n5, 308
Bowdin, John, 320
Bragg, William, 175n6, 308
Brashler, James A., 228n81, 308
Briggs, Charles A., 110, 308
Brill, A. A., 311
Bromiley, Geoffrey W., xxi
Bronowski, Jacob, 56n1, 308
Brown, Francis, 110, 308
Brown, Raymond E., 158n109, 164n21, 166, 166n123, 216n50, 263n51, 308
Buehl, Frants, 312
Bultmann, Rudolf, 115, 115n48, 136, 136n81, 137, 308
Burgess, Henry, 307
Burkert, Walter, 222n69, 309
Buttrick, George A., xix

Campbell, J. Y., 303, 303n2, 303n5, 304, 304n9, 309
Campion, C. T., 318
Carroll, Robert P., 246n10, 309
Cartlidge, David R., 47n16, 309
Case, Shirley Jackson, 279n78, 309
Cave, C. H., 314
Cave, F. H., 314
Cervantes, Miguel de, 107, 108
Chadwick, Henry, 309
Charlesworth, James H., 2n5, 309

Chaucer, Geoffrey, 11n44, 309
Clabeaux, John J., 96n16, 309
Clancy, Michael, 298n30, 309
Cline, Austin, 5n25, 309
Cockerill, Gareth Lee, 228n80, 309
Cohen, Nick, 176n11, 309
Collins, John J., 12n12, 93n13, 309
Collins, Raymond, 296n24, 309
Condon, Edward Uhler, 28n18, 309
Conner, Robert P., 5n25, 9n36, 309
Conybeare, Frederick Cornwallis, 98n21, 309
Conzelmann, Hans, 58n3, 309
Cook, Stephen L., 254n29, 309
Copernicus, Nicolas, 16n4, 45, 46, 46n13, 48, 309
Costandi, Mo, 7n31, 7n33, 309
Coxe, A. Cleveland, 204n24, 273n72, 310
Crombie, Frederick, 307
Cross, Frank Moore, Jr., 159n110, 310
Cuddon, J. A., 146n94, 310

Danker, Frederick William, 5n23, 10n43, 284n5, 308
Darion, Joe, 108
Darwin, Charles Robert, 28, 39, 175, 175n9, 270, 282, 310
Dave, 50n20, 310
Davies, G. Hinton, 187n22, 310
De lacy, Phillip H., 317
Desfor, Donald, 316
Dewey, Arthur J., 64n15, 108n34, 127n65, 310
Dibelius, Martin, 136, 136n80, 310
Dietrich, B. C., 318
Dillenberger, John, 89n6, 217n52, 265n57, 310
Dillon, John M., 253n26, 310
Dodd, C[harles] H[arold], 65n17, 303, 303n1, 303n3, 304, 304n6, 304n11, 310
Donaldson, James, xviii
Driver, S. R., 110, 308
Droge, Arthur J., 297n27, 310
Dungan, David L., 47n16, 309
Dunkly, James W., 309

Dunn, James D. G., 238n105, 310

Edmonds, J. M., 3n12, 320
Edwards, Jonathon, 246, 247, 247n13, 310
Ehrman, Bart D., 136, 136n76, 310
Einarson, Benedict, 317
Eissfeldt, Otto, 2n7, 76n34, 99n22, 310
Eliot, T. S., 144, 144n90, 310
Elliott, John H., 2n4, 203n18, 310
Estrada, Andrea, 11n47, 310
Evans, Craig C., 136, 136n75, 310

Falconer, William Armistead, 309
Fee, Gordon D., 125, 125n63, 310, 316
Feine, Paul, 151n102, 214n44, 237n101, 311
Ferguson, Everett, 188n25, 221n68, 223n74, 243n3, 252n25, 268n63, 311
Fevens, Thomas, 46n14
Fitzmyer, Joseph A., 9n37, 311
Fletcher, Joseph, 67n22, 299n33, 311
Foer, Franklin, 298n32, 311
Foerster, Werner, 263n53, 311
Forer, Ben, 51n21, 319
Fowler, Harold North, 249n15, 317
Frankfort, Henri, 271n70, 311
Frazer, James George, 3n10, 8, 8n35, 311
Freedman, David Noel, xvii
Fremantle, W. H., 146n96, 314
Freud, Sigmund, 189, 189n33, 311
Fried, Gregory, 313
Friedrich, Gerhard, xxi
Fuller, Russell E., 12n49, 311
Funk, Robert W., 101n26, 118n52, 135n72, 151n101, 162n116, 162n118, 200n7, 207n33, 208n34, 234n93. 242n1, 288n12, 311

Galilei, Galileo, 45, 46n13
Gallager, Richard, 285, 285n9, 311
Gamow, George, 80n35, 175n6, 175n7, 311

Gaster, Theodor H., 15n1, 111,
    111n41, 311
Gay, Peter, 3n8, 311
Gesenius, William, 97n10, 109, 110,
    308, 311, 312
Gilleland, Brady B., 144n91, 317
Goehring, James E., 312
Goodspeed, Edgar J., xx, 87n2,
    88n3, 110, 128, 143, 144,
    165, 170, 311
Goodwyn, Hannah, 188n23, 311
Goold, G. P., 145n92, 316
Grant, Frederick C., 206n26, 312
Graves, Robert, 34n25, 215n46, 311
Greig, J. C., 321
Grene, David, 314
Griffiths, Alan H., 110, 312
Grobel, Kendrick, 308

Hall, Howard Judson, 321
Harkness, Georgia, 82n37, 82n38,
    312
Harmon, William, 162n115, 314
Harris-McCoy, Daniel E., 188n28,
    312
Harrison, Peter, 316
Hartmann, Lars, 116n50, 135,
    135n73, 312
Hayes, John H., 1n1, 87n2, 101n27,
    194n36, 312
Haynes, Michael P., 262, 262n45,
    312
Heathcote, Arthur W., 314
Heber, Reginald, 177n13, 232n89,
    312
Hedrick, Charles W., xivn4, 9n38,
    31n20, 32n22, 43n6, 62n14,
    66n19, 66n20, 69n26, 74n28,
    81n36, 103n28, 105n29,
    115n46, 116n49, 134n66,
    135n69, 135n70, 141n86,
    144n88, 149n98, 150n99,
    155n105, 155n107, 159n113,
    163n120, 164n122, 179n14,
    195n39, 196n42, 200n6,
    203n19, 206n27, 206n29,
    209n35, 210n36, 213n40,
    213n42, 218n56, 218n59,
    220n65, 220n66, 234n91,
    236n99, 237n100, 260n41,
    263n54, 268, 284n4, 289n15,
    312, 313, 319
Hedrick, Charles W., Jr., 144n89,
    268n64
Heidegger, Martin, 66, 66n21, 313
Henley, William Ernest, 60n5, 65,
    65n18, 313
Henrichs, Albert, 246n7, 313
Hernando, James D., 260, 260n42,
    314
Hock, Ronald F., 69n25, 312, 314
Hoffman, Dustin, 70
Hollister, C. Warren, 3n13, 314
Holmes, Michael W., 12n49, 314
Holmes, Peter, 319
Holmon, C. Hugh, 162n115, 314
Holmyard, E. J., 34n24, 31
Hooke, S. H., 314
Hoover, Roy W., 213n41, 314
Hornblower, Simon, xx
Hultgren, Arland J., 234, 234n94,
    314

Isaac, Benjamin, 202n14, 314

Jacob, Edmund, 246n6, 314
Jeremias, Joachim, 142n87, 235n96,
    314
Johnson, Greg, 140n85, 220n64, 307
Johnson, James Turner, 2n2, 314
Johnston, George, 202n11, 314
Johnston, Harold Wetstone, 85n39,
    314
Jones, Donald L., 223n72, 314
Jones, Henry Stuart, 315
Jones, W. H. S., 314, 315
Jost, Madeleine, 109n36, 314, 315
Joy, Charles R., 319

Katzinis, Giannis, 68
Kaufman, Walter, 269n66, 315
Kearns, Emily, 61n9, 315
Kee, Howard Clark, 288n13, 311,
    315
Keener, Craig S., 162, 162n117, 315
Kim, Chan-Hie, 113n45, 315

King, Karen L., 249n17, 315
Kitchen, K. A., 2n3, 315
Kittel, Gerhard, xxi
Knickerbocker, William S., 309
Koester, Helmut, 117n51, 315
Kohlenberger, John R. III, 110, 315
Krause, Tom, 107n10, 108, 315
Kuemmerlin-McLean, Joanne K., 111, 315
Kuntz, Kenneth J., 18n9, 19n10, 35n27, 76n33, 315

La Bas, Philippe, 195n40, 315
Lake, Kirsopp, 202n8, 315
Leitch, James W., 309
Levi, Peter, 222n71, 217
Lewis, Naphtali, 224n75, 224n76, 249n16, 252n21, 252n23, 315
Lewis, Sinclair, 286n10, 315
Lewis, Theodore J., 61n7, 246n11, 315
Liddell, Henry George, 10n42, 315
Lindars, Barnabas, 166, 166n124, 315
Long, George, 307
Lovell, A. C. B., 174n5, 315
Luther, Martin, 88, 110, 166

Mack, Burton L., 136, 136n79, 316
MacRae, George W., 309
Magiorkinis, Emmanouil, 285n8, 316
Main, C. F., 313
Marcus, Ralph, 225n78, 314
Marsh, John, 308
Martin, Luther H., 253n27, 316
Mattill, A. J., Jr., 311
Maunder, Chris, 177n12, 195n41, 204n21, 215n45, 217n53, 231n85, 262n49, 263n52, 264n56, 278n77, 289n16, 308
McBride, Mary, 298, 299
McDonald, Lee Martin, 2n7, 313, 316
McKenzie, John L., xix, 243n2, 316
McKenzie, Roderick, 315

McLuskey, Fraser, 308
McLuskey, Irene, 308
Mendelsohn, Isaac, 225n77, 316
Merz, Annette, 136n78, 320
Metzger, Bruce M., 185n19, 212n39, 316
Meyer, Marvin [W.], 9n40, 171n1, 204n23, 272n71, 279n79, 280n81, 316
Michaels, J. Ramsey, 120n59, 316
Migne, J.-P., 316
Miller, Frank Justus, 145n92, 316
Miller, Robert L., 316
Milligan, George, 5n23, 317
Mills, Watson E., xix
Milton, John, 11, 11n45, 316
Moffatt, James, xix, 128, 143, 144
Montgomery, W., 318, 319
Morais, Betsy, 302n36, 316
Morris, Simon Conway, 176n10, 316
Moulton, James Hope, 5n23, 317

Newport, Frank, 290n17, 317
Nickelsburg, George W. E., 61n8, 317
Nickle, Keith F., 100n24, 317
Nicoll, W. Robertson, 317
Nietzsche, Friedrich, 269
Noll, Mark A., 2n2, 317
Noss, John B., 9n39, 317

Olmstead, Thomas J., 298
Oppenheimer, Aharon, 202n14, 314
Oskin, Becky, 26, 26n17, 317

Palmer, Jason, 3n11, 317
Papadiamantis, Aleksandros, 68
Parsons, Mikeal C., 313
Payne-Smith, [Jessie], 307
Pearson, Birger A., 308
Perrin, Bernadotte, 223n73, 317
Perrin, Norman, 234n92, 317
Persinger, Michael A., 5n25, 317
Phillips, J. B., xx, 129, 192
Phy, Allene Stuart, 2n2, 317
Planer, Felix E., 4n17, 317
Polt, Richard, 313
Potter, David S., 93n11, 318

INDEX OF MODERN AUTHORS   353

Potts, Richard, 57n2, 318
Preston, C. E., 146n94, 310
Purcell, Nicholas, 251n18, 318

Rackham, H., 309
Raffan, John, 309
Rajak, Tessa, 24n38, 318
Randall, John Herman, 3n8, 318
Rawley, Cliff, 43, 43n7, 318
Ray, Roger L., 262, 262n46, 287n11, 318
Reese, David G., 206n29, 318
Reinhold, Meyer, 224n75, 224n76, 249n16, 252n21, 252n23, 315
Reimarus, Hermann Samuel, 119n55
Reynolds, William J., 312, 321
Richardson, Ernest Cushing, 310
Rieu, E. V., 61n12, 314
Rios, Jame Martin del Campo, 5n25, 318
Roberts, Alexander, xviii
Robertson, Archibald, 307
Robertson, Noel, 318
Robinson, Edward, 97n20, 110, 308, 312
Robinson, James M., 118n54, 200n4, 308, 312, 318, 321
Robinson, John A. T., 173n3, 265n58, 318
Rogers, Eric M., 48on17, 318
Rotman, Youval, 318
Rousseau, Philip, 251n18, 318
Rowe, Christopher R., 120n58, 318
Rudolph, Kurt, 173n4, 318
Rusten, Jeffrey, 3n12, 320

Sagan, Carl, 15n2, 16n2, 16n5, 36n28, 59n4, 80n35, 175n6, 176n11, 318
Sage, Evan T., 144n91, 317
Sakenfield, Katherine Doob, xx
Sanders, E. P., 136, 136n77, 318
Schaff, Philip, xx, 310
Scheck, Thomas P., 314
Scholfield, Alwyn Faber, 307

Schweitzer, Albert, 119n55, 159, 159n112, 171, 171n1, 199, 199n3, 200, 219, 219n61, 220, 220n63, 316, 318, 319
Scott, Bernard Brandon, 234, 234n94, 319
Scott, Charles Archibald Anderson, 115n47, 319
Scott, Robert, 10n42, 315
Seng, Peter J., 313
Scheid, John, 4n18, 319
Shorey, Paul, 183n17, 317
Shriver, George, 41n4, 319
Sims, Walter Hines, 308
Simundson, Daniel J., 45n9, 319
Slick, Matt, 30n19, 319
Sloan, Christopher, 57n2, 318
Sloan, Robert B., 313
Smith, J. M. Powis, xxi, 110, 128, 143, 144, 165, 170
Smith, Joseph, 95
Soards, Marion L. 217n55, 319
Sondurlund, Sven K., 316
Spawforth, Anthony, xx
Spong, John Shelby, 294, 295
Stanglin, Doug, 22n14, 319
Stark, Rodney, 290n20, 294n21, 319
Stevens, Holly, 319
Stevens, Wallace, 107, 107n32, 319
Stimson, Dorothy, 45n10, 46n13, 46n14, 48n17, 270n69, 319
Sumney, Jerry L., 125n62, 319
Swanson, James A., 110, 315
Swete, Henry Barclay, 319

Tabor, James D., 61n13, 119n57, 126n64, 319
Talbert, Charles H., 204n22, 319
Tanglao, Leezel, 51n21, 319
Taussig, Hal, 17n6, 319
Tennyson, Alfred Lord, 17n8, 52n23, 319
Teselle, Eugene, 278n75, 319
Thackery, H. St. J., 225n78, 314
Theissen, Gerd, 136, 136n78, 320
Thelwall, S., 319
Thomas, Dylan, 75, 75n32, 320
Tillich, Paul, 175n8, 320

Trask, Willard R., 307
Traub, Helmut, 119n56, 320
Twelftree, Graham H., 234, 234n95, 320
Tyndale, William, 89

VanderKam, James C. 19n11, 320
Van der Linden, Sander, 189n32, 189n34, 320
Van Vorst, Robert E., 230n84, 239n107, 320
Verkuyl, Gerrit, xix
Versnel, H. S., 4n22, 320
Vonnegut, Kurt, Jr., 302, 320

Wace, Henry, xx
Waddington, W. H., 195n40, 315
Walker, Williston, 232n88, 320
Wallis, Ernest, 310
Ware, Timothy, 97n17, 320
Warmington, Eric Herbert, 246n8, 320
Warnock, Robert, xxi
Wasserman, Dale, 107

Watson, Duane F., 246n9, 320
Welch, Claude, 89n6, 217n52, 265n57, 310
Westcott, Brooke Foss, 88n4, 320
Wilson, John Francis, 112n43, 321
Wilson, Robert McLachlan, 311, 318
Wimsett, W. K., Jr., 107n34, 321
Winseman, Albert L., 290n18, 321
Wisse, Frederik, 202n9, 321
Woodwose, T. E., 301n34, 321
Woolf, Bertram Lee, 310
Woolley, Kate Wilkins, 60n6, 321
Wordsworth, William, 61n10, 62, 321
Wrede, William, 199, 199n2, 321
Wright, N. T., 316
Wycliffe, John, 89

Young, Louise B., 38n2, 308, 309, 311, 315, 318, 321

Zoll, Rachel, 22n14, 321
Zoroya, George, 71n27, 321

www.ingramcontent.com/pod-product-compliance
Lightning Source LLC
Chambersburg PA
CBHW021338300426
44114CB00012B/997